METACOGNITION
Process, Function and Use

METACOGNITION
Process, Function and Use

edited by

Patrick Chambres
Marie Izaute
Pierre-Jean Marescaux

Université Blaise Pascal
Clermont-Ferrand, France

KLUWER ACADEMIC PUBLISHERS
Boston / Dordrecht / New York / London

Distributors for North, Central and South America:
Kluwer Academic Publishers
101 Philip Drive
Assinippi Park
Norwell, Massachusetts 02061 USA
Telephone (781) 871-6600
Fax (781) 681-9045
E-Mail: kluwer@wkap.com

Distributors for all other countries:
Kluwer Academic Publishers Group
Post Office Box 322
3300 AH Dordrecht, THE NETHERLANDS
Telephone 31 786 576 000
Fax 31 786 576 474
E-Mail: services@wkap.nl

 Electronic Services < http://www.wkap.nl >

Library of Congress Cataloging-in-Publication Data

Metacognition: process, function, and use / edited by Patrick Chambres, Marie Izaute,
Pierre-Jean Marescaux.
    p.cm.
  Includes bibliographical references and indexes.
  ISBN 1-40207-134-5 (alk. paper)
  1. Metacognition. I. Chambres, Patrick, 1955- II. Izaute, Marie, 1965- III. Marescaux,
Pierre-Jean, 1958-

BF311 .M44892 2002
153—dc21

                                 2002075420

Contents

Contributors

Delphine BONIN, Laboratoire de Psychologie Sociale de la Cognition (UMR CNRS 6024), Université Blaise Pascal, 34, avenue Carnot, F-63037 Clermont-Ferrand cedex, France

Melanie CARY, Department of Psychology, Carnegie Mellon University, Pittsburg, PA 15213, USA

Patrick CHAMBRES, Laboratoire de Psychologie Sociale de la Cognition (UMR CNRS 6024), Université Blaise Pascal, 34, avenue Carnot, F-63037 Clermont-Ferrand cedex, France

Zoltan DIENES, Department of Experimental Psychology, Sussex University, Brighton, Sussex, BN1 9QG, England

Anastasia EFKLIDES, School of Psychology, Aristotle University of Thessaloniki, G-54006 Thessaloniki, Greece

Elsa EME, Laboratoire Language et Cognition (UMR CNRS 6096) - MSHS, Université de Poitiers, BP 632, 99 avenue du Recteur Pineau, F-86022 Poitiers Cedex, France

Fiona FITCH, Research Institute for the Care of the Elderly, St. Martin's Hospital, Bath, BA2 5RP, England.

Marie IZAUTE, Laboratoire de Psychologie Sociale de la Cognition (UMR CNRS 6024), Université Blaise Pascal, 34, avenue Carnot, F-63037 Clermont-Ferrand cedex, France

Peter JUSLIN, Department of Psychology, Umeå University, SE-90187, Uppsala, Sweden.

William L. KELEMEN, Department of Psychology, University of Missouri at St. Louis, 316 Stadler Hall, 8001 Natural Bridge Road, Saint Louis, MO 063121-4499, USA

Sachiko KINOSHITA, Department of Psychology and Macquarie Centre for Cognitive Science (MACCS), Macquarie University, Sydney, New South Wales, A-2109 Australia

Asher KORIAT, Department of Psychology, University of Haifa, I-31905 Haifa, Israel

Guy LORIES, Unité de Psychologie Cognitive, Université Catholique de Louvain, 10 Place du Cardinal Mercier, B-1348 Louvain-La-Neuve, Belgique

Pierre-Jean MARESCAUX, Laboratoire de Psychologie Sociale de la Cognition (UMR CNRS 6024), Université Blaise Pascal, 34, avenue Carnot, F-63037 Clermont-Ferrand cedex, France

Chris J. A. MOULIN, Department of Experimental Psychology, University of Bristol, 8 Woodland Road, Bristol BS8 1TN, England

Thomas O. NELSON, Department of Psychology, University of Maryland, College Park, MD 20742, USA

Nils OLSSON, Department of Psychology, Uppsala University, Box 1225, SE-75142 Uppsala, Sweden.

Laurence PAIRE-FICOUT, Laboratoire de Psychologie Sociale de la Cognition (UMR CNRS 6024), Université Blaise Pascal, 34, avenue Carnot, F-63037 Clermont-Ferrand cedex, France

Scott G. PARIS, Department of Psychology, 2008 East Hall, 525 East University Avenue, University of Michigan, Ann Arbor, MI 48109, USA

Timothy J. PERFECT, Department of Psychology, University of Plymouth, Drake Circus, Plymouth, PL4 8AA, England.

Josef PERNER, Department of Psychology, University of Salzburg, 34 HellbrunerStrasse, A-5020 Salzburg, Austria

Lynne M. REDER, Department of Psychology, Carnegie Mellon University, Pittsburg, PA 15213, USA

Jean-François ROUET, Laboratoire Language et Cognition (UMR CNRS 6096) - MSHS, Université de Poitiers, BP 632, 99 avenue du Recteur Pineau, F-86022 Poitiers Cedex, France

Florence V. SEEMUNGAL, University of Oxford, Center of Criminological Research and Probation Studies, 12 Bevington Road, Oxford OX2 6LH, England

Rachel SHITZER-REICHERT, Department of Psychology, University of Haifa, I-31905 Haifa, Israel

Sarah V. STEVENAGE, Department of Psychology, University of Southampton, Southampton, SO17 1BJ, England

Claude VALOT, Institut de Médecine Aérospatiale, Service de Santé des Armées (IMASSA-CERMA), Département de Sciences Cognitives et Ergonomie, BP 73, F-91223 Brétigny sur Orge, France

Charles A. WEAVER III, Department of Psychology and Neuroscience, Baylor University, Campus Box 97334, Waco, TX 76798-7334, USA

Foreword

New Theory and Data on Metacognitive Monitoring and Control in Different Contexts and by Different Individuals

Thomas O. Nelson
University of Maryland, USA

This book, divided into several sections (each containing several chapters), is timely in reporting new theory and data that help refine what is already known about metacognition (defined as people's cognitions about their own cognitions). New data are reported about metacognition during learning (especially *judgments of learning* that occur soon after studying new items) not only in traditionally examined people such as college students but also in children and in Alzheimer patients. Data are also reported about metacognitive monitoring during the reading of text, not only in college students but also in children. The above situations focus on the acquisition of new items from lists or from texts. However, the book also includes a chapter reporting data about metacognition during problem solving.

Besides the chapters on monitoring information in anticipation of future performance (sometimes called *prospective* monitoring), a chapter is included that offers data about the metacognitive monitoring of the retrieval of information from memory, where the emphasis is on the accuracy of *retrospective confidence judgments* not only in adults but also in children. This topic is of widespread interest both in traditional domains of cognitive psychology and in applications to domains such as forensics, where eyewitness reports are crucial to judicial decisions.

The above topics pertain to aspects of metacognition involving the *monitoring* of one's own cognitions. Two chapters also report new data about metacognitive *control*, both in terms of strategy selection and in terms of the metacognitive control of complex systems.

Besides the many new sets of data, several chapters focus on refinements of theories about metacognition. Particular emphasis seems to occur in several chapters on the role of context effects on metacognitive activity. This includes contexts in which people deliberately initiate metacognitive activity, contexts in which metacognition has a functional (i.e., instrumental) role in affecting performance, and a chapter on the unusual topic of using metacognitive knowledge to facilitate the flying of combat aircraft. A couple chapters focus on the implicit/explicit distinction to examine the interplay between metacognition and implicit/explicit memory and implicit/explicit knowledge.

New methodological contributions are offered by at least two chapters. One chapter examines the important but elusive topic of individual differences in metacognitive accuracy. The other chapter re-examines the confidence-accuracy relation in forensics and proposes a new measure of the confidence-accuracy relationship.

Thus the chapters contained herein offer both new theory and new data on the burgeoning field of metacognition. The contexts under investigation should help extend ideas about metacognition away from laboratory settings (although those are not disregarded) toward several useful domains of application. As such, metacognition is treated not only as an interesting intellectual topic but also as one that will help increase our understanding of applied situations where people are monitoring and controlling their own cognitive activity.

This wide scope of the book can be expected to generate widespread interest from readers in diverse domains and will also give traditional researchers of metacognition a larger perspective on the range of applicability to which ideas about metacognition can usefully be extended. This demonstrates that in contrast to some psychological phenomena that seem predominantly to be curiosities of the laboratory, metacognition has ramifications for diverse everyday settings and is therefore both of theoretical and applied interest.

Preface

Patrick Chambres, Pierre-Jean Marescaux, and Marie Izaute
Université Blaise Pascal, Clermont-Ferrand, France

While strict boundaries between research problems can certainly be identified in science, the boundaries are often more apparent than real. Doing research in a theoretical perspective is necessarily achieved within a specific pragmatic context. Inversely, an effective and valid study with a pragmatic aim cannot be conducted without some sort of theoretical framework, no matter how minimal. It follows that these two research approaches will overlap at some point. In the first case, knowledge of processes gained through theoretical research sheds light on behavior; in the second, the study of behavior can supply useful information for grasping psychological mechanisms. Added to this opportunity for mutual exchange between approaches, are studies which –although conducted outside the "official" field– use the knowledge acquired therein as a supplemental instrument for investigating some other specific area.

This book was designed to show how the concept of metacognition is used and studied from many different but complementary angles. Despite the common misconception that research dealing with the definitions and processes of metacognition is somehow separate from studies on its functions and roles, it is demonstrated throughout this book that many interesting connections can be made between the different perspectives. Going one step further, the book also strives to show that research in domains that are considered unrelated to metacognition but that use it as a sort of "tool", can afford interesting information for understanding metacognitive processes. The fifteen chapters in this book were brought together here for the purpose of highlighting these interconnections. The collaborating authors have taken the trouble to broaden the scope of their chapters to encompass a variety of topics in metacognitive research (e.g., Paris, Section 4 Chapter 1; Dienes & Perner, Section 4 Chapter 1). This "opening up" is so great in certain chapters that it is even difficult to unambiguously determine their main field of research. A good illustration of this is the chapter on retrieval mechanisms by Lories (Section 2 Chapter 3). The title of his chapter mentions retrieval of memory traces (the focus is on memory), and the first subtitle deals with metacognition and control (focus on metacognition); then the second part of the chapter discusses retrieval and feeling of knowing (joint focus on memory and metacognition), while still another part reviews the issue in problem solving.

This book should therefore be of interest not only to readers specifically interested in examining the field of metacognition from an essentially theoretical angle (What is metacognition and how does it work? By what mechanisms is metacognitive activity produced?), but also to persons more interested in a pragmatic perspective (Does metacognition play a significant role in performance? Does metacognitive activity always enhance if not direct ongoing behavior? Are some social situations more likely than others to spontaneously initiate metacognitive activity?). This book should also meet the needs of readers looking for additional theoretical information to enrich their own area of investigation and readers in search of tested methodological instruments likely to provide effective new measures of behavior. (How can a metacognitive approach facilitate our understanding of behavior?)

The interconnectedness and overlapping nature of the different chapters does not prevent the book from having a structure of its own. There are four partially-independent sections, each containing three to five chapters.

The first section is aimed specifically at illustrating the interconnections mentioned above. The introduction by Koriat and Shitzer-Reichert (Section 1 Chapter 1) stresses how the cognitive and developmental approaches, where the study of metacognition has been conducted in a relatively independent way, are nevertheless complementary in the breadth and depth they give to research on this topic. The authors start with a clear description of these two perspectives and their historical background. Next they present some arguments to defend the idea that undeniable benefits could be obtained by combining these points of view in current research. In their experimental work, these authors show quite nicely how the developmental study of metacognition could benefit by bringing to bear insights gained in cognitive psychology. Their study focuses on the processes that mediate metacognitive judgments and accuracy in young children, and shows that improved monitoring resulting from both practice and time is mediated by reliance on internal, mnemonic cues that are indicative of the extent to which studied items were mastered. This study thus contributes to bettering our knowledge of metacognitive processes, while reporting on some of the less well-understood aspects of metacognitive skill development.

In the same vein, the chapter by Efklides (Section 1 Chapter 2), framed in a problem-solving context, clarifies the mechanisms underlying metacognitive feelings (metacognitive experience) and the function of those feelings in cognitive processing. An interesting point is made regarding the affective nature of certain feelings (e.g., feeling of satisfaction). This chapter also provides some information on child metacognitive competence.

Less related to development, the other two chapters provide some valuable data and analyses that should contribute to fundamental research as well as to improving our knowledge of individual cognitive performance. Moulin, Perfect, and Fitch (Section 1 Chapter 3), who take a specific interest in the study of episodic memory deficits in Alzheimer's disease, furnish some crucial data in support of the dissociation between control and monitoring processes. This type of result represents an important advancement in the understanding of metacognitive mechanisms, since only a specific population like the Alzheimer's patients studied here could be used to experimentally test the dissociation hypothesis. Weaver and Kelemen (Section 1

Chapter 4) tackle another important question: What makes one person consistently more accurate in his or her metacognitive judgments than another person? This question is not really meaningful, however, unless the consistency of within-individual metacognitive performance is demonstrated. Variability in metacognitive performance is often observed and is sometimes analyzed *a posteriori*. The chapter by Weaver and Kelemen provides an in-depth analysis of this problem, but above all, it examines new data obtained in a study designed to address the following question: Is there evidence of a general monitoring ability?

The next two sections are more specific. Section 2 includes three chapters about the mechanisms underlying metacognitive activity. A very important theoretical question lies at the heart of all three of these chapters: Is metacognition necessarily a conscious process? Cary and Reder (Section 2 Chapter 1) launch this debate, while taking a relatively clear-cut stance. Based on their study of strategy selection in problem solving or task execution, they show that many strategy choices are beyond the individual's conscious awareness. They argue for an alternative view, in line with Koriat (2000) –either one must assume that a significant part of metacognition occurs implicitly (without awareness), or one must agree that if all metacognitive processing is under the individual's conscious control, then certain strategy-selection processes are not part of metacognition. In fact, Cary and Reder seem to agree that different degrees of metacognitive awareness are involved in controlling and monitoring performance. This first chapter, which is thus mainly in favor of metacognitive activity without conscious awareness, is balanced by the chapter that follows.

Kinoshita (Section 2 Chapter 2) provides quite a challenging point of view, claiming that metacognition and implicit memory are unrelated. Kinoshita first examines data presumed to support the idea that using a feeling of familiarity to give recognition answers is based on metacognition, (e.g. Jacoby, Kelley, & Dywan, 1989; Kelley & Jacoby, 1996). Then she discusses an alternative interpretation couched in the memory framework proposed by Moscovitch (1993, 1994). In this framework, explicit memory is partitioned into a memory module and a central memory system, with the feeling of familiarity being associated with the former system and metacognitive processes, with the latter. Faced with the sometimes difficult problem of obtaining experimental proof in support of a theoretical proposal, which is somewhat true of the problem treated here, Kinoshita proposes using computational modelling to take neuropsychological evidence into account in the memory module/central system distinction. There are some clearly interesting points in this chapter, which should help guide future research on the relationship between explicit memory, implicit memory, and metacognition.

In a less controversial chapter, Lories (Section 2 Chapter 3) also looks at control and monitoring processes, but this time, in cases where they are involved in procedure selection for solving problems by analogy. According to the author, memory retrieval plays an important role in this kind of task but retrieval theory nevertheless needs a monitoring and control component. The metacognitive approach seems to be the natural way to examine this possibility. One of the questions discussed by Lories is: How can I know whether one problem is analogous to another –or relevant to it– without retrieving it first and then comparing the two? Without providing a definitive answer to this question, Lories examines some old and new data, and proposes an interesting theoretical analysis of analogical problem solving. With a focus on structural similarities within problems, the factor at the core of his analysis is time. The idea is that retrieval may only gradually incorporate information about the structural aspects of problems.

These three chapters are not the only ones that deal with control and monitoring processes, especially with their conscious dimension. This issue is an irrefutably fundamental one insofar as it poses the problem of the very definition of metacognition. Throughout this book, readers will find many other points and findings that contribute to this debate, particularly in the chapters by Paris (Section 4 Chapter 1) and Dienes and Perner (Section 4 Chapter 1).

The third section of the book is mainly concerned with how metacognition influences performance. In the first chapter of this section, Paris presents his own conception of metacognition, which obviously contradicts Cary and Reder's (see Section 2 Chapter 1). According to Paris, metacognition should be regarded as thoughts about knowledge or thinking that can be about one's own mind or that of others, and can be shared with others. Paris introduces an important aspect of metacognition that is not developed in the previous chapters: its social dimension. An original idea in this chapter, one rarely found in the classical literature on metacognition, is that while many studies have demonstrated positive effects of metacognition on performance, such effects are not always observed. Paris states, "I believe that metacognition can sometimes be negative, destructive, debilitating, and dangerous" (Paris, herein see Section 3 Chapter 1). Many interesting examples are provided, such as "Doubts about the right course of action, uncertainty about which strategy to use, and confusion about attributions for performance may inhibit action altogether" (Paris, Section 3 Chapter 1).

The other three chapters deal with the connection between metacognition and performance, from three different perspectives. In the first, Rouet and Eme (Section 3 Chapter 2) try to understand why text-based learning disabilities sometimes persist even after pupils have achieved satisfactory reading and reading-comprehension levels. They show that at the age of 10 or 11, children still have much to learn about texts, text comprehension, and study strategies. In the second, Valot (Section 3 Chapter 3) looks at a very specific situation, flying a combat aircraft, to shed light on how knowledge can regulate activity. Valot's study is a good illustration of ecological research. The author is led to focus on an unusual metacognitive activity, controlling and monitoring a fellow crew member, which offers a new setting for the social approach to the study of metacognition. In the third perspective, the study by Chambres, Bonin, Izaute, and Marescaux (Section 3 Chapter 4) also revolves around the social aspect of metacognition. Two experiments clearly show that a social position of expertise has the power to spontaneously trigger metacognitive activity without specific prompting. Taking this result into account, the authors examine the question of the connection between metacognitive skills and social position, a connection assumed to be built through individual experiences.

The fourth and last section of the book is in response to a "policy" of the editors, who feel that it is always a good idea for researchers conducting studies in a specific domain to exchange information with others whose aims are different but who share problems and theoretical concerns. Dienes and Perner (Section 4 Chapter 1), who are well-known authors in the field of implicit learning, provide an excellent analysis of the relationship between the implicit/explicit distinction and metacognition. They first indicate how a representation can represent different contents implicitly or explicitly, and then use this to derive a hierarchy of knowledge explicitness. Within this context, they present their higher-order thought theory of consciousness. An important part of their chapter is devoted to the link between implicit learning and metacognition. They conclude their chapter with a comment that is perfectly in line with the editors' policy, and which clearly expresses the first step in the making of this book: "We hope we can tempt metacognition researchers to look at implicit learning more closely, and implicit learning researchers to look at metacognition more closely" (Dienes & Perner, Section 4 Chapter 1).

Some researchers were already involved in this endeavor in an interesting way. Marescaux, Izaute, and Chambres (Section 4 Chapter 2) demonstrate that a metacognitive perspective can be a good means for examining resistant problems: What is really implicit in implicit learning? The difficulty lies in finding a suitable measure of awareness. According to the authors, traditional metacognitive measures, precisely studied in metacognition research, are a complementary means for attacking such a problem.

The complementary role of metacognitive measures is also clearly established in the chapters by Olsson and Juslin (Section 4 Chapter 3) and Seemungal and Stevenage (Section 4 Chapter 4). Olsson and Juslin illustrate how alternative measures from the metacognitive literature can be fruitfully applied to the confidence-accuracy relationship in studies where eyewitnesses and earwitnesses are involved. In a forensic context, Seemungal and Stevenage investigate the role of a witness's state of awareness at retrieval time, on his or her ability to reliably match confidence and accuracy. These last two chapters are an excellent reply to skeptics who contend that some of what researchers produce is mainly only usable by themselves and by other researchers.

As this brief description brings out, the chapters in this book concern a number of different themes. To make the book easier to use and to help readers identify the major areas discussed by the author or authors in each case, the key themes are given for each chapter. The table below lists the codes used for the different themes covered.

Appl	Application
Cont	Influence of context
Defn	Definition of metacognition
Devl	Development aspects
Meth	Method
Perf	Metacognition and performance
Prob	Problem solving
Proc	Metacognition processes
Theor	Theoretical framework

For example, the reader can expect the following chapter to focus mainly on the theoretical aspects of metacognition and on the processes implemented in metacognitive activity:

Feeling of familiarity: Memory attribution versus memory module
Sachiko Kinoshita
Key themes: Theor / Proc

The table below showing the key themes for each of the different chapters will facilitate a topic-based use of the book.

Chapters	Appl	Cont	Defn	Devl	Meth	Perf	Prob	Proc	Theor
Koriat & Shitzer-Reichertt				■				■	
Efklides							■	■	
Moulin et al.	■							■	
Weaver & Kelemen		■				■			
Cary & Reder		■	■				■	■	
Kinoshita								■	
Lories								■	
Paris		■	■			■		■	
Rouet & Eme	■			■					
Valot	■			■					
Chambres et al.	■		■						
Dienes & Perner			■					■	
Marescaux et al.					■			■	
Olsson & Juslin	■				■				
Seemungal & Stevenage	■				■				

Acknowledgments

We would like to thank the many people who helped us in all stages of the production of this volume.

Our gratitude goes first to the contributors, many of whom are widely recognized as outstanding theorists, researchers, and practioners in the area of metacognition. We are deeply grateful to them for contributing their insights and efforts.

We would also like to thank the anonymous reviewers of an earlier version of this manuscript, we are indebted to them for their thoughtful analyses and constructive feedback.

Marianna Pascale, Michael Williams and Mary Panarelli, at Kluwer provided vigorous help in their production roles and Christiane Roll should be particularly acknowledge for her help and patience.

We particularily thank Paula Niedenthal who patiently corrected our English.

Emmanuel Merlin was enormously helpful in preparing the manuscript for production.

I

IS METACOGNITION
A DIVERSE DOMAIN?

Chapter 1

Metacognitive Judgments and their Accuracy
Insights from the Processes Underlying Judgments of Learning in Children

Asher Koriat and Rachel Shitzer-Reichert
Department of Psychology, University of Haifa, Israel

Key themes: Devl / Proc / Theor

Key words: Judgments of learning / Monitoring accuracy / Metacognitive development / Mnemonic cues / Delayed JOLs

Abstract: In this chapter we begin by examining the processes underlying metacognitive judgments, contrasting the two major approaches to the study of metacognition –the developmental and cognitive-experimental approaches. Focusing then on the monitoring of one's own knowledge during study, we point out the benefits of applying insights from cognitive psychology to the study of the determinants of monitoring accuracy in children. The results of two experiments suggest that similar processes underlie judgments of learning (JOLs) and their accuracy in adults and children.

A commonly held assumption among students of metacognition is that metacognitive judgments exert a causal effect on information processing and behavior. This assumption has been formulated in terms of the effects of monitoring on control (Nelson & Narens, 1990). Monitoring refers to one's subjective assessment of one's own knowledge whereas control refers to the regulation of behavior that is presumably based on the output of the monitoring system. According to this formulation, there is benefit in investigating the accuracy of metacognitive judgments because it has important consequences for the effective adaptation to reality.

1.   DEVELOPMENTAL AND COGNITIVE PERSPECTIVES ON METACOGNITION

Historically, the investigation of metacognitive processes has proceeded along two almost entirely separate lines. On the one hand, there has been extensive research in developmental psychology, spurred mainly by the work of Flavell (1979) and his associates, which emphasized the critical role of metacognitive processes in the development of memory functioning in children. On the other hand, there has been a line of investigation in cognitive psychology that has focused narrowly on several questions concerning the determinants and consequences of the monitoring of one's own knowledge.

Developmental work on metacognition has focused primarily on specifying the components of metacognitive abilities as they develop with age, and on their possible effects on memory functioning. The definition of metacognition is much broader than that which seems to underlie much of the cognitive work on metacognition. Thus, in Flavell's conceptualization metacognition is seen to encompass metacognitive knowledge, metacognitive experiences, goals and actions (see Flavell, 1979; 1999; Flavell & Wellman, 1977). Indeed, developmental research has addressed such questions as what children know about the strengths and limitations of memory in general and of their memory in particular, and what they know about task variables that affect memory performance (e.g., Kreutzer, Leonard, & Flavell, 1975). Such metacognitive knowledge is certainly critical in guiding the effective management of learning and remembering. Developmental work has also placed a heavy emphasis on strategies of learning and remembering, including knowledge about the benefits and costs of using strategies in general, the potential value of specific strategies, the choice of strategies, the ability to take advantage of a strategy following instructions to use it, and so on (Bjorklund & Douglas, 1997; Pressley, Borkowski, & Schneider, 1987).

The assumption underlying much of this work is that memory performance depends heavily on monitoring and regulatory proficiency. Indeed, developmental psychologists investigated the relationship between metamemory and memory skills and how both of these develop with age (see Schneider, 1985). Much of that work is correlational in nature, and some of it is primarily descriptive. Furthermore, some of the work on metacognitive knowledge has relied heavily on self-report techniques such as interviews or questionnaires (e.g., Kreutzer et al. , 1975).

In contrast, the study of metacognition by experimental cognitive psychologists has been more narrowly confined to several basic issues concerning the mechanisms of monitoring and control processes in memory (for reviews see Nelson & Narens, 1990; Koriat & Levy-Sardot, 1999; Schwartz, 1994). A great deal of the work has focused on within-individual variation to reveal the dynamics of metacognitive processes. Thus, within-subject correlations have been typically used to examine the accuracy of metacognitive feelings as well as the effects of metamemory on memory (e.g., Nelson, 1984; Koriat & Goldsmith, 1996). This research has given rise to the establishment of several experimental paradigms for examining the monitoring and control processes that occur during learning, during the attempt to retrieve information from memory and following the retrieval of candidate answers (e.g., Hart, 1965; Nelson & Leonesio, 1988; Koriat, Lichtenstein, & Fischhoff, 1980; Reder, 1987).

Several questions have been at the focus of investigation. First how accurate are metacognitive judgments, and what are the factors that affect their accuracy? (e.g., Schwartz & Metcalfe, 1994; Weaver & Kelemen, this volume). Second, what are the bases of metacognitive judgments, that is, how do people monitor their own knowledge? (e.g., Cary & Reder, this volume; Koriat & Levy-Sardot, 2001). Third, what are the processes that are responsible for the accuracy and inaccuracy of metacognitive judgments? For example, what are the processes that lead to illusions of knowing, that is, to situations in which people have strong, unwarranted confidence in their knowledge? (e.g., Benjamin & Bjork, 1996; Bjork, 1999; Koriat, 1998). Fourth, how do metacognitive judgments control and guide information processing and action? (e.g., Barnes, Nelson, Dunlosky, Mazzoni, & Narens, 1999; Son & Metcalfe, 2000). This question is predicated on the assumption that monitoring processes play a causal role in regulating cognitive processes and behavior (see Koriat, 2000). Finally, how do the metacognitive processes of monitoring and control affect learning and remembering? (e.g., Barnes et al., 1999; Koriat & Goldsmith, 1996).

Additional questions, of course, emerge in different contexts. For example, assuming that metacognitive processes are not activated routinely, the question then is what are the conditions that induce people to engage in metacognitive processes? (see Chambres, Bonin, Izaute, & Marescaux, this volume). Do metacognitive skills represent a stable and reliable dimension of individual differences? (see Weaver & Kelemen, this volume). Can metacognition be trained, that is, can procedures be devised that improve monitoring accuracy? (e.g., Dunlosky & Nelson, 1994; Koriat, et al. , 1980). These are but a few of the questions addressed by experimental students in their attempt to clarify the processes underlying metacognitive monitoring and control.

In contrast to the focus on process and on within-subject variation, developmental psychologists exhibit a tendency to treat metacognition as a series of skills. Hence the interest in individual differences and age differences, as well as in questions concerning the generality or task-specificity of metacognitive skills, and the extent to which such skills correlate with IQ or predict school achievement. This treatment of metacognition has also led to attempts to specify "deficiencies" that are characteristic of children at different ages, and to seek ways to remedy them.

There is certainly benefit in combining insights from the developmental and cognitive approaches to metacognition. The developmental approach provides breadth (see Paris, this volume): It offers a more comprehensive framework for the analysis of metacognition, and brings to the fore questions that have not attracted sufficient interest among cognitive psychologists. Apart from its emphasis on developmental issues, it has stressed the consequences of metacognitive processes, particularly as far as memory performance is concerned. The cognitive approach, on the other hand, provides depth: A more detailed, theoretically-driven analysis of the working of metacognition. It has also resulted in the development of several standard experimental paradigms that offer many opportunities for the study of various basic processes in metacognition in both children and adults. Although these paradigms are rather restricted, they can provide some insight into the internal dynamics of metacognitive monitoring and control (Barnes et al. , 1999).

All of the chapters included in this section can be seen to combine some aspects of the cognitive and developmental approaches in attempting to elucidate the processes underlying metacognition. Weaver and Kelemen's chapter is relevant to the conception of metacognition as a set of skills. As noted earlier, this conception underlies many of the studies that examined age-related differences in metacognition and the relationships between memory and metamemory. What is unique about the studies reported by Weaver and Kelemen is the inclusion of measures of individual differences in metacognitive accuracy that are based on **within**-person correlations. The results reviewed in that chapter question the possibility of a stable and reliable dimension of individual differences in monitoring proficiency. An important challenge is how to reconcile these findings with the systematic age-related differences observed in some aspects of metacognition.

The chapter by Moulin, Perfect, and Fitch, is representative of the recent attempts by developmental psychologists, cognitive psychologists and neuropsychologists to seek an explanation of memory deficits in terms of deficient metacognitive abilities. Not only do such attempts help clarify the nature of metacognitive deficiencies, but they can also contribute a great deal to our understanding of the processes underlying metacognitive judgments in general. An important feature of the results described by Moulin et al. on Alzheimer patients is that they suggest a dissociation in these patients between monitoring and control processes during the study of new materials. This dissociation runs counter the commonly held "monitoring-affects-control" hypothesis of self-paced learning (Nelson & Leonesio, 1988).

Efklides' chapter builds on the distinction advanced by Flavell between metacognitive knowledge and metacognitive experience (ME; see Efklides, in press). Whereas the former refers to long-term beliefs concerned with memory functioning, the latter refers to conscious affective or cognitive experiences that normally accompany on-line the monitoring and self-regulatory processes that take place during encoding and remembering (Brown, Bransford, Ferrara, & Campione, 1983; Paris & Lindauer, 1982). It is MEs that received greater emphasis among experimental cognitive psychologists (Koriat & Levy-Sardot, 1999). However, Efklides' study, which was carried out on 7th to 9th graders, emphasizes the richness of MEs, and their interrelations. Although the study embodies certain aspects of the developmental approach to metacognition, its main focus is to clarify the mechanisms underlying metacognitive feelings and the function of these feelings in cognitive processing.

The experimental work presented in this chapter attempts to import insights from cognitive psychology to the study of developmental aspects of metacognition. It concerns the monitoring of knowledge during learning, focusing on the processes underlying the accuracy of JOLs in children of two age groups. This work, like some of the recent studies referred to below, is intended to promote a greater crosstalk between developmental and cognitive students of metacognition.

2.   THE BASIS OF JUDGMENTS OF LEARNING AND THEIR ACCURACY

When studying new material, people normally monitor the extent to which they have mastered different parts of that material and control the allocation of learning resources accordingly. Memory performance, then, should depend not only on "memory" but also on "metamemory", that is on the extent to which a person is successful in monitoring the degree of knowledge of different items and regulating study resources accordingly. An important question in developmental research, then, concerns the extent to which the age-related improvement in memory performance might be mediated by improvement in the monitoring of one's own memory during learning. Several studies that examined this question have yielded inconsistent results (see Schneider, Visé, Lockl, & Nelson, in press). In this study we also investigate developmental trends in monitoring accuracy during learning, but our primary focus is on the processes underlying the accuracy of JOLs elicited during study. We wish to examine the bases for children's accurate monitoring and whether these bases are similar to those that have been found for adults.

Most of the developmental studies on monitoring have concerned calibration or absolute metacognitive accuracy (see Weaver & Kelemen, this volume) that is, the match between the predicted and actual overall memory performance. These studies have generally indicated that preschoolers and kindergarten children tend to overestimate their future memory performance, whereas schoolchildren's predictions tend to be more realistic (see Schneider & Pressley, 1997). In the present study instead we focus on resolution or relative accuracy, that is, the accuracy of JOLs in monitoring the relative recallability of different items, as indexed, for example, by a within-subject Goodman-Kruskal gamma correlation between JOLs and recall (see Nelson, 1984). Resolution, or relative accuracy, is critical for the efficient allocation of time and effort between different items in self-paced learning.

What are the determinants of JOLs and their accuracy? According to the cue utilization model of JOLs proposed by Koriat (1997), JOLs are inferential in nature, and rest on a variety of cues. Three classes of cues for JOLs were distinguished, intrinsic, extrinsic, and mnemonic. Intrinsic cues refer to inherent characteristics of the study items that disclose their a-priori difficulty. For example, in paired associates learning, the judged degree of associative relatedness between the members of the pairs is an important contributor to JOLs. Extrinsic cues pertain to the conditions of learning (e.g., number of presentations), or to the encoding operations applied by the learner (e.g., level of processing). Finally, mnemonic cues are internal, subjective indicators that signal to the person the extent to which an item has been mastered. Several types of mnemonic cues have been discussed as possible determinants of metacognitive judgments: the fluency of processing of a presented item (Benjamin & Bjork, 1996; Koriat, 1997), the familiarity of the cue that serves to probe memory (Cary & Reder, this volume; Metcalfe, Schwartz, & Joaquim, 1993), the accessibility of pertinent partial information about a memory target (Dunlosky & Nelson, 1992; Koriat, 1993), and the ease with which information is retrieved (Kelley & Lindsay, 1993; Koriat, 1993).

Further, Koriat (1997) proposed that intrinsic and extrinsic cues can affect JOLs directly, through the explicit application of a particular rule or theory. For example, a person may hold the belief that the same item is more likely to be remembered if it is presented several times than if it is presented only once, or that semantically related pairs are easier to learn and remember than unrelated pairs in paired-associates learning. Such beliefs may be applied directly in making a theory-based inference. However, intrinsic or extrinsic cues may also affect JOLs through their influence on internal, mnemonic cues. For example, an item seen previously may be processed more fluently than a new item (Jacoby & Kelley, 1987). Processing fluency, then, can serve as the immediate cue for JOLs.

The direct effects of intrinsic and extrinsic cues are assumed to involve an analytic, deliberate inference based on the person's a-priori theory about the memorial consequences of various factors. The effects of mnemonic cues, in contrast, are assumed to rest on the implicit use of a nonanalytic, unconscious inference rather than on a deliberate theory-based deduction (see Koriat, 2000; Koriat & Levy-Sardot, 1999). It is proposed that when intrinsic and extrinsic cues are directly consulted in making JOLs, the result is an information- (or theory-) based judgment of knowing. Mnemonic cues, on the other hand, give rise to a feeling of knowing, which can then serve as a basis for a judgment. Thus, the distinction between information-based and experience-based metacognitive judgments (see Koriat & Levy-Sardot, 1999) parallels in part Flavell's (1979) distinction between the effects of metacognitive knowledge and those of metacognitive experiences (see also Efklides, this volume).

The distinction between the analytic and nonanalytic inferential   processes mediating JOLs has important implications for JOL accuracy. When JOLs are based on the explicit application of a belief or theory (e.g., "I have poor memory for names", "associatively-related pairs are better remembered than unrelated pairs"), their accuracy should depend greatly on the validity of the underlying theories or beliefs. It is these theories or beliefs that have received a great deal of attention in the context of developmental studies of declarative metamemory (or metacognitive knowledge, Flavell, 1979). These studies suggest an age-related increase in the accuracy of children's beliefs about memory, and this increase should, of course, contribute to enhanced monitoring accuracy of theory-based JOLs.

The accuracy of heuristic-driven JOLs, in contrast, depends on the validity of the underlying cues. Although such cues can sometimes be misleading as predictors of memory performance (e.g., Benjamin, Bjork, & Schwartz, 1998), they are generally dependable because they are influenced by both intrinsic and extrinsic cues that affect learning and remembering (Benjamin & Bjork, 1996; Jacoby & Kelley, 1987). Therefore the accuracy of JOLs should generally increase as a function of the extent to which they are based on internal, mnemonic cues.

Koriat (1997) proposed that with repeated study of the same material the basis of JOLs changes from reliance on intrinsic cues towards increased reliance on internal, mnemonic cues. In support of this proposition, two changes were observed with practice studying the same list of paired associates. First, the accuracy of JOLs in predicting subsequent recall increased gradually from one study-test cycle to the next (King, Zechmeister, & Shaughnessy, 1980; Leonesio & Nelson, 1990; Mazzoni, Cornoldi, & Marchitelli, 1990; see also Weaver & Kelemen, this volume). Thus the within-participant cross-item correlation between JOL and recall increased from .66 on the first study-test cycle to .89 on the 4th cycle. This improvement in JOL accuracy was attributed to the increased reliance on mnemonic cues under the assumption that mnemonic cues closely reflect the cognitive processing of the items. Second, the correlation between JOLs and the a-priori difficulty of the paired associates, as rated by a different group of participants, decreased gradually with practice, averaging .93 and .73, respectively, for the 1st and 4th blocks. Judged item difficulty represents an intrinsic cue that can affect JOLs, and thus the changes in the JOL-difficulty correlation were seen to reflect decreased reliance on intrinsic cues with practice studying the same items.

In Experiment 1 we tested whether this presumed dynamics of JOLs also occurs in young school children. The question is whether children also reveal the assumed shift from reliance on intrinsic factors towards greater reliance on mnemonic factors with increased practice studying the same list of items. As noted earlier, developmental research have invested little attention in the nonanalytic processes underlying metacognitive judgments, and Experiment 1 may help remedy this situation by importing insights from the experimental-cognitive study of the dynamics of monitoring processes.

2.1 Experiment 1

Experiment 1 was modeled after Experiment 2 of Koriat (1997) but it was carried out on 2nd grade and 4th grade children. A list of paired associates, composed of hard and easy pairs was presented for four study-test cycles. Thus, apart from age, the experiment included an intrinsic factor (item difficulty) and an extrinsic factor (practice). Feedback about the correctness of the answers was also manipulated between participants.

2.1.1 Method

Participants. Participants were 32 second graders (mean age = 7.2 years) and 32 fourth graders (mean age = 9.7 years) from predominantly middle class homes. In each group participants were assigned randomly to the Feedback and No-Feedback conditions with the constraint that there was an equal number of boys and girls in each Age X Feedback condition.

Materials. The items were 24 pairs of Hebrew words that were selected on the basis of a preliminary study. In that study, 30 2nd graders and 30 4th graders were asked to rate 50 Hebrew pairs in terms of memorability. Specifically, they were asked to imagine that 100 children had studied these pairs, and to estimate how many of them would recall each pair, that is, would recall the response word when presented with the stimulus word. The median estimates were used to order the pairs in terms of judged a-priori difficulty. Twenty-four words were selected for which there was generally an agreement between 2nd and 4th graders, and were divided at the median into two sets of 12 easy and 12 hard pairs.

Procedure. Children were tested individually in a quiet room in the school, using a PC compatible laptop. They were instructed that they would have to study pairs appearing on the computer screen so that, during the test phase, they would be able to recall the response word when cued with the stimulus word. They were also told that at the end of each study trial they would have to estimate the likelihood of recalling the response word during the test phase. The elicitation of JOLs capitalized on the hot-cold game familiar to children, using a thermometer procedure devised by Koriat, Goldsmith, and Schneider (1999). The rules of the hot-cold game were explained, and participants were required to rate their JOLs on a 5-point scale depicted as a color drawing of a thermometer ranging from deep blue ("very cold", i.e., "no chance to recall the response word") to deep red ("very hot", i.e., "completely certain to recall the response word"). A large drawing of the thermometer was placed on the table in front of the child.

During the study phase the intact pair remained on the screen for 5 s, and was replaced by the statement "how sure are you that you will recall the second word later when you see the first word?" The child indicated his/her answer by placing a cube on one of the five colored segments of the thermometer drawing. When all the pairs had been presented for study, the test phase began: Each of the stimulus words was presented in turn, and the child had to speak aloud the answer. The stimulus word remained on the screen until the child responded, or until 10 s have elapsed.

The procedure was the same for the no-feedback and feedback conditions except that in the latter condition a sound was presented for 30 ms when the response provided was incorrect. (The instructions for the feedback condition included an explanation of the significance of the sound).

The study-test phase cycle was repeated three more times. The presentation of the items was random during all study and test phases.

2.1.2   Results.

The feedback manipulation had little effect and will not be discussed further. Considering first the results for the first block, the intrinsic factor of item difficulty had a strong effect on both recall and JOL. Recall for judged easy and hard items averaged 73.0% and 11.8%, respectively, and there was no effect of age. There was an Age X Difficulty interaction, however, with regard to JOLs: Whereas for easy items there was little difference between 2nd and 4th graders (the respective means were 4.06 and 3.92), for the hard items 2nd graders gave higher JOLs (the respective means were 3.51 and 2.99). Note that a rating of 3 was described in the instructions as "I may recall or I may not". If that rating is assumed to be roughly equivalent to a .5 probability, then the results would seem to suggest very inflated JOLs, with degree of overconfidence being stronger for the younger children (see also Schneider et al., in press).

We shall turn now to the effects of the extrinsic factor of repeated presentation. Figure 1 depicts mean recall (top panel) and JOL (bottom panel) as a function of presentation and item difficulty for each of the age groups. It can be seen that both age groups exhibited strong improvement in recall from 42% on the first presentation to 73% for the 4th presentation. JOLs also increased with presentation for both age groups, indicating that children's JOLs are also sensitive to the extrinsic factor of practice (cf. Moulin et al., this volume). This increase, however, was monotonic for easy items, whereas for hard items there was, in fact, a drop from the first to the second presentation. This pattern suggests that children in both age groups corrected their inflated JOLs in response to their low actual memory performance after the first presentation. It can also be seen that 2nd graders continued to provide higher JOLs than the 4th graders throughout the 4 presentations, but this age effect was entirely confined to the hard items.

We examine now the accuracy of JOLs in predicting inter-item differences in recall. For each child, a gamma correlation was calculated between JOL and recall across all 24 items (Nelson, 1984). Figure 2 (top panel) presents the means of these correlations as a function of presentation for each of the two age groups. An Age X Presentation X Feedback ANOVA also failed to yield any effect of feedback and therefore the results in Figure 2 are pooled across the two feedback conditions. However, there were significant effects for both age, $F(1, 55) = 13.91$, $p<.0005$, and presentation, $F(3, 165) = 13.99$, $p<.0001$.

The effect of age reflects the observation that the older children's predictions were more accurate than the younger children's predictions. This difference was significant ($p<.002$) even on the first presentation: Gamma correlation averaged .40 for the younger group and .66 for the older group. Note, however, that even the younger group's resolution was relatively high and significant ($p<.0001$). Thus, we have an indication of a developmental trend in monitoring skill but also for efficient relative monitoring even among 2nd graders.

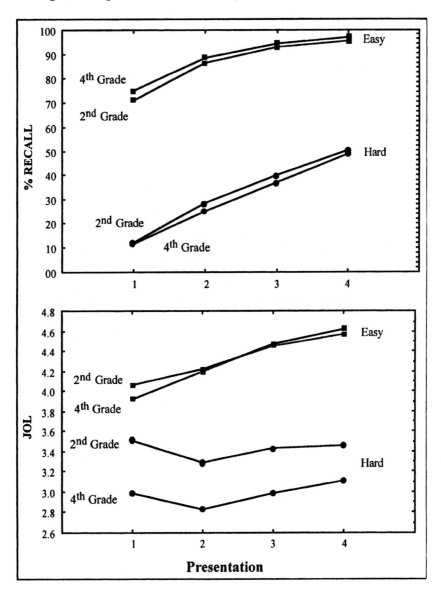

Figure 1. Mean recall (top panel) and JOL (bottom panel) as a function of presentation and item difficulty for 2nd and 4th graders (Experiment 1).

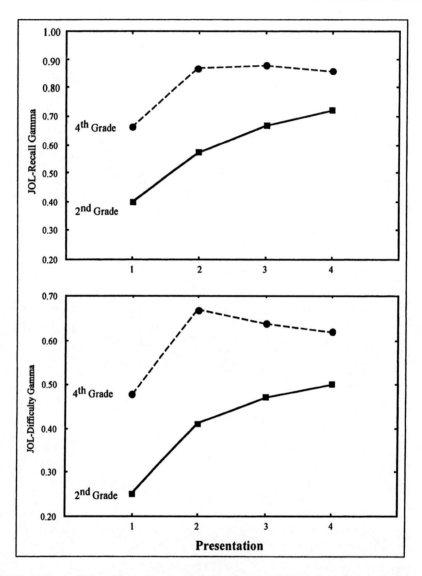

Figure 2. Mean within-subject gamma correlations between JOLs and recall (top panel) and between JOL and item difficulty (bottom panel), plotted as a function of presentation (Experiment 1).

As for the effects of presentation, the results replicate the pattern that has been observed previously with adults. The improvement in JOL accuracy with practice was more clearly seen in the younger children, possibly because of a ceiling effect that occurred for the older group. In fact, practice seemed to close the age gap so that the gamma correlation exhibited by the younger group on the 4th presentation was the same as that exhibited by the older group on the 1st presentation.

What are the implications of these results? According to Koriat (1997), the improvement in resolution occurs because of the increased reliance on internal, mnemonic cues that disclose degree of learning. Further unpublished work by Koriat and his associates with adults suggest that in fact two changes occur with practice studying the same list of items. First, mnemonic cues become increasingly more valid as predictive cues for recall, and second, the reliance on these cues increases with practice. If so, then we have here evidence that a similar reliance on internal cues occurs even in 2nd graders.

The second proposition of Koriat (1997), however, was not supported for children. According to that proposition, the increased reliance on mnemonic cues is accompanied by a decreased reliance on intrinsic cues. As can be seen in Figure 2 (bottom panel), the JOL-difficulty correlation (with difficulty scored dichotomously) actually increased rather than decreased with practice. This increase is evident for 4th graders between the 1st and 2nd presentations only, whereas for the 2nd graders there was a monotonic increase from the 1st to the 4th presentation. In fact, the similarity between the patterns depicted in the two panels of Figure 2 suggests that much of the improvement in the predictive validity of JOLs with practice was mediated by intrinsic cues.

The discrepancy between the children and adult results is interesting. At present we cannot tell whether it discloses a qualitative difference in the bases of JOLs for children and adults. As noted earlier, intrinsic (as well as extrinsic) cues can affect JOLs directly (through an analytic, theory-based process), but they can also affect JOLs indirectly, through their effects on mnemonic cues. Thus, it is possible that in children, much of the inter-item variance in mnemonic cues (e.g., processing fluency) is determined by intrinsic properties such as those captured by the judged a-priori difficulty of the items. In that case the results would be seen to accord with the proposition that practice does result in increased reliance on mnemonic cues even among children. It should be noted that in a post-experimental interview about the strategy used to memorize the pairs, 23% of the 4th graders and 10% of the 2nd graders mentioned reliance on the associative link between the two members of a pair. However, even those who did not mention such strategy indicated that some pairs were easier than others, and chose the strongly-related pairs as an example of the easier pairs. Thus, it is possible that children explicitly used that kind of declarative knowledge in making JOLs on the first presentation of the list. However, the observation that the JOL-difficulty correlation increased with practice suggests that even when young children do not take advantage deliberately of their a-priori knowledge that some items are easier to learn and remember than others, they can appreciate inter-item differences between the items after attempting to learn and remember them, and can then use mnemonic cues in making subsequent JOLs.

Some evidence for reliance on mnemonic cues also comes from the observation that for presentations 2-4, JOLs for different items on one presentation were highly correlated with the recall of these items on the previous test. This correlation was higher for the 4th graders and did not increase with presentation. Thus, for example, JOLs for presentation 2 correlated .76 and .92 for 2nd and 4th graders, respectively, with recall success on the previous test.

2.2   Experiment 2

Experiment 1 yielded some evidence that children's JOLs too exhibit improved predictive accuracy as a result of practice studying the same list of items. Experiment 2 explored one additional factor that has been found to affect JOL accuracy: The elicitation of JOLs immediately after study vs. its elicitation some time after study.

A robust finding that has been repeatedly observed by Nelson and Dunlosky (Nelson & Dunlosky, 1991; Dunlosky & Nelson, 1994, 1997) is the "delayed JOL effect": The accuracy of JOLs in predicting subsequent memory performance is substantially higher when JOLs are solicited some time after study than when they are solicited immediately after study. This effect was only observed when the JOLs were elicited by the stimulus word in the pair; not by the intact stimulus-response pair (Dunlosky & Nelson, 1992).

According to the monitoring-retrieval hypothesis of JOLs (Dunlosky & Nelson , 1997) this is because when JOLs are elicited immediately at the end of the study trial, the item is still in short-term memory and therefore the mnemonic cue associated with attempted retrieval has limited validity in predicting future recall. On the other hand, when JOL is delayed, the mnemonic cues associated with attempted recall tap the kind of retrieval from long-term memory that would be required during testing.

Experiment 2, then, had two aims. The first was to examine whether children's JOLs also exhibit sensitivity to the time at which JOLs are elicited. This possibility has been confirmed recently by Schneider et al. (in press). In their study, children (2nd graders, 4th graders and kindergarteners) made immediate or delayed dichotomous JOLs. Delayed JOLs were found to yield higher JOL-recall gamma correlations than immediate JOLs (.83 and .53, respectively in Study 1, and .75 and .18 in Study 2). These results not only indicate that young children are capable of monitoring their knowledge under favorable circumstances, but also suggest that their JOLs are affected by internal, mnemonic cues.

The second aim was to examine the hypothesis that the process underlying the delayed-JOL effect is the same as that underlying the effects of practice on JOLs. This hypothesis has not been tested so far on either adults or children. We have previously proposed that the improvement in JOL accuracy that occurs with practice derives from both the increased diagnosticity of the mnemonic cues underlying JOLs, and increased reliance on these cues. Similarly, the delayed-JOL effect has been explained in terms of a better diagnosticity of the cues underlying delayed JOLs compared to those underlying immediate JOLs. If so, we should expect an interaction between the effects of practice and the effects of delay so that both of these manipulations can be considered to constitute roughly alternative means to achieve the same goal. Therefore practice should have little effects beyond those that are due to delaying JOLs.

2.2.1   Method

Participants. As in Experiment 1, participants were 32 2nd graders and 32 4th graders. In each group participants were assigned randomly to the stimulus-alone and stimulus-response conditions.

Materials and Procedure. The same list of 24 Hebrew pairs as in Experiment 1 was used. The procedure was similar to that of Experiment 1 except for the following. First, in the stimulus-alone condition JOLs were cued by the stimulus word, whereas in the stimulus-response condition the intact stimulus-response pair was presented as a stimulus for JOLs.

Second, for each participant, the elicitation of JOLs was immediate for 12 items and delayed for the remaining 12 items. The assignment of items to the immediate and delayed JOL conditions was random except that in each condition there were exactly 6 easy and 6 hard items. For the immediate-JOL items the stimulus for JOL appeared immediately at the end of the study trial. For the delayed-JOL items, in contrast, the stimulus for JOLs appeared after all 24 items had been studied. The order of JOL elicitation for these items was such that the first 4 items studied that were assigned to the delayed-JOL condition, appeared first, in random order, then the next four items, and finally the last set of four items studied. Finally, unlike in Experiment 1, no feedback was given.

There were 4 study-test blocks. Participants were instructed about the difference between immediate- and delayed-JOL items, and were given practice with a 6-item list

2.2.2   Results.

Let us consider first the results for the first presentation. Recall was overall better for 4th graders than for 2nd graders in the first study-test cycle (47% and 42%, respectively). Recall was also better for the stimulus-response condition (47%) than for the stimulus-alone condition (41%), and for delayed-JOL (53%) than for immediate-JOL items (35%). However, there was an interaction such that the advantage of the stimulus-response condition over the stimulus-alone condition was found only for delayed-JOL items but not for immediate-JOL items.

With regard to JOLs, an interactive pattern was observed: There was little difference between immediate (3.65) and delayed JOLs (3.70) when JOLs were made in response to the stimulus-response pair. When JOLs were cued by the stimulus alone, in contrast, delayed JOLs were significantly lower (3.33) than immediate JOLs (3.98). These results suggest that delaying JOLs can mend the overconfidence experienced by children during study.

Note the interesting dissociation between the effects of JOL interval (immediate-delayed) on recall and JOLs in the stimulus-alone condition: Delaying JOLs improved recall significantly ($p<.0001$) but reduced JOLs significantly ($p<.0001$). The former effect is consistent with the finding that retrieval experience is more beneficial to recall when retrieval is difficult than when it is easy (Whitten & Bjork, 1977). The latter effect, on the other hand, presumably derives from the greater retrieval fluency that is experienced during immediate JOL compared to that characteristic of delayed JOL.

With regard to the effects of practice, the results were similar to those of Experiment 1, exhibiting increased JOL and recall with practice.

We turn next to resolution, that is, the accuracy of JOLs in predicting inter-item differences in recall. In the analyses of resolution we focused only on the results from the first three presentations because 12 participants exhibited little variance in JOLs on the 4th presentation. In addition, the results for the first 3 blocks were based only on 27 4th graders and 24 2nd graders because the remaining participants also yielded no variance in JOLs on one of these presentations.

First, consider the delayed-JOL effect. The results were consistent with those obtained for adults and with those reported by Schneider et al. (in press) for children: For the stimulus-alone condition the JOL-recall gamma correlation averaged .60 and .92 for the immediate and delayed JOLs in the first block. The respective values across all 3 blocks were .77 and .91. There was no similar difference for JOLs cued by stimulus-response pairs. We should also note that there were no significant age differences in JOL-recall accuracy, unlike what was found in Experiment 1 (see also Schneider et al., in press).

Second, the effects of practice on resolution were generally similar to those obtained in Experiment 1: JOL accuracy improved with practice. However, the results, presented in Figure 3 also disclose the expected interactive pattern between practice and delay. For three of the four conditions the JOL-recall correlation generally increased with practice, averaging .59, .80 and .85 for blocks 1-3, respectively. In contrast, delayed JOLs cued by the stimulus alone yielded a high resolution on the first block, consistent with the delayed-JOL effect, and this high resolution remained stable across blocks. In fact, practice seemed to achieve practically the same level of JOL accuracy as that achieved by delaying JOLs (cued by the stimulus alone). This pattern of results is consistent with the idea that practice and delay constitute alternative means for enhancing JOL accuracy, and that the effects of both are mediated by similar processes, presumably the increased diagnosticity of the mnemonic cues on which JOLs are based. We should stress, however, that because JOL accuracy was very high even on the first block for stimulus-alone delayed JOLs, the pattern of results depicted in Figure 3 could simply stem from a ceiling effect.

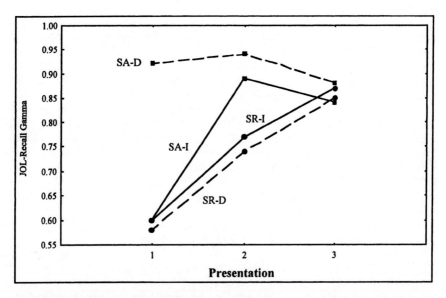

Figure 3. Mean within-subject gamma correlations between JOLs and recall plotted as a function of presentation for immediate JOLs cued by the stimulus alone (SA-I) and by the

stimulus-response pair (SR-I), and for delayed JOLs cued by the stimulus alone (SA-D) and by the stimulus-response pair (SR-D) (Experiment 2).

In sum, the present study concerned two factors that have been found to have marked effects on the accuracy of item-by-item JOLs among adults –repeated practice studying the same materials, and the elicitation of JOLs immediately after study or at some delay. The results obtained with adults suggest that the improved monitoring resulting from both practice and delay is mediated by reliance on internal, mnemonic cues that are diagnostic of the extent to which the studied items have been mastered. In this study we obtained results suggesting that children's JOLs are similarly affected by mnemonic cues, and furthermore, that the effects of practice and delay on JOL accuracy are mediated by similar processes. This study, then, provides some insight into the mechanisms underlying children's monitoring of their own knowledge during study, and the processes that contribute to the accuracy of that monitoring.

3.   CONCLUDING REMARKS

While the present study concerned metamemory in children, our main interest was not simply to assess children's monitoring proficiency or to examine age-related effects in that proficiency. Rather, the focus of the study was on the processes mediating metacognitive judgments and their accuracy in young children. As noted in the introduction, developmental studies in metamemory have been primarily descriptive and correlational, attempting to identify age differences in metamemory and their possible effects on memory performance. In contrast, the study of metacognition by experimental cognitive psychologists has concentrated more narrowly on testing specific hypotheses about the dynamics of metacognitive monitoring and control processes (e.g., Barnes et al., 1999; Koriat & Goldsmith, 1996; Nelson & Narens, 1990). Several recent studies, however, have attempted to bring insights from cognitive psychology to the investigation of developmental aspects of metacognition, concentrating on the on-line monitoring and control processes that occur during learning and remembering. For example, Butterfield, Nelson, and Peck (1988) applied experimental paradigms that have been in use in the study of adult metacognition to investigate developmental trends in the accuracy of the feeling of knowing. A subsequent study by Lockl and Schneider (submitted), while extending this study, also addressed the question of the basis of feeling-of-knowing judgments in children. With regard to monitoring and control processes during learning, both the Schneider et al. (in press) and the present study extended investigation of the accuracy of JOLs to children, focusing on the on-line monitoring of degree of learning that occurs in item-by-item learning (see Thiede & Dunlosky, 1999). A study by Dufresne and Kobasigawa (1989), however, provides important insight into developmental aspects of the control function. In general, the on-line monitoring of learning is important because it guides the allocation of study time and study effort among different items (Nelson & Leonesio, 1988). What Dufresne and Kobasigawa showed is that the main difference between younger and older children lies in the ability to put the output of monitoring to use in the self regulation of study time. A more recent study by Koriat, Goldsmith, Schneider, and Nakash-

Dura (in press; see also Roebers, Moga, & Schneider, in press) focused on the strategic regulation of memory performance during the report of information from memory. Their results indicate that young children, like adults, are capable of enhancing the accuracy of their memory testimony by screening out wrong answers under free-report conditions. The results also suggest a developmental trend in the level of memory accuracy that can be achieved through the strategic control of memory reporting.

These recent studies, among others, illustrate some of the benefits that ensue from the attempt to merge contributions from cognitive and developmental psychology in the investigation of metacognition. While the cognitive approach to metacognition stresses depth of understanding, the developmental approach offers conceptual breadth and richness. A combination of both approaches is likely to offer interesting and important new venues for investigation.

Authors' note
The experiments reported were conducted at the Institute of Information Processing and Decision Making, University of Haifa. We are grateful to Yaffa Lev for programming the experiments, and to Limor Sheffer for the analyses of the data. Correspondence concerning this chapter should be addressed to Asher Koriat, Department of Psychology, University of Haifa, Haifa 31905, Israel.
akoriat@psy.haifa.ac.il

Chapter 2

The Systemic Nature of Metacognitive Experiences
Feelings, Judgments, and their Interrelations

Anastasia Efklides
Aristotle University of Thessaloniki, Greece

Key themes: Prob / Proc / Theor

Key words: Feeling of confidence / Feeling of difficulty / Feeling of familiarity / Feeling of satisfaction / Metacognitiveexperiences.

Abstract: Metacognitive experiences comprise metacognitive feelings and metacognitive judgments or estimates evoked during a cognitive endeavour. The emphasis of this chapter is on the interrelations between metacognitive experiences and particularly between feeling of familiarity (FOF), feeling of difficulty (FOD), feeling of confidence (FOC) and feeling of satisfaction (FOS) in different phases of cognitive processing (i.e., in advance, during, and after task processing). It was assumed that these metacognitive feelings are products of inferential processes that make use of specific cues which are related to fluency or interruption of cognitive processing. Therefore, they are interrelated and form systems, in which the change of one metacognitive experience will influence the state of the others. Specifically, FOC was expected to be related to FOF, FOD, and estimated solution correctness (ESC), whereas FOS to FOC and ESC. These assumptions were tested in a study in which 274 students of 7th and 9th grade participated. They were required to solve two mathematical tasks, varying in their processing demands (task difficulty), and to rate on 4-point scales the above metacognitive experiences in three phases of problem solving. The results confirmed the systemic nature of the above metacognitive experiences, regardless of task difficulty. The phase of processing, however, did differentiate the relations between the metacognitive experiences studied. These findings explain various findings related to FOC and pose questions regarding the nature of metacognitive experiences.

Metacognitive experiences is a term coined by Flavell (1979) who posited that there are two forms of metacognition, namely metacognitive experiences and metacognitive knowledge. Metacognitive experiences constitute online metacognition, whereas metacognitive knowledge is knowledge we retrieve from memory (semantic or episodic; see Wheeler, Stuss, & Tulving, 1997) and regards goals, tasks, persons, and strategies. Metacognitive experiences comprise ideas, feelings, judgments, and metacognitive knowledge evoked during problem solving. In essence, metacognitive experiences are metacognitions available in working memory (see also Efklides, 2001; Efklides & Vauras, 1999; Lories, Dardenne, & Yzerbyt, 1998). The focus of this chapter is on metacognitive experiences and specifically on metacognitive feelings and judgments evoked during problem solving rather than on metacognitive knowledge (for a discussion of the similarities and differences between the two forms of metacognition see Efklides, 2001). This kind of metacognitive experiences is similar to the feelings and judgments studied in metamemory research such as feeling of knowing, feeling of confidence, or judgment of learning. Our research, however, differs from metamemory research in that it deals with feelings and judgments manifest in problem solving situations. More specifically, it deals with feeling of familiarity, feeling of difficulty, feeling of confidence, and judgment or estimate[1] of solution correctness (for an overview see Efklides, 2001).

Research based on metacognitive experiences in problem solving provides a new perspective to metacognition research and extends the scope of experimental metamemory research. It's advantage is that it shows the role of metacognition in everyday life situations. Specifically, it shows how metacognitive feelings and judgments influence online self-regulation in problem solving situations. The problem-solving situation that was depicted in the study presented in this chapter is school mathematics. Mathematics is used as a paradigm of school learning in which there is a lot of conscious and effortful processing and in which metacognitions in the form of metacognitive experiences and metacognitive knowledge is present. Furthermore, school mathematics represent a situation that is most common in educational settings. Thus, studying metacognitions in mathematics problem-solving bridges the gap between experimental metamemory research and educational research on metacognition and self-regulation.

From a theoretical point of view, the study of metacognition in problem-solving situations has a number of features that differentiate it from metamemory research and allow a richer picture of the phenomenon of metacognition. Firstly, in problem solving we do not have only one single metacognitive experience, such as feeling of knowing (FOK) or confidence, related to the retrieval of the response from memory. In problem solving we have construction of the response and during this process the person experiences a number of different feelings, judgments or estimates, or ideas (such as those mentioned above), which may be inter-related. For example, the person feels that the task is familiar and therefore not so difficult; or, the student experiences difficulty and thinks that s/he needs to use his/her brain to figure out the solution to the problem or recall the rule needed (Efklides, Samara, & Petropoulou, 1999); or, the student feels that the task is familiar but a lot of time is required for processing and therefore s/he cannot go on with problem solving. Therefore, if we want to understand the mechanism underlying the formation of metacognitive feelings or judgments, we need to take into consideration other metacognitive experiences present in the person's awareness. The constellation of metacognitive experiences may also explain the control decisions made by the person.

Another feature of metacognitions in problem solving is that some of the metacognitive experiences, such as feeling of difficulty, may recur and change as processing goes on. For example, students may start problem solving considering the problem easy and during processing become aware of difficulties. This awareness changes their initial perception of task difficulty (Efklides, Samara, & Petropoulou, 1996). Also, Efklides, Papadaki, Papantoniou, & Kiosseoglou (1997, 1998) found that students rated their feelings of difficulty in one mathematical problem relatively to the difficulty they had in problems previously processed. This implies that metacognitive experiences in problem solving make use of various cues depending on the context or features of the problem solving situation. Thus, the interrelatedness and dynamic nature of metacognitive experiences in problem solving is a phenomenon that needs to be investigated and explained. This kind of knowledge can contribute to our understanding of the formation and functioning of metacognition in general.

Another contribution of metacognition research in problem solving is its capability to reveal the relations of metacognition with affect. Metamemory research has focused mainly on the relations of metacognition with cognition. However, problem solving involves goals and outcomes that may have direct links to one's self and personal priorities or concerns. Thus, the difficulty experienced during problem solving may affect the person's motivation towards the task or the person's perceived capability to deal with the task at hand. In our research we have found that metacognitive experiences are influenced by one's existing self-concept (Dermitzaki & Efklides, 2001) but also provide intrinsic feedback to self-concept (Efklides & Tsiora, in press). They also influence causal attributions regarding ability, task difficulty, or effort (Metallidou & Efklides, 2001). These findings imply that metacognitive experiences may have much broader implications than just monitoring and control of cognition. They have effects on affect and are an indispensable part of self-regulation.

To sum up, the study of metacognition in problem solving allows for a broader conception of metacognition and its relations with cognition, affect, and volition. However, in order to be able to delimit which aspects of metacognition serve the functions we referred to above, we need to elaborate on the distinction between metacognitive feelings and metacognitive judgments.

Metacognitive feelings, like all other aspects of metacognition, convey information about cognition (Koriat & Levy-Sardot, 2000a); for example, that we already have a piece of information in memory. However, besides their informational / cognitive nature they also have an affective character. This is manifest in the quality of pleasantness or unpleasantness they have. For example, feeling of familiarity has a positive affective valence whereas feeling of difficulty a negative one. The question is what is the information conveyed by metacognitive feelings and why this information takes the form of affect. We will take up this point later on in this chapter. Suffice it for the moment to say that feelings, according to Frijda (1986), are signals of a continuous monitoring of good functioning. They reflect the smoothness or obstacles / interruptions occuring during processing, the match / mismatch between goal and actual conditions as well as the extent to which the outcome of performance suffices the person's concerns or goals. It seems, therefore, that the information conveyed by feelings is characterized by personal relevance and this gives them their affectivity.

Metacognitive judgments are cognitive in nature (Koriat & Levy-Sardot, 1999; Lories, Dardenne, & Yzerbyt, 1998; Lories & Schelstraete, 1998) and may regard the source or other aspects of one's memory (i.e., where, when, and how we acquired a piece of information (Johnson, Hashtroudi, & Lindsay, 1993), other aspects of memory such as frequency or recency of occurrence of a piece of information, judgment of whether learning has been achieved (Koriat & Shitzer-Reichert, this volume; Nelson, 1993) or whether the outcome of problem solving is correct, namely, judgment of solution correctness (Dermitzaki, 1997; Dermitzaki & Efklides, 2000). One could also ask for a judgment or estimate of effort or time spent on a task (Metallidou & Efklides, 2001; Efklides et al., 1996). Metacognitive judgments of this kind refer to qualities or features of one's own cognition or cognitive processing but not from the point of view of personal relevance, that is, of whether these features are in accordance with one's goals or concerns as feelings do. Of course, when one is asked to rate the strength of a feeling present in his/her awareness, this is also a judgment or estimate about the feeling.

Another kind of metacognitive judgments regards features of the task and task-processing. For example, how similar two tasks are (Efklides & Demetriou, 1989; Efklides, Demetriou, & Metallidou, 1994) in terms of surface and processing characteristics. This kind of judgment can be considered as online task-specific knowledge (Efklides, 2001) that draws a lot on one's metacognitive knowledge regarding tasks and their processing.

The distinction between metacognitive feelings and judgments suggests that there is a continuum in metacognitive experiences ranging from feelings that are marked with self-relevant goals or concerns to online task-specific knowledge that is driven mainly by task-relevant information. In all cases, metacognitive experiences are the interface between the person and the task at hand, with differing emphasis on the person, on cognition per se, or on the task at hand.

In this paper we shall refer to metacognitive experiences and their interrelations, as well as to their relations with other feelings such as being satisfied with the solution produced to a problem. Feelings like interest, liking a task, or satisfaction, are not usually considered metacognitive; however, they are closely related to the perception of the task and one's response to it and to the processing outcome. The metacognitive experiences we shall deal with are feeling of familiarity (FOF), feeling of difficulty (FOD), feeling of confidence (FOC), and feeling of satisfaction (FOS) as well as the judgment or estimate of solution correctness (ESC).

1.   RELATIONS BETWEEN METACOGNITIVE EXPERIENCES

In order to delimit the possible relations between metacognitive experiences we must first try to define each of them and the kind of information they convey.

Feeling of familiarity monitors processing fluency but also involves attribution about the source of fluency which is located in the past, that is, previous encounters with the stimulus (Whittlesea, 1993). **Feeling of difficulty**, on the other hand, monitors the obstacles or interruptions of processing (Frijda, 1986). Although there is no research to our knowledge on the nature of feeling of difficulty, one could assume that it reflects lack of fluency of processing in the sense of lack of availability of response, or in accessibility of relevant knowledge / procedures during online processing.

To the extent that both feeling of familiarity and feeling of difficulty monitor aspects of processing fluency, a relation should exist between them, and this relation should be negative. This was indeed found in Efklides et al. (1996). Furthermore, whereas feeling of familiarity is related to the frequency or recency of previous encounters with the stimulus (Efklides et al., 1996) or the perceptual similarity of stimuli (Whittleshea, 1993) feeling of difficulty is related to objective task difficulty[2] and personal factors that affect the accessibility of knowledge when needed. In our work(Efklides, Papadaki, Papantoniou, & Kiosseoglou, 1997, 1998; Efklides, Samara, & Petropoulou, 1999) we studied feeling of difficulty and factors that affect it, such as cognitive ability and personality, on the one hand, and task complexity / difficulty on the other (Efklides et al., 1997, 1998). Furthermore, we showed that feeling of difficulty is related to task-related control ideas or attributions about the source of difficulty such as ways and means instrumental for problem solving (Efklides et al., 1999). Therefore, feeling of familiarity and feeling of difficulty are related between them but the one cannot be reduced to the other.

Feeling of confidence is an experience related to the outcome of cognitive processing; it reflects the extent to which the answer / solution reached is accurate (Costermans, Lories, & Ansay, 1992). Confidence is usually measured as a judgment of the probability of an answer being correct, and in tasks such as eyewitness testimony or general knowledge tasks (Hollins & Perfect, 1997; Juslin, Olsson, & Winman, 1996; see also Olson & Juslin, this volume; Seemungal & Stevenage, this volume). It is also studied as a personal or gender characteristic with respect to overconfidence (Beyer & Bowden, 1997; Pulford & Colman, 1997; Stankov & Crawford, 1996; Yarab, Sensibaugh, & Allgeier, 1997).

Among the factors that affect the confidence-accuracy relationship is the type and difficulty of the task (Kebbell, Wagstaff, & Covey, 1996; Pulford & Colman, 1997), one's existing knowledge in the area of the question asked and one's awareness of lack of relevant knowledge (Allwood & Granhag, 1996). This suggests that metacognitive experiences conveying information about task difficulty, such as feeling of difficulty, or state of one's knowledge such as feeling of knowing, should be related to feeling of confidence.

Feeling of satisfaction has to do with the matching of the outcome to the goal set; it seems to be related to the monitoring of the extent to which our personal goals as well as standards or concerns have been met (Frijda, 1986). Satisfaction is usually studied with respect to well being and life satisfaction. Life satisfaction is considered to be related to personal goals and to the congruence between desired and achieved goals (Ardelt, 1997) or between "real" and "ought" self (Pavot, Fujita, & Diener, 1997). However, even at the task level the person may feel satisfied or not with the solution produced to the problem, depending on whether the solution matches the goal set. The matching process presupposes a judgment or estimate of solution correctness or accuracy of the response, because this is a cue that the goal has been achieved. It can be assumed that feeling of confidence provides such a cue. Therefore satisfaction should be related to confidence, although it cannot be reduced to it as shown in the case when one is confident that the solution produced is correct but is not satisfied with it, because s/he would like some other solution, perhaps more elegant or congruent with some criteria beyond correctness. Yet, despite the relative conceptual similarity between confidence and satisfaction, one does not find in the literature studies that relate the two feelings between them. Also, the relations between feeling of familiarity, feeling of difficulty, feeling of confidence and feeling of satisfaction have not been studied.

On the other hand, feeling of confidence and its relation to feeling of knowing has received considerable attention in recent research on metamemory (Costermans,

Lories, & Ansay, 1992; Miner & Reder, 1994; Narens, Jameson, & Lee, 1994; Nelson, 1996). Feeling of confidence regards items recalled whereas feeling of knowing items not recalled (Costermans et al., 1992; Narens et al., 1994) In this context, feeling of confidence has been related to feeling of familiarity (Costermans et al., 1992; Miner & Reder, 1994), to the amount of time allocated for searching memory (Miner & Reder, 1994; Robinson, Johnson, & Herndon, 1997) and to how rapidly an answer was given (Kelley & Lindsay, 1993). According to Robinson et al. (1997) reaction time (RT) and subjective assessments of cognitive effort (i.e., recognition vs. recall in eyewitness task) were both negatively related to confidence and accuracy. Subjective assessments, however, were superior predictors of confidence than RT, whereas RT was unique predictor of accuracy. What the previous findings suggest is that confidence is related to cues of fluency of processing (that is, feeling of familiarity) on the one hand, and cues of cognitive effort or time allocated for searching memory on the other. Time allocated for search or the subjective estimate of effort are indicative of the difficulty to access the answer, in other words, of the interruptions of processing. In fact the relationship between feeling of confidence and time for memory search is negative whereas in the case of ease of processing and speed it is positive. This implies that feeling of confidence should not only be related to feeling of familiarity but also to feeling of difficulty as a cue of processing interruption. The relationship with feeling of familiarity should be positive whereas with feeling of difficulty negative, because fluency of processing indicates availability of relevant knowledge or response and, indirectly, correctness of the answer. However, if confidence judgments make use of more direct cues or criteria pertaining to response accuracy, they should be closely related to estimate of solution correctness, and this relationship should be stronger than the one with feeling of familiarity or feeling of difficulty.

Further evidence on the relations between feeling of knowing and feeling of confidence suggests that whereas feeling of knowing is prospective in nature (the person judges the retrievability of an answer), feeling of confidence is retrospective, that is, it refers to one's belief that the answer produced is correct or accurate (Miner & Reder, 1994; Narens et al. , 1994; Nelson, 1996). Satisfaction is also a feeling following the production of the answer and, as assumed above, related to feeling of confidence. This implies that the relation of feeling of satisfaction with feeling of familiarity and feeling of difficulty, which precede performance output, will be indirect via feeling of confidence and estimate of solution correctness rather than direct.

A word of caution should be stated here: since feeling of confidence and feeling of satisfaction are retrospective rather than prospective in nature, feeling of confidence should be related to feeling of familiarity only when feeling of confidence is required prospectively, that is, before the actual answer is produced. For example, one can be asked how confident is that s/he can produce the correct answer to the question posed. In such a case the main source of information on which the person can base his/her judgment is processing fluency (that is, feeling of familiarity) and perceived obstacles (that is, feeling of difficulty) rather than the retrieved answer itself (or the estimated correctness of it). On the contrary, when feeling of confidence is required retrospectively it should be related mainly to the estimated solution correctness and feeling of difficulty experienced during the processing of the task rather than to feeling of familiarity or initial feeling of difficulty. Therefore, it is expected that prospective reports of metacognitive experiences will vary in their interrelations from retrospective ones.

Phase of processing. Obviously to test the above assumptions we need to have reports of metacognitive experiences at various phases of cognitive processing. Estimates of feeling of difficulty and other metacognitive experiences can be collected in advance of problem solving (right after the person comes across the problem), during solution planning, and at the output of response phase (after solution production). In the first phase one can ask for an estimate of the familiarity with the task (that is, feeling of familiarity) and feeling of difficulty, whereas in the other phases one can ask about the feeling of difficulty and about confidence felt with regard to the solution planned or the solution produced. One can also ask for the estimated correctness of the solution / answer planned or produced and the feeling of satisfaction from the solution produced. The metacognitive experiences of the advance (a) and planning (p) phase are essentially prospective whereas the metacognitive experiences of the phase after the response production (r) are retrospective.

Task difficulty. Besides the effect of phase of processing another factor that may affect the interrelations between metacognitive experiences is objective task difficulty, as stated before. The assumption is that the pattern of interrelations between feeling of familiarity, feeling of difficulty and estimated solution correctness with feeling of confidence would be invariant, independent of task difficulty, if these metacognitive experiences are the basic sources of information on which feeling of confidence is based. The relations between feeling of confidence and estimated solution correctness with feeling of satisfaction would also be preserved.

To conclude, having estimates of all the above metacognitive experiences allows us to study the interrelations between them, their possible systemic nature as well as their possible change along with objective task difficulty and problem solving phase. This decision was one of the aims of the study of Efklides et al. (1996, 1999). The data regarding the relations of feeling of familiarity, feeling of difficulty, feeling of confidence, feeling of satisfaction, and estimate of solution correctness are presented here.

The hypotheses tested in our study were the following:
1. Feeling of confidence is related to feeling of familiarity, feeling of difficulty, and the estimated solution correctness.
2. Feeling of satisfaction is a function of both estimated solution correctness and feeling of confidence.
3. The effect of feeling of familiarity on feeling of confidence will vary as a function of the phase of problem solving.
4. The pattern of interrelations between the above metacognitive experiences will be preserved regardless of objective task difficulty, although the strength of the relations will vary.

2.   METHOD

2.1   Design

Students of 7th to 9th grade were presented with two mathematical tasks differing in their complexity. Estimates of various metacognitive experiences among which were feeling of familiarity (FOF), feeling of difficulty (FOD), feeling of confidence (FOC), estimate of solution correctness (ESC), and feeling of satisfaction (FOS), were collected for each task during the various problem solving phases as shown in Table 1.

Table 1.
Metacognitive experiences involved in the study along the various phases of problem solving.

Phases	In advance (a)	Planning (p)	Output of response (r)
Metacognitive experiences	FOF, FODa	FODp, FOCp, & ESCp	FODr, FOCr, ESCr, & FOS

Students were tested in their classrooms. At the beginning of the testing session, they were given a pamphlet with instructions and an example so that they could grasp the idea of the phases and the scales for the various metacognitive experiences. After that, they were given the mathematical problems. The order of presentation of the two mathematical problems was counterbalanced.

When the participants were presented with the first problem, and before starting to work on it they were asked to give ratings on a questionnaire about the familiarity, difficulty, and other metacognitive experiences. This was the "in advance of problem solving" phase. Right afterwards, on the next page of the pamphlet, the problem was presented again, and students were instructed to think about the solution but not make the computations needed; they were also asked to give ratings about the metacognitive experiences. This was the "planning" phase. Finally, on a new page, the problem was presented again and students were asked to make the computations and give ratings on the metacognitive experiences questions. This was the "output of response" phase. For more details on the design and metacognitive experiences involved in the study, the reader can consult Efklides et al. (1999).

The same procedure was repeated for the second problem.

2.2   Participants

In all 274 students participated in the study. There were 84, 85, and 105 participants of 7th, 8th and 9th grade respectively. Their mean age was 13, 14, and 15 years. Both genders were about equally represented (133 boys and 141 girls). The participating students came from three different public schools of Thessaloniki, located in areas of different socioeconomic status. The participants represented the urban junior high school student population, considering that Greece has an egalitarian and centralized educational system.

2.3 Tasks

Two mathematical tasks were used. Both of them came from the mathematics curriculum of the 7th grade. The first task, the Fractions task, presented a series of fractions (1/3, 4/5, 4/6, 2/4, 4/7) and required students to place them in order of magnitude, from the smallest to the biggest. The second task, the Mathematical Expression task, presented the following mathematical expression [A=5.3^2 - (2 - 0.2X0.6) - 0.5^2 - 0.1^2] and required students to calculate it. This task was more complex than the first one, because it required knowledge of more rules and more solution steps than the Fractions task.

The estimates of the various metacognitive experiences were collected on a 4-point scale, ranging from 1: not at all; 2: a little; 3: enough; 4: very. The questions asked were: "How familiar are you with this task?"; "How difficult do you think the task is (was)?"; "How confident are you that the solution you planned / produced is correct?"; How satisfied are you with the solution produced?"; "How correctly do you think you answered this problem?".

3. RESULTS

The data were analysed with path analysis using the EQS statistical program (Bentler, 1993). This was necessary in order to test the hypotheses regarding the interrelations of metacognitive experiences and their relation with performance. The model specified by the hypotheses was firstly tested in the Fractions task. The model that fit the data was then applied to the data of the Mathematical Expression task, in order to find out if objective task difficulty influences the pattern of interrelations between metacognitive experiences. A series of ANOVAs was also applied in order to identify possible differences in the strength of metacognitive experiences between the two tasks and from one problem-solving phase to the next.

3.1 The interrelations of metacognitive experiences

The Fractions task. The model that fit the data of the Fractions task, $x^2(91)$ = 92.226, p = .444, CFI = .999, LISREL *GFI* = .962, Standardised *RMR* = .052, is given in Table 2.

Table 2.
The pattern of relations identified in the path analysis of the Fractions Task.

Dependent variable	Independent variable									
	Perform.	FOF	FODa	FODp	FOCp	ESCp	FODr	FOCr	ESCr	E
FOF	.149									.976
FODa		-.267								.964
FODp			.395							.919
FOCp	.146	.138	-.203	-.332						.849
ESCp			-.131	-.149	.505					.759
FODr				.221		-.198				.936
ESCr	.218				.215	.232	-.318			.753
FOCr					.114				.674	.678
FOS	.095				.090			.338	.418	.623

28   *Efklides*

A schematic representation of parts of the model is given in Figure 1. It shows that feeling of confidence in the planning phase (FOCp) was influenced by performance, feeling of familiarity (FOF) and feeling of difficulty of the advance (FODa) and planning phase (FODp) as predicted in Hypothesis 1. However, feeling of confidence at the output of response phase (FOCr) was directly influenced only by the respective feeling of confidence of the planning phase (FOCp) and the estimated solution correctness of the output of response phase (ESCr). The relationship with ESCr was particularly strong ($r = .674$). This suggests that there was an effect of phase of processing on feeling of confidence (as predicted in Hypothesis 3). Only feeling of confidence in the planning phase (FOCp) was based on feeling of difficulty of the planning phase (FODp) and on feeling of familiarity. This finding suggests that feeling of confidence before the solution production is an inference based on previous encounters with similar tasks (familiarity) and the subjective difficulty in the advance and the planning phase. At the output of response phase feeling of confidence (FOCr) is directly based on the estimate of solution correctness and indirectly to actual performance and feeling of difficulty of the same phase.

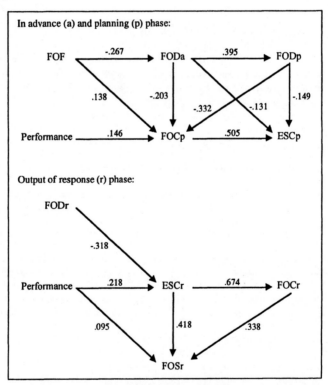

Figure 1. Effects of feeling of familiarity (FOF) and feeling of difficulty (FOD) on feeling of confidence (FOC), estimate of solution correctness (ESC) and feeling of satisfaction (FOS) as a function of the phase of processing in the Fractions task.

Note. The symbols a, p, and r denote the phase in advance of problem solving (a), during the planning phase (p), and the output of response phase (r), respectively.

The relationship of estimated solution correctness and feeling of confidence with performance right after the planning phase is probably due to the selection of the course of action at this phase which determines the solution production and the final performance. It seems that the planning of a solution already involves a prospective judgment of what the correct solution would be and this judgment is quite accurate.

Finally, feeling of satisfaction was mainly influenced by feeling of confidence and estimate of solution correctness of the output response phase (FOCr and ESCr) (as predicted in Hypothesis 2), but also by performance. Feeling of satisfaction was not directly related to feeling of difficulty. It was indirectly influenced by feeling of difficulty via estimate of solution correctness. The above findings suggest that feeling of satisfaction is monitoring performance outcome rather than the process through which this was achieved. On the contrary, estimate of solution correctness and feeling of confidence are directly related to the monitoring of how fluent, smooth, and uninterrupted the processing of the task is.

The Mathematical Expression task. The model that fit the data is given in Table 3. The fit indices were: $x^2(76) = 96.505$, $p = .056$, $CFI = .991$, LISREL $GFI = .958$, Standardised $RMR = .046$. For the basic relations identified in the model see Figure 2. The relations between feeling of confidence in the planning phase (FOCp), feeling of familiarity (FOF), feeling of difficulty in the planning phase (FODp), and performance were confirmed. The effect of estimate of solution correctness in the output of response phase (ESCr) on feeling of confidence of the same phase (FOCr) was also confirmed. Feeling of satisfaction was also found to be influenced by ESCr, FOCr, and performance as in the Fractions task. Therefore, some relations between metacognitive experiences seem to be stable, independently of task complexity, whereas others are not. This is in accordance with Hypothesis 4 which predicted moderating effects of task difficulty. However, Hypothesis 4 predicted effects on the strength of the interrelations and not on their pattern. What was also found in the Mathematical Expression task was an effect of feeling of familiarity on the estimate of solution correctness at the output of response phase (ESCr) besides the effect of feeling of familiarity at the planning phase. This suggests that when the person does not feel that the task is familiar and easy, this feeling persists until the end of the task processing and affects the estimate of solution correctness and indirectly the confidence in it.

Table 3.
The pattern of relations identified in the path analysis of the Mathematical Expression Task.

Dependent variable	Independent variable									
	Perform.	FOF	FODa	FODp	FOCp	ESCp	FODr	FOCr	ESCr	E
FOF										
FODa	-.168	-.164								.970
FODp		-.134	.474							.807
FOCp	.210	.207		-.300						.806
ESCp				-.220	.587					.700
FODr			.204	.159		-.155				.869
ESCr	.195	.157		-.205	.138	.283	-.303			.786
FOCr						.265			.538	.714
FOS	.118							.457	.332	.647

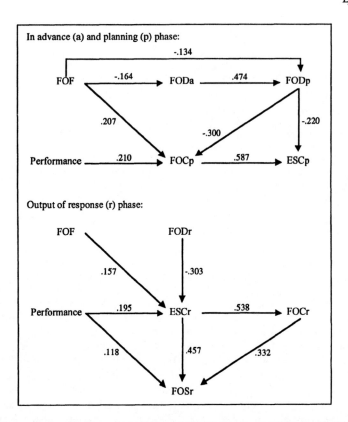

Figure 2. Effects of feeling of familiarity (FOF) and feeling of difficulty (FOD) on feeling of confidence (FOC), estimate of solution correctness (ESC) and feeling of satisfaction (FOS) as a function of the phase of processing in the Mathematical Expression task. *Note.* The symbols a, p, and r denote the phase in advance of problem solving (a), during the planning phase (p), and the output of response phase (r), respectively.

Phase and Task effects. The ANOVAs performed on the metacognitive experiences showed a significant effect of task and phase. Specifically, the Fractions task was judged easier than the Mathematical Expression task but performance was better on the latter. Confidence, estimate of solution correctness and feeling of satisfaction were also higher in the Fractions task than the Mathematical Expression task. Finally, whereas feeling of difficulty tended to increase from phase to phase in the Fractions task, the opposite happened in the Mathematical Expression task, where there was no significant difference between phases on feeling of difficulty and a marginal effect on feeling of confidence and estimate of solution correctness. The stability of feelings in the Mathematical Expression task along the problem-solving process may explain why the effect of feeling of familiarity on estimate of solution correctness in this task persisted even at the output of response phase. The initial subjective "data" on which feeling of confidence and estimate of solution correctness were based were not revised in face of the new processing data, unlike the Fractions task where the initial "data" were revised and the subsequent increased feeling of difficulty made the initial effect of feeling of familiarity to diminish.

4. CONCLUSIONS

The aim of this chapter was to delimit possible interrelations between metacognitive experiences with particular emphasis on the relations of feeling of confidence (FOC) and feeling of satisfaction (FOS) with feeling of familiarity (FOF), feeling of difficulty (FOD), and estimate of solution correctness (ESC).

Path analysis confirmed the hypothesized relations between the various metacognitive experiences but also the effect of phase of problem solving and of task difficulty. Specifically, our data, firstly, confirmed that FOC is influenced by FOF. This finding is in accordance with suggestions that link confidence to familiarity and feeling of knowing (Costermans et al., 1992).

Secondly, the relation of feeling of confidence with feeling of difficulty was demonstrated and this is in accordance with findings linking confidence to cognitive effort and time spent on the task (Robinson et al., 1997).

Thirdly, the relation of feeling of confidence with the estimate of solution correctness was established. The relation of FOC with ESC was particularly strong, and this suggests that the two of them monitor the same underlying process. For this reason, and since our data are correlational, we did not discuss issues pertaining to whether ESC precedes FOC or follows it. The models tested in path analysis entered the variables in the order in which they appeared in the questionnaire given to the participants and do not entail any temporal order between the two judgments.

Fourthly, although the effects of FOF on FOC were mainly evident in the planning phase, that is, when FOC was asked prospectively, the effect of FOD was present both at the planning and output of response phase (through its effect on ESC) and was relatively stronger than the effect of FOF. This implies a differentiation of the interrelations between metacognitive experiences according to the phase of processing. Fifthly, feeling of satisfaction was directly influenced by FOC and ESC rather than FOF and FOD. The effect of FOD on FOS was indirect via FOC or ESC. Therefore, FOC and FOS make use of different subjective cues although both FOC and FOS are related to performance outcome.

Finally, there were some effects of task difficulty on the interrelations of the metacognitive experiences studied, although the basic pattern of relations between FOF, FOD, FOC, ESC, and FOS was invariant across tasks.

The above findings pose significant questions with regard to the nature and functioning of metacognitive experiences in problem solving. One question pertains to the mechanism underlying the formation of metacognitive experiences and another one to the functioning of phenomenal experience, that is, the extent to which one's metacognitive judgments and/or metacognitive feelings about one's cognition make use of feelings and judgments already present in one's awareness.

In so far as the nature of metacognitive experiences is concerned, correlational data do not provide a firm basis for drawing inferences. Nevertheless, our data seem to point out that monitoring of the fluency or interruption of cognitive processing is fundamental not only for the formation of FOF and FOD, respectively, but also for judging the correctness of the processing outcome or response and the ensued confidence.

This finding supports the view that metacognition is inferential in nature (see Koriat, 1997; Lories et al., 1998; Weaver & Kelemen, this volume), making use of various cues, including mnemonic ones, such as fluency of processing (see also Koriat & Shitzer-Reichert, this volume). However, at the heart of FOC seems to be a mechanism that allows the estimation of solution correctness, even if the final response has not been formed yet, as it happens in the judgment of confidence in the planning phase. It seems that there is monitoring of the availability and/or accessibility of relevant knowledge and procedures that will be used for problem solving.3 This assumption is corroborated by studies showing the effect of availability of relevant knowledge or of alternative hypotheses on confidence (Arkes, Christensen, Lai, & Blumer,, 1987; Mckenzie, 1998). The availability along with the ease of accessibility of knowledge seems to form the basis of the prospective confidence judgment. At the output of response phase, the retrospective FOC seems to involve monitoring of the accessibility of knowledge and fluency of processing but also the correctness of the outcome of its application. This suggests that the person uses additional cues or criteria for judging solution correctness.

The correlation of FOC and FOS with performance suggests that the explicit criteria used for judging solution correctness by an observer (in our case, the experimenter) were at least partially used by the participants themselves. Whether the application of the criteria was explicit and analytic cannot be answered here. In conclusion, feeling of confidence when judged prospectively, makes use mainly of cues related to processing fluency / interruption as indicated by the respective FOF and FOD, as well as of knowledge accessibility; retrospective confidence, however, may in addition make use of cues related to performance outcome. For example, Seemungal and Stevenage (this volume) showed that confidence in the veracity of one's memories is boosted when the person can recall not only the event but also details of its context.

Feeling of satisfaction, on the other hand, seems to be based mainly on cues related to performance outcome and indirectly through ESC and FOC to processing fluency. Therefore, it seems to be more related to criteria pertaining to the quality of a response or answer rather than the fluency of the processing that led to the answer. One of the criteria used for a judgment of FOS is the confidence one has with respect to the accuracy of the answer.

Our findings, however, do not explain if FOC and FOS make use of the information provided by the monitoring process in an explicit manner, that is, after FOF and FOD have been formed and are available in one's awareness, or implicitly, without the mediation of the awareness of these two feelings. Koriat and Levy-Sardot (2000a) propose that subjective feelings serve an informational function, sometimes providing the basis for judgments and actions. Evidence in favour of explicit processing of the feelings and judgments available in one's awareness is the effects we found (see Tables 2 and 3) between feelings of the advance phase influencing the reported feelings of the planning phase, and feelings of the planning phase effecting the subjective reports of the output of response phase. It seems that participants kept track of the subjective experiences they had and the judgments they had made before giving their current judgment. More research is needed to unveil the possible implicit effects of the fluency / interruption monitoring on the formation of FOC.

More research is also needed in the case of satisfaction and its relations to the person's concerns and implicit or explicit criteria that underlie the formation of the feeling of satisfaction and the judgment of its intensity.

One final point we would like to stress regards the effect of task difficulty and phase of processing. The evidence we provided suggests that task difficulty influenced mainly the intensity of the interrelations between the metacognitive feelings rather than the pattern of the relations. This finding is in line with other research showing task effects on metamemory (see Weaver & Kelemen, this volume). The stability of the pattern of interrelations between metacognitive feelings, however, across tasks may not generalize to all metacognitive feelings and judgments. Leonesio and Nelson (1990) found that judgment of ease of learning (EOL), judgment of learning (JOL), and feeling of knowing (FOK) were largely uncorrelated. Therefore, it is essential to find out why some metacognitive experiences correlate between them and some not, what processes give rise to them and how these processes change as task processing goes on. It may be the case that metacognition starts at an implicit level, then gives rise to feelings, and later on it functions at two levels, one implicit and one explicit (see Cary & Reder, this volume) at the same time. Delimiting the effects of phase of processing on the processes that give rise to subjective experiences may offer insight as to this interplay between implicit and explicit level of functioning of metacognition.

In conclusion, our research showed that the feelings of familiarity, of difficulty, of confidence and of satisfaction are interrelated. This implies that there is either a common source (e.g., cues of fluency/interruption of processing), which are being monitored at an implicit level, and/or effects of particular aspects of subjective experience on other aspects of it at an explicit level. In the former case, the question that rises is why subjective experience takes various phenomenal forms. In the latter case, the question is how the interaction between components of conscious experience is being achieved and what this interaction serves. It seems that metacognition is still an unresolved enigma.

Notes

[1] The terms "estimate" of solution correctness and "judgment" of solution correctness are used as synonyms, the first denoting some kind of computation (Lewis, Canby, & Brown, 1946).

[2] "Objective task difficulty" can be defined, firstly, in terms of complexity, that is, number of steps required for the solution of the task (e.g., one, two or three operations), and type of procedure needed to be performed for the solution of the task, e.g., multiplication vs. addition. Secondly, in terms of conceptual demands. For example, in cognitive development it is known that children acquire some concepts later than others, e.g., the concept of fraction or ratio is acquired after the concept of integer (Efklides, Papadaki, Papantoniou, & Kiosseoglou, 1998).

[3] For a combined effect of cue-familiarity and accessibility heuristics see Koriat and Levy-Sardot (2000b).

Chapter 3

Metacognitive Processes at Encoding
Insights from Alzheimer's Disease

Chris J.A. Moulin, Timothy J. Perfect and Fiona Fitch
Research Institute for the Care of the Elderly, Bath, UK and University of Bristol, UK
University of Plymouth, UK
Research Institute for the Care of the Elderly, Bath, UK

Key themes: Appl / Proc

Key words: Dementia / JOLs / Repetition

Abstract: Researchers aiming to explain the episodic memory deficit in Alzheimer's
               disease have occasionally adopted a metacognitive framework to examine the
               role of memory monitoring as a possible contributory factor. In this chapter we
               briefly review the results of research into metacognition in Alzheimer's
               disease – with particular focus on item repetition. Here we consider what the
               study of Alzheimer's disease (AD) can contribute to our understanding of the
               bases on which metacognitive judgements are made. In particular, we
               concentrate on the cue utilisation approach (Koriat, 1997), describing work
               that suggests a dissociation between the mnemonic bases of metamemory
               control and metamemory monitoring during encoding. We present novel
               empirical data that examines the nature of metamemory monitoring at
               encoding for repeated items using a Judgement of Learning procedure (JOL).
               We find that a) in an AD group we can dissociate metamemory monitoring
               and control for repeatedly presented items and b) there is evidence that the ability
               to make JOLs that are sensitive to repetition of items is related to the
               awareness of repetition.

1.   ALZHEIMER'S DISEASE AND METACOGNITION

Episodic memory is the most profoundly affected cognitive domain in AD (e.g.
Grober & Kawas, 1997). Evidence from tests of episodic memory suggests that this

problem stems in part from a deficit in encoding processes (Christensen, Kopelman, Stanhope, Lorentz & Owen, 1998; Greene, Baddeley & Hodges, 1996). Unsurprisingly, a deficit in metacognition has been proposed as being a contributory factor in episodic memory dysfunction in general (Light, 1981; Shimamura & Squire, 1986). We aimed to assess the role of metacognition in the memory dysfunction in AD. Given that an episodic memory deficit may stem from dysfunctional encoding in AD, we made that the focus of our research.

In essence, previous research into metacognition in AD has tended to use a reversal of the standard developmental approach outlined by Koriat and Shitzer-Reichert (this volume); describing how people lose – rather than acquire – proficient memory processes. Previous research into metacognition in Alzheimer's disease (e.g. Pappas, Sunderland, Weingartner, Vitiello, Martinson & Putnam, 1992; Bäckman & Lipinska, 1993; Lipinska & Bäckman, 1996), has been largely equivocal, and based mainly on confidence judgements made at test and for general knowledge stimuli. Generally, the literature suggests that AD patients are as accurate as controls at ascribing confidence judgements at test. Only Pappas et al. consider metacognition for episodic (in contrast to general knowledge) stimuli. In their study, participants were asked to make item-by-item predictions of recall performance during the presentation of to-be-learned items. Pappas et al. were unable to draw conclusions about the predictive accuracy of metamemory judgements for recall because of floor effects in the memory performance of the AD group. For the recognition task, with superior performance, they found that AD patients did not predict memory performance as accurately as controls.

There are difficulties in concluding that people with AD have a metacognitive deficit on this basis. The standard conclusion is that metamemory is inaccurate when participants' predictions of performance fail to relate to how they actually perform: a word that is judged to be highly recallable should be more likely to be recalled than a word rated as less likely to be recalled. Clearly, problems occur with this approach when participants have an episodic memory impairment, since their likelihood of recalling *any* item is at floor. Additionally, the reason that an individual's metacognitive judgements lack predictive power at test may be due to processes that occur after study. It is conceivable that participants make appropriate predictions of recall during study that would be accurate were it not for an intervening episodic memory deficit. Even though accuracy measures indicate impairment, participants may accurately monitor the difficulty of different items to be learned, and control their encoding appropriately. In this case, then, using an accuracy-based measure of metacognition fails to focus on what occurs during the study phase.

In a series of experiments (Moulin, Perfect, & Jones, 2000a, 2000b, 2001) we adopted Nelson and Narens' (1990) framework and focused on monitoring and control aspects of metacognition in Alzheimer's disease. We offered a novel approach which overcame the confound with memory performance, and focused instead on processes occurring during encoding. Our rationale was straightforward; if metacognition is intact at encoding, then AD participants' monitoring and control should be as sensitive to item differences as controls' performance. To distinguish our paradigm from previous research examining metacognitive accuracy, we classified the measures as metacognitive sensitivity measures.

Firstly in this sensitivity approach, we presented participants with to-be-remembered stimuli with known objective qualities and examined the effect of those stimuli on predictions of future performance. This showed that AD patients are sensitive to stimuli during encoding (Moulin et al., 2000a). Like controls, AD patients allocate more study time to objectively difficult items and also make judgements of learning (JOLs) that reflect the objective differences in recallability (Rubin & Friendly, 1986) of the words. For instance, the AD group gave objectively easy words a mean JOL of 4.04 (out of 5) and difficult words a mean JOL of 2.83. In comparison, the older adult controls gave respective mean JOLs of 4.15 and 3.45.

There is a larger literature on global predictions in AD, where participants predict performance for a whole list of items. These studies find that before study, AD patients significantly overestimate their memory performance (e.g. Correa, Graves & Costa, 1996; McGlynn & Kaszniak, 1991). Again, we suggest that these traditional measures are not insightful about metacognitive processes that occur during encoding. Applying our sensitivity approach to global predictions we found that although AD participants make very inaccurate predictions of performance before study, they revise these estimates to more realistic levels after studying the list(Moulin et al., 2001). For instance, before studying a ten-item list, the mean AD prediction is 5.12 items (from 10), whereas after study the group's mean prediction is a much more appropriate 1.87 items. The mean predictions in the older adult control group are 5.94 (before study) and 5.37 (after study). We concluded from these findings that AD patients are sensitive to factors operating at encoding, and we argued that this sensitivity must be based on memory monitoring. This conclusion is in accordance with research that examined item-based metacognition at test in AD (Bäckman & Lipinska, 1993; Lipinska & Bäckman, 1996).

Here we expand on this previous research by focussing not on a) what a study of metacognition can tell us about Alzheimer's disease, but b) what the study of Alzheimer's disease can tell us about metacognition. Thus we aim to develop a cognitive perspective on the metacognitive abilities of people with AD. In particular, we believe that our research can illustrate important differences in the bases of people's JOLs. The distinction between (a) and (b) above resonates with Koriat and Shitzer-Reichert's comments about the two lines in which metacognition research has advanced. While the study of metacognition as a means of explaining memory deficits in a certain population is similar to the developmental approach to metacognition, the use of AD patients as a means to illuminate cognitive processes clearly contributes to our understanding of metacognition as an important part of human memory. Thus, like Koriat and Shitzer-Reichert's chapter, we hope that the empirical work presented here marries the developmental and cognitive approaches.

In order to examine the bases for people's metacognitive judgements we adopted Koriat's (1997) cue utilisation model. This makes a distinction between intrinsic, extrinsic and mneomic cues that are used to monitor one's own memory performance. Intrinsic cues are those which are central to the qualities of the to-be-remember stimuli themselves, such as word familiarity or pronouncability. Extrinsic cues are associated with factors operating at encoding, such as the number of presentations or the time available at study. Mnemonic cues arise from the learner's experience of learning and their privileged access to their memory system. Rather than an appraisal of an item or the conditions under which it was encountered, mnemonic cues are a bone fide evaluation of whether an item has been mastered. Intrinsic and extrinsic cues can be utilised directly during study – they are the application of a knowledge-based appraisal of performance, whereas mnemonic cues produce a 'feeling of knowing' that can be used to predict future memory performance.

Our previous research (Moulin, et al., 2000a) considered JOL sensitivity during encoding where there were clear objective differences between the words (e.g.

predicting recall for *tree* versus *impropriety)*. We selected the stimuli on the basis of their mean recallability – the likelihood that an item would be remembered in a free recall test(Rubin & Friendly, 1986). We showed that AD patients could assess the recallability of a word at study in line with the expected difficulty of that stimulus – i.e. predicted recall was lower for *tree* than *impropriety*. It is probable that this assessment was based on a mere evaluation of the intrinsic qualities of the to-be-remembered item, especially as the procedure exaggerated these aspects of the stimuli. We might therefore conclude that the ability to make JOLs on the basis of intrinsic cues is intact in AD. Naturally, we were interested to examine whether AD patients could also make JOLs on the basis of extrinsic and mnemonic cues, especially because JOLs have been shown to be more accurate when their mnemonic basis has been emphasised (e.g. delayed JOLs, Dunlosky & Nelson, 1992).

Alzheimer's disease offers an opportunity to research the relationship between extrinsic and mnemonic cues in metacognition during encoding. We found previously that AD patients are sensitive to intrinsic (e.g. objective item difficulty) and extrinsic (e.g. list length, Moulin, submitted) cues in their predictions of performance, but that ultimately, memory predictions bore a poor relation to actual memory performance. Is this because AD patients are unable to make a mnemonic consideration of the item's registration in memory? Here we describe experiments that aimed to consider the role of mnemonic and extrinsic cues on metacognition during encoding in AD.

We opted to explore metacognition for repetitions of items. There were two motivations for this. Firstly, we were driven by our foregoing research on sensitivity to objective qualities of the stimuli. Would AD patients be sensitive to objective qualities of to-be-remembered stimuli when the basis of a sensitive JOL relied on the storage of that item in memory, rather than an assessment of the item's characteristics? That is, would they be sensitive to extrinsic cues (the awareness of repetition and an appreciation of its benefits) and mnemonic cues (the strengthening of the memory trace associated with repetition)?

Secondly, AD patients have a particular deficit when learning repeated lists of items. Many clinical tests that assess episodic memory involve repeated presentations of stimuli to participants (e.g., the Californian Verbal Learning Test; Delis, Kramer, Kaplan & Ober, 1987). Such tests show that AD patients are unable to learn new items on a list and recall them to the same degree as controls (e.g. Brandt, 1991); AD patients have a characteristically shallow learning curve. Further support for this particular deficit comes from Greene, Baddeley and Hodges (1996), who suggested that people with AD approached multiple presentations of lists as if they were trying to remember a single unrelated trial. Our hypothesis was that this lack of ability to respond appropriately to repetition in AD was a metacognitive failure. Metcalfe (1994) suggests that monitoring and control of episodic memory enables the assessment of the familiarity or novelty of incoming events and the subsequent adjustment of attention or effort to those events. If AD participants are not sensitive to repetition, they will allocate resources to an already encoded item as if it is a novel item. The implications for this are that an AD participant would encode a repeated item for longer than a control participant would and would waste study time. This is of course not supported by the lack of a benefit of repetition in recall in AD: we return to this issue later in the chapter. Thiede (1999) has shown that in multi-trial learning monitoring accuracy and more effective self-regulation are associated with greater memory performance. Therefore, at this stage we assume that the most efficient encoding mechanism will be sensitive to item repetition.

To assess sensitivity to repetition we examined memory monitoring and control for a set of twelve items that were either presented once, twice or three times at study (Moulin, Perfect & Jones, 2000c). Specifically, we compared judgements of learning (JOLs) –an explicit measure of metamemory monitoring, and the allocation of study time (recall readiness)– a measure of metamemory control. Recall readiness also implies memory monitoring, since it is not possible to allocate study time appropriately without memory monitoring. At study, participants were given as long as they felt necessary to study each item – with the instruction to maximise recall. After study and with the item no longer in view, participants predicted future performance with a JOL, using a 5 point rating scale. When an item was repeated, the participant carried out the same recall readiness procedure and made a JOL again.

The memory performance (recall and recognition) indicated that participants from the AD and Older Adult Control (OAC) groups benefited from repeated presentation of to-be-remembered items. For the JOL data, we found that whereas the OAC group made predictions of performance that were in line with item repetition, predicting higher performance for items seen on the third occasion than on the first, the AD patients were insensitive to repetition in their JOLs. However, despite large group differences in study time, both the AD and OAC participants significantly reduced study time of an item as a function of how many times they had studied the word. Thus while the AD group showed the normal pattern of performance for study time, their explicit rating of how well they have learned the item (JOL) was insensitive to repetition.

These results are problematic for the monitoring and control framework (Nelson & Narens, 1990), because metamemory control (e.g. as measured by allocation of study time) is theorised to be reliant upon proficient memory monitoring (e.g. as measured by JOLs). How can AD affect monitoring and apparently not monitoring and control? Consequently we argued that the monitoring measure (JOLs) is tapping a different aspect of memory monitoring than is captured by the allocation of study time. In summary, both memory performance and study time were affected by the number of times an item has been studied, but for AD participants there was no conscious awareness of this at study. This suggests that in AD explicit memory is improved by factors that are not necessarily being monitored at encoding. This conclusion is consistent with other research showing that memory performance can benefit from factors that are non-monitored. For example, Jameson, Narens, Goldfarb and Nelson (1990) used a near-threshold priming paradigm with a student population and introduced the idea that there were both non-monitored and monitored components in the successful retrieval on an item.

If there is a metacognitive deficit as observed in our previous research, then it is that the AD group is not consciously aware of the benefits of repetition. This research left us with two questions. First, was the pattern of JOLs in the AD group a product of the time spent studying items? Previous research has identified that study time and JOLs are usually reliably related. Perhaps the lack of sensitivity in the AD group's JOLs is due to the differences in study time. It is conceivable that the propensity to spend less time studying previously presented items is a natural aspect of processing at encoding that is actually unhelpful to people with AD. If we assume that an AD participant fails to adequately encode an item the first time they encounter it, then the next time they see the to-be-remembered item, they would benefit from studying that item for as long as it takes to master that item. Instead, our data suggests that they actually study the item for less time. Even though the monitoring of the items registers no difference in the degree to which it has been learnt(the lack of sensitivity in the JOL), the AD participant skips over the item in the same manner as a control participant. Perhaps this propensity to allocate study time in the same manner as a non-demented participant means that the AD group fails to show sensitive JOLs and also fails to benefit from repetition. The AD group may fail to shift their JOLs with repetition because they do not judge the items as being any better learnt. This suggests that the AD patient is not basing their JOL either on extrinsic or mnemonic cues. However, if study time is fixed at longer presentation rates, does the AD group become more aware of repetition in their JOLs?

Second, we were interested in whether the JOL effect was driven by the memory deficit: was the AD group unable to detect repetition of items consciously and thus unable to make JOLs that were reflective of item repetition? That is, it is only possible to make an extrinsic appraisal of memory processes on the basis of repetition if you are actually *aware* of the repetition of the item. There is evidence that the ability to detect repetition at test is in deficit in AD. Downes (1988) investigated memory for repetition in demented, depressed elderly and normal elderly groups. In his study, participants were presented words either once, twice or four times and participants had to estimate at test how many times a word had been seen at presentation. Downes found that the AD group could not discriminate between singly presented and repeated words. However, a second phase of this experiment used word fragment completion to assess implicit memory. It was found that although the demented group did not show explicit awareness of repetition, their probability that word fragments would be completed increased as a function of presentation frequency, suggesting a benefit to implicit memory for repetition during encoding. This suggests that AD participants may be unaware of repetition during presentation, but that uncontrolled aspects of their memory performance may nonetheless benefit from repetition. Thus, AD participants may not control and monitor memory appropriately during a learning task because they are not aware that some items were repeated, even though implicitly, performance may benefit.

With the data presented here we aimed to replicate the findings of the previous study and answer these two questions. We removed the recall readiness aspect of the experiment, and had each word appear for a fixed presentation time. If this influenced the JOLs of people with AD, it could indicate that their memory monitoring was intact, but related to study time. Also, instead of testing recall and recognition performance, we gave participants a yes/no recognition test, followed by an estimate of how many times they had studied each item. Was the lack of sensitivity related to the inability to remember how many times a word had been presented?

In summary, AD patients – who are not aware of repetition – offer the opportunity to disambiguate extrinsic and mnemonic bases of JOLs. Whereas an extrinsic JOL made on the basis of knowledge of repetition and its effects relies on an awareness of repetition, presumably, mnemonic cues rely only on the appraisal of the item itself. Is the failure to be sensitive to repetition in AD the mere product of an inability to remember whether an item has been presented before or not, and thus the failure to use an extrinsic cue for the JOL?

2.   METHOD

2.1   Participants

There were sixteen AD patients and sixteen age and education matched controls. The AD patients had a diagnosis of probable or possible AD (McKhann, Drachman, Folstein, Katzman, Price, & Stadlan, 1984). These patients were recruited from a hospital-based memory clinic and were diagnosed by independent clinicians. Patients were diagnosed as being demented with the DSM III-R (American Psychiatric Association, 1987) criteria and as having AD by the NINCDS-ADRDA criteria (McKhann, et al., 1984). If there was a suggestion of a psychiatric disorder, patients were also assessed by a psychiatrist. Patients with a history of stroke or depression were excluded from this study. Patients with a Hachinski score (Hachinski, Linnette, Zilhka, DuBoulay, McAllister, Marshall, Russel, & Symon, 1975) that indicated they might have a vascular component to their dementia were also excluded. The AD group had a mean Mini-Mental State Examination (Folstein, Folstein, & McHugh, 1975) score of 16.69 (4.41). They had a mean age of 75.00 (6.59) and were educated for a mean of 10.50 (1.82) years.

The older adult control (OAC) group was recruited from a panel of older adults who had expressed an interest in participating in research. All OAC participants were screened for dementia. The OAC participants who were part of the volunteer panel received a small remuneration for their time. The mean age of the OAC group was 75.62 (5.71) and they had a mean of 12.56 (3.83) years of formal education. There were no differences in the mean ages of the groups, $F<1$, although the difference in the groups' education levels approached significance, $F (1, 30) = 3.78$, $MSE = 8.99, p=0.06$.

2.2   Materials and Design

There were two phases to this experiment: presentation (study) and recognition (test). At presentation, words were presented individually on a computer screen. There were 3 levels of repetition for 12 items, meaning that there were 24 trials (i.e., four items presented once, four items presented twice, and four items presented three times). The 12 items were those used in a previous study (Moulin et al., 2000c) and were all items with a high probability of free recall (Rubin & Friendly, 1986). The 24 trials were presented in a pseudo-random order with no word repeated immediately on successive trials. The order of items was counterbalanced, with half of participants receiving items in one order, and the other half in the reverse order. The list was designed in such a way that there was an even distribution of items presented once, twice and three times throughout.

2.3   Procedure

Participants were tested individually in a quiet room. They were instructed that this was a memory task, and that they should try to remember each word as best they could. They were told that there would be repetition of some of the items. Words were presented individually in a booklet form. AD participants were given 8s study time and the older adult controls were given 4s(the approximate average times spent studying the items under recall readiness instructions in our previous research). Immediately after study, the word was removed from view, and participants predicted recall using a JOL. Participants were reminded of the JOL with a prompt to judge how easy the word was to remember on a five point scale (1 = very hard to 5 = very easy) after each presentation. Participants declared their JOL verbally, and the experimenter advanced the presentation phase.

Immediately after presentation there was a visually presented yes/no recognition test. This consisted of 12 targets and 12 distracters (matched for recallability) presented in a pseudo random order. Participants responded verbally to the test items, indicating yes if they had seen the word before, or no if it was a new word. If the participant indicated that they had seen the word before, they were asked to estimate how many times they had seen the word at presentation. They indicated this verbally using a five-point scale: once, twice, three times, four times or more than four times.

3.   RESULTS

3.1 Memory Performance

The memory performance was assessed by analysing the number of hits for each level of item repetition. The mean hits are shown in Table 1. A 2x3 (group x repetition) repeated measures ANOVA assessed recognition performance. There was the expected main effect of group, $F (1, 30) = 18.47$, MSE = .12, $p<.001$, with the older adult controls out-performing the AD group. There was a main effect of repetition, $F (1, 30) = 16.85$, MSE = .03, $p<.001$, with participants recalling more of the more frequently presented items. There was also a significant interaction, $F (1, 30) = 7.16$, MSE =.03, $p<.05$, which is difficult to interpret because of the obvious ceiling effects in the OAC group. In any case, simple main effects make it clear that recognition in both groups benefits from repeated presentation during study (AD: $F (1, 15) = 12.80$, MSE =.05, $p<.005$; OAC: $F (1, 15) = 5.00$, MSE =.03, $p<.05$).

Table 1.
Means (and Standard Deviations) for Recognition (proportion of items correctly recognised), Frequency (participant's judgement of number of presentations) and JOL (prediction of future recall on 5 point scale, will definitely recall = 5, will definitely forget = 1).

Presentation	AD				OAC			
	1	2	3	FP	1	2	3	FP
Recognition	0.50	0.69	0.80	0.21	0.94	0.97	1.00	0.01
	(0.34)	(0.34)	(0.31)	(0.26)	(0.11)	(0.08)	(0.00)	(0.03)
Frequency	0.80	1.25	1.41	0.33	1.27	2.00	2.81	0.01
	(0.75)	(0.75)	(0.64)	(0.48)	(0.30)	(0.49)	(0.44)	(0.03)
JOL	3.73	3.68	3.81		3.43	3.51	3.66	
	(0.49)	(0.71)	(0.63)	-	(0.43)	(0.47)	(0.57)	-

Notes: AD = Alzheimer's disease group (*n*=16), OAC = Older Adult Control group (*n*=16), FP = False Positive errors on recognition test, JOL = Judgement Of Learning.

We also consider the recognition errors – false positives (Table 1). These were calculated as the proportion of the twelve distracter items that were judged to be old. A one-way ANOVA indicated that there was a significant difference in the number of false positive errors made by each group, $F (1, 30) = 9.04$, MSE = .04, $p<.01$, with the AD group making more of these errors. Therefore, we appreciate that the recognition performance in the AD group could be inflated by guessing, but we assumed that it would be equal across each level of item repetition.

3.2 Frequency Judgements

The frequency data were estimates of the number of times a participant judged they had seen the word at study. If the participant erroneously judged an old item to be new, the frequency judgement was given as zero (no presentations). The judgement of 'more than four times' was scored as five. With these criteria, the mean frequency judgement for each level of item repetition was calculated. We included false positives in this analysis – these were interpreted as items with zero presentations. The mean frequency judgements are given in Table 1. A 2x4 (group x repetition) repeated measures ANOVA analysed these data. There was a main effect of group, $F (1, 30) = 13.87$, MSE =.77, $p<.001$, with the OAC group judging that they had seen the items more frequently. There was a main effect of repetition, such that items seen more frequently are judged so, $F (1, 30) = 536.00$, MSE = .12, $p<.001$. There was also a significant interaction, $F (1, 30) = 96.86$, MSE = .12, $p<.001$. The means indicate that this is due to the AD group showing less of a shift in estimates of frequency across repetition. This was confirmed with Student's t-tests between the observed mean prediction and the actual number of times the item was presented. The AD group show no significant discrepancy between estimates and actual repetition for items presented once, $t(16) = -1.08$, $p<.3$, but they show a significant difference for items studied more than once (twice: $t(16) = -4.02$, $p=.001$; three times: $t(16) = -9.99$, $p<0.001$). The older adults show the reverse pattern, significantly overestimating the number of times items were presented when only studied once, $t(16) = 3.60$, $p<0.005$; but making accurate estimates of frequency for items presented more than once (twice: $t(16) = 0$; three times: $t(16) = -1.70$, $p<.12$). For the distracter items, the AD group shows a significant discrepancy too, $t(16) = 2.74$, $p<.01$, whereas the OAC estimates are not significantly different from zero, $t(16) = 1.46$. This indicates that the AD group significantly overestimates the number of presentations of items that were not seen at study. Despite this indication of inaccurate estimates of repetition in absolute terms using one sample t-tests, the simple main effects make it clear that the AD group are still responding to item repetition in the estimates of frequency made at test(AD: $F (1, 15) = 78.76$, MSE = .14, $p<.001$; OAC: $F (1, 15) = 621.85$, MSE = .11, $p<.001$). In summary, there are the expected differences between the two groups in their ability to estimate frequency at test: we replicate Downes (1988), in that the AD group is relatively insensitive to frequency of presentation.

3.3   Judgements of learning

We calculated a mean JOL for each level of item repetition for each participant. These mean JOL ratings (Table 1) were analysed using a 2x3 (group x repetition) repeated measures ANOVA. There was no main effect of group, $F (1, 30) = 1.32$, MSE = .79, $p<.27$, indicating that both groups make roughly the same mean predictions of performance. There was a main effect of repetition (replicating our previous work), $F (1, 30) = 4.42$, MSE = .09, $p<.05$, indicating that JOLs were higher as a function of item repetition. There was no significant interaction, $F<1$, indicating that the groups did not vary with regard to how their JOLs changed as a function of item repetition. Because we strongly expected an effect of repetition, and for this to vary across groups, we carried out the within group simple main effects regardless of the lack of an interaction. These indicated that whereas the OAC group showed a small, marginally significant repetition effect, $F (1, 15) = 4.19$, MSE = .10, $p=0.06$, the AD showed no effect at all, $F<1$.

To assess whether awareness of repetition was driving the groups' JOLs, we added the frequency estimates into an analysis of covariance. The first step was to measure each participant's awareness of repetition. To do this we created a slope variable for each participant's four mean frequency judgements, where x were the number of presentations and y were the mean frequency judgements. For this statistic, a gradient of 1 indicated an appropriate awareness of repetition, and a gradient of less than 1 meant that the estimates of frequency were relatively insensitive to item repetition (and underestimated the number of presentations). The mean slopes (and standard deviations) for the AD and OAC groups respectively were: .36 (.16), .91 (.15). A one-way ANOVA indicated that the AD group were less sensitive to repetition at test than the control group, $F (1, 30) = 96.86$, MSE = .02, $p<.001$. The effect of this variable as a covariate on the mean JOLs ANOVA was to remove the significant main effect of repetition, $F<1$. The effect of group and the interaction remained non-significant. This analysis indicates that accounting for awareness of repetition at test removes any significant differences in JOLs at study across repetition.

4. DISCUSSION

The analysis of JOLs is the crux of this chapter. In a previous study (Moulin et al., 2000b) we found that people with AD made JOLs which were not sensitive to item repetition, although their study time did vary accordingly. Older adults made JOLs and allocated study according to how many times they had studied to-be-remembered items. There is evidence from Alzheimer's disease that control (as measured by recall readiness) and monitoring (as measured by JOLs) are therefore reliant upon separate processes. JOL sensitivity to repetition seems to be impaired in AD whereas the allocation of study is comparable with controls.

There were two motivations for the present study. We were interested in the effect of fixed study time on JOLs and the relationship between estimates of repetition at test and JOLs across item repetition. First, we consider the effect of study time. In this study we find results that support the findings of our previous work. The simple main effects indicate that the AD group fails to show an effect of repetition on their JOLs, whereas there is a marginal effect of repetition in the old. From this study we find that the AD participants insensitivity to repetition is not driven by the amount of time at study. In effect, this means that giving AD participants a longer time at study does not increase the sensitivity of JOLs to repetition. Therefore, we can rule out the possibility that the results of our previous study were due to the effect of the recall readiness instruction on JOLs. This finding resonates with two known effects in the literature. Firstly, it is similar to the finding that AD memory performance is still worse than controls even after twenty times the presentation rate (20s versus 1s, Heun, Burkhart, Wolf & Benkert, 1998). We have extended this finding to metamemory: even when study time is extended in the AD group, they still make JOLs that are not reflective of actual performance[1]. Secondly, the lack of any benefit of extended study time or repetition in either group is reminiscent of the Labor-in-Vain effect(Nelson & Leonesio, 1988), whereby very large increases in study time have been shown to have very little effect on memory performance in normal populations.

The completion of this work has allowed us to triangulate on an issue that puzzled us in the first study. The argument involves two contradictory predictions, and cannot be easily resolved: when a participant sees an item for a second time, it is reasonable that they should both study it for less time, and they should rate it as more recallable. In contrast, when they study an item for a shorter time, independent of the number of presentations, they should judge the item as less likely to be recalled. If a participant bases their JOLs on study time or vice versa then study time should decrease as JOLs increase (for a model of self-regulated study, see Thiede & Dunlosky, 1999; but also Mazzoni & Cornoldi, 1993; Son & Metcalfe, 2000). However, if the participant is seeing the item for a second time, then JOLs should increase as study time decreases. Because of this contradiction, it was difficult to find the basis of the AD group's metacognitive deficit. In this study, there were no differences in study time across repetitions, because presentation rate was experimenter-controlled. The findings were that the AD group still could not make appropriate JOLs. This is suggestive that the deficit in memory monitoring in AD is more than a confusion of study time and repetition, and a bone fide lack of memory awareness.

The second issue we were interested in was the relationship between JOLs and explicit judgements of repetition. We felt that by measuring the awareness of repetition as well as the sensitivity to repetition in JOLs, we could examine extrinsic and mnemonic cues in metacognition. If the metamemory deficit in AD is not ameliorated by fixing study time, then the lack of sensitivity to repetition must be based on a lack of an explicit knowledge (or awareness) of repetition, thus a failure in the extrinsic cues. In this study we were able to test this hypothesis in part because we asked for estimates of frequency at test. The AD group was impaired relative to the OAC group in its ability to estimate the frequency of an item and an analysis of covariance provided some statistical support for the fact that awareness of repetition is behind the sensitivity to repetition in JOLs. We acknowledge that our frequency measure is made at test, not during study. This is a possible limitation, and further research should examine the relationship between JOLs and awareness of repetition during study. However, our results suggest that AD patients cannot – or do not – use either mnemonic or extrinsic cues in their JOLs for repeated items.

We feel that our results are pertinent to the discussion of the basis on which Judgements of Learning are made. Koriat (1997) has argued for a cue-utilisation approach to JOLs, whereby JOLs are inferential judgements based on 'beliefs and cues that are more or less predictive of future memory performance' (p.365). This is opposed to a trace access account, where JOLs are predictive of memory performance because JOLs and recall are both sensitive to trace strength. As far as our work is concerned, we find in favour of the cue-utilisation approach. Presumably, trace strength cannot be driving both JOLs and recall since in two studies we have shown that the AD group has memory performance that was sensitive to item repetition where predictions of performance were not. In contrast, we argue for the cue utilisation account, since we find an association between awareness of repetition at test, and level of JOL at study. We suggest that one of the extrinsic cues on which JOLs are inferred, item repetition is useless in AD, since they are not aware of repetition. We find that AD patients are impaired in terms of estimating repetition at test, and so is their sensitivity to item repetition.

Our other chief finding was that if we compare the present work with our previous report, fixing study time has no influence on either group's recognition or JOLs. This is a potentially contentious issue that needs further research because previous studies have shown that there is a strong relationship between JOLs and study time. To recapitulate, we feel that our AD group data suggests that recall readiness and JOL measures can be dissociated, and in the present study, the JOL magnitude was unaltered by fixing the study time. Again this relates to cue utilisation in JOLs. That study time and memory performance can be modified by repetition in AD, but that JOLs fail to pick up on these mnemonic cues suggests that an appraisal of memory processes at encoding as measured by JOLs is not necessarily an essential part of normal encoding processes. The mnemonic cue of 'feeling of knowing' that is available for conscious report seems unlikely, therefore, to be the basis by which we allocate resources at study, or benefit from repetitions during study.

5.   CONCLUDING REMARKS

The most interesting finding thrown up by this research concerns what the study of Alzheimer's disease can contribute to our understanding of metacognitive processes. We return to the dissociation between control and monitoring measures found in this population. We propose that in AD, explicit memory monitoring and control may be impaired, but the automatic aspects of metamemory functioning that occur during study are intact. This parallels the distinction between implicit and explicit memory in Alzheimer's disease, where generally, it has been shown that whereas explicit memory is in deficit in AD, the automatic, or implicit aspects of memory are preserved (Koivisto, Portin, Seinela, & Rinne, 1998). This suggests that the allocation of study time does not necessarily reflect deliberate metamemory control processes, but is rather an automatic response to repetitions of stimuli, at least in this population. Nelson and Narens (1990) suggest that metacognitive research proceeds through "...monitoring constructs typically being operationalized via an introspective report(e.g. EOL judgement) and control constructs being operationalized by some other empirical outcome (e.g. elapsed time during self-paced study)" (p.131). Our results indicate that in memory impaired populations the comparison of metamemory monitoring as explicit declarations with less direct measures of control, may not be useful for understanding the separate contributions of monitoring and control. The most important aspect of this work is that the dissociation found between these two measures of metamemory leads us to think more carefully about the nature of metacognition, especially with reference to clinical populations. In populations where participants appear unaware of their level of performance, it is simplistic to conclude that they are not therefore successfully processing the items in a memory test. We hope therefore, that this chapter illustrates the benefit of applying the cognitive perspective of metacognition to a memory-impaired group. We show another combination of the developmental and cognitive styles of enquiry in metacognition.

Notes.
[1] Incidentally, we examined the recognition and JOL performance in our original paper (Moulin et al., 2000c) and the present study in a 2x2x3 ANOVA (experiment x group x repetition). For both the analyses of JOLs and recognition there were no main effects of experiment and no interactions with experiment(all Fs<1) indicating that the fixed study time had very little bearing on either groups' memory or metamemory functioning.

Chapter 4

Comparing Processing-based, Stimulus-based, and Subject-based Factors in Metacognition
Evidence Against a General Metacognitive Ability

Charles A. Weaver, III and William L. Kelemen
Baylor University, Texas, USA
California State University-Long Beach, USA

Key themes: Cont / Perf / Proc

Key words: General metacognitive ability / Individual differences reliability of metacognition

Abstract: We investigated the reliability of individual differences in metacognitive accuracy in two experiments, examining within-subjects performance on 4 different tasks: (a) ease of learning judgments, (b) feeling of knowing judgments, (c) judgments of learning, and (d) text comprehension monitoring. In addition, we tested the same individuals twice (with a one-week delay). If a general metacognitive factor exists, we would expect to find reliable correlations between metacognitive accuracy across the four tasks. Additionally, we would expect significant test-retest correlations: metacognitive accuracy on a given task should be consistent even if the tests are separated by a one-week delay. Although individual differences in memory and confidence were stable across both sessions and tasks, differences in metacognitive accuracy were not. These results argue against the notion of general metacognitive factor.

The topic of consciousness has received a great deal of attention in recent years. Any number of prominent psychologists (e. g., Damasio, 1994; Nelson, 1996a; Reder, 1996; Weiskrantz, 1997), philosophers (Dennett, 1991; 1996) and others (Crick, 1994) have tackled the centuries-old questions of consciousness. For reasons that are not entirely clear, the resurgence of interest in consciousness has not extended to the field of metacognition, at least not fully. Metacognition rarely rates more than a mention in these sources, and usually less than that. But the maturation and expansion of research in metacognition over the past decade has led to a number of real advances in our understanding of what happens inside the proverbial "black box".

Like any cognitive task, metacognition can be studied in several different ways. Researchers could choose to study sources of differences between groups –to examine the effects of various study conditions on judgments, for example. Alternatively, researchers could focus on differences between *individuals* –what makes one person consistently more accurate than another? Almost all research in metacognition has focused on the first set of questions. As a result, we now have a good understanding of many conditions which can cause metacognition to be more or less accurate.

Our focus, though, is on the second task. What makes one individual consistently more accurate in their metacognitive judgments than another individual? In the course of answering that question, however, it became clear that while most researchers *assumed* reliable individual differences exist, there is little evidence to support this assumption (see Kelemen, Frost, & Weaver, 2000, for a review). This changed the nature of our task to an even more basic question: are individual differences in metacognitive performance reliable? If not, the question of the source of those differences becomes moot.

1.   SOURCES OF INDIVIDUAL DIFFERENCES IN PERFORMANCE

Past research has focused on a number of variables that can produce (or obscure) differences in metacognitive performance. We classify these factors into three broad categories: (a) differences due to task demands (b) difficulties in reliability of measurements, and (c) differences in ability. Most research over the past decade, including virtually all the research conducted in our labs, has focused on task demands (e.g., Frost & Weaver, 1997; Kelemen, 2000; Kelemen, Frost, & Weaver, 2000; Kelemen & Weaver, 1997; Slife & Weaver, 1992; Weaver & Bryant, 1995; Weaver, Bryant, & Burns, 1995; Winningham & Weaver, 2000). In addition, several critical issues concerning the measurement of metacognitive performance have also been identified. Relatively few studies, however, have investigated differences in ability (e.g., Schraw, Dunkle, Bendixen, & Roedel, 1995). Even in these cases, it is unclear whether such differences are best viewed as "state-based" –in which case individual differences in metacognition need not be stable across situations or individuals –or "trait-based"– in which case individual differences should be stable. It is possible –even likely, as some have argued (e.g., Nelson, 1988)–that current measurement procedures do not permit the routine detection of individual differences in metacognitive ability.

2.   DIFFERENCES DUE TO TASK DEMANDS

For both pragmatic and conceptual reasons, task demands have been the subject of more thorough scrutiny. Task factors can be controlled more precisely, and they generally produce robust and reliable effects. We view task demands as having two subcategories: differences which can be induced by *processing factors*, such as the effect of specific instructions or procedures; and *stimulus factors*, those differences which can be attributable to the test materials themselves.[1] Most theoretical accounts of metamemory rely extensively on processing and stimulus factors (see Koriat, 1997; Nelson & Narens, 1990; Schwartz, 1994; Schwartz, Benjamin, & Bjork, 1997).

2.1 Processing factors

Begg, Duft, Lalonde, Melnick, and Sanvito (1989) found that judgments of learning (JOLs) were most accurate when the prediction task involved the same processing factors, independent of the specific cue used to elicit the prediction. We have found similar effects using paired associates (Kelemen, Winningham, Renken, Frost, & Weaver, 1998) and text comprehension (Renken & Weaver, 2000; Weaver, Winningham, & Renken, unpublished). In the text comprehension studies, predictions for recognition were most accurate when participants saw the specific question stem and alternatives to be included on the final test. (Predictions were much worse when they were told at time of prediction *which* of the alternatives was correct, however). For recall, predictions were best when only the question stem was presented. In both cases, we argue that the predictions are most accurate because they most closely mirror those conditions present at the ultimate test. This general finding has been called "transfer-appropriate monitoring."

Practice tests can improve metacognitive performance. Using paired associates, King, Zechmeister, and Shaughnessy (1980) found improved predictions for participants given additional tests compared to those given additional study, because participants used the results of these additional tests as a basis for their JOLs. Kelemen & Winningham (unpublished) showed that practice improved metacognitive accuracy, even when different items were included in each practice trial. Participants completed five separate testing sessions, each containing a unique set of vocabulary items. Mean memory monitoring accuracy increased during the first three sessions before reaching asymptote. Apparently, increasing familiarity with the testing procedures can improve metacognition, although the precise source of participants' improvement is still under investigation.

Beneficial effects of practice tests have been shown using texts. Glenberg, Sanocki, Epstein, and Morris (1987) found that participants used self-generated feedback from pretest questions to improve their metacognitive performance on closely related posttest items (Experiments 6-8). Inserting adjunct questions during reading improves comprehension monitoring (Glover, 1989; Pressley, Snyder, Levin, Murray, & Ghatala, 1987). Rawson, Dunlosky, and Thiede (2000) have shown that simply rereading a text before making predictions of future performance improves metacognitive accuracy.

The timing of judgments can affect metacognitive accuracy dramatically. One of the most robust findings in metacognition is the *delayed-JOL effect* (Nelson & Dunlosky, 1991). Judgments of learning for paired associates are more accurate after a delay compared to immediate judgments. The finding is observed in recognition tests (Begg et al., 1989; Thiede & Dunlosky, 1994) and is sensitive to the type of encoding procedures (Dunlosky & Nelson, 1994). Koriat's work with children reported in this volume shows a similar finding in 2nd and 4th graders. Delayed JOL accuracy also extends to more complex tasks (e.g., remembering categorized lists of items), but only if participants make a retrieval attempt at time of JOL (Kelemen, 2000). Some evidence suggests that delayed-JOL accuracy is in part a memory effect (Kelemen & Weaver, 1997; Spellman & Bjork, 1992), but the practical advantage of delayed-JOLs is substantial, regardless of the theoretical explanation.

2.2 Stimulus factors

Stimulus variables refer to effects produced by the experimental materials themselves. In standard verbal learning studies, they include concreteness, relatedness, and range of difficulty for the paired associates. In text comprehension monitoring these include the genre of text (e.g., narrative vs. expository), length, and text readability.

Begg et al. (1989) found that participants provided higher JOL ratings for concrete and common words, though these factors did not produce better performance on recognition tests. The relatedness of stimuli can also influence memory monitoring accuracy. Rabinowitz, Ackerman, Craik, and Hinchley (1982) used lists of word pairs with varying degrees of association. JOLs were higher for more related word pairs than for less-related words, even when the instructions for encoding successfully increased memory performance for the less-related words. Dunlosky and Schwartz (1995) also reported that predictions of performance for free recall are based on relational information between items. Mean JOL ratings were higher when the words the words were related. In addition, the magnitude of item-by-item JOLs increased as participants discovered that the stimuli were related.

The overall difficulty and range of stimuli also can affect observed metacognitive accuracy. For example, Schraw and Roedel (1994) found that overconfidence is due to both test-based errors (related to the materials themselves) and person-driven errors. Test difficulty accounted for most of the overconfidence in comprehension monitoring. These differences persisted when the different tasks were matched for difficulty. Schraw, Dunkle, Bendixen, and Roedel (1995) compared performance across a large number of tasks. In Experiment 1, participants estimated confidence in their answers to questions in a variety of domains (geographical distances, knowledge of presidents, caloric value of food, running speed of animals, mathematical word problems, spatial judgments, general knowledge, and reading comprehension). Confidence scores were correlated across tasks, but the accuracy of these judgments was inconsistent across domains. (Metacognitive performance was somewhat correlated across tasks when they were matched on difficulty, format, length, and inferential demands, however.) This finding is consistent with Maki and Berry's (1984) earlier finding that "structural" variables such as length, serial position, and hierarchical level of text sections were related to metacognitive performance, but not memory performance.

In general, items from a relatively narrow difficulty range constrain metacognitive accuracy. Nelson, Leonesio, Landwehr, and Narens (1986) found that the correlation between FOK judgments and memory performance was higher when questions were more normatively different. Schwartz and Metcalfe (1994) also found that the range of recognition difficulty for general knowledge questions reliably altered metacognitive performance. Thus, when comparing metacognitive accuracy across tasks or populations, investigators should be sensitive to the normative difficulty of items being tested. These results also make clear some of the measurement difficulties which can influence observed performance. Like any kind of correlational analysis, restriction of range can artificially constrain correlations between predicted and actual performance (see Weaver, 1990, and Weaver & Kelemen, 1997, for a further discussion of these problems).

In the domain of text comprehension, Weaver and Bryant (1995) found that metacognitive accuracy in text comprehension varied as a function of readability. Texts that were too easy or too difficult for readers produced lower correlations between predicted and actual performance; predictions were most accurate when the texts were of a "standard" level of difficulty, approximately equal to the level of participants' reading ability. Weaver and Bryant's results show clearly the interaction between stimulus and processing variables. They proposed that for each individual, there is some intermediate level of cognitive effort that produces maximal metacognitive performance, what they called the "optimum effort hypothesis" (however, see Lin & Zabrucky, 1998).

2.3 Unreliability of Measurement

In addition to the restriction of range problem mentioned earlier, other potential difficulties for assessing metacognitive accuracy have been identified (for a review, see Schwartz & Metcalfe, 1994). While an extensive discussion of these issues is beyond the scope of this article, several issues are sufficiently important to demand mention. Perhaps the most important of these is which measure should be used to assess the relationship between prediction and performance. Difference scores (e.g., Hart, 1965, see also the predictive accuracy quotient used by King et al., 1980), correlation coefficients (Pearson's r, Goodman & Kruskal's Gamma (G), and Phi), and signal detection analyses have all been used to assess metacognitive accuracy. There is now considerable evidence suggesting that the nonparametric Gamma correlation is the best measure of *relative metacognitive accuracy* (Nelson, 1984, 1996b; Wright, 1996).[2] Because G treats only the rank of the underlying distribution of data, however, the potentially interesting magnitude of judgment differences cannot be determined (Schwartz & Metcalfe, 1994). Therefore, *absolute metacognitive accuracy* is often assessed by plotting actual performance as a function of predicted performance (i.e., a calibration curve). If judgment and performance measures occur on the same scale, this procedure provides an index of overconfidence or underconfidence known as *bias*. Identical calibration curves can produce different Gs, depending on the distribution of judgments (Weaver & Kelemen, 1997). In addition, processing variables can differentially affect these measures: Koriat (1997) found that practice improves relative accuracy but lowers absolute accuracy.

In text comprehension monitoring studies, it is critical to allow participants ample opportunity to demonstrate their knowledge. Glenberg and his colleagues observed low metacognitive accuracy when one test question was used per text (e.g., Glenberg & Epstein, 1985, 1987; Glenberg et al., 1987). However, Weaver (1990) demonstrated that metacognitive accuracy for texts could be improved substantially merely by assessing memory with several questions for each text. In short, stable and accurate measures of metamemory require adequate memory assessment.

Are measures of metacognition typically reliable? Maki, Jonas, and Kallod (1994) examined the internal reliability of predictive and post-test judgments for 12 sections of text. They calculated 12 Gamma correlations for each participant based on random groups of 6 judgment-test dyads. Cronbach's alpha was high (above .90) for both pre- and post-test judgments. This finding suggests that G itself is a reliable metacognitive measure, but does not address whether differences between individuals are stable.

Reliability can also be computed for sets of judgments made on distinct items. Alternate-forms and split-half reliabilities have been used to examine whether metacognitive accuracy is consistent for the same metacognitive task using different stimuli. Thompson and Mason (1996) elicited predictions of memory performance for faces, adjectives, and general knowledge questions, and then repeated this procedure two weeks later using alternate test forms. They computed G between predictions and actual performance as a measure of metacognitive accuracy during each session. Finally, Spearman rho correlations were computed between Gs derived from alternate test forms and also from split-halves of each individual test. Only 1 of the 19 reported correlations reached statistical significance at the .05 alpha level.

Nelson (1988) observed a similar lack of reliability using feeling of knowing judgments. In unpublished work, Nelson and his colleagues had previously observed a lack of stability in FOK ratings and postulated that this variability might be due to inadequate set size. Nelson computed split-half reliabilities for FOK accuracy using groups containing 30, 70, or 110 questions. The Spearman rho correlations between the two groups ranged from -.18 to -.02, and none were reliably different from zero. Note that the standard deviations of the FOK accuracy scores were large (.27 to .14), suggesting that these null results were not due to a restricted range of difficulty. Thus, the only two published studies designed specifically to test the reliability of predictions of performance for different sets of items show a complete lack of reliability (Nelson, 1988; Thompson & Mason, 1996).

3.   SUBJECT-BASED FACTORS

Metacognitive accuracy may be influenced by differences between participants. For example, Moulin, Perfect, and Fitch report differences in memory monitoring and control in Alzheimer's patients compared with healthy older adults in this volume. There is some question, however, whether metacognition is best viewed as a stable general trait or represents more of a malleable idiosyncratic state. This dichotomy is somewhat contrived, because "state" and "trait" explanations are not mutually exclusive. Metacognitive accuracy could still be affected by temporary states even if reliable individual differences (traits) are observed.[3] Nevertheless, these terms have an intuitive appeal and we view them as a useful framework for past findings.

3.1   State-based explanations

Numerous physiological and environmental effects on metacognitive accuracy have been reported. These factors often have differential effects on metacognition compared to memory performance. Nelson et al. (1990) tested mountain climbers at altitudes up to 20,000 feet and found that metacognition became inaccurate while memory performance was unaffected. Slife and Weaver (1992) reported that severely depressed individuals showed both memory and monitoring deficits. Mildly depressed patients showed no memory impairments, but metacognitive accuracy was lower.

Pharmacological manipulations also produce reliable differences in metacognition. Nelson, McSpadden, Fromme, and Marlatt (1986) tested intoxicated participants and found impaired memory performance, but FOK accuracy was unaffected. A subsequent JOL study replicated the memory impairment due to alcohol, but also showed reduced immediate JOL accuracy (Nelson et al., 1998). Kelemen and Creeley (2001) tested for state-dependent memory and metamemory effects using caffeine (4 mg/kg). Caffeine modestly improved free recall, but metacognitive accuracy was not affected by drug states during encoding and retrieval. Finally, other drugs (e.g., lorazepam and nitrous oxide) can influence metacognition (Bacon et al., 1998; Dunlosky et al., 1998).

3.2   Trait-based explanations

There is some evidence supporting a stable trait view of metacognition. Walczyk and Hall (1989) parsed out "cognitively reflective" versus impulsive children with a Matching Familiar Figures Test. Reflective students were more likely to detect inconsistencies and employed superior metacognitive strategies than impulsive students.[4] Maki and Berry (1984) found that participants who scored above the median (in test performance) gave higher ratings to items they answered correctly than to those they answered incorrectly. Participants below the median did not. Thiede (1999) found that students differing in monitoring ability and study regulation showed different test performance in a multitrial task. Finally, Schraw et al. (1995) found limited support for a trait-based view of metacognition once task demands were controlled, although this study also used postdictions rather than predictions of performance.

4.   IS THERE EVIDENCE FOR A GENERAL MONITORING ABILITY?

Most researchers in metacognition implicitly assume that metamemory *performance* is a reflection, to some degree, of an underlying metamemory *ability*. Such an assumption seems reasonable. After all, memory performance certainly reflects an underlying ability –those who perform above average on one test are more likely to perform above average on others. The same is true of judgments– individuals who are confident in one situation are more likely to be confident in others. It seems logical to assume the same would be true of metacognitive accuracy. At present, however, there is surprisingly little empirical support for any such kind of global metacognitive ability. Despite the success of past research in isolating numerous factors that influence metacognitive accuracy, there has been no consistent evidence for a general metacognitive ability.

4.1   Stability between tasks and over time

Few studies have been designed specifically to test the reliability of prospective metacognitive judgments over time (Thompson & Mason, 1996) or across tasks (Leonesio & Nelson, 1990). The same is true for the reliability of text comprehension monitoring judgments. Glenberg and Epstein (1987) found unstable individual differences in text comprehension monitoring over an interval ranging from 1 to 7 days, although this was not their primary concern. Maki and Swett (1987) found that the correlation between the accuracy of predictive judgments and confidence postdictions for text was not reliable (Pearson r = .04). Given the increasing interest in metacognition, it is surprising that so little attention has been focused on the apparent instability of these judgments.

Kelemen, Frost, and Weaver (2000) investigated the reliability of individual differences in metacognitive accuracy in two experiments, examining *within-subjects* performance on four different tasks: (a) ease of learning judgments (**EOL**) (b) feeling of knowing judgments (**FOK**) (c) judgments of learning (**JOL**), and (d) text comprehension monitoring (**TCM**). In addition, we tested the same individuals twice (with a one-week delay). If a general metacognitive factor exists, we expected to find reliable correlations between metacognitive accuracy across the four tasks. Additionally, we expected significant test-retest correlations: metacognitive accuracy on a given task should be consistent even if the tests are separated by a one-week delay.

EOL judgments were made using 15 pairs of Swahili-English word pairs from Nelson & Dunlosky's (1994) norms (e.g., *wingu - cloud*). Prior to study, individuals provided a self-paced judgment as to how difficult each pair would be to learn, ranging from 0% ("most difficult to learn") to 100% (labeled "least difficult to learn"). Following all EOL ratings, participants studied the paired associates for six seconds each, and were later tested using a cued-recall procedure.

JOLs were made for unrelated pairs of English concrete nouns (e.g., *letter - mountain*). Either immediately after studying each item (Immediate JOLs), or after all items had been studied (Delayed JOLs), individuals rated the likelihood that on a later test they would recall the second word given the first as a cue, using a similar 0%-100% scale. After a ten-minute distractor task, they were given a cued-recall test over the paired associates.

FOKs were collecting using 25 general knowledge questions developed by Nelson and Narens (1980; e.g., *What is the name of the organ that produces insulin?*). Individuals attempted to answer all 25 questions; the questions were shown again, and this time individuals judged the likelihood of recognizing the correct answer when presented in a four-alternative multiple-choice test. After all FOK ratings, the four-alternative multiple-choice test was administered. Following Koriat (1993, 1995), FOKs were collected on *all* 25 items, with no feedback provided. More typical FOK procedures elicit judgments only for *incorrect* items, and we used this format in Experiment 2.

To assess text comprehension monitoring, individuals read four narrative texts developed by Weaver and Bryant (1995). Immediately after reading a text passage, participants made a judgment as to how well they would perform on a later four-alternative multiple-choice test over the material. After providing these ratings, the test was given.

We compared ratings of predicted performance with actual test performance separately for each participant. We used Kruskal-Goodman's G as our primary indicator of metacognition accuracy (We also computed bias and discrimination scores where possible; these results were similar to G). A more detailed discussion of the procedures, analyses, and results can be found in Kelemen et al. (2000); we present only the highlights here. In Experiment 1, we found both memory performance and confidence to be at intermediate levels, avoiding possible floor or ceiling effects. As a check on the efficacy of our procedures, we examined metacognitive accuracy for each separate task. We also found significant metacognitive accuracy in all tasks, and the magnitude was similar to those obtained in past research (cf. Kelemen & Weaver, 1997; Leonesio & Nelson, 1990; Nelson & Dunlosky, 1991, 1994; Weaver & Bryant, 1995). Furthermore, we replicated Nelson & Dunlosky's (1991) delayed-JOL effect, with delayed JOLs significantly more accurate than immediate JOLs.

Next, we examined whether memory, confidence, and metacognitive accuracy were consistent across the four tasks. For example, would a confident (or accurate) participant in the EOL task also be confident (or accurate) in the JOL task? Component measures of metacognitive accuracy (i.e., memory and confidence) themselves were quite consistent between tasks: measures were significantly correlated between tasks in 51 out of 80 cases, about 64%. In marked contrast, metacognitive accuracy (the correlation between confidence and memory) itself was not consistent: very few (2/24, about 8%) of the Gs were consistent between tasks, little better than would be expected by chance. We also examined whether memory, confidence, and metacognitive accuracy were consistent within a given task over the one-week interval. For example, would a participant with high performance in the EOL task on Day 1 also perform well in the EOL task one week later? Test-retest performance was even more striking. Component measures displayed significant test-retest reliability in all tasks: memory and confidence scores were stable in every case (10/10). In contrast, none of the four test-retest correlations of G were reliably non-zero.

We modified the tasks in Experiment 2 to make the various metacognitive tests more similar. (The procedures used in Experiment 1 were based on commonly used procedures for each task, resulting in superficial differences in the number of questions and judgments.) Experiment 2 confirmed our previous findings. Both memory and confidence were consistent between tasks (memory and confidence scores were significantly correlated between tasks in 67% of the cases (32/48). In contrast, only 3 of the 24 correlations (12%) of metamemory accuracy (G) across tasks were non-zero –and two of these were in the unexpected direction! Test-retest differences were even more pronounced: both memory and confidence scores showed reliable test-retest correlations in all four tasks (8/8). Examination of metacognitive accuracy values showed the opposite pattern: none (0/4) of the test-retest correlations of G were reliably non-zero. These results from Experiments 1 and 2 are displayed in Figure 1.

The summary of these results is simple but powerful: while memory performance and confidence were stable across both time and task, metacognitive accuracy was not. Therefore, individual differences in metamemory accuracy do not appear to be reliable. Arguing in favor a null hypothesis is always tricky, but our data allow us to address many of the obvious criticisms and potential (alternative) explanations: Could the null results arise because of unreliability of the component measures? We found that both component measures when treated independently were reliable across conditions, and produced reliable corrections within conditions. Using the two most commonly accepted ways of assessing reliability –test-retest and split-half– we found substantial reliability among the individual component measures. We are satisfied that our measures were sufficiently reliable. Perhaps the procedures employed here were ineffective. The magnitude of observed metacognitive accuracy (G) in all tasks was comparable with previously published norms (see Kelemen et al., 2000, for further details). Furthermore, we obtained a reliable delayed-JOL effect (Nelson & Dunlosky, 1991) with the appropriate manipulation. In every kind of test were used, our results fit squarely into other findings on similar tasks.

Is the null outcome a function of insufficient power to detect differences? We had sufficient power to detect small (but reliable) correlations between other variables. More importantly, the magnitude of differences between reliability of component measures and unreliability of metacognitive accuracy was enormous: across the various tasks, mean correlations for the component measures were significant in nearly 2/3 of possible cases (83/128). Test-retest correlations for the component measures were significant in every case (18/18). Across task correlations for metacognitive accuracy were significant (in the prediction direction) in about 6% of the cases (3/48). Test-retest correlations were no better: none of the cases were significant (0/8).

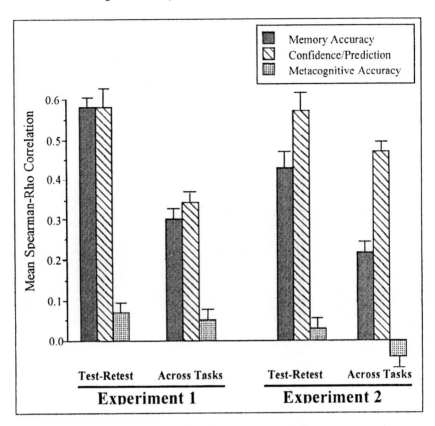

Figure 1. Mean test-retest and across-task reliability (with standard errors) for memory performance, confidence/predictions, and metacognitive accuracy in Experiments 1 & 2. (Adapted from Kelemen, Frost & Weaver, 2000)

Ruling out other explanations, we are forced to conclude that unlike memory and other cognitive traits, metamemory performance does not seem to be a product of an underlying unitary ability. Rather, metamemory accuracy appears to reflect differences attributable to external factors: conditions at time of judgment, the type of items being used, delay between prediction and test, type of processing used, familiarity, retrieval fluency, and so forth. As such, our results converge with those of other researchers who now characterize metamemory as an inferential process (see Schwartz, Benjamin & Bjork, 1997, for a review), one influenced by the cues which are used at time of judgment (see Koriat, 1997, 1998).

Author Notes
This work was supported by a Baylor University Research Council award to the first author, and was written in part during a sabbatical granted by the College of Arts and Sciences. The first author wishes to express appreciation to Wallace Daniel, Dean of the College of Arts and Sciences, for proving the support necessary to complete this project. The authors thank Asher Koriat, Ruth Maki, Tom Nelson, and Roddy Roediger for insightful comments on an earlier version of this manuscript. Send correspondence to Charles A. Weaver, III, Department of Psychology and Neuroscience, Baylor University, Waco, TX 76798-7334, E-mail: Charles_Weaver@baylor.edu.

Notes

[1] Of course, the two factors need not be independent. Most stimulus variables, for example, produce changes because of the processing they induce. By "processing factors", we mean those variables which produce differences over and above those 'naturally' induced by the stimulus materials. Likewise, processing factors can be manipulated even without changing stimuli.

[2] Gamma correlations range from -1.0 (perfect negative correlation) to +1.0 (perfect positive correlation), with 0 representing complete lack of predictive accuracy. Unlike other correlation coefficients, G is not interpreted in terms of variance accounted for, but rather has a probabilistic interpretation. Specifically, if an individual gives two items different JOLs and only one of these items is correctly recalled, the probability (P) that the correct item was given a higher JOL is determined by the equation: $P = 0.5 + 0.5G$.

[3] We thank Asher Koriat for his input on this point.

[4] Patton, Weaver, Burns, Brady, and Bryant (1991) failed to replicate this finding in adult college students.

II

WHAT IS METACOGNITION
IN RELATION TO COGNITION?

Chapter 1

Metacognition in Strategy Selection
Giving Consciousness Too Much Credit

Melanie Cary and Lynne M. Reder
Carnegie Mellon University, USA

Key themes: Cont / Defn / Prob / Proc / Theor

Key words: Metacognition / Strategy selection / Cognitive processes / Adaptivity / Implicit learning

Abstract: Many researchers believe that metacognitive processes regulate strategy selection. Another common assumption is that metacognitive processes, such as strategy selection, entail conscious processing or decision making. In this chapter, we examine whether conscious awareness is a critical aspect of strategy selection. We review evidence that first establishes that strategy selection varies both across and within individuals in response to dynamic features of the environment. Then, we present evidence that strategy adaptation can occur without (a) conscious consideration of different strategies or (b) conscious awareness of factors influencing one's strategy use. Specifically, shifts in strategy use occurred when people seemed to be unaware (a) that there were shifts in their strategy use or (b) that there were changes in the characteristics of the environment that, nonetheless, affected their strategy use.

Conscious awareness is generally believed to be a necessary condition of metacognition (e.g., Paris, this volume). Some researchers clearly express this belief, as evidenced by the recent statement that "metacognition is an essentially conscious activity" (Darling, Sala, Gray, & Trivelli, 1998, p. 89). Many others tacitly hold this assumption, as noted by Tulving (1994). However, a few researchers have recently proposed an alternative view of the role of consciousness in metacognition by suggesting that there are metacognitive processes that do not depend on conscious awareness (Koriat, 2000; Sun, 2000). From this perspective, metacognition involves a combination of explicit and implicit processes.

Additionally, metacognitive processes have frequently been proposed as the mechanisms that regulate strategy selection (e.g., Dunlosky & Hertzog, 1998; Nelson & Narens, 1990; Roberts & Erdos, 1993). In this chapter, we examine whether conscious awareness is a critical aspect of strategy selection. In doing so, we establish that strategy selection varies across and within individuals in response to dynamic features of the environment. We present evidence that this strategy adaptation can occur without awareness of the environmental changes that affect adaptation and without awareness that shifts in strategy have occurred. Therefore, we contend that if metacognition is dependent on conscious awareness, then not all strategy selection involves metacognitive processes.

1.   METACOGNITION AND STRATEGY SELECTION

Consistent with the view that metacognitive processes are involved in strategy selection, several researchers have suggested that two principle components of metacognition are monitoring and control of cognitive processes (e.g., Metcalfe, 1996; Nelson, 1996). This conception of metacognition underlies the edited book "Metacognition and cognitive neuropsychology: Monitoring and control processes" (Mazzoni & Nelson, 1998). Monitoring involves assessing information about one's knowledge and performance. Monitoring processes do not inherently require conscious awareness, but the term "metacognitive monitoring" typically refers to processes that do. Control involves self-regulative processes that direct and modify one's behavior, such as processes that govern the selection of strategies for accomplishing tasks.

Monitoring and control of cognitive processes are central to everyday functioning. Consider the processes involved in selecting which procedure to use to calculate a tip. A person can calculate the tip mentally, use paper and pencil, or use a calculator. Further, the person must initiate the processes responsible for each step in obtaining the tip (e.g., round up bill total to the nearest dollar, locate calculator). Understanding how it is that people self-regulate and how these control processes are affected by monitoring is important for understanding human behavior and cognition. Do people shift among available strategies or processes to perform a task? Do people evaluate how they are doing while performing a task or a series of tasks? Do people measure what they know in order to select the most appropriate strategy?

Monitoring and control processes are almost certainly interdependent. Some metacognitive researchers have proposed that there is a causal link between metacognitive monitoring and metacognitive control (e.g., Barnes, Nelson, Dunlosky, Mazzoni, & Narens, 1999). Generally, monitoring processes must exist, because strategy use has been shown to be influenced by the prior success of each strategy (e.g., Reder & Schunn, 1999). The information gleaned from monitoring may be used later to facilitate selection of the best strategy when the person re-encounters a problem of the same type. Consider children's selection of a strategy for solving simple addition problems. Siegler (1987) showed that young elementary school children use a variety of addition strategies and do so in a way that is adaptive to different types of problems. Children tend to use the strategy that produces the most beneficial combination of speed and accuracy for a particular problem. Specifically, children choose faster strategies (e.g., retrieval) when these strategies produce a correct answer. They choose slower strategies (e.g., counting) when these strategies yield a correct answer and the faster ones produce errors. Presumably, cognitive processes monitor the speed and accuracy of each addition strategy by problem type, and this information influences which strategy is used on a particular problem. The question arises as to whether a child's selection of a strategy results from deliberate consideration of the choices and conscious awareness of their prior success rates or from more autonomous, implicit processes. Is conscious control a general requirement of strategy selection? Must an individual be aware of the prior history of success with each strategy?

1.1 Overview and organization of the chapter

We argue that a great deal of strategy selection happens without conscious deliberation or awareness of factors influencing one's choice. The term "strategy selection" may seem to suggest that the process involves a type of deliberate choice, but we believe this process often lacks conscious deliberation. Therefore, we also contend that if *metacognition* is understood as a property of mind that requires conscious awareness, then much of cognitive monitoring and control occurs without metacognitive involvement.

It is important to note that in this chapter we do not distinguish between strategies and procedures. Readers may believe that it would be more appropriate to refer to some of the strategies that we discuss as procedures. Both of these terms refer to means that people may use for accomplishing a task. We are interested in the nature of the mechanisms that result in an individual using one of multiple means for accomplishing a task, regardless of whether the alternatives are procedures or strategies. Furthermore, we believe that the presented effects and conclusions hold for both strategies and procedures.

The rest of this chapter is organized in the following manner: First, we establish the need to posit strategy selection in performance by illustrating that there is strategy variability in people's performance of multiple tasks, not only between but also within individuals. Second, we discuss factors that affect strategy selection, focusing on two types of factors that were proposed by Reder (1987, 1988). In examining these factors we demonstrate that strategy variability can be caused by sensitivity to features in the task and the task environment. Where possible, we report participants' levels of conscious awareness of changes in the task features and their shifts in strategy. Lastly, we consider more generally the necessity of conscious awareness for strategy adaptation. We will conclude that strategy selection can occur implicitly, without conscious consideration of alternative strategies.

2.   STRATEGY VARIABILITY

Until relatively recently, the accepted view of performance assumed that the cognitive scientist was to identify *the* procedure used to perform a task. Developmental psychologists assumed sequential or stage-like use of alternative strategies, with more sophisticated strategies being adopted later. More recently, people have provided evidence for the notion of strategy variation within a person performing a task (e.g., Erickson & Kruschke, 1998; Lemaire & Reder, 1999; Lovett & Anderson, 1996; Reder, 1982, 1987, 1988; Siegler, 1988). Consider strategy selection in question answering. In the 1970s and 1980s, the dominant view was that people *first* search memory for the answer when a question is posed. If, and *only* if, that search fails, then people attempt an alternative strategy. This type of view was apparent in several theoretical perspectives, such as SOAR (Laird, Newell & Rosenbloom, 1987) and the Distribution of Associations model (Siegler & Shrager, 1984).

Early evidence that people vary in question-answering strategies was provided in Reder (1982). Participants in that study read brief stories and then were asked to make judgments about each of a series of statements that, based on the stories, were highly plausible, moderately plausible, or implausible. Some participants were asked to discriminate previously read assertions from statements that were not part of the story. These participants were only tested with highly plausible and moderately plausible statements. Other participants were asked to judge the plausibility of each test statement. In addition to the judgment task manipulation, Reder also manipulated the delay between when participants read a story and when they were tested on it: Testing was immediate, 20 min later, or 2 days later.

The results of that study indicated that people can use either a direct retrieval strategy or a plausibility strategy and that people do not always try direct retrieval first. When judgments are made immediately after reading a story, the statements in the story should be relatively accessible from memory; however, after a 2-day delay the information should be less accessible. Participants who were tested immediately were much more likely to first try direct retrieval than participants tested with a 20-min or a 2-day delay. Importantly, this was true regardless of whether participants were asked to judge plausibility or asked to make recognition judgments. Participants who were tested after a 2-day delay had a tendency to try a plausibility strategy first, using retrieval as more of a backup strategy. In sum, Reder (1982) demonstrated that the two judgment strategies had shifting propensities for individuals to try a particular one first.

There is a variety of other evidence for strategy alternation within individuals, some of which will be discussed in more detail below. Reder (1987, 1988) provided evidence that for each test statement there is a strategy selection phase in which individuals making story fact verifications select among plausibility and direct retrieval. Strategy variation has also been documented in an air traffic control task (Reder & Schunn, 1999; Schunn & Reder, 1998), as well as in the problem solving and arithmetic domains. Lovett and Anderson (1996) had participants perform a problem-solving task in which there are two alternative strategies available for the first step in attempting a solution. They found that individuals solving a series of these problems varied their use of the two alternative strategies, rather than each person only using one strategy across several problems. Lemaire and Reder (1999) examined strategy selection in an arithmetic verification task. Again, individuals used a variety of strategies when performing multiple verifications. Because the selection of a strategy for each verification problem was influenced by features of the problem, an individual's strategy use varied across problems. As mentioned earlier, children solving simple arithmetic problems sometimes achieve the answer by retrieval and other times by using one of a variety of different strategies, such as adding by counting up from the larger number (Siegler, 1987, 1988). Variation in strategies for simple arithmetic is not limited to children. Adults performing a running arithmetic task that required multiple additions used retrieval on some steps and counting on others (Cary & Carlson, 1995). Furthermore, individuals appeared to fluently switch between addition strategies without deliberately choosing one strategy over another.

3. FACTORS AFFECTING STRATEGY SELECTION

Given that we have established that people select among multiple strategies for task performance, and they seem to vary in their preferences within the same task, can we specify the factors that influence the strategy selection process? For example, in question answering what determines whether a person searches memory for an answer or infers an answer? Reder (1987, 1988) emphasized two types of factors that affect strategy selection: intrinsic and extrinsic. Intrinsic factors involve people's familiarity with features of the task, problem or question, such as familiarity with terms in a problem. Extrinsic factors involve features of the general context in which a task is performed, such as task instructions and prior history of success with a strategy.

3.1 Intrinsic factors

Many of the experiments described in Reder's (1982) work could be explained by postulating that a person shifts strategy preference before reading the question. Experiments that involve a change in base rates of success, specific advice about the best procedure for the next question, or a delay between study and test all allow participants to decide *a priori* which strategy is likely to prove more efficient. In real life people do not necessarily know the age of the relevant memories when they are queried. Therefore, it might be reasonable to assume that the decision to use plausible reasoning rather than searching memory is based on attributes of the question rather than the tacit knowledge "I have come back 2 days later and thus the information must be old."

A study reported by Reder (1988) provides evidence that people's strategy selection can be influenced by intrinsic features of a task; in this case features of a test statement. The study consisted of two experimental sessions that occurred 2 days apart. Participants read 5 stories in the first session and 5 stories in the second session. After each story in the second session, participants were tested on the immediately preceding story and one of the stories read 2 days earlier. At the beginning of each test, participants were informed as to which story would be tested from 2 days prior. Because the test statements were presented randomly, rather than blocked by target story, participants did not know which of the two stories a statement was related to until after they read the statement. Thus, a critical difference between this study and the Reder (1982) study discussed previously is whether or not participants would know the age of the relevant material prior to reading the test statement. As in the earlier study, half of the participants made recognition judgments and half made plausibility judgments.

The results of that study indicated that participants in both the recognition and plausibility conditions used both direct retrieval and plausibility strategies to make their judgments. Importantly, the selection of a strategy was influenced by the age of the relevant story. When test statements were related to the immediately preceding story, the data indicated that participants tended to use the direct retrieval strategy. However, when test statements were related to a story from 2 days earlier, participants tended to use the plausibility strategy. The data also indicated that participants did not always try retrieval before using the plausibility strategy. Hence, participants were able to adjust or make their strategy choice after seeing the test statement, and the strategy selected was influenced by an intrinsic feature of the probe. These results suggest that when a problem is presented there is an initial evaluation phase that influences strategy use.

When a person initially evaluates a question or problem, how do intrinsic factors influence which solution strategy is tried first? In the case of question answering, by what means does age or familiarity of the material lead a person to decide to use a plausibility strategy first rather than search memory first? We argue that one of the criteria used in this decision is a quick *feeling of knowing* or familiarity that comes from features of the question or test statement. A strong feeling of knowing is likely to lead someone to try retrieval first, while a weak feeling of knowing is likely to result in the use of some other strategy. Furthermore, this feeling of knowing is not based on searching for the answer (Reder, 1987, 1988; Reder & Ritter, 1992). There is evidence that people can know whether they will be able to answer a question *before* they can find the answer in memory. The first evidence for these claims came from studies that used a "game show" paradigm.

In non-experimental settings, most people have observed that television game show contestants appear able to indicate whether or not they know an answer before they have retrieved it from memory, often before the entire question is read to them. Conceivably all people can do this on a more regular basis. Reder (1987) tested this idea by using world knowledge questions in a paradigm intended to be treated like a game show. Participants were asked questions like "Which ship carried the Pilgrims to America in 1620?" and "What was the name of the clown on the *Howdy Doody* television show?" Half of the participants were asked to estimate whether or not they thought they would be able to generate an answer for each question. When they answered "yes" they were then asked to come up with an answer. The other half of the participants were simply asked to answer each question. All participants were encouraged to respond as rapidly as possible. Participants in the answer condition began articulating the answer more slowly than participants in the estimate condition indicated whether or not they thought they could answer the question. Participants in the answer condition were also slower to respond "don't know." This effect was not due to a speed-accuracy tradeoff, because participants in the answer condition correctly answered 74% of the questions they attempted, and participants in the estimate condition correctly answered 88% of the questions they attempted. A control experiment that required participants in both conditions to press a key also found that participants in the answer condition responded more slowly than those in the estimate condition. These data are consistent with the idea that there is a feeling-of-knowing mechanism that allows people to evaluate whether or not they are likely to know the answer to a question before they can actually answer the question.

Conceivably the ability to rapidly evaluate one's knowledge about a question could derive not from a rapid feeling of knowing, but rather from an early stage of retrieval (see Nhouyvanisvong & Reder, 1998; Miner & Reder, 1994 for reviews). Reder and colleagues (Reder, 1987; Reder & Ritter, 1992; Reder & Schunn, 1996; Schunn, Reder, Nhouyvanisvong, Richards, & Stroffolino, 1997) conducted experiments to try to rule out this alternative. They manipulated feeling of knowing by manipulating participants' familiarity with intrinsic features of the questions or problems. Generally when a target item has been seen recently or frequently, familiarity with the item should be high and the item should be relatively accessible from memory. Hence, items with high familiarity should produce a high feeling of knowing.

Reder (1987) manipulated familiarity with test questions in the game show paradigm by priming terms in the questions. For one-third of the game-show questions two terms in each question were previously rated by the participants for co-occurrence (e.g., "How often do golf and par appear together?"). Question difficulty was also manipulated by dividing questions into three levels of difficulty based on norms developed by Nelson and Narens (1980). As in the preceding experiment, half of the participants estimated whether they knew the answer and the others simply answered the question if they could.

As predicted, questions that contained primed terms gave people the impression that they knew the answer to questions that they could not answer. Easier questions should already afford a high feeling of knowing and, thus, priming cannot and did not raise the tendency for participants to think that they knew the answer. However, for harder questions, participants in the estimate condition judged that they could answer more primed questions than unprimed questions. Their ability to correctly answer those questions did not increase with their first impression that they knew the answer. In contrast, for participants in the answer condition there was no effect of priming on proportion of questions attempted. Rather, the effect of priming appeared in the time to respond "don't know" to questions that were not attempted. Participants in the answer condition were slower to respond "don't know" for primed questions than for unprimed questions, suggesting that they were searching longer for an answer to primed questions. These results support the ideas that feeling of knowing is influenced by recent exposure to features of the target item and that this feeling affects whether and how long people search for the answer. Research by Metcalfe, Schwartz, and Joaquim, (1993; Schwartz & Metcalfe, 1992) also emphasizes the role of familiarity with question features. They found that priming of cues in a paired-associate study increased feeling of knowing without affecting memory performance.

Feeling of knowing mechanisms can also be used for initial strategy selection in arithmetic verification problems (Reder & Ritter, 1992). Participants solved "sharp" problems and either addition (Experiment 1) or multiplication (Experiment 2) problems, such as 14#17, 37+15, and 19*13. The "sharp" operator (#) was designed to be fairly equivalent to multiplication in computational difficulty. Participants were presented with a large number of problems, many of which were repeated up to 20 times. When each problem was presented, participants had approximately three-fourths of a second to select between calculating or retrieving the answer. Participants received a 10 times greater reward for selecting retrieval if they could answer correctly within 2 sec. Occasionally participants were presented with operator switch problems in which a practiced problem had its operator switched to a different operator. For example, 19*13 may have been presented several times and then for the first time 19#13 was presented. There are a few important aspects of the results. First, frequency of exposure affected participants' tendency to believe that questions could be answered by retrieval. With each re-presentation of a problem, participants were more likely to select retrieval for solving that problem. They also became faster at correctly answering the problem. Critically, as participants acquired experience with a problem they were more likely to select retrieval when an operator switch problem was presented. In fact, regression analyses indicated that it was experience with the operand pairs, not the entire problem, that predicted tendency to select retrieval. These results suggest that familiarity with terms of the problem, rather than the ability to retrieve the answer, drives feeling of knowing.

Additional evidence indicates that strategy selection was not due to information from an early stage of retrieval (Reder & Ritter, 1992; Reder & Schunn, 1996; Schunn et al., 1997). Reder and colleagues examined the possibility that operator switch problems gave a high feeling of knowing because the wrong answer was being retrieved in from memory. Some evidence against this alternative account comes from Reder and Ritter's study. Their participants were much less likely to choose retrieval for operand reversal problems (e.g., 23x12 vs. 12x23) than for previously encountered problems or for operator switch problems. In other words, their participants failed to indicate a feeling of knowing for problems to which they did know the answer when the problems looked different, while at the same time they quickly responded retrieve, indicating that they felt that they knew the answer, to problems that looked familiar even though they had never been seen before.

More recent work experimentally de-coupled familiarity with the arithmetic operands from familiarity with the answer (Schunn, et al., 1997). This was accomplished by blocking participants from calculating the answers 5 times out of 7 presentations for a set of special problems. For these problems participants made the initial retrieve-compute decision, but instead of providing an answer on most of the trials the screen was cleared, and the participant was instructed to continue on to the next problem. To ensure that participants could not learn that the special problems were never answered, participants were occasionally required to answer them. These infrequently answered problems were one-fourth of all problems in the experiment. In other respects, the experiment resembled the Reder and Ritter (1992) study. As before, participants were presented with a series of multiplication and sharp problems with repetition of individual problems. On each trial, participants made a rapid decision as to whether they would retrieve or calculate the answer. By frequently blocking participants from solving the special problems, familiarity with the problems and learning of the answers were different than for regular problems.

If feeling of knowing is due to an early stage of retrieval, then participants should rarely select retrieval for the infrequently answered problems, because the answer is not associated with the problem on most trials. However, if this feeling is based on familiarity with features of the problem, then participants should select retrieval for the infrequently answered problems as a function of the amount of exposure to the problem, because problem familiarity is increased with each exposure. The predicted pattern of strategy selection for the normal problems (i.e., the ones answered each time they are presented) is the same under each hypothesis: Participants should select retrieval for the normal problems as a function of the amount of exposure to the problem. As predicted by the familiarity hypothesis, for both infrequently answered problems and normal problems the probability of selecting retrieve was a function of exposure, and the same function appeared to underlie strategy selection in both problem conditions. Thus, the tendency to select retrieval was affected by exposure to the problem itself and was not dependent upon exposure to the answer. This result provides strong evidence for the role of the intrinsic factor of problem familiarity in initial strategy selection.

There are other task domains in which intrinsic features have been shown to affect strategy choice. Problem schemata for word algebra problems have been cued by superficial problem features (Hinsley, Hayes, & Simon, 1977). Strategy selection in problem solving has been influenced by how close in absolute distance each strategy will get one to the goal state (e.g., Lovett & Anderson, 1996). Analogical remindings are also influenced by superficial similarity between the current problem and the remembered analogy (Ross, 1984, 1989).

3.2 Extrinsic factors

There are a variety of extrinsic factors that also affect strategy selection, including task instructions, advice about what strategy will work, the availability of working memory support, and prior history of success with a strategy. For example, Cary and Carlson (1999) demonstrated that the strategy that people use to solve a complex problem is influenced both by the availability of working memory aid and the availability of a worked example problem. Participants could use one of multiple strategies to solve each of several income calculation problems. When an example problem was provided, participants were more likely to select the illustrated solution strategy than when no example was provided. Participants provided with working memory aid, via the availability of paper and pen, tended to settle on using a problem-solving strategy that corresponded with the conceptual structure of the task, whereas participants without this memory aid tended to settle on using a different strategy, one that minimized demands on working memory.

A strategy's past history of success appears to be a primary extrinsic factor that affects strategy selection. The influence of this factor has been shown to affect strategy choice in several domains, including runway selection in an air traffic control task (Reder & Schunn, 1999), story question answering (Reder, 1987), equation verification (Lemaire & Reder, 1999), and simple problem solving (Lovett & Anderson, 1996). In general, people tend to be sensitive to base rates of success and select a strategy based in part on what has been successful in the past.

Reder and Schunn (1999) studied strategy adaptivity to changing base rates using an air traffic control task. Participants had to land planes selecting between a short and long runway. There are various rules for the task including rules that govern when a short runway can be used for different types of planes. A long runway can always be used for all planes, but 747s always require a long runway. When most of the planes that must be landed are 747s, participants should try to avoid using the long runway for smaller planes. When there are few 747s, use of the long runway for short planes does not matter, and it is more efficient to land all planes on the long runway. To investigate whether people adapt in this way, Reder and Schunn varied the proportion of 747s in different blocks of the experiment. For example, for some participants the proportion of 747s was 25% in the first block of trials, 5% in the second block, and 50% in the third block. To assess strategy adaptivity, they looked at how frequently participants selected the short runway when both runways were open and could be used. They found that participants generally adapted in response to the proportion of 747s and did so in the expected directions: When the proportion of 747s increased participants increased their use of the short runway, and when this proportion decreased participants decreased their use of the short runway. Interestingly, strategy adaptivity varied across individuals with some participants being more adaptive than others. Furthermore, inductive reasoning and working memory capacity were positively correlated with individual differences in adaptivity (see Reder & Schunn, 1999; Schunn & Reder 1998 for more information).

In one of the experiments described by Reder (1987), participants judged the plausibility of statements based on the story they had just read. Some of the plausible test statements had been presented earlier as part of the story and some of the implausible test statements were identical to statements in the story except for one word whose opposite meaning had been substituted. Thus, participants could use either a retrieval strategy or a plausibility strategy to make judgments. The proportion of test statements that could be judged based on an explicitly presented statement in the story varied both across participants and across the experiment. For the first 6 of 10 stories, the successfulness of the retrieval strategy differed for the two groups of participants. For participants in the direct retrieval bias condition, 80% of the plausible statements had been presented in the stories and 80% of the implausible statements were contradictions of statements that had been presented. In contrast, for participants in the plausibility bias group only 20% of the plausible statements had been presented and 20% of the implausible statements were contradictions of presented statements. For the last 4 stories in the experiment, the percent of statements that could be verified using direct retrieval shifted to 50% for both groups.

Direct retrieval should be a faster process than judging plausibility at the short delay used in this study, and direct retrieval can only occur when the test statement or its contradiction had been presented in a story. Hence, Reder examined the difference in response time for stated probes and not-stated probes. During the bias manipulation (i.e., stories 1-6), this difference between stated and not-stated probes was much greater for participants in the direct retrieval bias condition than for participants in the plausibility bias condition. These data indicate that participants in the retrieval bias condition used the retrieval strategy, even though the task required judging plausibility, whereas participants in the plausibility bias condition were much less inclined to use retrieval. When the proportion of previously presented test statements changed to 50%, the response time difference between stated and not-stated probes was equivalent for the two groups of participants. That is, from the first to second part of the study, the response time benefit for previously presented statements decreased for participants in the direct retrieval bias condition and increased for participants in the plausibility bias condition.

Furthermore, when the data are analyzed with regard to the difference in response time between moderately and highly plausible statements, the data indicate a complementary shift in the tendency to use the plausibility strategy. During the bias manipulation, the response time benefit for highly plausible statements was larger for participants in the plausibility bias condition. When the bias was removed, this benefit decreased for participants in the plausibility bias condition and increased for participants in the retrieval bias condition. Hence, the data strongly suggest that as the retrieval strategy became less successful for participants in the direct retrieval bias group they became less likely to use it, and as the retrieval strategy became more successful for participants in the plausibility bias group they became more likely to use it. These results are consistent with the idea that people are sensitive to base rates of success with a strategy and this sensitivity can produce changes in the likelihood of selecting a particular strategy.

Participants in that study were questioned at the end of the experiment regarding their level of awareness. They were not consciously aware of either the strategies that they were using or the different base rates of success for using retrieval. Regardless of bias condition, the participants thought that they had used direct retrieval to judge plausibility. They also did not differ in their guesses of base-rate as a function of condition.

Lemaire and Reder (1999) found evidence that strategy selection in arithmetic verification can be sensitive to a strategy's base rate of success without participants conscious awareness of these base rates. Their participants were presented with a series of correct and incorrect multiplication problems and asked to indicate whether each one was true (e.g., 6 x 32 = 192) or false (e.g., 8 x 7 = 58). There were two kinds of false problems. Parity match problems had a false answer with an odd-even status the same as that of the correct answer (e.g., 8 x 7 = 58), whereas parity mismatch problems had a false answer with an odd-even status different from the correct answer (e.g., 8 x 7 = 57). Participants were faster at rejecting parity mismatch problems than parity match problems, indicating that people can use violations of the parity rule to rapidly reject false problems. In other words, participants sometimes used a parity-check strategy to reject problems. Lemaire and Reder manipulated the proportion of false problems violating the parity rule. For participants in the high mismatch condition, 80% of the false problems violated the parity rule, and for participants in the low mismatch condition 20% of the false problems violated the rule. In this way, the base rate of success for using the parity-check strategy differed for the two groups of participants. This difference in base rate was reflected in the rejection response time advantage for parity mismatch problems, relative to parity match problems. The parity effect for participants in the high mismatch condition was almost twice that of participants in the low mismatch condition. This differential parity effect can be interpreted as participants being more likely to use the parity-check strategy when it had a higher base rate of success.

Lemaire and Reder's (1999) participants were not aware of either their use of the parity-check strategy or the percentage of parity mismatch problems. Only 5 of 32 participants reported using any strategy other than verification, and only 2 of those participants reported using the parity-check strategy. When participants were asked to guess what percentage of the problems were parity mismatch problems, their responses did not differ for the two conditions (high and low mismatch). Approximately half of the participants in each condition estimated that more than 50% of the incorrect problems violated parity, and the other half estimated that less than 50% violated parity. Thus, the participants did not seem to have explicit access to the relevant proportions that were influencing their strategy selection.

Lovett and Anderson (1996) found evidence that base rates of strategy success affect strategy selection regardless of whether participants' deliberately tried to use them. The task was Lovett's Building Sticks Task (BST) in which participants must build a stick of a target length by adding and subtracting sticks from an infinite resource of sticks of 3 different lengths. The lengths of the target and resource sticks vary from trial to trial. There are essentially two strategies that participants can use for solving the task. Neither of these strategies is inherently correlated with perceptual features (i.e., the lengths) of the various sticks, hence base rates of success with each strategy can be varied independently of whether or not perceptual problem features "suggest" one strategy over the other. Participants solved twenty blocks of BST problems. The base rate of success for each strategy was varied across groups of trials. For example, participants received 5 blocks of trials with one strategy working most of the time, then five blocks with that strategy working less frequently, and so on. Participants' strategy choices generally tracked the variable base rates of success of the alternative strategies.

As with the two previous studies, awareness was not critical for base rates to affect strategy selection. Sixteen participants claimed to have solved the task by looking at the lengths of the sticks, and twenty participants claimed to have solved the task by choosing the more successful strategy. However, when strategy selection was investigated as a function of which of these two strategies participants reported using, there was no difference between the two groups in the proportion of trials on which they selected the more successful strategy. Thus, participants' likelihood of selecting a successful strategy was not affected by whether or not they reported using base rates of success, even though the base rates influenced strategy selection.

4.   STRATEGY ADAPTATION AND CONSCIOUS AWARENESS

We have established that people select among strategies, do so with variability, and select strategies adaptively in response to changes in intrinsic and extrinsic factors. The critical issue on which we now focus is whether or not participants adapt as the result of conscious monitoring. First consider whether adaptation to changing base rates of success is due to conscious monitoring. The evidence discussed earlier indicates that this is unlikely. In Reder (1987), Lemaire and Reder (1999), and Lovett and Anderson (1996) most participants were not aware of either base rates of success or changes in base rates of success. Many participants were not even aware of which strategies they had used to accomplish the task.

There are other tasks that show sensitivity to base rates without awareness. Participants in a study by Reder and Weber (1997) performed a spatial localization task. On each trial a target appeared in one of four spatial locations on the screen, and participants responded by pressing one of four buttons to indicate the location of the target. On most of the trials a distractor as well as a target was presented. The probability of a distractor was systematically varied across these four locations, such that 60% of the distractors occurred in one position, 30% in another, 10% in another, and no distractors appeared in the other position. Reder and Weber found that participants were slower to respond to the target as a function of distractor location. Participants were slowest when the distractor appeared in a location that rarely contained it, specifically the 30% or 10% position. However, when the distractor appeared in a frequent (i.e., 60%) location participants responded as fast as they did when no distractor was present. Although participants learned to ignore the distractor when it occurred in a frequent location, as indicated by their latency patterns, when participants were questioned at the end of the study about the distribution of distractors across the four locations, they were not aware of the different rates of presentation. Most participants reported that the distribution of distractors was even across the positions, the distribution was random, or they paid no attention to the distractors. In sum, participants showed sensitivity to the rates at which distractors were presented in various spatial locations without conscious awareness that there were different rates.

Chun and Jiang (1998) demonstrated that implicit learning of display contexts can help direct spatial attention to the location of a target. Their participants had to locate and identify a target in a display with several distractors. The context of each target was operationalized as the spatial layout of objects present on a trial. For half of the trials, the contextual configurations were yoked to target locations such that the target position could be predicted by the configuration of the other elements in the display. For the other trials, the configurations were unique and random. Participants detected targets in the repeated configurations more rapidly than targets presented in unique configurations. This benefit was maintained even when the actual distractor objects changed halfway through the experiment. Thus, participants' strategies for locating and responding to the target differed for the learned repeated configuration and the unique configurations. Importantly, this learning occurred without participants' conscious awareness of the repeated configurations. At the end of the experiment participants were given a recognition test of the configurations, and their hit rate and false alarm rate were the same (i.e., presented and not-presented configurations were indistinguishable). Only 3 of the 14 participants noticed that there were repeated configurations, and their hit rate was the same as their false alarm rate. Additionally, the latency benefit for repeated configurations did not differ for the aware and unaware participants. Clearly, conscious awareness of the repeated contexts, or even that there were repeated contexts, was not necessary for participants to learn about them or to have this knowledge affect performance (see Marescaux, Izaute, & Chambres, this volume, for a discussion of implicit learning and metaknowledge). This is yet another example of strategy selection occurring without conscious awareness of the factors that influence which strategy is used.

Sometimes the impression of conscious control of strategy choice may be illusory. In some tasks, participants may observe what they are doing and confabulate an explanation for their behavior that may or may not be accurate. Regardless of explanatory accuracy, when the rationale for strategy selection only comes after one's behavior it is not conscious deliberation that affects the regulating processes and strategies that are evoked.

Is performance better when participants are (or report being) aware of the factors that influence their strategy selections? The answer is "not necessarily." Recall Lovett and Anderson's (1996) study with the Building Sticks Task, in which participants' strategy selection was sensitive to base rates of success. Performance was no better for the participants who were aware of different base rates of success than for those who were not aware.

There are several factors that might affect whether or not a person is aware of the strategy that she has selected for performing a task. People are likely to be aware of the strategy selected when they are required to report it, as in the feeling of knowing and game show paradigm experiments previously discussed. When a particular strategy does not lead to a successful outcome, individuals may be inclined to assess the strategy that they are using in order to modify it or switch to a potentially more successful strategy. For example, a tennis player may wonder "Why are my tennis balls going into the net?" The timeframe of the unit task is also likely to influence people's awareness of their strategy selection. For processes that take on the order of a second to complete, there is no time for introspection to affect performance or strategy selection. There may be conscious strategy selection and metacognition for tasks that take several seconds (or longer) to complete, because there is more time to think about or reflect on what one is doing. The ease with which a task can be performed likely affects awareness, with easier tasks associated with less awareness. It may be that more difficult tasks elicit more awareness because they are more error prone or take longer to execute. Similarly, the degree of experience a person has with a particular type of task can influence his awareness of his strategy use. With practice the performance of some simple skills can become relatively automatic in nature (e.g., Shiffrin & Schneider, 1977), essentially eliminating the need for strategy selection.

5.   CONCLUSION

This chapter has reviewed evidence that people's actions are influenced by features of the task, features of the environment, and their success at using specific strategies. Remarkably, this adaptation often occurs without any awareness of what procedures or strategies are being used, the base rates of types of stimuli in the environment, or the success of a given strategy. A number of these strategy choices, such as retrieving versus reasoning to the answer, have often been discussed as examples of behaviors that are subject to metacognitive control. Therefore, if people in the field maintain the position that metacognition requires conscious awareness, then we would argue that cognitive monitoring and strategy selection often occur without metacognitive intervention.

One way to respond to the evidence and claims that we present is to exclude a requirement of conscious awareness from the concept "metacognition" and distinguish between conscious and non-conscious (or explicit and implicit) metacognitive processes. Some researchers have recently adopted this view. For example, Koriat (2000) proposed that there are both information-based metacognitive judgments that involve conscious awareness and experience-based metacognitive judgments that are implicit in nature. Additionally, Sun (2000) argued that metacognition is not necessarily explicit nor implicit, but rather is a combination of both types of processes. For further discussion of the relationships between explicit knowledge, implicit learning and metacognition see Dienes and Perner (this volume).

Perhaps there are different degrees of metacognitive awareness that are involved in the control and monitoring of performance. For example, Carlson (1997) suggested that there are three levels of metacognitive awareness for problem solving (cf. Valot, this volume). He proposed that a problem solver's cognition can be reflective, deliberate, or routine. When problem solving is quite difficult, people may reflect on their problem-solving activities. The intermediate level refers to instances when a person considers alternative strategies and deliberately decides which strategy to try. In skilled problem solving, cognition is routine in that one does not deliberately select among strategies, but knows what to do and does it.

Whether or not one considers conscious awareness as a requirement of metacognition, it is important for people to know that cognitive monitoring and control often occur without awareness of either the factors that are influencing strategy selection or the strategies that are being used. Hence, when researchers find individual variability in strategy use they should not assume that strategy selection was the result of conscious deliberation.

Author note
Preparation of this chapter was partially supported by grants 2-R01-MH52808 and 5-T32-MH19983 from the National Institute of Mental Health.

Chapter 2

Feeling of Familiarity
Memory Attribution versus Memory Module

Sachiko Kinoshita
Macquarie Centre for Cognitive Science (MACCS), Sydney, Australia

Key themes: Proc / Theor

Key words: Familiarity / Perceptual fluency / Attribution / Recognition memory / Repetition priming

Abstract: In this chapter, I will defend the intuitively plausible notion that implicit memory and metacognition are unrelated. I will do this in the context of studies that examined the relationship between recognition memory and perceptual fluency. Specifically, I will argue against the view that perceptual fluency, a product of implicit memory, gives rise to the feeling of familiarity in recognition memory via a process of attribution, a metacognitive process.

Intuitively, implicit memory and metacognition seem to be at the two opposite ends of the spectrum -as suggested by Reder (1993) in the first book to relate metacognition and implicit memory, one is "seemingly conscious and control-oriented", and the other "occurring without subjects' awareness" (p. ix). Indeed, one assumption common to different versions of multiple memory systems view is that there are two separate memory systems: One that subserves explicit, conscious memory and the other that subserves implicit memory which is unconscious and runs automatically. It would seem natural to assume that metacognition, whose function is to monitor and control cognitive processes, would be associated with the conscious process, but not with the unconscious process.

Contrary to this intuitive notion, there is a popularly held view of recognition memory that suggests that there is a close link between metacognition and implicit memory (e.g., Jacoby & Whitehouse 1989; Kelley & Jacoby, 1996). This view, referred to as the memory attribution view, suggests that a common component underlies performance on recognition memory test, an explicit memory test, and repetition priming effects, a product of implicit memory. Specifically, proponents of this view argue that a basis for the feeling of familiarity is the ease of perceiving events in which the feeling of familiarity is inferred or attributed from perceptual fluency. Further, they suggest that this process of inference/attribution is similar to other heuristic processes that are described as metacognitive, such as Tversky and Kahneman's (1973) availability heuristic.

In this chapter, I will defend the claim that metacognition and implicit memory are unrelated, by presenting a critique of the memory attribution view. I will first review experimental findings that are cited as support for this view, and will argue that such support is found only under limited conditions. I will then discuss an alternative interpretation of the basis for the feeling of familiarity. This interpretation is couched within a framework of memory proposed by Moscovitch (1993; 1994), which views the feeling of familiarity as a product of explicit memory. Specifically, the framework partitions explicit memory into a memory module and a central memory system, and regards the feeling of familiarity as being associated with the former system, and metacognitive processes as being associated with the latter. In this way, I defend the position that metacognitive processes do not share a common component with implicit memory processes.

1.   THE MEMORY ATTRIBUTION FRAMEWORK

The most clearly articulated statement suggesting a common element between metacognitive processes and implicit memory was made by Kelley and Jacoby (1996): In their words, "metacognition and implicit memory are so similar as to not be separate topics" (p. 287). Their claim is based on the memory attribution view, which is couched within the dual-process model of recognition memory. According to the model, recognition judgments are driven by two separate processes: the recovery of the context in which the recognition probe was studied, and a familiarity process (Atkinson & Juola, 1973; Mandler, 1980).

Jacoby and colleagues (e.g., Jacoby, Kelley, & Dywan, 1989; Kelley & Jacoby, 1996) proposed that the feeling of familiarity arises as a result of an automatic attribution of perceptual fluency, which is the ease of perceiving events. Items that have been encountered earlier produce repetition priming effects, that is, their perceptual fluency is enhanced. This enhanced perceptual fluency is a product of implicit memory. Jacoby and colleagues went on to argue that conversely, subjects can detect the ease of perception of an item and use the relative perceptual fluency to infer their study status. That is, when an event (e.g., a recognition probe) is perceived fluently, the fluency is attributed to a recent encounter with the stimulus and hence gives rise to the feeling of familiarity. Kelley and Jacoby (1996) described this attribution process as a metacognitive mechanism, in that it is an inferential process, rather than being based directly on the output of retrieval processes. But it is also described as nonanalytic, because subjects are said to be unaware of the source of the feeling of familiarity. Kelley and Jacoby (1996) used this nonanalytic nature of feeling of familiarity to explain why recognition judgments based on feeling of familiarity, as against those based on recollection of context, have a more automatic character, such as their relative speed (speeded recognition judgments rely on a greater extent on the feeling of familiarity) and the lack of control (they afford less control).

1.1   Empirical evidence 1: R and K responses

In evaluating the view that the feeling of familiarity is based on the output of implicit memory, I first turn to studies that used a modified recognition test in which subjects are requested to distinguish between two types of "old" responses: R (or Remember) and K (or Know) responses. The distinction was initially proposed by Tulving (1985) in which R responses are "old" responses accompanied by conscious recollection of the probe's prior occurrence and its context, and K responses which are not. Because K responses, by definition, are not accompanied by recollection of context, they seem an ideal tool for tapping the feeling of familiarity proposed by the dual-process models of recognition memory.[1]

Work by Gardiner and colleagues has demonstrated dissociative effects of many factors on the R and K responses. For example, Gardiner (1988) reported that levels-of-processing and generate-versus-read manipulations enhanced R responses but not K responses. Similarly, dividing attention at study was found to impair R responses but not K responses (Gardiner & Parkin, 1990). Based on the fact that these same factors also have little effect on performance on perceptual implicit memory tests, Gardiner (1988, Gardiner & Parkin, 1990) has suggested that K responses are based on the same process that produce repetition priming effects in perceptual tests. Such a position is entirely consistent with the memory attribution view. However, it should be noted that the observed dissociation between R and K responses generally reflects the fact that there are factors that affect R responses but not K responses. The converse, in which factors affect K responses but not R responses is rarely observed. In particular, from the view that perceptual fluency is automatically attributed to the feeling of familiarity, it is expected that factors that are known to reliably affect performance on perceptual implicit memory tests (e.g., a change of modality between study and test) would similarly affect K responses. In fact, studies that have specifically looked for such evidence did not find support for this prediction (e.g., Gardiner, 1988; Rajaram, 1993, Experiment 1). In line with this absence of perceptual effects on K responses, Gardiner (Richardson-Klavehn, Gardiner, & Java (1996) has recently retracted the earlier claim that the process responsible for repetition priming also produces the feeling of familiarity, as tapped by K responses.

1.2   Empirical evidence 2: Correlation between naturally produced fluency and recognition memory

Another line of evidence used to support the attributional view of feeling of familiarity came from studies that reported a relationship between the fluency of processing at test and the probability of calling an item "old" in recognition tests. Typically, in these studies, recognition probes are presented under degraded conditions, and perceptual fluency is measured in terms of accuracy or speed with which the item is identified (e.g., naming latency, the number of key presses required to progressively demask the item for identification). Earlier studies provided correlational evidence between measures of perceptual fluency and recognition memory judgments. For example, Johnston, Dark and Jacoby (1985) reported that nonwords that had been studied earlier and then presented for a recognition memory test under a visual noise mask were more likely to be judged old if they were more quickly identified.

It should be noted however, as has been pointed out by Watkins and Gibson (1988), a correlation between natural variation in perceptual fluency and recognition judgments does not constitute evidence that perceptual fluency was a **causal** basis of recognition judgments. Consider the following possibility. Under data-limited conditions (e.g., when items are presented under a visual noise mask), the process of recognizing the item in episodic memory presumably cannot start until the recognition probe is resolved, that is, until the item is identified. Implicit memory could affect the ease of identification, that is, studied items may be easier to identify than unstudied items. Therefore more "old" recognition judgments may be made to items that are easier to identify because of their (objective) study status than items that have not been studied earlier and are hence more difficult to identify. Such a mechanism could produce the correlation observed between perceptual fluency that varies between items and the probability of "old" judgments. However, note that the described mechanism does not necessitate the notion of memory attribution. The covariation between perceptual fluency and "old" recognition judgments is merely mediated by the objective status of the item, and the mechanism described above has nothing to say about how the feeling of familiarity arises.

It may also be expected that if the feeling of familiarity is based on automatic attribution of perceptual fluency, the dependency between the two should be ubiquitous. Contrary to this expectation, such a relationship is not always found. In the study by Johnston, Dark and Jacoby (1985) described above, the relationship between perceptual fluency and recognition judgements was not found for word targets. A study reported by Verfaellie and Cermak (1999) involving normal and amnesic subjects is also informative in this regard. In their Experiment 2, normal and amnesic subjects initially saw 40 words, and were later tested for recognition of these words. The recognition probes were presented through a visual noise mask, which was gradually and continuously clarified until subject pressed a key. At that point, subject identified the word and then gave a recognition judgment (i.e., whether or not the word had been studied). Verfaellie and Cermak reported that the pattern of relationship between recognition judgment, the actual study status of the item, and perceptual fluency (as measured by the density of masking at the point at which the word was identified) was different for normal and amnesic subjects. Specifically, amnesic subjects showed the same dependency between the probability of "old" judgments and perceptual fluency (higher probability of old judgments for items that were identified more fluently) for studied and unstudied items, but normal subjects showed this relationship only for studied items and not for unstudied items. Verfaellie and Cermak took this absence of relationship for the unstudied items to suggest that the relationship between perceptual fluency and recognition judgments is "unlikely to reflect the use of fluency heuristic as a basis for recognition in nonamnesic controls" (p. 203).

1.3   Empirical evidence 3: Experimenter-manipulated fluency effects on recognition judgments

As mentioned earlier, it is only the demonstrations of experimenter-manipulated perceptual fluency effects that provide evidence that perceptual fluency is the causal basis of "old" judgments. In contrast to relatively numerous findings of correlation between naturally produced variation in perceptual fluency and recognition judgments, findings of positive effects of experimenter-manipulated perceptual fluency are few (Johnston, Hawley, & Elliott, 1991; Rajaram, 1993; Whittlesea, Jacoby, & Girard, 1990). In a paper reporting a series of failures to find such evidence, Johnston, Hawley and Elliott (1991) concluded that such effects of experimenter-manipulated perceptual fluency on the probability of "old" judgments is found only when the overall recognition performance is poor. It should be added to this that an effect of experimenter-manipulated fluency has been found when recognition judgments were speeded (Rajaram, 1993; but see also Kinoshita, Karayanidis, Woollams, & Tam, 1997).

As an example of the first condition, Whittlesea, Jacoby and Girard (1990) presented subjects a list of seven words in rapid succession, for 60 ms each, followed by a eighth word, which served as the recognition probe. As would be expected from such a difficult encoding condition, the overall recognition performance was low (hit rates around .6 and false alarm rate around .2). Whittlesea et al. manipulated perceptual fluency of the recognition probe by presenting test words through a dynamic noise mask and varying the mask density. They reported that subjects were more likely to judge an item as having been presented earlier if it was perceived more easily (i.e., when the mask density was low).

I (Kinoshita, 1995) have previously argued that the finding of experimenter-manipulated perceptual fluency effects on recognition judgments under the condition in which recognition performance is low as in the study described above may be interpreted in terms of demand characteristics. Specifically, faced with a difficult discrimination between old and new items on the basis of strength of memory trace, subjects may adopt a deliberate decision strategy based on more salient factors, which include perceptual fluency. A finding reported by Merikle and Reingold (1991) supports this possibility. In their experiment, subjects were shown pairs of words at the rate of 500 ms per pair, and were required to read aloud one word of the pair cued by an arrow pointing to it. The uncued words (that did not require a response) formed the target set in the subsequent test phase. In the test phase, subjects were shown a list of words presented against a mottled background, and were asked to decide whether or not the word had been presented earlier (recognition test, an explicit memory test) or whether the word was presented under high- or low contrast condition (contrast decision task, an implicit memory test). As would be expected for words studied under a poor encoding condition, recognition performance was low, and in the initial block, was at chance. However, performance improved across blocks. Merikle and Reingold noted that a similar improvement in recognition performance across blocks has been observed in a previous study that involved poorly encoded stimuli (Mandler, Nakamura, & van Zandt, 1987), and interpreted the improvement in terms of a change in the basis for subjects' recognition decisions. Specifically, during the early trial blocks, subjects follow the instructions and attempt to decide whether each word is old or new. But if no conscious information relevant to the old/new decision is available, then across blocks, subjects may "adopt a more passive strategy and simply base their decisions on general impressions", hence "the recognition task would in fact become an indirect task" (p. 231).

While such a decision strategy is consistent with the idea that subjects may base their recognition decisions on perceptual fluency, Merikle and Reingold's description is far from the possibility that it reflects an "automatic" attribution process. In particular, there is no evidence that the phenomenology of familiarity, that is, the "feeling" of re-experiencing an earlier event, arises from the ease of perception. The fact that the Merikle and Reingold (1991) found the coupling between perceptual fluency and recognition judgments only towards the end of experimental session suggests that the decision strategy reflects a conscious, deliberate effort on the part of subjects to optimize performance. Moreover, the "relationship" between perceptual fluency and probability of old judgments is also found even when the test items have never been studied. Verfaellie and Cermak (1999, Experiment 1) showed subjects during the initial study phase forty trials in which only a mask was presented but told them that single words were presented at a speed too quick to allow perception. In a subsequent test phase, normal subjects were equally likely as amnesic subjects to depend on the perceptual fluency for making recognition judgments. This contrasts with their finding in Experiment 2 described earlier, in which items were actually presented during a study phase. In that experiment, normal subjects showed a much weaker relationship between perceptual fluency and recognition judgments. This pattern of findings is more compatible with the view that normal subjects rely on perceptual fluency as a basis for making recognition judgments only as a fallback strategy in the absence of a reliable basis for making old-new discriminations. Finally, the fact that Whittlesea et al. (1990) did not observe an effect of manipulation of perceptual fluency when subjects were informed of the manipulation suggests that the attribution process is cognitively penetrable. These considerations sit at odds with the claim that the attribution of perceptual fluency to feeling of familiarity is automatic, as suggested by Jacoby and colleagues.[2]

So far, I argued against the evidence for perceptual fluency as the **causal** basis for the feeling of familiarity in recognition judgments based on studies in which recognition performance was poor. However, experimenter-manipulated perceptual fluency effects on recognition judgments have been found when recognition level was relatively high when the judgments were speeded (e.g., Rajaram, 1993). Also, rejection of the memory attribution view begs a question, namely, where does the feeling of familiarity come from? Recognition judgments reflecting the feeling of familiarity do seem more automatic in character than recognition judgments based on the recovery of context, in that a feeling of familiarity seems to occur both involuntarily and rapidly. An attractive feature of the memory attribution framework was that it provided an explanation of this automatic character by pointing to its nonanalytic nature (cf. Kelley and Jacoby, 1996). If the memory attribution framework is to be rejected, how can this automatic nature of feeling of familiarity be explained?

In the next section, I will outline an alternative framework that explains the source of familiarity, and why it has the automatic quality. I will then extend the framework to explain why experimenter-manipulated fluency is found when recognition judgments are speeded.

2.   THE MEMORY MODULE FRAMEWORK

2.1 Moscovitch's multiple memory systems framework

As mentioned earlier, multiple memory system models typically assume the existence of two separate systems, one associated with explicit, and the other associated with implicit memory (e.g., declarative vs. procedural memory systems, episodic vs. semantic memory systems). Within these accounts, retrieval of contextual information is related exclusively to one (the explicit) memory system. One problem with these accounts, then, is to explain how recognition judgments, which are after all, judgments of explicit memory, can be made without the retrieval of contextual information: That is, they do not readily provide a mechanism for context-free feelings of familiarity that is nevertheless a part of explicit memory.

In contrast, Moscovitch (1992) has suggested that there are two components within explicit memory. He emphasized the role of phenomenological awareness of the study episode in defining implicit and explicit memory: Explicit memory, but not implicit memory, is associated with phenomenological awareness of the study episode. According to Moscovitch, expressions of memory unaccompanied by the phenomenological awareness such as repetition priming effects (implicit memory) are supported by perceptual input modules located in the posterior neocortex. Phenomenologically aware forms of memory (explicit memory) on the other hand are supported by two separate systems: An associative memory module, which is identified neuroanatomically with the medial temporal lobes/hippocampus (MTL/H) and related limbic structures, and a nonmodular, central system, which is identified with the prefrontal cortex. The latter system is responsible for intentional, strategic retrieval such as demanded in a recall task when minimal cues are provided at retrieval and subjects need to generate their own retrieval cues (e.g., "What words did you see in this experiment?"). The MTL/H system, on the other hand, Moscovitch argued, satisfies the criteria of a module as suggested by Fodor (1983). That is, it is an information processing device that is domain specific, mandatory, informationally encapsulated, and have shallow output.

Because retrieval is assumed to be mandatory, given an appropriate cue, the cue can spontaneously trigger the recollection of a studied word. This process of interaction between a retrieval cue and stored memory trace that produces the contents of retrieval is referred to as ecphory (Tulving, 1983). Ecphory is assumed to occur automatically: As long as the retrieval cue matches the stored memory trace, phenomenological awareness that the event was experienced in the past occurs involuntarily (as can be seen in everyday experience of meeting someone on the street and recognizing the person), that is, it arises without the intention to retrieve the event. In contrast, the frontal system is responsible for the metacognitive processes that control retrieval: For example, generating own cues to facilitate retrieval (as in free recall when minimal cues are given), and monitoring the output of the memory module for veridicality and logical consistency (without which can result in confabulation, see Moscovitch, 1989). The frontal system is also responsible for the retrieval and monitoring of contextual information (source monitoring). evidence for the distinction between these two systems can be found in the pattern of memory deficits observed in frontally-impaired patients. for example, korsakoff patients who have frontal lobe dysfunction in addition to the core memory dysfunction have been observed to show source amnesia (e.g., Schacter, Harbluk & McLachlan, 1984). patients with frontal lobe dysfunctions have also been reported to show disproportionate impairment in recall, which demands more strategic retrieval, relative to recognition (e.g., Shimamura, Janowsky & Squire, 1991).

The assumption that the feeling of familiarity reflects the operation of a memory module explains why some types of recognition judgments, namely, those based on a feeling of familiarity, have an automatic quality. Because they are produced by a memory module, they have the characteristics of modular processes, such as mandatoriness and fast responding, unlike those that rely on the metacognitive processes at retrieval. At the same time, this framework suggests that recognition judgments are necessarily judgments of explicit memory, thus being consistent with the observation that experimenter-manipulated perceptual fluency generally has little effect on recognition judgments.

2.2   Why does experimenter-manipulated fluency affect speeded recognition judgments?

As mentioned earlier, one exception to the absence of experimenter-manipulated effects of perceptual fluency has been reported when recognition judgments were speeded (Rajaram, 1993). In this study, each recognition probe was preceded by a very brief presentation of a prime which was consciously unavailable to subjects, which was either the same or different from the probe. Previous research (e.g., Forster & Davis, 1984) has found facilitation to responses to the probe when the masked prime is the same as the probe, which Rajaram has interpreted in terms of facilitation of perceptual processing of the probe. In line with the view that perceptual fluency enhances the feeling of familiarity, subjects made more "old" judgments to probes preceded by the same rather than different primes. Further, this effect of masked priming on recognition judgments was limited to those that subjects subsequently classified as K responses and not R responses.

We (Kinoshita, et al., 1997) replicated this finding using the same speeded recognition judgments as Rajaram used, but failed to observe the effect of masked priming when the recognition judgments were not speeded. Initially, this finding seemed compatible with the dual-process model of recognition memory, which assumes that the familiarity process is more automatic and hence is faster-acting than the context retrieval (recollection) process (e.g., Jacoby, 1991). When recognition judgments are not speeded, subjects shift their basis of judgments from the familiarity process to a more time-consuming, but more reliable context retrieval process and hence the effect of experimenter-manipulated fluency is eliminated. What argued against this interpretation was the fact that the recognition judgment latency was actually faster to those that were subsequently classified as R responses rather than K responses. Assuming that the R responses reflect the context retrieval process and K responses reflect the familiarity process, this pattern is contrary to what is expected from the dual-process view of recognition memory that assumes that the feeling of familiarity process is the faster acting process.

Instead, we interpreted the observed pattern within the one-process account of R and K responses in which K responses reflect an unsuccessful outcome of a context retrieval process (Donaldson, 1996; Hirshman & Master, 1997). Slower recognition judgments for items that are classified as K responses would follow naturally from this account, because these are items for which sufficient contextual information cannot be retrieved to reach a high criterion for an "old" response. Since R and K responses both reflect the operation of a context retrieval process, the absence of experimenter-manipulated fluency effect is also expected from this account. The question, then, is why was there an effect of experimenter-manipulated fluency when recognition judgments were speeded, and why was it apparent only for those that were classified as K responses?

To answer this question, it is useful to draw a parallel between the feeling of familiarity in recognition memory and the feeling-of-knowing (FOK). In the FOK paradigm, subjects are asked to recall an item, for example, in response to a general knowledge question (e.g., What is the name of India's 'holy' river?"). When the subject is unable to provide an answer, he/she is asked to rate his/her FOK. Such FOK ratings are generally positively correlated with performance on a subsequent objective memory task, for example, in an eight-alternative recognition test. This ability for subjects to monitor the presence of information in the memory store that they are unable to retrieve has been a puzzle for FOK researchers.

To date, two main classes of explanation has been put forward to explain the basis of FOK ratings for which the answer cannot be retrieved (for a review see, Nelson, Gerler, & Narens, 1984). One class of explanations, called the inferential models, suggests that there is a monitoring mechanism that is separate from the memory retrieval process. The assumption is that subjects have no way of monitoring directly the presence of a solicited target in store and must infer it from a number of cues. The cue familiarity mechanism proposed by Reder and colleagues (e.g., Reder, & Ritter, 1992), in which subjects base their FOK rating on the familiarity of the question, rather than what they can recall about the answer, is an example of such a process. Another class of models, which is termed the trace access models, in contrast, presumes that subjects have partial access to, and are able to monitor some aspects of, the target item. In defense of this approach, Koriat (1993) has argued that one need not assume a FOK monitor that is separate from the act of retrieval itself. In his model, FOK ratings are based on the accessibility of correct and incorrect information about the target. Thus, for example, if a subject is unable to recall the answer to the question "Corsica island belongs to what country?" and rates his/her FOK, it may be based on what the subject can recall about the wrong answer "Italy", rather than the correct answer "France". According to Koriat (1993; 1994) then, FOK is based directly on the product of the retrieval attempt, rather than a separate internal monitor that has privileged access to unretrieved information. However, this monitor does not know about the source of information: The high FOK rating may be based on the amount of information retrieved about the wrong answer (in this case, Italy) or the correct answer.

In the same way, then, rather than being a product of an inferential or attribution process as suggested by the proponents of the memory attribution view, the feeling of familiarity used in recognition memory judgments may be tied directly to the active retrieval of information pertaining to that stimulus. Within this view, familiarity is simply a measure of the (total) amount of information retrieved about the recognition probe. It is a "scalar" based on the sum of information from undifferentiated sources, just as an FOK rating is based on information retrieved about an incorrect or correct answer. It is suggested that when subjects make a speeded recognition judgment it is based on this global feeling of familiarity. Because it is based on unverified sources, experimenter-manipulated perceptual fluency could inflate "old" judgments. Further, such effects are likely to be seen for weaker memory traces which would otherwise not have reached the criterion for an "old" response, thus resulting in the apparent dissociation between R (reflecting stronger memory traces) and K responses (reflecting weaker memory traces for which retrieval of context was unsuccessful). In contrast, when recognition judgments are unspeeded and hence there is time to reflect on the sources of familiarity (i.e., when metacognitive processes have time to kick in), subjects are likely to discount the inflated perceptual fluency for primed items. The pattern of effects of experimenter-manipulated fluency on R and K responses under speeded and unspeeded conditions can be explained in this way, without recourse to the notion of memory attribution.

2.3   The relationship between feeling of familiarity, metacognition, and recognition judgment

It may be noted that this view of familiarity as a global scalar index is similar to that shared by models referred to as global matching models (for a review, see Clark & Gronlund, 1996). While these models differ in detail, they share the assumption that the cues available at test are combined into a single joint probe, and are used not to retrieve particular piece of information in memory but to access memory broadly, activating information stored about multiple events in parallel. The result of this global access to memory is a scalar index that is variously called familiarity, match, activation, or strength.

While Moscovitch (1992) did not specify in detail how ecphory (the interaction between a retrieval cue and stored memory trace) occurs, the global matching models may be said to fit his framework quite well. in section 2.1, I pointed out that the assumption that the feeling of familiarity reflects the operation of a memory module explains why the feeling of familiarity has the attendant characteristics of a modular process, as described by Fodor (1983). Here, the characteristic of shallow output is relevant. According to Moscovitch (1992), this means that the output produced by the memory module (the MTL/H complex) is not properly interpreted in relation to other memories, consisting of fragmentary elements that are combined without regard to their internal consistency (as exemplified in confabulations seen in frontally-damaged patients, for an example, see Moscovitch, 1989). It can be seen that this description of shallow output also fits well the view of familiarity as a global scalar based on undifferentiated sources, both valid and invalid.

It should be pointed out however, that under typical conditions in which recognition memory is tested, that is, where judgments are not speeded and the level of performance is relatively high, recognition judgments are unlikely to reflect just the operation of the memory module. Even in cases where recognition probes reinstate the studied items as a whole (in contrast to free recall, where minimal retrieval cues are given), the output of the memory module needs to be monitored for veridicality and logical consistency. This would require the operation of the central system (neuroanatomically identified with the prefrontal cortex). The need for a process in addition to the familiarity monitoring process has also been acknowledged by the proponents of the global matching models (Clark & Gronlund, 1996). It would be an interesting challenge to integrate the neuropsychological evidence for the distinction between a memory module and the central system with computational modeling.

3.   SUMMARY AND CONCLUSION

In this paper, I argued against the view that the feeling of familiarity in recognition memory arises as a result of attribution of perceptual fluency, which is output by the same process that is responsible for producing repetition priming effects. I discussed three lines of evidence that have been cited in support of this view, namely, the correlation observed between naturally varying fluency and recognition judgments, the effects of experimenter-manipulated perceptual fluency on recognition judgments when overall recognition performance is poor, and the effects of experimenter-manipulated fluency when recognition judgments are speeded. The correlational evidence has been pointed out as not providing definitive support for the view that the relationship between perceptual fluency and recognition judgments is causal. The second line of evidence was explained in terms of demand characteristics, and the third line of evidence was argued as better interpreted within an alternative view of feeling of familiarity.

According to this alternative interpretation, based on a framework of memory proposed by Moscovitch (1992), the feeling of familiarity is ascribed to a memory module within explicit memory located in the medial temporal lobe-hippocampal (MTL/H) complex. This module is distinct from the frontal system which comprises the other component of phenomenologically aware memory and is related to the various metacognitive processes involved at retrieval. In this way, I defend the position that implicit memory and metacognition are unrelated.

At the same time, however, the MTL/H complex responsible for producing the feeling of familiarity is assumed to have the characteristics of a "module". This therefore provides a ready explanation for why recognition judgments based on the feeling of familiarity, as when recognition judgments are speeded, have the characteristics of automatic processes.

The possibility of a memory module within explicit memory that is distinct from metacognitive processes has not received as much attention as the distinction between implicit and explicit memory processes. This is mainly because explicit memory has been seen as a unitary process. However, dissociations observed between different types of explicit memory tests (e.g., free recall, cued recall, recognition) attest to the involvement of different retrieval mechanisms. In particular, different tasks demand varying degree of strategic retrieval and hence metacognitive processes. The current framework would be useful in guiding research on this issue.

Notes

[1] More recently, an alternative one-process interpretation of R and K responses has been proposed (Donaldson, 1996; Hirshman & Master, 1997). Specifically, proponents of this view suggest that R and K responses do not reflect the operation of separate recognition processes, but that K responses simply reflect the unsuccessful outcome of a search for context. My own interpretation of R and K responses is consistent with this one-process view, and I do not regard K responses as recognition judgments based purely on the feeling of familiarity **process** that is separate from the context retrieval process. Whether a subject's response is based on a particular process cannot be guaranteed by instruction, just as any task cannot be assumed to be process-pure. I argue further that under the typical condition in which recognition judgments are not speeded, K responses reflect such unsuccessful outcome of a search for contextual information. Evidence consistent with this interpretation will be discussed later in relation to the finding of experimenter-manipulated perceptual fluency effects on K responses.

[2] More recently, Whittlesea and Williams (1998; 2000) refined Jacoby's attribution hypothesis and suggested that the feeling of familiarity does not result from fluency per se, but it results instead from perceiving a discrepancy between the actual and expected fluency of processing. Their claim is based on the finding that nonwords which are easier to name because of their orthographic regularity and similarity to existing words (e.g., HENSION) produced more false alarms (37%) than words (e.g., STATION, 16%) or difficult nonwords (e.g., STOWFUS, 9%). Since words were named faster than easy nonwords which were in turn named faster than difficult nonwords, the original perceptual fluency view would have predicted greater false alarms to words than the easy nonwords. Instead, Whittlesea and Williams (2000) claimed that the elevated false alarm rate to the easy nonwords resulted from the perception of a discrepancy between the expected and actual fluency of processing: Fluent processing of the easy nonwords violated the subjects' expectation that nonwords would be named slowly, causing a perception of discrepancy. One problem with the discrepancy hypothesis is that by the authors' own admission (Whittlesea & Williams, 2000, p. 559) the hypothesis is vague, and the definition of perceived discrepancy could run into circularity. Take the processing of "easy" nonwords for example. These items are processed **objectively more** fluently than the "hard" nonwords, and objectively **less** fluently than words, as measured by naming latency. However, the recognition false alarm rate to the easy nonwords was higher than both easy nonwords and words. In the absence of a clear measure of discrepancy of perceived processing, there is a danger that the discrepancy hypothesis would be able to explain any data, and is simply unfalsifiable.

Chapter 3

Familiarity and the Retrieval of Memory Traces
Metacognitive Aspects

Guy Lories
Université catholique de Louvain, Louvain-la-Neuve, Belgique

Key themes: Prob / Proc / Theor

Key words: Metacognition / Problem solving / Feeling-of-knowing

Abstract: Cue familiarity has been proposed as a mechanism by which the Feeling of Knowing and illusions of knowing might be established. Kamas and Reder (1995) describe a 'partial matching' process that would determine familiarity and may play an important role in explaining various shortcomings of metacognitive heuristics. This process is developed into the more ambitious Source of Activation Confusion model (SAC) in later work (Nhouyvanisvong & Reder, 1998; Schunn, Reder et al., 1997). We examine two domains for which the mechanism has been proposed and discuss a number of theoretical opportunities the proposition offers.

1. METACOGNITION AND THE CONTROL OF RETRIEVAL

It is one of the strong points of the human information processing system that it makes purely associative access and retrieval possible very effectively. Memory retrieval plays an important role in various tasks. It is important in question answering but also in many other areas like problem solving, for instance, when an old problem provides a solution to a new one.

The mechanism of retrieval would therefore deserve a theory of its own but it is not perfectly understood yet. It has extraordinary successes (genial intuitions) but also very common failures (the tip of the tongue, the Moses effect[1]). Moreover, it has recently become clear that the retrieval process is not always as easy as it seems: retrieval loads working memory (Anderson, Reder and Lebière, 1996) and proceeds by successive retrieval attempts until success occurs.

Because retrieval also has this psychological cost, calculations regarding the probability of a successful retrieval are involved in our decisions to pursue or abandon a particular memory search (Anderson, 1990). When trying to answer a general information question, retrieval efforts will cease after a while or will even never start (Glucksberg and McCloskey, 1981). The theory of retrieval should therefore involve a component of monitoring and control and the metacognitive approach seems natural.

Metacognitive aspects provide an interesting angle because a number of conditions should be met for metacognitive processes to be *adaptive*. Control may only rest on metacognitive processes if these processes are *fast* enough (e.g., Kamas & Reder, 1995). The output of metacognitive processes must also be *accurate* enough and predict reasonably well the result of the various strategies that can be chosen. Finally, the *cost* of the metacognitive activity itself should be low enough; in any case it should be lower on average than the cost of an error in choosing a response strategy. These conditions provide strong constraints on theorizing and, specifically, on what mechanisms may be thought to underlie various metacognitive activities.

Another set of constraints that metacognition imposes comes from a potential 'bootstrap' problem. Although, as suggested by Koriat (1993, 1995, 1999), monitoring may rest on the product of attempted retrieval, adaptive control of retrieval operations in general seems to require information about the object to be retrieved *before* the object itself is retrieved. For instance, the domain or specific characteristics of the sought for answer should be identified and this introduces the "bootstrap" problem. How do I know whether I know the answer before I retrieve it? Or even whether it is the answer at all? In problem solving, for instance, how can I know whether a problem is analogical to another -or even relevant- without retrieving it first and considering both. In reading, how can I know that an element of information from memory is/will have to be linked to a text element before I have read and understood the text and retrieved the element?

One fairly general solution to these problems has actually been proposed that apparently satisfies these constraints (Kamas & Reder, 1995). The proposition they make is that familiarity is the main heuristic during an initial, rapid, stage of retrieval or processing. Other mechanisms can be thought to take over later on, that may rest on various sources of information, but the initial rapid familiarity based mechanism is thought to be responsible for adaptively controlling cognitive strategies, in particular the decision to attempt retrieval or not. The familiarity mechanism is also thought to rely on a specific form of 'sloppy' encoding that is responsible for a number of inaccuracies observed in metacognitive research and described at length in Kamas and Reder (1995).

The rapid FOK solution when generalized in this way, leads a kind of dissociation assumption. There would be a fast and a slower metacognition. Dissociations are something that should be introduced with caution. Occam's razor, an old philosophical principle, recommends that concepts or hypotheses be introduced only when absolutely necessary. In the present case there may be arguments in favor of a *theoretical continuity* between the controlling and the controlled processes. First, it is a matter of theoretical parsimony. Our general cognitive theory should fit reasonably well with our theory of metacognitive processes. Second it is also economical *for a cognitive architecture* to use the same processes in cognition and metacognition. If the fast encoding on which metacognitive decisions are based is intrinsically sloppy or inaccurate in some sense, it raises questions regarding its role in relation with further -and slower- cognitive mechanisms.

We will first consider some aspects the Kamas and Reder (1995) proposition in its broadest interpretation and examine how it applies to two specific cases, one is the case of the FOK and one is the case of analogical retrieval. Next we will consider how it fits with these theoretical continuity constraints.

2.   RETRIEVAL AND THE FEELING OF KNOWING

Regarding the Feeling of Knowing (FOK) in particular, it has been suggested for quite a time that, during an initial stage, memory retrieval is mainly guided by familiarity (Miner & Reder, 1994). It has been proposed that a rapid FOK develops during this early stage and that, in answering general information questions, this rapid FOK may involve *cue familiarity* only (e.g., Kamas & Reder, 1995. Reder & Ritter, 1992). Cue familiarity would determine the first impression of knowing the answer to a question (rapid, initial, FOK). This processing of the cues would be superficial and would easily allow for mistakes and for illusions of knowing.[2]

Evidence has accumulated to support the view that this rapid FOK is useful in guiding retrieval behaviour. The role of familiarity has been repeatedly confirmed and it is cue familiarity more than familiarity with the answer that seems important (Reder & Ritter, 1992; see Nhouyvanisvong & Reder, 1999 for a review). It is likely that these considerations of familiarity, among others, determine the choice of a strategy to answer questions either by retrieving the information directly if it appears to be available, either by figuring out a plausible answer either, as in the case of arithmetic, by computing an appropriate response (Reder, 1982, 1987).[3]

As discussed above, the adaptive/controlling function carries a number of empirically testable implications. For an adaptive function to be fulfilled, speed and accuracy conditions should be met. Regarding *speed*, results like Glucksberg and McCloskey (1981) have shown that fast decisions of ignorance can be made; and that such decisions can actually be made faster than retrieval. Reder (1982, 1987) has shown that a strategy of plausibility can be used instead of a retrieval strategy to answer questions and that the choice of strategy can be made very rapidly and even without any added cost. The time to make the strategy choice in favour of retrieval and the time to actually retrieve the answer did sum up to the average retrieval time obtained in a control condition. This suggests not only that the decision can be fast but also that there may even be a continuity from the processes involved in a rapid FOK and in the final answer since apparently no processing time is lost.

Regarding *accuracy*, the situation is more complex. Most correlations obtained between the FOK and a criterion task (usually a recognition test) are significant but so low that one can wonder how such a noisy channel may be of any use. There are many reasons why the FOK validity as a predictor is low. One is that the task predicted by the FOK in most FOK experiments is to recognize the correct answer among distracting items. The most important factor of success or failure in such a task is probably the choice of the distracting items: there is no way to make sure that effective distracting items will be found precisely for the questions that have a low probability of recall. Moreover, the FOK is generally asked from the subjects only for the items they fail to recall. Therefore the subjects, when they give a rating, are actually attempting to predict recognition success on a very special subset of items

(items they failed to recall). The subjects may be able to do much better when predicting success on the whole population. Izaute et al. (1996) have already shown that this is an important factor in the low validity of the FOK but one might argue that their result is obtained on too long a time scale to really support the theory presented here.

In two recent experiments (Lories & Petre, unpublished) we show that accuracy can be obtained for speeded decision. We use an adaptation of the 'game show' paradigm (Reder, 1982) to compare the accuracy of the FOK as a predictor of response correctness in several conditions of time pressure. The participants are asked to press a button when a question is presented that they think they can answer but they are given only a short time window in which to make this decision. The time window has been calculated to allow the participants only a constant fraction of the time necessary to read the question on average. Later in the experiment, the participants are given the questions they have not previously accepted. They succeed or fail. The accuracy of their initial decision can then be assessed using –for instance– gamma coefficients or signal detection theory. This accuracy is compared under various conditions of time pressure (using a shorter or longer time window). The results support the idea of an initial, fast, FOK that may based on cue familiarity because they show that accuracy and speed can be obtained simultaneously: accuracy, when properly defined, remains high even at high speed.

This result therefore contributes to support the idea that a rapid FOK can be used effectively for monitoring and control. It does not by itself guarantee that it is based on familiarity. The question acts as a cue and takes some time to read. The progressive processing of the cue may have a number of consequences. Moreover, in these results, accuracy seems to increase progressively with time. Although one might argue that it is due to an increase in the amount of information retrieved and maybe even to an increase in the probability of retrieving the target itself, this nevertheless suggests some sort of continuity from familiarity –as a first effect of cue presentation– and target retrieval –that eventually will occur. One may wonder how special familiarity is and why it is an important concept here. Of course familiarity is a simple intensity value, but so is the amount of information retrieved, for instance. We will first discuss the differences that may exist between early familiarity and later effects of cue presentation.

3.   FAMILIARITY BASED MODELS AND THE FOK

Two types of models have been proposed to explain the results obtained in this domain. They have been introduced as more or less equivalent by Kamas and Reder. One is the SAC model (Kamas & Reder, 1995; Schunn et al., 1997), the other is a mechanism of partial matching (Kamas & Reder, 1995). Both attempt to explain why the FOK can be accurate but also why it can be in error.

What makes the detail of the FOK results difficult to explain is probably the false alarms (Koriat, 1999). Although one might try to explain the FOK by an 'early' read of some elements of the answer, this does not work well because it is also necessary to explain why false alarms occur i.e., why we can have the feeling that we know an answer (the FOK) when we actually do not. Given that the FOK is studied on omission errors, there can simply be nothing to read, 'early' or not, in this case. The models proposed must solve this problem. Therefore they must somehow, introduce *a difference* between what is used to build the FOK and what is to be retrieved. This makes the idea of familiarity important because familiarity can be based on something simple and different from actual retrieval. At the same time, satisfying this requirement will necessarily tend to contradict our 'continuity' requirement.

The *partial matching* hypothesis is a simple way to go. The question cue is represented by a vector of features and so is the response to be given. The model postulates that only some of the features of the cue are encoded and matched against the features of the response when computing familiarity. The idea is that using only part of the available cues may lead to providing an illusory FOK (or an inappropriate response, as in the Moses effect, for instance). The problem, of course, is to explain why some elements of information are encoded and matched and some are not but attentional hypotheses are possible.

The *SAC model* (Source of Activation Confusion) is a network model in which each node represents some element of the problem or memory structure to be retrieved. Work on retrieving the solution of arithmetic problems best illustrates this. Schunn et al. (1997) model the result from Reder and Ritter (1992) described above. The subjects are given the task of solving arithmetic problems either by retrieving the answer from memory either by calculating. They are given only a very short time window in which to decide which of these strategies they will use. Once their decision is made they are given just enough time to calculate or just enough time to retrieve, according to their choice. The accuracy of their strategy choice is the object of interest. Specific and interesting errors occur. The material involves two different arithmetic operations that are proposed repeatedly on various combinations of operands. The frequency of the operands in the material determine a feeling of familiarity that turns out to be independent of the operation actually realized. The subjects apparently consider as familiar some combinations of operands that have already occurred but with a different operator.

The SAC model explains these 'false alarms' by a *confusion of activation sources* in working memory. The representation is such that each node encodes one possible operand or one possible operation. Each problem is represented by the simultaneous activation of the appropriate operands and operation. The input activation to a specific combination of operands and operation propagates and eventually activates a node that represents the problem. Because of a *fan effect* around operations, the operation may fail to act as an effective discrimination cue. Although the fan effect may be considered a slightly ad hoc explanation because it depends on specific aspects of the experimental material, the general point is that discrimination between sources of activation may fail causing the confusion among new and old combinations of operands. The model is richer that the partial matching hypothesis because it helps imagine specific reasons why the encoding is imperfect (like the fan effect).

The *partial matching* and the *SAC* explanations can be made compatible by simply postulating that nodes exist to represent features (Kamas and Reder, 1995). A vector of features is then represented by a pattern of activation over a set of nodes. This comparison makes it apparent that they actually involve two kinds of encoding difficulties. First, attentional factors and the encoding context can prevent some features from being encoded or preset them from playing their role once encoded. Second, the vector/nodes representation also imposes limitations. A vector of features, by definition, does not have a rich internal structure. In particular, if two features are set (are 'ON' in the vector) they are implicitly supposed to describe a single object. For instance, a structured object like an arithmetical operation can be encoded only by building some internal structure into the vector and by 'repeating' the features to encode the two numbers (the first n vector components are used for one number, the next n components for the other etc.). Although such a vector actually has two parts, one for the first number and one for the second but the model does not take this into account explicitly. Only the experimenter 'knows' that. So apparently, the representation cannot easily accommodate and process structural information.

In the SAC model also it is possible that some elements simply fail to be encoded (again, nodes may fail to be activated for attentional reasons). In the SAC model as it is used by Schunn, Reder, Nhouyvanisvong, Richards and Stroffoli (1997), what is lost, though, is the exact relation between operand and operation. This loss is attributed to a fan effect in the arithmetic task but it can be noted that encoding a relation over a set of nodes is a problem *in itself*. This particularity is used by Shafto and McKay (2000) to provide an explanation of the Moses effect that is close to the SAC model but does not call for a specific fan effect hypothesis in explaining the failure of discrimination.[4] So a second explanation for the shortcomings of familiarity as a metacognitive cue would be that the exact relations between elements of the representation cannot easily be encoded and influence familiarity.

The above considerations create no particular problem for a model of fast FOK decisions but they involve a difficulty with what we have called the *continuity* condition. The problem is that if some information, relational or other, is not represented properly from the start, it becomes difficult to understand how it could ever be used. In other words, given the strong mechanisms that are postulated (the fan effect, attentional failure, but maybe also the more general failure to represent relational information easily), it is unclear how the SAC model could ever be able to discriminate correctly between previously learned or unlearned problems that would involve the same operands with a different operation. The same reasoning applies for the Moses effect in Shafto and McKay's (2000) approach. This may not seem important but relations may come to play an important role, as in the following task.

4.   RETRIEVAL AND PROBLEM SOLVING

Although Kamas and Rederdo commit themselves on the exact reasons why the matching process and familiarity are 'sloppy' so to speak, they suggest that a role for familiarity also exists in analogical problem solving and this places an accent on the role of relational information. According to the problem solving literature, retrieving a problem that is analogical to a target problem is largely a matter of superficial content familiarity. The elements mentioned in the problems must be similar but the role of the *relations* between them is more complex. The relations apparently do not need to be identical in both problems for retrieval to occur although retrieval may benefit from this identity, especially if attention has been drawn explicitly towards the structural similarities (Holyoak & Koh, 1987). At the same time, to be of any use at all, an analogy must be real; it must rest on *structural* similarities i.e., on the fact that similar relations can be detected between different elements and on the fact that the corresponding elements of the two problem structures map onto each other. Thus analogical problem solving is a critical case. Relational information *must* be encoded and used at some point for analogical problem solving to succeed.

The computational burden of finding analogical problems by mapping potentially comparable structures is enormous. Obviously, each element in a structure must map into the appropriate element of the candidate 'analog' structure. This requirement may force to consider all the possible ways of mapping the problem at hand to all candidate problems. This task is computationally intractable. Therefore, some theories of analogical problem solving like MAC/FAC (acronym for 'Many Are Called, Few Are Chosen') actually postulate a retrieval stage (MAC) and a mapping stage (FAC). The retrieval stage is independent of the mapping stage and mapping is attempted only on the most likely candidates (Gentner, Rattermann & Forbus, 1993; Forbus Gentner & Law, 1994). Familiarity of content is used to select a small number of potentially interesting structures and mapping is accomplished only later and only for the structures that have been considered plausible in this first step. The model postulates that retrieval is not guided by structural similarity but only by something like element-wise (superficial) similarity. This first stage would be compatible with the hypothesis of a vector representation that has a weak structure.

The overall structure of the MAC/FAC theory is obviously similar to the Kamas and Reder solution already described but one complication stems from a series of experiments by Wharton et al. (1994) that does not seem to support this analysis of the problem solving literature. Wharton et al. provide results to suggest that retrieval of a short narrative is influenced by *structural* features of the cue. The participants in their experiments are given a more or less coherent cue and asked to retrieve a short narrative episode from a series of such episodes they have been presented earlier. The structurally coherent cue is a sentence involving two characters of the original narrative. The specific terms designating the characters have been replaced by terms that have a similar meaning but that are either more, either less specific than the original terms (e.g., 'businessman' for 'executive'). The structurally incoherent cue is the same sentence as the structurally coherent cue, but with the roles of the characters reversed. Wharton et al.'s subjects retrieve the episode more easily from a coherent cue. In some experimental conditions there were two possible episodes for a same cue and the effect was demonstrated by showing that the episode retrieved tends to be the one with which the assignment of roles is congruent (i.e., the one that makes the cue 'coherent').

According to the general MAC/FAC theory, the first step (MAC) must be fast because it must be computationally simple. On the other hand, retrieval must produce the full target problem with its details for the mapping to occur. So at one point it is clear that computational complexity prevents the processing of relational information, but, eventually, relational information *must* be made available. The critical point is just *how, and how early* relational or structural information should enter the picture. A complete separation appears slightly artificial.

One open question with the Wharton et al. paper is thus whether an effect of structural coherence of the cue ('structural similarity') on retrieval would be found when the response is to be given within a restricted time window. To support Wharton's conclusions, the early structural similarity effects should not be attributed to a contamination by the 'second' stage, the stage in which retrieval has already taken place. We ran such an experiment (Lories, Engels and Petre, unpublished), replicating Wharton et al's design and although the results are complex, they suggest that a structural similarity effect does appear early under time pressure.[5] This makes it more difficult to believe that clear cut transitions do exist between a first stage of retrieval that would be based on element similarity only and a second stage that would properly process structural information.

It is important to note that the experimental situation in the Wharton et al. paper has been designed specifically to detect even weak effects. Actually the point made by Wharton is that structural information does have a small but non negligible effect, but we know from the same data that the main factor of retrieval is superficial (non structural) information. Technically, the result rests on the comparison between two cues in one case, on the comparison between two target for a same cue in the other. In both cases general similarity effects have been 'neutralized' experimentally. This suggests that similarity with the cue (a source of familiarity) may be essentially computed from non-structural information, (information that ignores role assignment in Wharton's case) but there remains an effect, however small, that seems to create problems for a theory that postulates independent stages.

Some theories of analogical problem solving recognize these problems and postulate a progressive constraint satisfaction dynamic network (Thagard, Holyoak, Nelson, & Goschfeld, 1990). In this case structural information enters the picture progressively through the interplay of all constraints and 'features/nodes'. The problem is that the whole process is hypothetical and difficult to analyse, but it preserves a form of continuity between processes.

Yet at this point there is no direct way to impose this conclusion. For instance, some authors (Ripoll, 1998, 1999) have suggested that, at least in experts, a complex encoding strategy may be used that detects relational features and encodes them as such using supplementary vector features for the relational information. This would help 'explain away' results like Wharton's.[6] It would explain an early processing of at least some of the relational information in analogical problem solving. There would be limiting conditions, however. The theory would be strongly limited in explaining the details of the dynamics of relational information. For instance, if relational information plays a role in retrieval because it is encoded in specific vector components, it should play this role early because by definition it is no longer different from 'ordinary' information. One interesting empirical question would become whether 'partial' encoding in early processing can be 'corrected', so to speak, with time or not. The Moses effect, for instance, does not seem to depend on available response time (Reder & Kusbit, 1991; but see also Shafto & McKay, 2000). From this point of view more research would be needed regarding the time course of information processing in the paradigms we have discussed.

5.   CONCLUSIONS

At this point, our short review of empirical results confirms that the fast familiarity-based FOK is reasonably accurate, even in a fast paced task, to help make metacognitive decisions. This suggests that a fast, effective form of metacognitive decision might be based on a preliminary treatment of information. According to Kamas and Reder (1995) this processing stage is in a sense 'sloppy' and may rest on partial matching of a feature vector. This suggests that relational information might not be processed easily in the early stages of retrieval when familiarity is computed because such a representation is not the most adequate to deal with relational information. This 'sloppiness' would be a condition for the fallibility of the FOK.

A first interpretation of this idea is that there would be a clear-cut separation between the early stage of retrieval and further processing. Whether the accuracy of an early metacognitive decision significantly increases with time is still under investigation, but we nevertheless find it difficult to accept the idea of a clear-cut separation between a fast form of information processing (that would not use relational information) and a slower one (that would). The reason is that this second form of information processing must necessarily come into play at some point and we feel that this makes the separation quite artificial. It leads to paradigms of speeded decision in which any effect of relational information on a 'fast' task can always be interpreted (and dismissed) as a contamination by the second, slower, stage. It is sufficient to imagine that the slow stage is not quite as slow as one had expected.

Some results (Wharton et al., 1994) also suggest that analogical retrieval is influenced by relational information and, maybe, even early. This contradicts the usual results of the problem solving literature and the MAC/FAC conception of a first stage of retrieval that would be based on superficial (non-structural) similarities. We have considered several possible explanations but, here again, the idea of a clear-cut separation between a first and a second stage seems artificial. Some other models of retrieval clearly postulate an integrated process in which relational information progressively enters the picture. For instance, the solution proposed in problem solving by Thagard, Holyoak, Nelson and Goschfeld (1990) is to postulate that relational information is incorporated only progressively during the processing of the cues.

This may be especially true on a long time scale, when reading a complex verbal stimulus like a question or a sentence. One of the problems in the experiments we described is that the time scale is relatively broad. On such a time scale, cue encoding is bound to be progressive simply because reading the question or cue sentence is a constructive and progressive activity anyway (e.g., Kintsch, 1988,1998). At first only a few words can be used for the match and they are used independently and not integrated.[7] One consequence of this is again that it becomes difficult to avoid the contamination argument in most cases. So on a reasonably large time scale it may be better to postulate one mechanism with a complex dynamics.

Even on a shorter time scale though, it is possible to believe that whatever happens during retrieval naturally at first depends on a superficial processing of the cue and then increasingly on structural aspects (relations between elements of the cue) as time passes.[8] There is evidence that processing of relational information is slower than element-wise processing on a short time scale. In a paired associate learning task, Gronlund and Ratcliff (1989) have shown that associative information was available later than the information about each element of the pair. Their subjects must respond 'old' only to pairs of elements that have been presented together and not to pairs made of elements that have both been presented but separately. The subjects must provide an answer within a specific time window. They exhibit a maximal tendency to false alarm around 700 msec, which Gronlund and Ratcliff interpret as the effect of a slower processing of associative information. They suggest that global matching memory models, in particular convolutional models (Murdock, 1982, 1987; Hockley & Murdock, 1987) provide a framework to understand these phenomena but the literature regarding these models has not developed a detailed representation of the time course of processing for relational information.

What should we conclude? At this point we can stick with a 'partial matching' approach and a MAC/FAC-like model, adopting, for instance Ripoll's solution presented above. Existing data do not actually coerce us into abandoning that position. This position also agrees with a simple interpretation of Kamas and Reder's (1995) propositions but leads to problems in experimentally defining the length of the first stage. Alternatively, we may assume that the retrieval dynamics is at first –but only at first– independent of relational information and that retrieval itself may proceed in such a way that it incorporates information covering the structural aspects only progressively. This is closer to the approach taken by Holyoak et al. It preserves what we have called a continuity requirement, it is more parsimonious, and it generates a number of questions regarding the dynamics of relational information processing.

Notes

[1] The Moses effect appears when a subject attempts to answer a question like 'How many animals did Moses take with him on the Ark'. The answer is usually something like two of each and it is given without considering that Noah built an Ark and not Moses.The effect can be understood as resulting from inappropriate but converging activations.We return to this later (see, for instance, Reder and Kusbit 1991).

[2] The existence of such illusions are an important fact because they are not compatible with the intuitive theory that the FOK would be caused by an 'early read ' of the answer. In the absence of an answer there is just nothing to read, early or not (e.g., Koriat, 1999).

[3] Even when the subject does not answer there seems to be a relation between the time taken to respond 'Don't Know' and the FOK expressed later on (Costermans, Lories & Ansay, 1992).

[4] In the SAC arithmetic example, relational nodes are explicitly defined (there is a node that explicitly encodes the operation) but this node is 'neutralized' by the fan effect and this is how the exact relation between operands is lost. It is destroyed by interference. In the 'mega-Moses effect', Shafto and McKay (2000) use a 'node structure theory' in which specious priming of an erroneous response is possible through shared nodes (these nodes represent features that are common to Noah and Moses in the Moses effect). They explain the illusion in a straightforward manner but they need a specific process for conscious (and correct) comprehension.

[5] It should also be noted that the time scale of the Wharton experiments and even of our own is much longer than the time scale of a FOK experiment using the game show paradigm. We can imagine that much smaller processing times would simply support the general view of the problem solving literature. Yet this raises a time scale problem.

[6] The proposition has merit. In a sense, such a hypothesis is necessary anyway if a proper encoding of relational information is to be made possible (we have seen that the proper features or nodes necessary to encode the relation must exist). One should also note that for the general MAC/FAC mechanism to be effective, it is necessary that problems involving similar objects tend to have similar structures. In other words some of the non-structural features may be redundant with elements of structural information. In everyday life it may be, that the environment is 'just so'. The nature of things may be such that problems that involve similar objects may just tend to have similar structures. The role of relational information may be limited to real world material or expert subjects and it may be completely absent from experiments that use 'toy' problems for which good encoding schemes do not pre-exist. From that point of view, Ripoll's solution does not make unreasonable assumptions.

[7] On a larger time scale yet, a macroscopic approach is possible. The results may be seen as depending only on what has been encoded or not but encoding can be restarted and therefore in a sense corrected.

[8] Although it could seem strange to postulate a differential processing or time course of relational and non relational information, it is worth noting that some neuro-physiological evidence supports the idea of a dissociation between relational and non relational information. Some models of the role of the hippocampus in memory suggest that the hippocampus is specifically devoted to the flexible encoding of arbitrary associative information, i.e., binding specific elements in specific functions. Although some results have cast a doubt on this interpretation because damage to the hippocampus does not always preclude the processing of relational information, recent conceptions suggest that a proper division of labor between the hippocampus and the cortex can explain the data. Cortical structures would learn associative information only slowly, after recurring presentations and provided that the task requires that this information be taken into account. The hippocampus would learn it flexibly and immediately but retrieving this information may be the ultimate step of the retrieval process.

III

WHEN AND HOW IS METACOGNITION EFFECTIVE?

Chapter 1

When is Metacognition Helpful, Debilitating, or Benign?

Scott G. Paris
University of Michigan, U.S.A.

Key themes: Cont / Defn / Perf / Theor / Devl / Proc

Key words: Functional perspective / Development of metacognition / Consequences of metacognition / Definition of metacognition

Abstract: Psychologists in many fields are interested in metacognition because it focuses attention on how people monitor and control their own thinking. Cognitive psychologists often analyze the bases and accuracy of metacognition in memory whereas educational psychologists study the role of metacognition as instrumental in self-regulated learning in academic domains. The structural and functional perspectives on metacognition are contrasted. I suggest that a functional analysis of metacognition; should be anchored in a theory, should be sensitive to changes due to development and learning, should identify context and motivating conditions, should be interpreted relative to sociocultural practices of the local community, and should examine the potential consequences of specific metacognitions. Attention to these five factors may allow researchers to identify the circumstances that make metacognitions useful, harmful, or innocuous for the person.

Whenever metacognition is discussed among psychologists, such as the conference that was the basis for this volume, two related issues emerge quickly. The first concerns the definition of metacognition and the second concerns the role of consciousness. A fundamental question is whether metacognition implies awareness of thoughts and conscious control of thinking or whether metacognition can be implicit and unconscious. This question has been raised often (e.g., Hacker, 1998; Schraw & Impara, 2001) and is unlikely to be resolved through consensus because researchers become attached to their operational definitions and methodological orientations that often lead to opposite answers. I want to address such definitional issues at the beginning of this chapter, though, because they frame the interpretations of how metacognition is studied, how it operates, and why it is important. I begin with an historical analysis of the term and proceed to a functional analysis of metacognition in children's thinking.

1.   COMMON ROOTS OR PARALLEL GROWTH?

Metacognition was first introduced into modern psychology in the 1970s by John Flavell and his colleagues who conducted research on children's metamemory. Historically, this approach to thinking was revolutionary for child development, especially since it occurred when Piagetian approaches dominated analyses of children's mental development and cognitive psychology was an emerging field. Verbal reports about cognition seemed like introspection and too radical and unreliable of a method to use with children. However, the early enthusiasm about metamemory quickly spread to other domains, such as attention, learning, and communication, and the broader term of metacognition gained popularity. Flavell (1979) described metacognition in terms of person, task, and strategy knowledge whereas Brown (1978) interpreted metacognition in terms of processes such as planning, monitoring, and regulating. Research in the ensuing ten years did not use a single definition. Instead, researchers discussed both knowledge and processes about mental states, abilities, and operations as metacognitive (Alexander, Schallert, & Hare, 1991). Paris and Winograd (1990) described these twin emphases as self-appraisal and self-management of thinking and they are evident in many different studies of metacognition. These different functions are sometimes referred to as monitoring (i.e., appraisal) and control (i.e., management) and reveal the reciprocal nature of influence from task-mind and mind-task respectively.

Surprisingly, metacognition became a popular construct in many fields in psychology without a strict definition or attachment to a specific theory. Maybe that is why it was adopted easily and incorporated in so many different kinds of research. Developmental researchers began to study the ontogeny of metacognition in various domains. They examined at what ages young children gained various kinds of knowledge about the mental world and posited that children's early theories of minds, both their own and others, are cornerstones of children's theories about the world, along with biological and physical theories (Wellman & Gelman, 1992). The developmental researchers' goals for metacognition were mostly descriptive and epistemological. In contrast, educational researchers examined how children understood knowledge and processes relevant to reading (Brown, 1980), mathematics (Schoenfeld, 1992), and many other educational topics (Hacker, Dunlosky, & Graesser, 1998). Educational researchers studied how metacognition was related to age, achievement, motivation, and intelligence (e.g., Borkowski, Carr, Rellinger, & Pressley, 1990; Swanson, 1990). They also incorporated the term into teaching and learning and studied how metacognition could be enhanced through instruction, particularly instructional conversations that focused on the use of specific strategies (Palincsar & Brown, 1984; Paris, Cross, & Lipson, 1984). Educational psychologists regarded metacognition as a tool to facilitate learning and teaching rather than an object of study in its own right.

Metacognition experienced parallel popularity in cognitive psychology and most frequently in studies of adult memory. Nelson (1996) described this movement as a new way to study the old problem of consciousness, a topic rooted in philosophy as much as psychology. Many of the studies focused on **monitoring** cognitive states and subsequent **control** of cognitive processes. Both monitoring and control were studied as subjects attempted to learn or remember information and the measures determined (a) the basis for a metacognitive judgment and (b) the accuracy of a metacognitive judgment. Nelson and Narens (1990) described three important examples of metacognitive research within the tradition of cognitive psychology; feelings of knowing (FOK), judgments of task difficulty and ease of learning (EOL), and judgments of learning (JOL). Although research on subjective experiences such as FOK predated Flavell's work, the topic of metacognition provided a conceptual framework for it. Research on adults' subjective feelings about memory and knowledge grew independently of metacognitive research in developmental and educational psychology and flourished because it fit within information processing models of memory. This line of inquiry focused squarely on metacognition as the topic of study and analyzed the accuracy and reliability of the feelings and judgments under different conditions of recall, recognition, and motivation as described in Koriat and Shitzer-Reichert (this volume).

Another line of inquiry about metacognition arose in cognitive psychology that focused on the uses of such knowledge for answering questions, selecting strategies, and guiding thinking (Metcalfe & Shimamura, 1994). This split reflects the dual nature of metacognition as both knowledge and process. There were other branches within this growing tree of psychological research, but it seems to me that the branches of research became more independent and less connected over time. The reasons for this insularity are partly because of differences in theoretical perspectives, partly because the methods and subjects were different, and partly because the research was motivated by different goals. As a result, educational, developmental, cognitive, and clinical research on metacognition have grown independently and may differ widely in their views of metacognition as well as the methods employed to study it. Thus, controversies about metacognition may reflect fundamental differences in metatheoretical approaches.

Many of the chapters in this volume can trace their roots to cognitive psychological approaches to metacognition which are often based on information processing models and research that is laboratory-based. My approach is rooted in children's purposive behavior, such as goal-oriented learning, that typically occurs in schools. The core difference is that I am most interested in analyzing how metacognition contributes to the successful accomplishment of a cognitive action, whereas other researchers are interested in the accuracy of the metacognition alone. I offer several points of clarification about an approach to metacognition that is grounded in developmental and educational issues and how it may appear at odds with approaches grounded in cognitive psychology.

First, I think it is important to define metacognition in a manner that separates it from other types of cognitions. For me, that has always had two key characteristics; one, the particular metacognition must pertain to a cognitive (as opposed to a noncognitive) state, ability, or process and two, that any metacognition must be available for public scrutiny. Usually, this means metacognition is verbalized, reported, and conscious but other ways of sharing knowledge publicly are possible. The main reason that I favor a definition of metacognition as conscious, aware, and often deliberate is that it allows these kinds of thoughts to be measured, verified, or disproved. If they are not public or not measurable, how can their veracity or function be assessed? If metacognitions are defined as a broad category including unconscious and unmeasured thoughts, then they cannot serve useful explanatory roles because they are not available for empirical testing.

I also think that metacognitions need to be separated from other types of cognitions if they are to be analyzed for their distinctive attributes and functions. The usual dualism of behavior versus mind has been expanded to include dualistic types of mental events, cognitions and metacognitions. If these two types are both defined as potentially implicit and unconscious, then they are not distinguishable. Metacognition may become gratuitous if it is not clearly differentiated from other kinds of thinking. Thus, I favor a restricted definition of metacognition that permits empirical verification and accords metacognition a status clearly distinct from other cognitions. In this view, any cognition may become the object of another cognition and thus, a metacognition. There may be many other kinds of implicit and unconscious feelings, dreams, and associations about cognitions, but they should be studied as a class of cognitions different than people's awareness of their own thinking. There may be many thoughts and feelings that influence how, when, and why people think in particular ways, but not all of these processes are metacognitive, verbal, conscious, or easily measured. I am most concerned with a subset of thoughts that influence thinking that are conscious and reportable, and I think the value of a restricted definition of metacognition is greater explanatory power within the subset.

A second point of clarification follows directly from this definitional confusion because awareness influences other processes. Cary and Reder (this volume) assert that metacognition can be implicit and unconscious. Likewise, they do not distinguish between mental procedures and strategies, and thus they conclude that awareness (i.e., metacognition) is not required for selective and adaptive use of strategies. Their data are compelling and it is possible, within their defined use of strategies and metacognition, that people often are unaware of their own strategic behavior. My concern is that an approach that does not distinguish between conscious and unconscious processes or between procedures and strategies is obfuscating an important feature of human reasoning, the role of overt and deliberate knowledge in the guidance of thinking. I think that a restricted definition of metacognition and strategies as explicit, conscious, and often deliberate processes accords them special status and allows more precise research and explanation. The distinction between implicit processes and explicit strategies is important because it focuses attention on the role of awareness in guiding thinking. For example, a problem may be solved or a text read with automatic processes or similar strategies applied in a deliberate manner. The difference between these two conditions is important and requires separate terms for the cognitive processes employed.

A third point of clarification concerns the fate of conscious processes, such as metacognition, in both learning and development. My view is that conscious processes give way to automaticity with practice and development and that unconscious execution of the skill or knowledge is preferred because it requires fewer resources and is both faster and more efficient. In this view, metacognition is cumbersome and less preferred while problem-solving. Examples of automated cognitive skills are numerous, such as decoding words while reading or direct retrieval of information from memory. I believe that metacognitions and strategies are special cases of the larger set of mental thoughts and procedures that are important during learning and then become transformed and embedded in automatic sequences of thinking and acting. To distinguish the developmental course of these cognitions and to identify how teaching influences such automatization requires distinctive constructs. The questions of how, why, and when such transformations occur are important from developmental and educational perspectives. They may be less important to cognitive psychological views that focus on accuracy and reliability of metacognitions. However, the difference between a deliberate use of a strategy and the automatic use of a skill, even when they appear behaviorally similar, is an important distinction in analyses of learning and development.

Fourth, research that focuses on epistemological questions of when people can "have" certain metacognitions or if those metacognitions are accurate is most relevant to structural, or morphological (Nelson, this volume) models of the mind. They focus on questions of what metacognition is and where it fits in a taxonomy of other kinds of cognitions. In contrast, research that focuses on the operations of metacognitions, that is, how people use their knowledge about mental states and abilities to guide and regulate their actions are more concerned with functional models of metacognition in teaching, learning, self-control, and intervention. For example, it may be humorous if a child reports that he learns best when he crosses his fingers and arms, but it is a functional and important behavior if he does so every time he is asked a question. Accuracy of the metacognition may not always be as important as the frequency and persistence of the enacted belief. The differential focus on structural versus functional models of metacognition exacerbates the differences among approaches to metacognition. My contention is that many of the disparate views about metacognition, including some that may be reflected in this volume, can be traced to different orientations about the definition, measurement, and models or metacognition in different branches of psychology.

2.   A FUNCTIONAL ORIENTATION TO METACOGNITION

The focus of this chapter is on the functional role of metacognition in thought and action. **Functional** is a key term because it aligns our analyses to the instrumental roles that metacognition might play in contrast to **structural** analyses that examine the existence and quality of thoughts as ends in themselves. There is a long history of different methods and purposes associated with structuralism and functionalism in psychology that are reflected in different approaches to the study of cognition today. The early structuralism of Wundt and Titchener combined associationism with the experimental method and legitimized the study of consciousness. It has always surprised me that the early functionalism of William James and John Dewey did not enlist more support. Their core ideas about the utility, purposes, and contexts of thinking have been resurrected in contemporary theories of situated learning (e.g., Lave & Wenger, 1991) but remain peripheral to many cognitive approaches. Schunk (1996) summarized some key points about the functionalist perspective that are similar to my approach to metacognition.

"Functionalists were interested in how mental processes operate, what they accomplish, and how they vary with environmental conditions. They also saw the mind and body not as existing separately but as interacting with each other. Functionalists opposed introspection as a method, not because it studied

consciousness but rather because of how it studied consciousness. Introspection attempted to reduce consciousness to discrete elements, which functionalists believed was not possible. They contended that studying a phenomenon in isolation does not reveal how it contributes to an organism's survival (Schunk, 1996, p. 27)."

Analyses of metacognition for its own sake carry the same risks as introspection, namely, thoughts dissociated from actions, purposes, and contexts. I want to emphasize these contextual and instrumental features of metacognition explicitly because these features are missing in experiments in which subjects are asked to judge their FOK or JOL about esoteric topics. Analyses of metacognition without purpose or context provide little information about how people regulate their own thinking, and they may be as uninformative as early studies of introspection. I think research needs to identify the conditions, motivation, and consequences of metacognition in order to understand the functions it serves. A functional perspective on metacognition leads to five claims. Metacognition:

5. Requires anchored theoretical analyses,
6. Develops throughout childhood and the acquisition of expertise,
7. Is motivated by actions of self and others,
8. Is influenced by sociocultural practices, and
9. Has a range of consequences from negative to positive.

I shall address each of the first four claims briefly and give more attention to the consequences of metacognitions.

2.1   Anchored Theoretical Analyses

Metacognition has been an orphan construct, adopted by researchers in some areas more than others. Educational theories have adopted metacognition as an essential ingredient of self-regulated learning (Paris & Paris, 2001; Pintrich, 2000; Zimmerman & Schunk, 2001). Developmental approaches, such as theory of mind (Wellman & Gelman, 1992), emphasize the mental topics of young children's language and thinking more than metacognitions as a component or stage in a larger theory. Metacognition has spawned a great deal of research by cognitive researchers with information processing methods who have elaborated metacognition as components in chains of production sequences. It is often inserted in box and arrow diagrams of information processing with two-headed arrows connecting it to multiple other boxes to illustrate how it can influence different thinking processes at different times (Pintrich & Schrauben, 1992). Unfortunately, diagrams of constructs surrounded by circles of metacognition or connected by two-headed arrows are uninformative because they only illustrate a variety of potential, reciprocal, and unknown interactions among mental processes.

I think part of the reason that metacognition has received "enthusiasm without adoption" is due to the historical turmoil in psychology that surrounded the introduction of the term "metacognition". The enthusiasm for studying metacognition in America occurred at the infancy of cognitive psychology when information-processing theories challenged traditional theories. For developmental and educational researchers, metacognition was introduced amidst a general orientation of constructivism when the views of Vygotsky and situated learning were only barely visible on the horizon. Instead of overarching theories about learning or development, research in the 1970's and 1980's was focused on distinct areas of academic learning. Thus, research on metacognition fit perfectly into analyses of children's reading, writing, mathematics, and problem-solving (e.g., Brown, Bransford, Ferrara, & Campione, 1983; Paris & Winograd, 1990). Metacognition became absorbed by academic content areas such as reading because awareness of thinking was shown to be instrumental in children's learning. For example, there has been considerable research that shows that good readers, compared to younger or less able readers, have more awareness about reading strategies and they display more planning and monitoring while they read (Paris, Wasik, & Turner, 1991). Similar findings in other content areas reinforced the value of metacognition as a general feature of children's thinking and learning. This led to the popularity of metacognition in many theories of self-regulated learning (see Zimmerman & Schunk, 2001). However, metacognition remains theoretically disconnected from many mainstream theories of learning and development.

I want to suggest a few ways that metacognition can be anchored in other theories. First, I think that metacognition can be connected to research on theory of mind. Wellman and Gelman (1992) identified three foundational theories of children's cognitive development, biology, physics, and psychology, in which children construct theories of variables and causal relationships. Using their psychological knowledge about people, children create a theory of mind and surely metacognition must be a part of their growing knowledge. To date, however, most research on topics within theory of mind have focused on very young children and the distinctions they draw between their mind and others or between accurate and inaccurate beliefs that people hold. Paris and Byrnes (1989) described children's emerging theories of self-regulated learning and it seems plausible that other "theory theories" can be generated using theory of mind as a conceptual anchoring point.

A second type of theory that might provide a foundation for metacognition is theories of self development. Harter (1999) describes normative developmental changes in children's self-representations and it is clear that children's thinking about themselves and others, their person cognition and social cognition, is intertwined with their thoughts about their own intelligence, thoughts, and abilities. Metacognition is thus a feature of self-referenced processes including thoughts about self-efficacy, self-control, and self-competence. Moreover, Harter (1999) views the child's construction of self as a function of internal factors that can be either rational or irrational and external factors that can be positive or negative. Her approach is contextual and functional as is evident in her description of three positive functions of self-representations.

*"Self-processes perform **organizational** functions in that they provide expectations, predictive structure, and guidelines that allow one to interpret and give meaning to life experiences and to maintain a coherent picture of oneself in relation to one's world. Structures that serve to define the self also cement social bonds and foster appropriate social behavior as well as self-regulation. Self-processes also perform **motivational** functions in that they energize the individual to pursue selected goals, they provide plans and incentives, and they identify standards that allow one to achieve ideals in the service of self-improvement. Finally, self-processes perform **protective** functions toward the goal of maintaining favorable impressions of one's attributes and more generally to maximize pleasure and minimize pain (Harter, 1999, p. 10)."*

Metacognition can profitably be anchored to theories of self-development because one's reflections, awareness, and cognitive monitoring all contribute to one's self-concept and identity. For example, Paris, Byrnes, and Paris (2001) suggest that children become self-regulated partly as they experiment with possible identities and roles in which they enact coherent behaviors in order to be recognized by others as like X, where X is an aspired identity or possible self (Markus & Nurius, 1986). One's thinking about self can include metacognitions about one's abilities and potential development. Although we generally view metacognition in positive roles, I will later discuss how metacognition can lead to negative self-evaluations too (e.g., I'm not smart enough to be an engineer) and maladaptive attributions. Such negative thoughts can inhibit action or lead to self-destructive behavior (e.g., I'll feel stupid if I get a low test score so I'll just put C for all the answers). Self-referenced theories anchor metacognition to larger purposes and consequences in the individual's life and thus are consistent with a functionalist perspective. They are also inherently developmental.

A third way to anchor analyses of metacognition is to relate metacognition directly to theories of teaching and learning. In fact, research on metacognition has largely focused on these topics but in a subsidiary role. For example, reciprocal teaching (Palincsar & Brown, 1984) has been widely cited as an effective instructional technique for enhancing reading comprehension because it provides explicit instruction on strategies such as paraphrasing and summarizing the meaning. It also is effective because it allows tutor and tutee to exchange roles thereby increasing awareness of the importance of the target strategies, although metacognitive assessments are often missing from such instructional interventions. Children acquire three kinds of metacognitive knowledge during reciprocal teaching, **declarative knowledge** about strategies (e.g., what strategies are relevant), **procedural knowledge** (e.g., how to apply them), and **conditional knowledge** (e.g., why they are useful). What remains unexplored are the ways that metacognition functions in various kinds of learning (e.g., project-based learning) as well as various kinds of teaching (e.g., Socratic dialogues or direct explanation). Anchored analyses in teaching and learning both offer promising conceptual frameworks for future research on metacognition.

2.2   Developmental Dimensions of Metacognition

Because metacognition has been studied in distinct domains, such as academic subject areas, the developing awareness of children is tied to particular tasks. For example, in the area of reading, we know that 4 year olds are often unaware whether pictures or print should be read. We know that 8 year olds do not understand how to identify main ideas or see the need for re-reading as a means to enhance comprehension. A host of similar naïve understandings and misconceptions could be listed for reading, mathematics, and scientific thinking, many of them due to inaccurate metacognition. There is great value to the domain-specific descriptions of children's emerging awareness of variables that affect cognitive performance. Knowing what children know about cognitive tasks and how they think as they attempt to solve them provides a great deal of information that is diagnostically valuable. Indeed, it points the way for future instruction.

What I am advocating is syntheses of these developmental markers into larger theories of metacognitive development. Perhaps this can be accomplished best in coordination with my first point about anchored analyses. For example, if metacognition is embedded in theory of mind, or more broadly, theory theory, then it might be possible to chart the kinds of metacognition that children acquire about their own minds from infancy through adolescence. Research on the earliest evidence of children's theory of mind is substantial now but there is considerably less known about children's developing understanding of the many topics within cognitive psychology such as memory, decision-making, and problem-solving.

Theory of mind is age-dependent and usually examines children's emerging theories but development of metacognition is not solely dependent on development during childhood. We could also examine developmental changes in metacognition about tasks as a person goes from novice to expert. There may be similarities in the instrumental roles of metacognition whether the naivete is due to age or lack of experience but it is important to acknowledge and study both kinds of developing competence. Soviet theories proposed that involuntary actions became voluntary during learning and then were later automated into involuntary actions. Perhaps metacognition becomes important in some stages of learning, whether primarily bound by age or practice, and is less important at other points during learning.

If metacognition is cast in a framework of self-development, then perhaps the markers of awareness about personal cognitions and social cognitions can be organized by age. For example, Harter (1999) provides a neo-Piagetian model of normative stages of self-development that includes implicitly many metacognitive evaluations of self and others at each stage. The result is a differentiation of multiple Me-selves, the objects of self-analysis, and the possible identities that the person can assume. Harter (1999) charts the child's emerging awareness of "self-guides" from using external standards in early childhood to internalizing others' opinions in late childhood to recognizing conflicting self-guides in adolescence to personal choices of self-guiding standards in late adolescence. Metacognition enables deeper insights at each stage because the I-self processes of thinking and abstraction develop as well as the content of the self-evaluations.

2.3 Motives for Metacognition

One of the fundamental problems with research on metacognition has been the exclusive focus on the quality of the reported thoughts or the connections between metacognition and performance. Rarely is attention given to the reasons why an individual engages in metacognition at all. Vygotsky (1962) warned of the dangers of decontextualized cognitive analyses that lead to thoughts thinking themselves. Strictly cognitive analyses of metacognition run the same risk. What is needed, in my opinion, are analyses of the conditions and contexts that initiate or support metacognition. These may originate in the self or others, during task engagement or during reflection, but it seems useful to specify the events that lead to metacognition. Such analyses are usually irrelevant or eschewed by researchers pursuing structural models of metacognition.

Why do people think about their thinking? Usually people engage in metacognition because they need to make a choice or a decision and are unsure which action to take. Metacognitive thinking is associative and ruminative as often as it is sequential and systematic. There are two classes of stimuli for metacognition, thoughts engendered by the self and by others. Self-initiated metacognition has two primary sources. First, we pause to examine our own thinking when things do not make sense. Uncertainty and confusion lead us to monitor the meaning of our understanding. For example, as I read or listen, I might ask, "Does this make sense?" My efforts to check and repair comprehension lead me to examine current knowledge and to analyze or revise cognitive processes so that I take actions such as re-reading or paying closer attention. It is closely aligned with equilibration as a Piagetian motive for dialectical thought processes that seek the coherence and balance of understanding. Affective reactions entailed by "feelings of knowing" or "tip of the tongue" also motivate the individual's desire to know or display accurate knowledge to others. Whether a specific instance of cognitive monitoring is conscious or not is a testable question within my operational definition but not in a model that does not draw a distinction between monitoring that is done with or without awareness.

The second source of self-initiated metacognition is evident when we consider our self-presentation to others. "Does she think I'm clever or forgetful or clumsy?" My analysis of the question is a metacognition about someone else's thinking that influences my behavior if I desire the other person to have particular thoughts about me. My belief about her thoughts, coupled with my desire to present a positive self-image, stimulate me to say or do specific things that I think will promote the desired impression. It is similar to impression management in social psychology. It is also similar to the belief-desire-action sequence of young children's theory of mind. Personal desires to make sense of events and personal desires for self-presentation motivate metacognitive processes such as evaluating, planning, and monitoring.

The second class of motives involve other people who cause an individual to think about cognitive states and abilities. Again, sense-making and self-presentation are obvious interpersonal stimuli for metacognition. Imagine another person who asks, "Why did you say that?" or "What does that mean?" Both engender self-examination of personal intentions and understanding. Or imagine the occasion when a person says or does something that is confusing and you ponder, "Is he trying to be humorous?" or "Is he lying to me?" or "Doesn't he know that I know that too?" or "Does he think I'm stupid?" The other person provides cues for us to examine what we are thinking and how we are acting. The outcome of the metacognitive deliberation may be a revised conversation or self-presentation so that the other person thinks what we want him or her to think about us.

There are other possible motives for metacognition to be sure, but these few illustrate both internal and external causes to jump off the automatic track of routine behavior and to engage in self-examination. When the targets of the self-examination are cognitive knowledge and abilities, the outcomes are metacognitions. If I ask, "Do I look fat in this coat?", the self-evaluation is not metacognitive, but if I ask, "Does she think I look fat in this coat?", it is a metacognition about someone else's thoughts. My point here is that we need to restrict our analyses to metacognition and what motivates people to think about cognition. Without considering the reasons for being metacognitive, it is impossible to examine the consequences of metacognition, and without examining the consequences, we cannot determine if the thoughts are functional, useful, adaptive, or valuable for the individual.

2.4 Contextual Influences on Metacognition

A functional perspective on metacognition is situated by necessity. By this, I mean that metacognition cannot be extricated from the context and appraised or studied independent of the task and purpose. The perspective on situated learning espoused by Lave and Wenger (1991) embeds thinking in the practices of a group, so by extension, metacognition should also be examined as part of the community's practices. It is surprising to me that situated learning perspectives have not incorporated metacognition into their frameworks. I would like to suggest that there are several likely ways that this could be done.

First, metacognition can be regarded as a practice if we consider the ways that communities make thinking public. For example, teachers who emphasize "learning to learn" skills in class may explicitly describe tactics for studying and learning. I think the key feature of all metacognitive interventions in schools, including my program called Informed Strategies for Learning (Paris, Cross, & Lipson, 1984), reciprocal teaching (Palincsar & Brown, 1984), and transactional strategy explanations (Pressley, Woloshyn, & Associates, 1995), is the public discussion about how to think. Conversations about cognition at the child's level and with children as active participants helps them become aware of how they think and other possible ways to tackle problems. Likewise, parents who provide an academic focus in their homes are likely to engage in conversations about thinking, reasoning, remembering, and learning frequently and with insights that children can discern.

Second, ordinary and daily practices might have an implicit focus on metacognition, but the same practices may also be accompanied by explicit teaching. Declarative, procedural, and conditional knowledge about strategies may be taught directly to students in classrooms learning to read or to children at home learning to control impulses or to children in museums learning to appreciate paintings. Teaching, rewards, sanctions, and encouragement to talk about thinking or to be reflective are embedded in daily practices that vary widely among schools and families within countries as well as between cultures.

Third, metacognition may be influenced by implicit cultural beliefs. American society emphasizes achievement, rationality, individualism, and personal responsibility that all support metacognition as a means of self-control and self-improvement. Other societies may emphasize collectivism or spiritualism or mysticism in ways that demote metacognition from any central role and regard it as superfluous, unnecessary, or undesired. I have always thought it is presumptuous and self-aggrandizing that academics establish the premiums on certain cognitive and now metacognitive processes that are the desired ends of schooling at the expense of many other talents of children. My point here is simply that metacognition is valued, expressed, taught, and supported to different degrees by different communities and the origins and practices that imbue metacognition with value should be studied.

2.5 Consequences of Metacognition

Finally, I come to the instrumental role of metacognition, and the answer to the question, "Does metacognition matter?" Yes, I think it could matter, might matter, can matter, but not always. Furthermore, I believe that metacognition can sometimes be negative, destructive, debilitating, and dangerous. It is unclear why these consequences have been neglected in past analyses of metacognition. I will give prototypical examples of the positive, negative, and neutral consequences of metacognition.

2.5.1 When is Metacognition Helpful?

Metacognition can enhance performance on cognitive tasks such as remembering and reading. The initial and sustained excitement in educational psychology about metacognition is due largely to the benefits that accrue from deliberately thinking about what we know and how we go about knowing. The research presented in this volume makes this point abundantly clear. What I want to do is categorize the situations in which metacognition is formative, that is, when thinking about thinking leads to better ideas, decisions, actions, and performance. There are three exemplary situations.

First, metacognition is important during the initial acquisition of a skill or during early encounters with related tasks. The child, for example, needs to become familiar with the task requirements, the goals, and the tactics that enable completion whether the task is adding numbers, reading words, or assembling toys. Becoming aware of the problem space and the available resources can enable different approaches to the task. Good teachers, parents, and coaches break complex skills into parts and help children see how to do each one and then how to put the pieces together. Vygotsky called this "defossilization" because it takes an intact behavior and breaks it into components. It is like the disassembly of an automatic routine and involves awareness of the elements, their relations, and the tactics for reassembling them.

It is important to note that dissecting whole actions into parts and piecing them together sequentially does **not** mean that this is the usual way that children learn the skill or that there is one best way to help others become aware of task features. Too often, componential analyses have presumed that learning is linear reassembly of dissociated pieces but this confuses the analytical tool with the learning process. Breaking apart complex tasks is only helpful if it increases awareness of previously unknown facts and relations. Otherwise, decontextualized analyses of pieces of complex acts can be tedious and boring. All metacognitions are not equal. Repetitive, trite, and uninformative metacognitions may discourage learning rather than inspire it. That is why coaching, parenting, and teaching include a range of pedagogical styles that are more or less effective at fostering children's awareness of key variables during initial learning.

Thus, a second occasion in which metacognition is formative is during instruction. Not all teachers are adept at defossilizing behavior and explaining the components. Just as the new learner needs to know the task requirements and heuristics or strategies that can be applied, the teacher needs to be aware of the task features and how to present them to individual students. Teachers also need to understand how to stimulate the learner's metacognition. Good teachers know how to explain the processes of thinking at the level that the learner can understand and employ. This principle of teaching is also evident in coaching athletic and musical skills. Instruction then is in the "zone of proximal development." Effective teaching involves both subtle and direct stimuli for metacognition. Subtle stimuli might include questions, counter-intuitive examples, comparisons among possible solutions, or prompts to reconsider the steps taken. Direct stimuli might include explanations of errors or discussions about alternative routes to successful task completion. It seems obvious that metacognition can be reciprocal and interactive between learners and teachers. The key feature is that skilled teachers use optimal amounts of stimuli and explanations so that learners are motivated, challenged, and successful in their actions.

A third occasion in which metacognition is beneficial is during trouble-shooting. Those occasions include any monitoring initiated by the person such as responses to clarify understanding or enhance self-presentation. Monitoring meaning or checking to see if others perceive you as you intended, usually lead to actions that improve comprehension or one's image, although it is possible that the person's metacognition can be erroneous and the subsequent decision inappropriate. When monitoring is intentionally directed toward self-improvement and becoming aware of what one did wrong or right, it can lead to more effective future actions. The intent of metacognitive monitoring is repair and revision if needed so it is usually beneficial, proactive, and formative.

2.5.2 When is Metacognition Benign?

Thinking about thinking can be irrelevant or pointless or ruminative or whimsical or humorous or deceitful or playful. It may serve many functions that are perfunctory and innocuous compared to improvement of understanding and self-presentation. It is erroneous and presumptuous to think that people constantly try to monitor and control their own thinking. Metacognitions are often unrelated to behavior, choices, and decisions and often can be neutral, benign, or harmless. Here are three paradigmatic cases when metacognition seems benign.

First, metacognitions can be elicited from others and the person's response may be contrived or inaccurate. For example, if I ask you, "How did you remember the grocery list?" and you do your best to tell me what you did but are unsure if you really used the tactics you reported, I would say that your metacognition might be benign. If you had no commitment to the methods or conviction in your response, I would be even more assured that the metacognitive report was fabricated at the point of prompting. Unfortunately, many research methods elicit metacognition from subjects without ascertaining commitment or conviction. Think-aloud protocols, ratings of strategies, surveys of study methods, and multiple-choice tests of metacognition may all yield responses that are benign. They are benign partly because they are detached from the performance and the reports have no consequences for the subject. That does NOT mean that subjects lie or make false responses, but it does mean that subjects may not be invested in the tactics they report. Elicited metacognitions run the risk of contrived responses in order to avoid looking ignorant. Analyses of accuracy alone miss the central point of the metacognition in this case.

A second occasion in which metacognition is benign involves situations in which people try to appear clever or more intelligent than they are. When people report that they think in certain ways but are not accountable to prove it, there is room for distortion. They may describe their actions as planful and strategic. They may discuss deliberation and reflection as decision-making tactics. They may take elaborate steps to describe what they did retrospectively without much concern whether it is factual or not because they want to present themselves in a positive manner. Some of this may be deliberate, but that usually involves intentional deception by people who fear that others will think them dull so they try to create false impressions. There is a lot of metacognitive work going on here but it is mostly benign, if you consider self-congratulation harmless. Children, though, may unwittingly try to please others with positive metacognitive responses. So, when we ask 7-8 year olds, "Did you say the names of the words so you could remember them?", they nod vigorously that they did. When we ask, "Is it a good idea to look at the pictures before you read the story?", many children infer that the right answer is Yes, so they agree that they would look at the pictures. Self-presentation of positive images of students who try hard, are virtuous, and act strategically are evident in first grade and university alike. Children receive kinder evaluations of their ingratiating behavior then adolescents, however. In both cases, though, self-presentation of thoughtfulness in order to impress others is largely benign.

A third example of benign metacognitions is the case of "feeling of knowing" (FOK) or "tip of the tongue" phenomena. There is ample evidence that people recognize that they know or can recall a bit of information with a slight cue but cannot recall it without a cue. These situations are usually without consequence, however, because it makes no impact on the person. FOK reactions are often followed by cues supplied by others so that recall is possible. FOK may lead to a search for additional cues or requests for aid but they are rarely met with negative social reactions or personal recriminations of faulty memory. Thus, they are socially and personally benign. Koriat (this volume) shows that FOK can be influenced by monetary reward which may reveal how little motivation subjects usually have in these experiments and how malleable is their metacognition when there is little at stake.

2.5.3 When is Metacognition Debilitating?

Metacognition has been described only in positive terms, largely due to the embeddedness of the construct as a useful guide in academic learning within educational psychology accounts. Cognitive psychology models that are concerned with monitoring and control functions usually presume positive values for the metacognitive tactics as well as the outcomes, another limitation in decontextualized memory experiments. When the term is anchored in other theoretical perspectives and viewed functionally in terms of various outcomes, it is clear that metacognition can be debilitating. In fact, metacognition may underlie a range of clinical problems ranging from mild delusions to pathological breaks with reality. Consider a trio of examples when metacognition can lead to negative consequences.

The first example is the most frequent, and perhaps the mildest, way in which metacognition can lead a person astray – negative self-evaluation. The issue is not the occasional self-deprecating evaluation about isolated occurrences of forgetfulness or poor performance, but rather, the persistent and deep-seated belief that the person lacks ability on particular tasks. It is clearly an attribution to low ability and if the domain is highly valued, by self or others, the person suffers from lowered self-worth. The clearest example is school failure for a student who wants to succeed and values academic achievement. Repeated failure or low performance in the face of high value and high effort contributes to a negative self-image. Another example is the depression that many adolescent girls experience about their appearance (Harter, 1999). Social rejection can also stimulate metacognitive reflections that can be self-defeating.

The consequential problem is not simply low self-esteem or self-worth but the actions that emanate from the self-doubts, low expectations, and negative beliefs. These self-processes organize and motivate behavior that may lead to depression, aggression, or suicidal ideation. Because people act according to their feared identities as well as their aspired identities, children and adolescents may begin to act in ways that identify themselves as "school failures" but in disguised terms. Thus, frustrated students may act out in class with aggressiveness or anti-social behavior. They may engage in risky behavior as displays of noncompliance. They may overtly show disdain and devaluation of academic tasks. They may direct all their effort to avoiding demonstrations of failure rather than achieving success. An excellent example of the consuming nature of this negative affect and failure-avoiding work is described in a book called **Faking It** (Lee & Jackson, 1992) about Chris, a university student with learning disabilities, who struggled to come to terms with his difficulties reading and writing.

A second example of the potentially negative consequences of metacognition concerns obsessive thinking. It is literally possible to become "lost in thought" when one ponders mental states, abilities, and choices of actions. At times, this may result only in delayed responding such as considering how to tackle a problem or whether it is better to re-read the chapter or take notes on the material. But on other occasions, doubts about the right course of action, uncertainty about which strategy to use, and confusion about attributions for performance may inhibit action altogether. For example, when students are given large projects to complete in school that require independent thinking, plans, and revisions, like dissertations in graduate school, there is a hidden threat for some students. The assignment appears too unstructured and success is entirely determined by their own actions and they do not know how to begin or are afraid of taking the wrong path. So they procrastinate or cheat or set low goals or display helplessness. Passivity is especially likely among students who have experienced failure before so even creative assignments are regarded as looming threats to self-worth (Covington, 1992).

I think it is important to point out that these negative metacognitions are not restricted to low-achieving students. Many highly competent students have negative self-evaluations of themselves because they compare their performance to the very best of their peers. When students in the 90th percentile feel like failures compared to students in the 99th percentile, they may think debilitating thoughts and pursue self-destructive behavior. Similarly, helplessness and self-inhibition are responses among successful students who feel threatened by challenges of independent thinking. Graduate schools have many students who are compliant, good at following directions, good at emulating their mentors, but unable to be creative and independent. They may obsess over criticisms of their own work and others, exhibit frustration with apparent obstacles to their own success, take on additional tasks that prevent success, procrastinate, revise and change proposals repeatedly, or attribute blame to external factors – all as metacognitive efforts to avoid self-initiated work. Obsessively thinking about one's course of action can lead to no action at all.

The third example of negative consequences of metacognition is delusional thinking. It is related to obsessive thinking and biased, negative self-evaluations but includes a larger range of dangerous thoughts. Delusions about one's abilities may be revealed in thoughts such as, "I'm so smart that this teacher cannot even understand me", or, "This person is too stupid to appreciate my work." Exaggerated claims about one's own ability or lack of ability in others is self-serving and self-protective of one's self-worth, but they can lead to highly inappropriate actions. For example, the deluded person might feel unconstrained by social rules or so "special" that the rules do not apply and thus act out their fantasy about being smarter or better than others. Delusions may lead to anger and aggressiveness to "show the other person" or "to get even". People with low self-esteem are especially vulnerable to delusions about their own abilities and others and find power in their attempts to control or subjugate others. Deriding spouses, minorities, or helpless victims might all be outcomes of delusional metacognitions about the abilities and competence of self and others. All might be negative outcomes of self-protective processes born of fear of low self-worth and defensive reactions.

There are, of course, other kinds of delusions that may be less severe. People often think about what others think and then recycle that thought to recursive thinking such as, "I think that he thinks that I don't know about X but I really do know about X and I don't want him to know that I do." People can become deluded about intentions, emotions, and knowledge. Repeated thinking about what one knows/feels/wants and what others know/feel/want may confuse what is real from what is self-serving. Over time, the person may not be able to distinguish what they think is the case from other evidence. It is also possible that the repeated delusional thinking leads to internal arguments with the self or imaginary others that may lead to psychoses in extreme cases. Will we become delusional or psychotic if we keep thinking about metacognition? I doubt it. I hope we are not led to negative self-evaluations or helplessness either. Debilitating metacognition is possible but can be avoided with both self-regulating processes and support from other people.

3.   SUMMARY

My main point has been to show that metacognition can be viewed profitably from a functional perspective and this perspective reveals consequences of thinking about thinking that can be positive, neutral, or negative. The interpretation of the consequences depends on situated understanding of the role of metacognitions for the person and the motives for metacognition and the contextual influences. I argued that these interpretations would benefit from being anchored in mainstream theoretical approaches such as theories of mind, theories of self development, or theories of teaching and learning. Theories provide conceptual terms and explanations of cognitive, self-directed processes like metacognition and are necessary if metacognition is going to be given any explanatory role in behavior. I believe that the interpretation of the functions of metacognition can only be achieved with a personal, autobiographical, and developmental understanding of what the person thought and why. Some might say this is almost clinical interpretation and I would not object. This approach is intended to move the study of metacognition beyond thinking for its own sake and into analyses of the personal and long-term consequences of metacognition for the individual. If it is successful, I suppose it is meta-functional.

Chapter 2

The Role of Metatextual Knowledge in Text Comprehension
Issues in Development and Individual Differences

Jean-François Rouet and Elsa Eme
CNRS and University of Poitiers, France

Key themes: Appl / Devl / Perf

Key words: Comprehension / Education / Learning / Strategies / Text

Abstract: We investigated the acquisition of metatextual knowledge in children from grades 3 and 5 (Study 1) and in college students (Study 2). Metatextual knowledge is defined as the knowledge a person possesses about texts and text comprehension activities. We found that metatextual knowledge evolves from superficial to semantic characteristics of texts and situations. Metatextual knowledge was significantly related to comprehension performance. We also found individual differences in students' metatextual knowledge, especially on items related to advanced text features and regulation strategies. The educational implications of these findings are briefly discussed.

As computerized information technologies make their ways into homes, classrooms and school libraries, students frequently find themselves studying complex online documents (e.g., interactive encyclopedia, Web sites). Students are often requested to search through large information databases, to select, compare and integrate multiple information sources, and to make use of sophisticated forms of reasoning *about* and *with* documents (Britt & Gabrys, in press; Dillon, 1994; Rouet, Britt, Mason & Perfetti, 1996). Learning in autonomy with the help of computer technologies is believed by many to be a way to develop students' motivation, their creativity and their learning skills. Yet, with or without computers, many students in secondary and higher education experience serious difficulties when performing document-based learning tasks: Some students fail to locate relevant information (Guthrie, 1988; Gillingham, 1996); others "get lost in hyperspace" (Edwards & Hardman, 1988; Dillon & Gabbard, 1998). Some students only achieve a superficial "cut-and-paste" type of information processing

(Scardamalia, & Bereiter, 1987), with limited ability to *evaluate* and *transform* source information in meaningful ways (Rouet, Favart, Britt & Perfetti, 1997; Wiley & Voss, 1999).

The present paper attempts to shed some light on individual variables that underlie complex information processing skills. We claim that text-based learning difficulties have to do with what students know (or don't know) *about* texts and comprehension tasks, or "metatextual knowledge". Our main contention is that very few students have achieved a sufficient level of metatextual knowledge by the time they begin secondary education. We also believe that a significant proportion of students still need to learn more about texts and comprehension tasks as they enter college (Hacker, 1998). In the present paper we try to present a rationale and some empirical data to support those claims.

We start with a brief review of the role of metacognition in reading comprehension as assessed in previous studies. Then we outline two recent empirical studies. Study 1 aimed at providing a fine-grained description of metatextual knowledge in 3rd and 5th graders and its relationship with reading comprehension. Using similar materials and procedure, Study 2 revealed substantial progress, but also serious gaps in college students' metatextual knowledge. We discuss the implication of these findings for literacy education in the secondary grades.

1.   METACOGNITION AND TEXT COMPREHENSION: A BRIEF REVIEW

Text comprehension involves several types of cognitive processes organized in a hierarchical fashion. Lower-level processes include lexical access, syntactic parsing and the extraction of semantic propositions. Higher-order processes include the formation of a macrostructure, the integration of text information with previous knowledge (i.e., situation model construction), and the selection of relevant information according to reading purposes or objectives (Kintsch, 1998).

Most authors acknowledge that expert comprehension requires the use of context-sensitive, goal-based heuristics (van Dijk & Kintsch, 1983; van den Broek, Young, Tzeng & Linderholm, 1999). Expert readers have to plan, control and regulate their own activity (Brown, Armbruster & Baker, 1986; Paris, Wasik & Turner, 1996). In other words, expert comprehension requires some form of metacognition. The various approaches to this broad, somewhat ill-defined concept have either focused on the *processes* or on the *knowledge* involved in metacognitive regulation of comprehension behavior. As Fischer and Mandl (1984, p. 250) wrote "... *Flavell's metacognitive thinker knows a lot but has no executive device to make use of knowledge and Brown's executive does much but does not know much*". However, metacognition theoreticians generally acknowledge the need to define both knowledge structures and control mechanisms that underlie the concept of metacognition (see Paris, this volume). In complex areas like language comprehension, the acquisition of metacognitive skills is often mediated by language (e.g., questions, directions, explanations). Therefore there is most likely a positive relation between readers' ability to express their metacognitive knowledge, and their actual use of expert strategies.

1.1 The acquisition of metatextual knowledge

Evidence for the strategic nature of expert comprehension may be found in studies of children's text comprehension. When learning to read and comprehend texts, children experience various types of difficulties. Some are due to poor decoding skills or other problems at the lexical level (Perfetti, 1985); other are linked to higher-level comprehension processes, e.g., generating inferences, resolving anaphora, or identifying main ideas (Oakhill, 1994). Yet other sources of difficulties seem related to children's lack of sensitivity to the requirements of comprehension tasks. For instance, they may fail to consider reading objectives, or they may have trouble locating key information in text (Cataldo & Cornoldi, 1998).

Part of children's comprehension difficulties seem related to their lack of explicit knowledge of the cognitive requirements of text comprehension. Myers and Paris (1978) found that 8 year-olds are aware of basic features of texts (e.g., that sentences are organized into paragraphs), but they ignore specific functions of paragraphs, as well as the function of initial and final sentences. Their study suggested that by Grade 6 most children can define these features. Yuill and Oakhill (1991) showed that 9 year-old good and poor readers both mention speed and accuracy when asked to define what makes a good reader. However, "not knowing the words" is more frequently mentioned by poor readers. Lovett and Pillow (1995) found that 9 year-olds are able to make a distinction between different reading objectives (i.e., to memorize vs. to comprehend). However, they need concrete purposes (e.g., comprehend in order to build a game). In the absence of such concrete objectives, even 10 year-olds seem less able to adjust their strategies (Lovett & Flavell, 1990).

Thus, previous studies have provided evidence of a relationship between children's knowledge about texts and text processing (or metatextual knowledge) and their actual performance in comprehension tasks.

1.2 Metatextual knowledge and expert comprehension

While there has been a large number of studies of metacognition and text comprehension in children, there is surprisingly less evidence of the role of metacognition in adult text comprehension. Lorch, Lorch and Klusewitz (1993) report that college students are aware of the specific demands of a wide range of comprehension tasks (e.g., from leisurely browsing a magazine to preparing an exam). However, other studies suggest that adult readers vary in their ability to manage complex comprehension situations.

Fischer and Mandl (1984, Experiment 1) asked college students with little previous domain knowledge to study a 1700-word social sciences text for recall and comprehension. The students were identified as poor- or good readers based on a combination score of recall, comprehension and reading time. After reading, subjects were asked to explain their reading strategies. Good and poor readers reported different types of strategies: Good comprehenders more often sought to identify the main goals and issues dealt with in the text; they performed a fine-grain diagnosis of reading difficulties and described flexible and adaptive strategies. Poor readers were not as specific in their descriptions; they reflected on their general capacities as learners, and expressed concerns about their comprehension performance. Poor comprehenders' metacognitive control seemed to be little more than some fuzzy awareness of their likely failure. The authors concluded that it might be worth to train poor comprehenders to use specific "preventive" strategies rather than general "summative" strategies.

Wagner and Sternberg (1987, Experiment 1) asked college students to read a series of text passages followed by comprehension questions. Based on the latency and accuracy of answers, the authors distinguished easier (gist, main idea) and more difficult types of trials (detail, analysis). They found that some students tended to spend more time on the most difficult trials. Moreover, differential allocation of time predicted a significant proportion of the total comprehension score, independent from reading speed, reading ability and verbal reasoning. They concluded that skilled readers adjust their reading rate to the perceived difficulty of the comprehension task.

In a second experiment, Wagner and Sternberg (1987) provided students with various types of advance information about the difficulty of each trial. Better able students made use of text difficulty ratings to plan their passage reading order. They also focused on sentences marked as important, but there was no relationship between this strategy and comprehension performance. The authors concluded that planning plays an important role in comprehension activities, and that some types of adjunct information may facilitate planning in more able students.

Studies have also found individual differences among adults in tasks that involve searching lengthy texts for specific information. Dreher and Guthrie (1990) asked 16 year-old high school students to search a textbook presented on a computer screen in order to answer simple and more complex questions. Based on students' search time, they identified efficient (i.e., faster) and less efficient (i.e., slower) searchers. They found an interaction between question complexity, search efficacy and the distribution of search time: For complex questions, more efficient searchers tended to spend more time selecting target passages in the table of contents or in the index, while less efficient searchers spent more time reading contents. This finding suggests a difference in planning activities: efficient searchers spend more time identifying potentially relevant categories; they make better choices and do not have to process as much irrelevant information.

Finally, individual differences have been evidenced in tasks that require the integration of multiple sources of information. Rouet, Favart, Britt and Perfetti (1997) obtained evidence that "discipline expertise", i.e., experience in the problems and document types typical of a discipline, in this case history, influences the evaluation and use of documentary evidence during historical problem-solving. They also observed large interindividual variations in study strategies, document evaluation and use within groups of novice and expert historians. They concluded that knowledge of the rhetorical properties of texts play an important role in the acquisition of discipline expertise.

So far metatextual knowledge has been mostly studied in children and teenagers. Moreover, methods of investigation differ across populations, which makes it difficult to picture the general evolution of metatextual knowledge throughout secondary education. The main purpose of our studies was to obtain a comparable set of data about metatextual knowledge in primary school children (Study 1) and in college students (Study 2).

2. STUDY 1: ASSESSMENT OF METATEXTUAL KNOWLEDGE IN 8 AND 10 YEAR-OLD CHILDREN

2.1 Rationale

Even though previous studies have provided evidence that metatextual knowledge actually develops throughout the elementary grades, the evidence generally deals with global aspects of metacognition. However, metacognition involves a variety of finer grain dimensions: knowing about the structural and functional properties of texts, getting prepared for comprehension activities, evaluating one's comprehension performance and potential problems, and knowing about ways to improve comprehension. Moreover, within each dimension, part of the knowledge might be acquired early while some other aspects might be acquired later. For instance, the functions of texts' basic features (e.g., heading, paragraphs) may be known by 5th graders, while more complex aspects (initial sentences, tables of contents, indexes) may be learned later in secondary or higher education. Finally, knowledge about a particular aspect of texts or comprehension activities may develop gradually with a qualitative shift from superficial or structural knowledge, to deeper or functional knowledge.

In a recent study (Eme & Rouet, 2001) we assessed metatextual knowledge in 8 and 10 year-old students. We aimed at providing evidence of the differential development rate of various aspects of metatextual knowledge. We also wanted to examine the relationships between several dimensions of metatextual knowledge, on the one hand, and children's' reading comprehension performance, on the other hand.

2.2 Method

2.2.1 Participants

The participants were 84 children from suburban and rural areas in Western France. 42 children were at Grade 3 (22 females and 20 males, mean age 8 years and 8 months, SD = 4.1 months); 42 were at Grade 5 (20 females and 20 males, mean age = 10 years and 11 months, SD = 5.8 months). The children were recruited through their families and participated voluntarily in individual sessions.

2.2.2 Materials

The materials included a metatextual knowledge questionnaire and a text comprehension task.

The metatextual knowledge questionnaire was build according to the distinction between three metacognitive dimensions of comprehension (Jacobs & Paris, 1987; Paris & Jacobs, 1984): Evaluation, planning and regulation. Items representative of each dimension were formulated or borrowed from previously published questionnaires (Ehrlich, Kurtz-Costes, Rémond & Loridant, 1995; Myers & Paris, 1978; Paris & Jacobs, 1984). We took into account cultural differences, the age levels considered and the conditions of application of the questionnaire (i.e., individual as opposed to collective). In addition, we added a fourth subset of items aimed specifically at evaluating metatextual knowledge, i.e., knowledge about structural of functional properties of written discourse (e.g., "what is a table of contents? What is it used for?").

The basic form of the questionnaire included 23 items. 19 were short answer open questions, 3 were multiple choice questions (Q13, Q17 and Q23) and 1 was a self-estimate of comprehension level (Q4, a 10-point scale). The number of items varied across subscales with 5 items about evaluation (Q1-5), 6 metatextual knowledge items (Q6-11), 7 planning items (Q12-18), and 5 regulation items (Q19-23). The complete list of items is presented in Tables 1 through 4 below.

2.2.3 Procedure

The children were interviewed individually at their homes during the months of March and April 1999. First, they completed the reading comprehension task. After a short break (5-10 min.), they answered orally the metatextual knowledge questionnaire. The interviewer wrote down their answers on a standard scoring sheet. The session lasted approximately 40 minutes.

2.3 Results

2.3.1 Data scoring

There was a large variation in the content and style of answers to the open-ended questions. A fine grained analysis of the transcriptions led to the identification of 3 to 6 main types of answers per item. A scoring template was designed by listing each item, defining its answer types and providing examples for each type. The answer types were hierarchized according to their level of precision and/or their elaborateness. Answer types reflecting functional properties of texts or strategic behavior were assigned a higher level of elaborateness. For each item, a "no/other" category was created by grouping (a) "don't know" answers or a lack of answer; (b) irrelevant, unplausible or unscorable answers (e.g.; "an index is like a finger", "I never go backwards when I read", "(in the initial sentences) the events can be magic").

Two independent judges scored the whole set of data according to the scoring template. In case of multiple answers the scorers retained the most elaborate answer. Inter-scorer reliability was 95.8% for Grade 3 protocols and 95.5% for Grade 5 protocols. Discrepancies were resolved through discussion; which led to slight revisions of the scoring template.

What do 8 and 10 year-olds know about texts and text comprehension?

Evaluation of comprehension. A majority of children reported that they do not always understand what they read (60% and 64% at Grades 3 and 5, respectively), with or without a justification for their answer. However, they believed that they correctly understood the text that they had just read (83 and 86%). They awarded themselves good or very good comprehension scores: 83% of the 3rd graders and 79% of the 5th graders assigned themselves a score of 7 to 10 (on a 0-10 scale). Most of the children associated their own reading difficulties with decoding or lexical knowledge (57% and 50%). They also attributed other people's comprehension difficulties to insufficient attention or vocabulary problems (67% and 76%). Few subjects mentioned higher-order processes, e.g., "get the meaning, important ideas" (12% and 21%).

In short, even though most children acknowledged that reading comprehension can sometimes be a problem, they had a positive appreciation of their performance on the particular task they performed as part of the experiment. Moreover, they focused on rather *basic causes* of poor comprehension (e.g., word identification), and they seemed to ignore more *elaborate* comprehension processes (e.g., main idea construction). Finally there was little or no evolution between Grades 3 and 5 for the evaluation subscale.

Knowledge of text features. A majority of children were able to define a *title* (88% and 90%), but few mentioned the function of titles in text comprehension (24% and 21%). For the definition of *paragraphs* (Q7), we observed a developmental trend: 33% of 3rd graders either failed to provide an answer or gave inappropriate answers (e.g. "a sentence"; "it is behind the text"). At Grade 5, only 7% of children did so. While most of the children at both grades defined paragraphs according to their structural features (e.g. "when you skip a line"), 19% of 3rd graders and 41% of 5th graders were able to define the function of paragraphs in text comprehension (B and C answers, e.g., "corresponds to an idea, a topic").

About half of the children acknowledged the importance of *initial sentences* (57% and 36%), but less than a third of them mentioned their introductory function. Similarly, over two thirds of the children at both grades acknowledged the importance of *final sentences* (Q11) but, to a majority of them, they have to be there only to tell "the end of the story". Other functions (e.g., conclusion, transition) were seldom mentioned. Finally, a minority of 3rd graders provided an acceptable definition for a *table of contents* (38%) or an *index* (12%); the percentages increased at Grade 5 (67% and 35%, respectively), but few children could explain what these devices are used for (table of contents: 24%; index: 2%).

In summary, some children could provide structural (elementary) definitions of text features, but very few provided functional definitions. The proportion of *structural*, but not *functional* definitions, tended to increase between Grades 3 and 5. The function of complex devices, such as the table of contents or the index, was seemingly ignored by most children.

Planning comprehension tasks. Most of the children acknowledged that the purpose of reading a story is to retain its main points rather than its literal wording (79% and 98%). However, few of them selected rewriting as an efficient strategy in order to remember a text (19% and 31%). They preferred to "think about the fact that (they) have to remember" or to "repeat the words" (79% and 62%). 74% of 3rd graders and 67% of 5th graders could not mention an activity that could facilitate comprehension before they start reading (Q15). Even though most of them made a distinction between "reading for fun" and "reading to learn", they only mentioned that the latter requires more effort. Only 14% considered specific objectives or reading strategies, unless they were explicitly warned that they would be asked questions after reading (41% and 50%).

Fixing comprehension problems. When asked how to deal with *words* (Q19) or a *sentences* (Q20) that they don't understand, the children generally mentioned external sources of help (e.g., dictionary or adult assistance, 67% to 95% across items and grades) rather than repair strategies (e.g., use context, etymology or syntax). Most of them cited poor reading or understanding as a reason for *reading again* some part of a text (Q21) with (A+B answers: 69% and 60%). References to global coherence (C) or information search (D) were much less frequent (10 and 12%). About two thirds of the children were able to mention at least one piece of advice in order to help those who have trouble understanding what they read. About half of the answers focused on decoding skills or external assistance. The improvement of competence was defined in wholistic terms, e.g., "practice more". Comprehension techniques or strategies were non-existent. The notion that 3rd and 5th graders have little awareness of control strategies seemed confirmed by the distribution of answers to Q23. In this item, 10 strategies were described, and the child was asked to tell for each of them whether it was useful, useless or troublesome for comprehension. Many children omitted "imagine oneself in the story" or "make a drawing", whereas a majority selected "repeat the words" as a useful strategy. 45% of 3rd graders and 21% of 5th graders evaluated correctly less than 5 strategies out of 10 proposed.

The pattern of answers to regulation questions looked similar to that of planning questions: Most of the participants had some awareness of appropriate behavior to fix word or sentence comprehension problems, or to improve one's reading comprehension skill. However, their definition of control strategies focused on lower levels of processing and external sources of assistance, reflecting dominant reading practices at school or at home. More specific, functional comprehension strategies were rarely mentioned or identified as useful ones.

2.3.2 Simple vs. elaborate metatextual knowledge

The initial qualitative analysis allowed us to set up a general quantitative scoring scheme for the questionnaire. For each item, we made a distinction between "simple", "elaborate" and "other" answers. *Simple answers* focused on structural rather than functional text features; they focused on lower-level, general aspects of reading comprehension (decoding, attention), or on external factors. They corresponded to partial, superficial knowledge of text comprehension activities. *Elaborate answers* were based on semantic, functional text characteristics. They referred to higher-level comprehension processes: Main idea comprehension, learning, selecting information. They seemed to reflect a more analytic, thorough knowledge of text comprehension activities. Finally, *other answers* included "don't know" and irrelevant answers. Correspondence between categories and levels were established jointly by the two authors, following a procedure similar to that of Paris and Jacobs (1984). Scores of 1, 2 and 0 were granted to simple, elaborate and other answers, respectively. Items 3 and 4 of the evaluation scale were recoded with respect to actual comprehension performance (0= large overestimate; 1= small overestimate; 2: correct estimate).

A score was computed for each participant and each subscale in order to obtain a quantification of differences across grades. Raw scores were converted into a percentage of the maximum possible score in order to control for the different number of items across subscales. Furthermore, children at each grade were assigned to one of three comprehension subgroups, according to their actual performance at the reading comprehension task (poor, medium or good comprehension).

Figure 1 shows the average metatextual knowledge scores as a function of subscale, grade and comprehension level. We found a significant relation between comprehension level and the metatextual knowledge score (for more details about statistical procedures see Eme & Rouet, 2001). Poor comprehenders obtained lower scores than good comprehenders at the four metacognitive subscales. However, the contrast between the two extreme groups was stronger for the evaluation subscale, which resulted in significant level x subscale interactions at both grades.

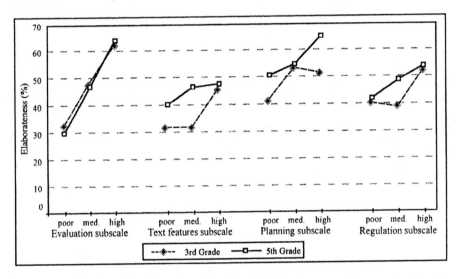

Figure 1. Level of metatextual knowledge elaborateness as a function of grade (3rd, 5th) and comprehension performance (poor, medium, high).

2.4 Summary and discussion

In line with previous studies (e.g., Paris & Jacobs, 1984), we found a developmental evolution of metatextual knowledge between grades 3 and 5. The pattern of answers suggested a distinction between simple and elaborate forms of knowledge. Simple knowledge is characterized by either an emphasis on superficial characteristics of texts and comprehension activities, whereas elaborate knowledge conveys semantic features of texts and higher levels of processing (e.g., main idea construction). Furthermore, we found a relationship between metatextual knowledge and comprehension performance.

Our data suggest that at Grade 5 there are still wide gaps in children's metatextual knowledge about texts and reading comprehension. Most children ignore the function of higher-level devices (e.g., table of contents, index). Moreover, a significant proportion of 5th graders could not cite one specific rhetorical function of initial or final sentences. The lack of functional knowledge about text features may be related to failure to perform comprehension-based learning tasks. For example, recent observations by Rouet and Chollet (2000) suggest that 9 year-old children generally make little use of the table of contents or index when asked to locate specific information in a junior encyclopedia. Most of them flip through pages, looking for a picture or keyword related to the item to be found. In the present study, the children seldom mentioned specific ways of getting prepared to study (Q15), or techniques that help remember the contents of a text (Q17). Finally most of them did not mention a relevant strategy to solve comprehension problems by themselves (Q20).

Based on the data, there are reasons to believe that the development of metatextual knowledge continues throughout the secondary grades and, possibly, in higher education. The purpose of our second study was to assess metatextual knowledge in undergraduate students.

3.   STUDY 2: INDIVIDUAL DIFFERENCES IN COLLEGE STUDENTS' METATEXTUAL KNOWLEDGE

3.1   Rationale

At the present time there is no single psychometric instrument to assess metatextual knowledge throughout the elementary and secondary grades. As a first step toward designing such a tool, we wanted to assess undergraduate students' metatextual knowledge with a procedure as close as possible to that of Study 1. Such an approach would allow an indirect comparison of children and adults' metatextual knowledge.

3.2   Method

3.2.1   Participants

Thirty three undergraduate students from a French university participated in fulfillment of a course requirement. No participant had taken any course in comprehension or metacognition prior to the study.

3.2.2   Materials and procedure

The questionnaire was the same as in Study 1 except for some minor modifications: Two multiple choice questions in the children's version were replaced by open-ended questions. Two items which were dependent upon the particular comprehension task performed by the children were replaced by equivalent questions. Finally, the wording of some items was changed so as to fit the participants' background (e.g. university vs. primary school). The questionnaire was administered collectively as part of an optional class to groups of 10 to 12 students.

The experimenter read out loud each question one at a time. Students wrote their answer on an answer sheet. One to three minutes were allowed for each question.

The scoring sheet used in Study 1 was adapted to fit differences in vocabulary and knowledge between the two populations. Eight new categories were added to take into account new types of answers. Five new categories concerned the function of text features (Q6-11); the three others dealt with the role of knowledge in comprehension (Q5), skimming (Q12), information search (Q16). All these new answer types were categorized as "elaborate" according to the framework described above. All the answers were scored by the same two judges as in Study 1. Inter-scorer agreement was 93.1% and discrepancies were solved through discussion.

3.3 Results

Only the main results will be reported here. For more details see Eme and Rouet (2001).

For the *evaluation* items, we found that some characteristics of children's answers were still present. For instance, when asked about sources of comprehension difficulties (Q1 and 5), a significant proportion of students mentioned lower-level processes: Word identification, lexical knowledge, attention (Q1, 33%; Q5: 58%). Higher-level processes, such as text coherence, study strategies, knowledge activation were mentioned by a minority of students (Q1, 33%, Q5: 36%).

Most participants displayed elaborate knowledge about basic *text features*: Titles (100%); paragraphs (76%); table of contents (85%). However, other features seemed harder to define. 58% of the participants could not define an index; a significant minority failed to provide elaborate definitions of first and last sentences (25% and 49%, respectively).

The evaluation was also clear for *planning* activities. Most participants cited skimming as a means to deal with time constraints (Q12, 79%), they mentioned underlining, taking notes, self-questioning as comprehension-fostering activities (Q14, 61%; Q16; 64%) or selecting information in order to write a summary (Q18, 58%). However, only a minority cited specific ways to get prepared to study (Q15, 39%) or to improve recall (Q17, 33%).

Finally, few participants cited elaborate *regulation* strategies. 30% cited the use of context or syntax as a means to understand difficult words (Q19), and 42% did so for difficult sentences (Q20). 21% mentioned locating information or global integration as reasons to re-read (Q21), and 24% cited the acquisition of specific strategies as a means to improve reading comprehension (Q22).

The answers were converted into quantitative scores using the same procedure as in Study 1. For the purpose of global comparison across studies, mean percentages for each subscale as a function of age level (8, 10 year-olds and adults) are showed on Figure 2.

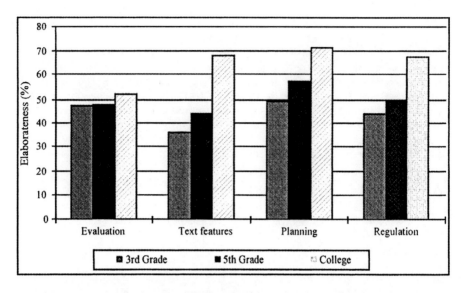

Figure 2. Metatextual knowledge as a function of subscale and age level.

As shown on Figure 2, college students obtained far better scores than children on all the four subscales. However, there was still a large range of scores in the adult sample, especially for the evaluation and regulation subscales. 25% of subjects obtained scores lower than the theoretical mean on those scales.

4.   GENERAL DISCUSSION

The study of skilled comprehension has shown that good comprehenders are generally able to provide accurate descriptions of their strategies. Although essentially procedural, text comprehension and study strategies seem accessible to conscious thinking and verbalization (Afflerbach, 1990). The present studies attempted to use a questionnaire in order to assess the evolution of metatextual knowledge in children and college students.

The first study presented in this paper shows that by the age of 10-11 years (i.e. after 5 years of exposure to print and reading activities), children still have a lot to learn about texts, comprehension and study strategies. Their answers suggest an overwhelming concern for lower-level processes: Identifying words, accessing their meaning, paying attention to what they read. Most children cannot assess accurately their own level of comprehension. They ignore the functional properties of most text features and higher-level structuring tools like tables of contents and indexes. They show little planning and comprehension activities, little adjustment to specific task demands. Finally, children seem to have very few means to deal with comprehension difficulties. Most of them rely to external sources of assistance (either parents or teachers). In short, our data suggest that the average 10 year-old pupil has a fairly good mental model for reading words, but not for comprehending or studying texts. These observations add to the existing literature on the development of metacognition (Gombert, 1990; Myers & Paris, 1978).

Among the limitations of the present study, it should be pointed out that part of our data is "negative evidence". That children did *not* mention strategies or text features does not mean that they could not use such strategies or features when reading. However, the converging evidence across items and the global relationships between metatextual knowledge and text comprehension suggests at least some correspondence between children's answers and their actual comprehension behavior. Evidence is still missing, however, on the functional relationships between students' explicit knowledge and their actual learning strategies (see Koriat, this volume).

Considering that reading comprehension skills are seldom taught explicitly beyond primary schools, it is little surprising that, in times when almost 50% of teenagers take some kind of higher education, many undergraduate students show rather poor strategic skills. Even though the comparison between the data of Study 1 and 2 shows a massive (and predictable) increase in metatextual knowledge from 5th Grade to college, it is clear that some students still can't define advanced features of texts (e.g., what is an index, what is it for?), or evaluation and regulation activities. Because the sample used in Study 2 is of limited size and from a specific population (3rd year undergraduate psychology students), these data call for some replication. However, they corroborate other views of metacognition at the college level (e.g., Hacker, 1998). Moreover, there is now some clear evidence that academic success is predicted in part by students' text processing skills (e.g., Lonka, Lindblom & Maury, 1994).

The bigger picture suggested by our results is that teenagers learn progressively to deal with reading assignments of increasing complexity throughout secondary education. In French middle and high schools, current educational policies leave it almost entirely to the student to acquire the literacy skills and knowledge requested to succeed in their further academic or vocational projects. Most students in Study 2 must have acquired their emerging metatextual knowledge in implicit ways, through the various text-based tasks that they were assigned in high school science, literature or history programs. However, a large number of 17 year-olds simply continue to apply the rudimentary comprehension behavior that they have learned initially, with little strategic improvement (Guthrie, 1988). It is worth asking whether more explicit types of training might help a larger proportion of students master such skills before they become a prerequisite for further progress (see Britt & Gabrys, in press). Given the mixed results of metacognition training programs for children in the elementary grades (Brand-Gruwel, Aarnoutse & van den Bos, 1998), we suggest that strategic skills should be taught in *continuation* rather than in *replacement* of basic reading skills. Therefore, teaching advanced text processing skills might be more realistic an agenda for *secondary*, as opposed to *primary* education. As complex information technologies continue to pervade our everyday environment, it seems a natural consequence that the training of information processing skills be continued beyond elementary grades. A challenge for further studies will be to identify relevant objectives and methods for the education of literate citizen in the information society.

Chapter 3

An Ecological Approach to Metacognitive Regulation in the Adult

Claude Valot
Institut de Médecine Aérospatiale, Service de Santé des Armées, Brétigny-sur-Orge, France

Key themes: Appl / Cont / Perf

Key words: Ergonomics / Metacognition / Dynamic environment / Regulation of activity

Abstract: The analysis of metacognition in a professional context sheds light on how knowledge can regulate activity. For individual and collective tasks, metacognitive knowledge is noted as helping operators perform complex tasks. It helps regulate the operation of cognition, not in view of improving its performance but to adjust its use according to the constraints at hand. Metacognitive knowledge helps regulate the imprecision of cognitive operations rather than their accuracy.

1.   INTRODUCTION

Working situations are a unique environment to help better understand metacognition. Operators must develop a specific knowledge of their own competencies to correctly manage risks resulting from task complexity, uncertainties of decision-making or the entrapping consequences of technological innovations. Cognitive ergonomics increasingly attempt to grasp what specifically in metacognitive knowledge plays a key role in regulating activity.

Two complementary approaches to metacognition are available in order to analyze metacognitive processes involved in these activities.

The first one consists in studying interactions, in laboratories, between, for example, memory, metamemory and the "feeling of knowing". This creates a relevant framework, where data and behaviors can be easily confronted, and matched with one another, in order to eventually model metacognitive functions. The comparison between cognition and metacognition is accurate, but could lead to a normative interpretation, and thus to viewing metacognitive regulation as a sort of ideal efficient cognition. This is illustrated by the following questions (Koriat, 1996): How is the operation of cognition controlled? What processes are in charge of checking its accuracy? These questions, which focus on the nature of metacognitive processes, address metacognition according to accuracy and to the possible relationships developed between reality as it is observed, cognitive processes and quality of control.

The second way to approach metacognition is inspired by the ergonomic perspective mentioned earlier. Metacognitive functions can be addressed according to their interaction with the environment and its constraints. This approach of metacognition can be called "ecological".[1] Operators' performance level, when confronted with difficult and risky situations, not only results from a specific involvement of memory or from decision-making processes. The different cognitive functions co-operate and compensate each other, in order to develop the behavior best suited to the constraints encountered, and to the capacities operators believe they are endowed with. A person's knowledge of his/her level of competence in a specific situation leads this person to develop compensation strategies to eventually obtain a certain effectiveness, taking into account interactions between environmental constraints and cognitive capacities.

The ecological analysis, mentioned earlier for regulation in a professional context, would rather envisage regulation as taking into account human limits and specificities in relation to the activity's environmental constraints. Its final goal is to find the adequate strategy integrating limits and constraints, in view of developing a satisfactory compromise.

This ecological approach of metacognition, which will be detailed later, is founded on the analysis of human activities in complex work situations. This complexity makes it possible to observe how operators develop behaviors suited to the risks encountered. Another advantage could be found in that approach of metacognition: in complex work situations, metacognition is "in action" and behavior could be easily compared with self-reports from operators.

A number of steps are required to correctly obtain an ecological analysis of metacognition. Ecological studying of metacognitive mechanisms in the adult first requires a short description of concepts such as metacognitive knowledge and the interest of an ecological reading. Two researches on the activity of single-seater and two-seater combat aircraft pilots will be used to illustrate this approach. Finally, the ecological role of metacognition will be modeled.

2.   METACOGNITION AND ECOLOGICAL APPROACH

2.1   Metacognitive knowledge

In keeping with the perspective of conscious metacognitive activity and the need for a higher process to execute regulation, Pinard (1992) suggests the possibility of a *metacognitive capacity*. This capacity would aim at deliberately and consciously taking over the way a person's cognition operates. It would cover *metacognitive knowledge* (facts as well as strategic elements involved in production and regulation), and *cognitive activity* organized around self-regulation. This includes i) the level at which metacognitive knowledge is activated in a given situation, ii) the preparation, follow-up and verification activities carried out during the action, and iii) metacognitive experience providing an immediate *internal feedback.*

The same author also insists on the need to add a new level: *metaconsciousness,* which involves charge taking of the person for his/her own cognitive operations. Metaconsciousness is organized around a person's feeling of self-efficiency, self-awareness, and this person's style of causal attribution. This consciousness may be associated to more familiar concepts in ergonomics, such as being engaged in an activity, and prioritizing and economizing behaviors.

For Shaw, Mace and Turvey (1995), metacognitive knowledge is a result of coping with working process instability, variety of professional context or variability of cooperation situation. These situations provide metacognitive experience, which reinforces or modifies a person's metacognitive knowledge. Experience and metacognitive knowledge can interact, when the metacognitive knowledge on a specific class of situation generates a conscious metacognitive experience, derived from the difficulty encountered in finding a solution to the situation. The next step is to select a strategy integrating this newly acquired experience. Metacognitive experience seems to be a leading driver in the feedback persons develop out of their mode of operation.

2.2   Ecological approach

The term "ecological" expresses the focus attached to the taking into account of environment to better understand person's behaviors. An ecological analysis of metacognitive knowledge is based upon conditions of this knowledge generation. According to Flavell, the interaction between a person and his/her environment is all the more important when the person's activity stimulates a thought process highly conscious of the challenging importance or novelty of the activity. Among other things, this includes the learning curve in new situations or when decisions are important and risk-ridden...

Ecological approach to metacognition introduces not only to an instantaneous dimension of a person but also to his past cognitive events. A large number of confrontations to highly challenging situations and strategies integrating lessons drawn from metacognitive experience, feed-back on one's performance contribute highly to the building of metacognitive knowledge. Metacognition obviously operates by calling on a combination of mechanisms. Some of these involve short-term regulation and are hardly inspected by the person; they generate awareness only as the action occurs. Others are more closely linked to mental representations and to activity tracking over the long-term. The way these different moments of metacognition interact seems to indicate that strategy selection mechanisms are connected to a person's own history. These moments were a conscious and active concern during a first stage, when the person was confronted to a context. They were then gradually integrated into acquired and non-conscious behavioral automatic processes. It becomes almost impossible to verbalize the assessment of a previously acquired cognitive operational mode. This expertise is no longer conscious; however, it is only during a confrontation with a new or no longer familiar context that a person becomes aware of a difficulty and of explicit cognitive limits.

In this ecological view, there are grounds to say that a pure self-analysis of metamnemonic mechanisms seems to be very rare when dealing with clear-cut and streamlined tasks. The real nature of metacognition only reappears when dealing with more complex tasks, where selecting the right strategy is important or challenging.

Metacognitive knowledge could be considered as gradually merging into the body of behavioral automatic processes, as facts eventually come to prove the correctness of the regulation strategy implemented by the person.

3.   METACOGNITION IN ACTION

Numerous facts to analyze metacognition used in interaction with a person's environment rise up when trying to understand how operators behave. The management of dynamic situations, problem-solving or decision-making are areas where the involvement of metacognition is closely studied. The nature of this involvement should be briefly addressed, to better understand how, in the work situations, metacognition is specifically called upon.

3.1   Managing dynamic situations

Dynamic environments are characterized, among other things, by the quick pace at which situations change and by the difficulty to anticipate in complex contexts, which is why operators have to integrate cognitive costs and the knowledge they have of their own actions (Samurcay & Hoc, 1988). Another element, noted by Critchfield (1996) can be added: in experiments, tasks carried out under an increasing time pressure lead subjects to develop a double-tasking system to maintain their performance while conducting a self-observation exercise. The greater the time pressure, the more important the second task becomes.

Amalberti and Hoc (1988) note anothercognitive dimension in their research on the way human beings manage timeframes. Human beings have several internal and external timeframes, which may come into conflict when a dynamic process is managed. These authors stress that some behaviors on the job can only be understood by taking into account personal and biased interpretations applied to the management of individual resources.

3.2   Problem-solving

Logic and rationality of human operation have long permeated the analysis of problem-solving mechanisms. New approaches to problem- solving dramatically change the way this question is now analyzed. Bastien and Richard (1995) sum up this change: "we moved from notions highlighting the role of logic and reasoning towards new ideas that increasingly focus on the role played by the activation of knowledge (...) according to problems previously solved by the human subject" (p. 379).

This interpretation of problem-solving leads directly to metacognition. Among the various elements used to develop compromises aimed at solving a problem, self-knowledge of a person's skills, and feedback on how these skills were implemented are of utmost importance. Operator preference, motivation factors, limitations of the cognitive system, knowledge of the entire catalogue of available responses are key criteria which help understand how problems are solved (Amalberti, 1995).

Davidson, Deuser and Sternberg (1994) suggest a definition of problem-solving integrating the specificities of metacognition: "Problem-solving is the active process of trying to transform the initial state of a problem into the desired one. Metacognition helps the problem solver (1) recognize that there is a problem to be solved, (2) figure out what exactly the problem is, and (3) understand how to reach a solution." (p. 208). These authors believe that when studying how metacognition is involved in problem-solving, the important part is not the exactness of the result provided by the subject, but the way the problem was identified and the kind of response adopted. The subject is setting up a cost-effectiveness analysis, integrating motivation and environmental constraints. In their approach, authors highlight the importance of interindividual differences in the solutions provided. They also point to possible improvements in problem-solving performance, which could result from training operators on the identification and selection of various cognitive strategies. Jausovec (1994) shows that metacognition is an important success factor in the case of open problems calling on a subject's creativity. Subjects who tap their metacognitive knowledge to a maximum, and who implement better-suited strategies obtain the best performance.

4. EXPERIMENTS ON THE ADULT'S METACOGNITIVE ACTIVITY IN COMPLEX PROFESSIONAL SITUATIONS

In highly complex tasks, operators run the risk of quickly being confronted with limitations in skills and know-how, because of the nature of the task. Operators can no longer be sure the activity will be successful in any circumstances, when various parameters come into play, such as autonomous processes, automatic control systems, uncertainties in the definition of tasks, and finally, limited timeframes for complex decision-making.

This potential fragility in dynamic environments is reinforced by the research on safety and risks, which **supports** that, whatever the industry involved, most accidents originate from moves made by humans: errors, poorly suited decisions, misunderstandings between operators and their assistance systems. These human errors place operators in a delicate position: operators are indispensible, but are also aware of being a major risk factor. Operators are regularly confronted with complex situations, and with uncertainties on their own performance level. For this reason, their attention cannot be limited to environment changes or pitfalls; they must also pay great attention to their own behavior. This is even more so the case when they run the risk of operating at the border of their cognitive skills.

This control of activity, and the knowledge thus accumulated, is left at the discretion[2] and initiative of operators: technical systems cannot contribute much to helping operators in adjusting and monitoring their activity. Operators invest strong skills in these activities, because the nature of the job and their own professional value rely on their ability to simultaneously take into account dynamic processes, organizational features, and their own behavior. The nature of these interactions has long been pointed out. Bainbridge (1980) notes that operator knowledge brings together process elements, and elements pertaining to the operator's personal behavior and cost of this behavior.

4.1   General experimentation principles

To appreciate the interest of an ecological view on metacognition, two experiments are proposed. They have in common to analyse role and content of metacognitive knowledge of operators involved in tasks highly dynamic, risky and of a high level of cognitive complexity. The professional frame used for these experiments is the flying of combat aircraft. These experiments try to find out how and when metacognitive knowledge is involved in strategies developed by subjects.

Another important question will be addressed by the second experiment. In many cases, a team of operators (or at least two) must combine their efforts to pursue a collective activity. Performance is directly linked to this co-operation, where regulated cognitive activity is no longer limited to the individual. Information sharing, communication, and decision-making are significantly improved when operators take the cognitive capacities of their partner(s) into account. It is thus interesting to try and find the guidelines ruling this quite paradoxical metacognitive activity, which deals with "the other party's" cognition. This approach is already included in the previous framework of conscious and verbalizable metacognitive knowledge. However, it presents an additional specificity: dealing with the cognitive activity of another party, with which it is essential to fruitfully co-operate.

Methods and protocols were designed in the following way. The environment was deliberately chosen to be professional. It is assumed that subjects are well trained and familiar with the situations under study. Operators' metacognitive knowledge must come freely into play, and its consequences on strategy development must lead to observable behaviors. The task must be sufficiently demanding to place strong constraints on execution and thus push operators towards the limits of cognitive competence.

The mere analysis of observable behavior is not sufficient for interpretation. Observation must be supplemented by verbalization to better understand the subjects' strategies and metacognitive knowledge. The best possible situation is an experimental set up, in an environment which can be reproduced, where all subjects are placed in a working situation, and where behaviors can be observed in detail.

Flying a combat aircraft is a situation meeting all the criteria mentioned above. Two different tasks were defined to meet all the criteria involved.

• *Flying a single-seater combat aircraft,* on a low altitude mission. The mission called for a single plane, and the pilot was free to adapt the route, around various constraints referred to in the mission plan (points to reach, deadlines, compulsory route sections). Eight single-seater pilots flew a mission in a very realistic full-flight simulator, all with the same mission plan and operational conditions. They were all provided with the documents and tools usually available for this type of mission. The mission was demanding but corresponded to their skill level. It was recorded, to serve as reference during the self-confrontation interview carried out after the flight.

• *Flying a two-seater combat aircraft.* The principles adopted here were similar to those in the single-seater. Eight crews were given the same mission plan, corresponding to their skill level. The flight was recorded, and used for self-confrontation during the after flight interview.

In the "single-seater" environment, interviews focused on analyzing the gaps between the flight described in the mission plan, the plan developed by the pilot (or crew) and the actual flight. The purpose of the analysis is to assess how metacognitive knowledge can contribute to understanding the reasons for the arrangements or modifications between these three different types of flight.

For the "two-seater", interviews aimed at identifying what amount of knowledge of the other's cognition was available and actually used during the planning stage and the actual flight.

4.2   Results of experiments on individual regulation (single-seater planes)

The observation of the various stages involved shows the following results:

• all pilots successfully fulfilled their mission, in all aspects (points to reach, deadlines, routes);
• each pilot developed a specific flight plan to meet mission goals;
• all actual flights differed from the planned flights
• all pilots were highly skilled, but actual navigation was always very different from their plan, despite the availability of very accurate assistance systems.

As a first tool for analysis, different forms of "flight" could be distinguished. The first one is the *mission order* on which pilots had the possibility of developing their own "customized" flight plan, since they were in charge of designing it to fit their needs. This *planned flight* is the second form of flight. The third form of flight is the *actual flight* performed. That is to say the actual path and the lever of observance of flight timing and navigation.

Gaps observed between flight plan and actual flight are interesting in terms of metacognitive regulation. Two facts seem to come into conflict: pilots did not navigate accurately during their flight, but they all managed to successfully carry out their mission within its pre-defined limitations. Some evidence of this adjustment could be observed in path accuracy and schedule respect. Although they have aboard a precise navigation system, the flight by one pilot in the single-seater experiment (Figure 1) shows large discrepancies between the planned flight and the actual flight.

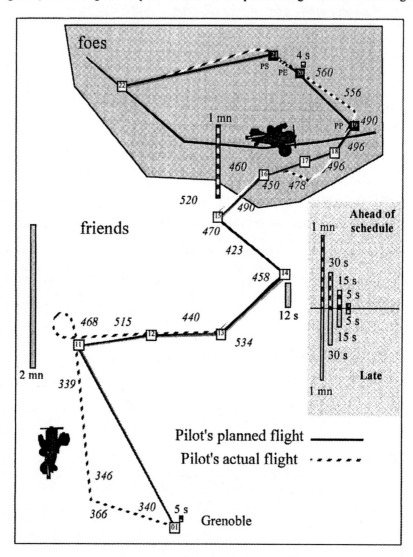

Figure 1. Discrepancy observed between the planned flight and the actual flight by one pilot in the single-seater experiment.

This pilot was 2 minutes late then 1 minute ahead during this flight. In the same manner, this path was up to 10 or 5 nautical miles away from the planned path. The figures all along the path indicate the aircraft speed. Speed values change noticeably in spite of a planned speed of 450 knots. Friends and foes are two classical areas for combat aircraft: in foe area threat avoidance, maneuver and speed have more strict rules than in friend area. Each pilot was asked to describe strategies and knowledge attached to this management of time and path. In each case pilots used a specific form of verbalization. The relationship between the cognitive knowledge expressly mentioned by pilots during the interviews and the gaps observed helps better understand how these gaps come about, and how they relate to each pilot's metacognitive regulation.

The following sentence: "I'm not able to perform reliable checks after the front line so, for my part, before the front line I check navigation accuracy because later I'll be overburdened..." is a representative example. This sentence is typically a heuristic; that is to say a local rule usable only in a given context. This kind of knowledge is directly linked to metacognitive knowledge and each pilot is endowed with a significant directory of metacognitive heuristics.

These heuristics associate systematically different form of facts: on the one hand a cognitive constraint, a threshold, and a preferred action, and on the other hand, a situation management constraint, and a metacognitive connotation (Figure 2).

A constraint on cognitive activity	A threshold	A preferred action	A management constraint	A metacognitive connotation
I'm not able to perform reliable checks ...	*after the front line ...*	*so, for my part, before the front line ...*	*I check navigation accuracy ...*	*because later I'll be overburdened ...*

Figure 2. Example of heuristics with metacognitive connotation.

The constraint on cognitive activity is a result from previous experience. This result is associated with situation references used to apply that heuristic. The metacognitive connotation defines a specific part of knowledge, which contains a reference to metacognition but not directly expressed. The overburdened state, at this flight step, connotes a metacognitive reference: a consciousness of a cognitive state is associated on the one hand with the origin of this state and on the other hand with the effect on flying.

More generally speaking, interviews demonstrate that each pilot integrated domain-related metacognitive knowledge, with double characteristics. This specific knowledge is essential to make sure the task is carried out with adequate performance quality, and at the same time, they point to fragile cognitive activities arising from the constraints encountered in these situations.

These various aspects of metacognitive knowledge highlight the limits observed by pilots on the way their cognition operates in flight.

All the heuristics gathered can be described in five main families of metacognitive knowledge:
- *Chronological distribution of tasks.* Scheduling the tasks, to make sure the cognitive possibilities of control checks and action are never exceeded during the various flight phases when numerous actions overlap: "I only check the fuel

before banking to be sure not to forget it, and to make sure other flight phases are not overloaded with useless checks...".

• *Risk management.* The pilot can only distribute his attention between roles and actions up to a certain point; beyond this point, excessive sharing can lead the pilot to run the risk of losing control of the situation. The pilot must be careful to limit risk-taking according to available cognitive capacities: "I only quickly glance inside the cockpit, otherwise I run the risk of not seeing an obstacle and not being aware of the time spent dealing with a problem..."

• *Management of memory during the flight.* Many inputs from the flight plan must be memorized during the flight. The problem is memory overload. Pilots know which flight stages are less demanding, and use this time of relative availability to specifically bring the data to be memorized back to mind. They know that during intense action phases, they will not be able to consult the documents or texts involved. "I take advantage of high altitude flying to go over the flight plan again, and to memorize again the main low altitude flight phases..."

• *Keeping track of a highly dynamic activity.* For the pilot, flying a combat aircraft at low altitudes and high speeds requires carrying out a great number of actions, control checks, and constantly anticipating and assessing the situation. All these requirements operate in different timeframes. The pace of activity is imposed to the pilot, who must absolutely stay abreast of these dynamic tasks, by correctly anticipating variations in constraints during flight phases, according to the various choices made and solutions selected.

• *Distribution between pilot actions and automated systems.* The on-board availability of numerous automated systems represents a gain and an extra-burden for the pilot. The gain is that delegating tasks to the automated systems can decrease his workload. However these systems need to be controlled to make sure they are reliable. The confidence the pilot has in these systems, the appreciation he may have of his own capacities to fully and intelligently use these tools and to understand how they work make up metacognitive knowledge, and have a great influence on the strategies selected to control the flight.

These heuristics are two-sided. On the one hand, they are like signs of past difficulties encountered in dealing with environment (technical and operational). In that way, they belong to metacognitive knowledge. On the other hand, they help the pilot to plan his activity to avoid cognitive pitfalls and improve efficiency. They are also regulation tools for short and long term activity planning.

It seems difficult, at first, to always find a consistent relationship between metacognitive knowledge, pilot strategies and mission achievement. When confronted with demanding and complex situations, pilots only moderately embark on accurate situation processing, and seem to tolerate important gaps. The heuristics they express are also quite limited in scope. Surprisingly, coherence may be found in the purpose of this knowledge: helping manage the level of looseness and imprecision pilots can allow themselves throughout the mission.

Too much imprecision can jeopardize the mission and even make it impossible. Conversely, over-accuracy throughout the flight is penalizing, because it over-engages cognitive capacities. This situation typically calls for the management of cognitive resources. The pilot must find the right trade-off between a certain level of control, the complexity of the task elaborated, and an appropriate performance level.

Figure 3 illustrates this variability in trade-offs between situation constraints and the capacities of cognitive operations; they are used to manage the mission.

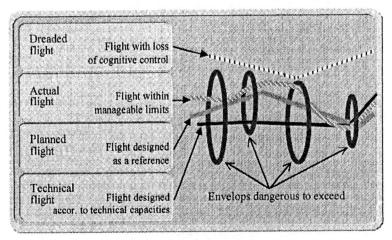

Figure 3. Pilot's four flights.

The mission was originally designed and defined by taking into account the system's technical capacities, resulting in a "technical" flight. Pilots, when preparing for the mission, developed a "planned flight" based on the representation they had of their cognitive skills. They employed a set of metacognitive heuristics helping chain actions together, to make sure these actions can be managed within the constraints expected. This construction produces a specific result, since the sophisticated mission the pilot could theoretically develop in the quiet atmosphere of the planning room may exceedingly expose this pilot to the limiting effects constraints have on the way cognition operates.

The "actual flight" is the pilot's adaptation, in situation, according to the difficulties actually encountered out of all those expected and planned. Heuristics are still present, but of another nature. They help select options answering the constraints encountered.

A final generic flight is available in the pilot's mind, during planning as well as during execution: "the dreaded flight", bringing together all the conditions pilots dread. Pilots consider then that constraints encountered and their effects would greatly exceed available processing capabilities and knowledge.

The actual flight and its tolerated approximations make up a sort of envelope within which the pilot wants to remain, somewhere between the "planned flight" and the "dreaded flight", which remains a limit to be avoided.

4.3 Results of experiments on collective regulation (two-seater aircraft crew)

In a two-seater aircraft, tasks are allocated as follows: one of the crewmembers is in charge of flying the aircraft (short-term time frame), and the other of navigating

Valot

(long-term time frame). Voice is almost the only communication mode available, and remains an irreplaceable channel to exchange information. Communication is intense in this distribution of tasks; during the average 45mns long flight, a great number of verbal exchanges are carried out. 412 sentences are expressed from pilot to his navigator, but the navigator expresses 655 sentences to the pilot.

A part of these sentences is data driven according to aircraft technical systems. But observations and interviews show that the navigator's position in the crew involves a great amount of metacognition. The navigator not only processes questions on the aircraft's course, but also items dealing with the pilot's cognitive state. To this end, the navigator has extensive knowledge of the pilot's mood and capacities, and acts different levels: on the aircraft's itinerary, using professional know-how, and on the nature of information passed on to the pilot, on the way this information is passed on, and on the scheduling of this information.

Navigators develop a cognitive management of their pilot. This management is supported by a specific knowledge. The navigators know the consequences of the constraints encountered during a flight may have on the other crewmember cognitive functions.

Various risk factors or symptoms of limitation are associated to heuristics so as to recover part or all of the crewmember's cognitive capacities. Figure 4 illustrates this with relationship between some cognitive risk factors and response heuristics; some strategies to strengthen the other's cognitive processes are listed.

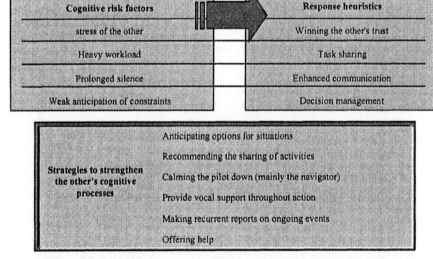

Figure 4. Relationship between cognitive risk factors and response strategies.

Each navigator has his own way of achieving this regulation. Behavioral indicators, such as the number of communications and their content, quite accurately testify to the quality of decisions made by pilots when the flight needs to be adapted to an external event.

Figure 5 shows an example of these management strategies. An "anticipating options" strategy is analyzed with the amount of anticipated information provided by two navigators having different skill levels. The flight was divided in 9 legs containing, for each, a specific constraint to deal with (instrument flight, interception, failure, target...). For each leg, sentences expressed by pilots or navigators were analyzed retaining sentences, which express material to help pilot or navigator to anticipate coming events.

Better-adapted decisions are made by pilots kept well up-to-date by their navigators on the upcoming events and on possible options.

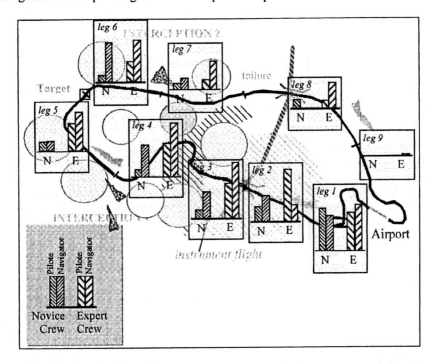

Figure 5. Proportion of anticipation statements throughout the flight according to experience.

This "metamanagement" essentially goes from navigator to pilot, since only the navigator has the time and information required to execute this dual task. This task is, to a large extent, based on metacognitive knowledge of the "other": what information is required for the pilot to effectively react to the upcoming event, and when is this information needed? Like in any other professional situation, regulation is opportunistic: the navigator can choose not to tell the pilot an error was just made, and only provide the corrected information later. This strategy smoothes the relationships between crewmembers, and results in a situation controlled through managed imprecision.

5.   METACOGNITION, AN ASSET FOR INDIVIDUAL AND COLLECTIVE EFFECTIVENESS

Controlling a process such as flying an aircraft is strongly marked by deadlines at which decisions must be made. Decision-making is optimized if it also takes into account a person's capacity to execute the decision process within an adequate timeframe. This reference to the self and to the knowledge one has of one's competence turns this judgment into a typically metacognitive mechanism (Jensen & Benel, 1977). As indicated by Riley (1996) or Amalberti (1996), risk management might be one of the major drivers behind metacognitive knowledge. Having to assess the relevance of know-how, having to estimate the relevance of one's knowledge and one's competence, becomes crucial when the integrity of a person and the safety of a technical system and its human and economic environment depend on these assessments. Operator skills will increase, if this person is able to take the activity performed into account, either to add value to it, or to question its relevance.

The development of metacognitive knowledge can be envisaged as a "reinvestment" into the knowledge of one's competence, to turn it into an adaptation tool.

Bandura (1977, 1992) suggests a distinction between *expecting results*, which is a person's perception of the behaviors required to reach a goal, and *expecting effectiveness*, which deal with this person's belief of personal abilities to effectively carry out this behavior. "Effectiveness" places us in an operative and situated framework, where the capacity of implementing knowledge in a given context is just as important has having this knowledge.

5.1   Metacognition in uncertain and unstable situations

It is now time to return to the role played by metacognitive knowledge in the way a person operates. The ecological approach mentioned earlier sheds some light on this role. Thanks to Bateson's (1995) work on ecology of mindsets, the ecological approach offers an interesting opportunity to return to the concept of feedback. The way operators use metacognitive knowledge highlights the way they typically control activities: in very dynamic situations, heuristics used by operators do not seem sufficient to guarantee that further developments will meet expectations.

For Bateson, the informative value of feedback regulation is included in a bipolar system. Information involves what is being observed as well as what is not being observed. For an operator, information on performance can be expressed in terms of success/failure. For example, after a flight, the pilot's feedback on the flight is not only information as to its success, but can go much further. A flight modestly but correctly performed may be a non-failure, and the pilot may be quite satisfied with it, given the circumstances. Another day, a flight below the pilot's expectations will be experienced as a non-success, even though it looks like a success. A well-controlled flight will not necessarily be seen as a success, if the pilot believes sheer luck unexpectedly chipped in and helped out.

We now encounter another difficulty. The time between feedback and the next opportunity for this pilot to confront this newly enhanced knowledge to a real situation. Here again, an important combination comes into play. Background features, which were assessed and helped develop skills at the time, might not be encountered again before long. The memory of the control level obtained previously might have faded away, or have changed in nature.

In the framework of these combinations of support and distrust, even an operator endowed with genuine cognitive skills, significant know-how and proper training cannot be sure that the "next flight" will be flown in an ideal and well-controlled fashion. Even though this pilot can "reasonably" believe hazards will stay under control and that the flight will remain within a favorable envelope, numerous uncertainties still plague the situation: will the maneuvers be carried out correctly? Will an adequate answer to failures be provided? What will be the reaction to possible errors? In this context, over-rigid or over-specific heuristics are too prone to failure. Having an image of absolute skill and control could be deceitful and generate risks, because the diversity of situations the pilot must always be ready for would not be faced.

Metacognitive knowledge is a loop process: experiencing the situation as it is lived by the operator, then becoming aware of one's adaptation level, continuing with the development of heuristics, and finally anticipating new situations to come. Each transition stage provides an opportunity to transform and screen knowledge. This screening seems to correspond to limitations, once cognition biases are taken into account, but human actions do not seem notably degraded by their existence. They probably help protect a person's emotional make-up, and take part in its construction. Their heuristic nature makes them opportunistic, they only appear now and again, and are quite uncertain. However, all operators have them and use them.

It is important to note that, except in very limited professional contexts, individual professional feedback on performance is for the most part left to random confrontations and to the power play ruling any organization. This is most certainly a new area for investigation, since in numerous dynamic environments, the reinforcement of a person's metacognitive skills could be a way to increase operator effectiveness, individually as well as collectively.

5.2   Metacognition in ergonomics: regulating activity

Defining how operator activity is self-regulated provides inputs on the use of metacognitive knowledge. According to the operator's autonomy on the job and to the regulation requirements imposed by the task, it might seem possible to have differences in the way the operator's personality is expressed; selection of the metacognitive knowledge requiring implementation could also differ. However, it is necessary to determine a sufficient match between the operator and the processes and strategies employed throughout the activity.

This problem needs to be placed back in perspective. Operators have a specific autonomy level, defined by the organization of tasks or by their arrangement in a professional environment. If we consider autonomy to be the social expression of the "room for maneuver" within which a person can execute a specific professional activity, the way this autonomy is "occupied" is specific to the person.

Another dimension plays a great role on the job: "the pleasure derived from smooth operations". Metacognition models reported earlier use the monitoring of activity as the foundation of metacognition, since this monitoring results from and feeds into metacognitive activities. However, these models do not describe how this control loop materialized by metacognition is adjusted and fine-tuned at individual level.

The metacognitive monitoring of activity results in observations of gaps, and in performance assessment, which must be linked to satisfaction or dissatisfaction, depending on whether the person eventually notes that personal objectives were met or not. This pleasure derived from a job well done is closely connected to "resistance points" in the task, which can only be lifted through operator initiative and autonomy: differences existing between theoretical organizations and practical life, space occupied by human interactions, be they collective or hierarchical...

Self-confidence mechanisms express the pleasure of controlling an activity, which contributes internally to fine-tuning the way metacognitive knowledge is used. Being in possession of a metacognitive knowledge well adapted to the skills required by the situation probably reinforces this pleasure.

6.   CONCLUSION

The characteristics of dynamic environments (uncertainty, complexity, deadlines, impossibility to have complete knowledge) represent a problem for operators. These items are strongly associated to metacognitive control and regulation. Highlighting the role played by metacognition in ergonomics will undoubtedly help better understand operator activities. The existence of metacognitive knowledge provides information on the instability and uncertainty plaguing professional environments, and sheds light on the uncertainty persons may experience as to whether the personal skills available will be sufficient to meet situation demands. Situations are unstable, and operators are always uncertain about their professional performance.

This provides us with some keys to better understand how operators face the constraints of dynamic situations. They might not always have the best-suited skills, complexity may be challenging, but they usually manage to adequately control the situation. Studies of metacognition on the ergonomics of dynamic situations can undoubtedly contribute to help better understand the goal operators set for themselves when designing their activity. Seeing the role of metacognition from this new angle can also further contribute to fundamental metacognition research. Metacognitive knowledge is given an "ecological" dimension, modifying the analysis of performance and the role played by metacognition in the way the human mind operates.

Notes

[1] Ecological approach could be considered as a specific interest for studies of a person's interactions with environment, in the functional framework described by S.G. Paris in the same chapter.

[2] According to Maggi's (1996) interpretation, i.e. a job organised at operators' "discretion" allocates some initiative to these operators in making choices and decisions. Areas of action are allocated to operators, in a process ruled from the outside, and operators can make choices and decisions within this framework of dependence.

Chapter 4

Metacognition Triggered by a Social Aspect of Expertise
A Study in Speaking English as a Foreign Language

Patrick Chambres, Delphine Bonin, Marie Izaute and Pierre-Jean Marescaux
Université Blaise Pascal, Clermont-Ferrand, France

Key themes: Appl / Cont / Devl / Perf

Key words: Metacognition / Social aspects of expertise / Social interaction / English as a foreign language (EFL)

Abstract: The main goal of this study was to show how the social dimension of academic expertise affects cognitive and metacognitive activities in the context of speaking English as a foreign language. Two studies are reported in which pairs of French students interacted in English. The first study showed that students randomly said to be experts in English performed better than students said to be nonexperts. The second study replicated this effect, but showed that it was slightly modulated by the students' actual expertise in English. This research clearly supports the claim that in communicative interaction, what individuals are told about their own and their partner's expertise along a comparative dimension (here, English proficiency) is a determinant of the quantity and quality of their performance. A fictitious expert position, for example, has the power to promote metacognitive activity. These studies suggest that academic performance should be investigated not only from a cognitive and didactic standpoint, but also in terms of the social aspects of academic expertise.

1. INTRODUCTION

Research on metacogntion attempts to tackle various important questions. Koriat and Shitzer-Reichert (Chapter 1 Section I) report five of them: First, how accurate are metacognitive judgments, and what are the factors that affect their accuracy? Second, how do people monitor their own knowledge? Third, what are the processes that are responsible for the accuracy and inaccuracy of metacognitive judgments? Fourth, how does metacognitive monitoring control and guide information processing and action? Finally, how do the metacognitive processes of monitoring and control affect actual memory performance? The following chapter is an attempt to shed light on another important question: What makes people trigger metacognition?

According to Scott Paris, "... metacognition cannot be extricated from the context and appraised or studied independent of the task and purpose." (Paris, Chapter 1, Section 3). This means that the context in which people are required to perform a task is one of the important factors that determines cognitive and metacognitive activity. This suggests that modifying the characteristics of the situations in which people are involved could be an effective means of promoting people's metacognition and cognition without providing specific instructions (e.g., Chambres, 1993; Chambres, 1995). Manipulating the context would be an interesting means of improving cognition and metacognition in "less competent" subjects who are known to have difficulty producing efficient cognitive and/or metacognitive activity, or at the very least, do not do so spontaneously (e.g., Jacobs & Paris, 1987; Palincsar & Brown, 1987; Rouet & Eme, this section). When explicitly prompted along these lines, they have been shown to improve their performance (e.g., Cross & Paris, 1988; Jacobs & Paris, 1987; Paris, Cross, & Lipson, 1984; Paris & Oka, 1986; Palincsar & Ransom, 1988; Pressley, Borkowski, & O'Sullivan, 1985; Raphael & Pearson, 1985). Nevertheless, in cases of explicit induction of cognitive and metacognitive activity, the performance of low-achievement subjects rarely equals that spontaneously produced by the "more competent" subjects, and their performance deteriorates when the assistance or external prompting is no longer provided (e.g., Borkowski, Carr, Rellinger & Pressley, 1990; Duffy & Roehler, 1989; Pressley, Borkowski & O'Sullivan, 1985; Schunk & Rice, 1987).

Because any context is composed of many different elements, studying its impact on cognitive and metacognitive activity requires identifying and manipulating only some of its characteristics. Given that many situations in which people perform are social situations, we focused on the social aspects of context, and more precisely on how different positions of expertise[1] might influence metacognitive and cognitive activity. The purpose was to show that even without providing specific instructions to people asked to carry out a task, it was nevertheless possible to lead them to perform differently and to have more or less metacognitive activity depending on their social position of expertise (see also Valot, this section). Why choose position of expertise?

It has been shown that when two persons are physically or mentally together, they are led to compare themselves along many different dimensions, with many different goals (e.g., Brickman & Bulman, 1977; Gilbert, Giesler, & Morris, 1995; Goethals, 1986; Wood, 1989, 1996). When comparisons are made along an achievement dimension, individuals explicitly or implicitly assign each other positions of competence. Being more competent or less competent than others (relative competence) is the typical characteristic used to define experts and novices, respectively (e.g., Caverni, 1988; Frensch & Sternberg, 1989). Thus, an interaction between students with different levels of competence in an educational setting can be likened to an interaction between people with different levels of expertise (Chambres, 1995).

What is interesting is that the metacognitive superiority of experts has also been demonstrated for a variety of tasks and activities (e.g. Baker, 1985; Borkowski, Carr, Rellinger, & Pressley, 1990; Elio & Scharf, 1990; Lovelace, 1984; Lovelace & Marsh, 1985; Pressley, Borkowski & O'Sullivan, 1985). Experts' metacognitive superiority is probably due to their competence level, but it is also reasonable to claim that this superiority is due to their social position of expertise. It has been demonstrated that the social aspects of expertise can play a significant role in performance. For instance, the idea that beliefs about *relative proficiency* have an effect on how well a foreign language is used has already been demonstrated. A few findings (e.g., Gass & Varonis, 1985; Selinker & Douglas, 1985; Zuengler, 1989) indicate that an individual's ability to communicate effectively depends on how competent he/she feels (amount of expertise) compared to the conversation partner. The main finding has been that participants who believe they are more competent (more expert) than their partner on the comparative dimension in question dominate the situation. They generally take control over the interaction by playing the main role in the negotiation of meaning (Long, 1983; Pica, 1987), by interrupting or asking more questions to help their partner make statements that are clearer (Woken & Swales, 1989; Zuengler, 1989), and by providing most of the topics of discussion[1] (Takahashi, 1989; Zuengler, 1989). It has also been shown in educational settings that part of the cognitive efficiency of students sometimes stems more from their social position as experts (i.e., their public recognition as experts) than from their true capacities (Chambres, 1995; Chambres & Marescaux, 1998). Moreover, students' performance on a reaction time test before and after relative outcome feedback has been shown to change as a function of the relative position assigned (Rijsman, 1974, 1983). It has also been found that average students' self-beliefs are mainly determined by the specific social position of competence they are assigned (e.g., Chambres & Martinot, 1999, Experiment 4). Some studies have also demonstrated that expertise positions could determine the way people produce metacognitive activity (e.g., Chambres, 1995). Together, these results suggest that the performance of people in general, and of students in particular, depends not only on their true competence level (expert or nonexpert) but also on their perception of their relative degree of expertise.

Because people interact with many others, during their lifetime, they are led to experience numerous expertise positions. For instance, after having spent 3 years studying psychology at the university, a student should perceive her/himself as more expert than the first-year student with whom he/she is talking about research. On the other hand, only shortly afterwards, that same student may perceive her/himself as less expert than a conversational partner who is finishing a PhD. This is also the case in job contexts, where many people frequently have to alternate between interacting with superiors and interacting with subordinates. According to multiple-trace theories (e.g., Hintzman, 1986; Nosofsky, 1986), the everyday episodes we experience are memorized and later activated in similar situations. Moreover, Monteil showed that cognitive performance depends on the degree of consistency between the actual social context of performance and students' prior relevant social experience (Monteil, 1988, 1991, 1992; Monteil, Brunot & Huguet, 1996). For this reason, usual expertise and expertise assigned to people were simultaneously examined in the second experiment.

The main goals of the studies presented below can be summarized as follows: to show that different positions of expertise affect performance by changing the way individuals carry out metacognitive and cognitive processing, and to examine the interaction between the current and usual positions of expertise.

2.   STUDY 1

The academic context of this study was speaking English as a foreign language (EFL). Participants took a bogus English test and were then randomly assigned a nonexpert or expert position. Next they performed a metacognitive task in which they examined an essay in order to give advice to the writer. Then, working in pairs in which one student was assigned an expert position and the other, a nonexpert position before the interaction began, the participants had to converse in English as they jointly carried out the same metacognitive task. Last, participants were tested on what they had learned from the essay and then filled out a questionnaire about how they felt during the experiment.

2.1   Method

2.1.1   Participants

The participants were 30 twelfth-grade students. Their average age was 17 years 6 months. They worked in pairs. Each pair contained two same-sex students with a very similar grade-point average in English and a very similar score on the English pre-test. They were selected from two different classes to minimize familiarity within the pair.

2.1.2   Material and procedure

The study had four main phases:

1. *Preliminary expertise assignment.* The participants took an English test to assess their academic standing in English. Then each one was arbitrarily assigned a fictitious position of expertise (expert position vs. nonexpert position). (Contact authors for more details).

2. *Main experiment.* The main experiment took place four days later. The idea was to examine the students' English speaking behavior in order to infer three types of information for each student: (1) attitudes and feelings about the interactive situation, (2) planning, control, and regulation (metacognition), and (3) English speaking skills.

First, in two different rooms, two students with the same academic standing in English were individually given an English essay supposedly written by an anonymous student with the same proficiency in English. The task, which lasted 15 minutes, was to write down some pieces of advice (metacognitive activity) to help the writer improve his or her essay.

Next, the students were brought into the same room. They were told that, based on the initial test, they were better (expert position) or worse (nonexpert position) than their partner. In each pair, the nonexpert student was attributed a fictitious score between 125 and 131 and the expert student was attributed a score between 173 and 179. After being assigned to their positions of expertise, the participants were given 10 minutes to converse and write up a joint list containing pieces of advice about the essay they had examined individually beforehand. Their conversation was taped.

3. *Knowledge assessment.* The students' knowledge was assessed after the experimental phase. The participants were given 10 minutes to write in English what they could remember from the essay, by answering the following questions. Q1: What was the purpose of the essay? Q2: What are the advantages of urban life and rural life according to the author? Q3: What are the disadvantages of urban life and rural life according to the author?

4. *Post-experimental evaluation.* The post-experimental evaluation was designed to determine how the students felt while interacting with their partner. A questionnaire containing two questions ("Did you feel at ease during the interaction with your partner? Was speaking in English with a French partner a natural situation?") each accompanied by a continuous rating scale was administered. The scale was a horizontal line 100 mm long labeled with an extreme attitude at the left end and the opposite attitude at the right end. Participants were told to draw a vertical stroke through the scale, according to how they felt. Before the participants left the experimental room they were told they could freely talk about their feelings regarding the interaction situation. They were also informed of the real purpose of the study and told that the grade they had gotten on the English test was totally fictitious.

Students assigned the expert position, which granted them the social resource of expertise, were expected to be more dominant (e.g., produce more words, use fewer compensatory strategies), feel more at ease, and exhibit higher cognitive performance (e.g., have better recall scores) and metacognitive performance (e.g., give more pieces of advice) than students assigned the nonexpert position.

2.2   Results

Because the performance of students within each pair was dependent, one-factor analyses of variance (ANOVAs) with assigned expertise position as a within factor were performed on the different measures.

2.2.1   Students' attitudes and feelings while interacting (metacognitive experience)

The number of words produced by each member of a pair (AF1) was computed, because this parameter is usually considered as a sign of dominance in an interaction (Takahashi, 1989; Zuengler, 1989). Contrary to predictions, there was no significant effect of expertise on the number of words (AF1) produced while interacting (assigned nonexpert position (ANEP) = 152 vs. assigned expert position (AEP) = 168; $F(1, 14) = 1.63, p > .20$). Given that people have difficulty conversing in a foreign language (e.g., Poulisse, 1987; Faerch & Kasper, 1983), two compensatory strategies were identified: language switching (use of French words), and avoidance (totally or partially giving up on a message). ANEP students did more language switching than AEP students (ANEP = 3.07 vs. AEP = 1.47; $F(1, 14) = 8.73$, $p < .01$). They also produced more avoidance behavior (ANEP = 1.26 vs. AEP = .33; $F(1, 14) = 6.53$, $p < .005$). Assigned nonexperts felt less at ease than students with an expert position (ANEP = 47 vs. AEP = 64; $F(1, 14) = 7.72$, $p < .01$). They also reported that talking in English with a French-speaking partner was less natural than did assigned experts (ANEP = 45 vs. AEP = 61; $F(1, 14) = 4.39$, $p < .05$).

2.2.2 Students' metacognition

Previous work on text comprehension has shown that advice given to a writer is a good means of assessing metacognitive capabilities and metacognitive performance (e.g., Englert & Raphael, 1989; Englert, Raphael, Fear & Anderson, 1988; Garner & Alexander, 1989; Garner, Macready, & Wagoner, 1984; Jacobs & Paris, 1987; Paris, Lipson, & Wixson, 1983; Paris & Oka, 1986). Four "metacognitive" parameters were examined to evaluate metacognition: the number of pieces of advice students gave about the target essay before they were assigned a nonexpert or expert position, the number of pieces of advice students produced orally, the number of justifications associated with each orally-produced piece of advice, and the number of criticisms-clarifications-suggestions the students produced while interacting.

As expected, before being assigned a nonexpert or expert position, students of both types wrote the same number of pieces of advice about the target essay (ANEP = 3.73 vs. AEP = 4.27; $F(1, 14) = .63$, $p > .45$). During the interaction phase, there was an unpredicted lack of a significant difference between the number of pieces of advice produced orally by ANEP students and by AEP students (ANEP = 3.07 vs. AEP = 3.73; $F(1, 14) = 2.05$, $p > .10$). However, ANEP students gave fewer advice justifications than AEP students (ANEP = 2.60 vs. AEP = 4.00; $F(1, 14) = 9.44$, $p < .01$). There was no significant difference between ANEP and AEP students on the number of criticisms-clarifications-suggestions (ANEP = 1.20 vs. AEP = 1.87; $F(1, 14) = 1.68$, $p > .10$).

2.2.3 Students' cognition (implicit learning)

The idea here was to find out how much participants learned (implicitly[2]) from the target essay. A global "cognition" parameter was defined on the basis of the students' answers to assessment questions Q1, Q2, and Q3.

Contrary to predictions, ANEP students were significantly better at recalling information from the essay than AEP students (ANEP = 3.60 vs. AEP = 3.07; $F(1, 14) = 8.25$, $p < .01$).

2.3 Discussion

This study was conducted in order to determine whether a fictitious position of expertise can significantly affect students' metacognitive performance. The results revealed two important points. First, even though students assigned a fictitious expert position did not produce significantly more words than their partners, they behaved more like experts than the fictitious nonexperts did. In particular, they rarely displayed nonexpert behaviors like language switching or avoidance. Their position also led them to feel more at ease during the interaction phase than their nonexpert partners. Moreover, there was a correlation between the number of partner approvals (e.g., "OK, "I agree with you", "you're right") given by ANEP and AEP students, and the number of justifications for each piece of partner-produced advice (ANEP / AEP, $r = .82$, $p < .0002$; AEP / ANEP, $r = .78$, $p < .0007$). Another correlation was between the number of approvals (AF6) directed at the partner and the number of criticisms-clarifications-suggestions (e.g., "I don't think that giving more details is a good way to improve the text", "what do you mean by a better organization?", "we should first compare our pieces of advice, and then select the ones we agree about", "we should give an example of a sentence giving an opinion") that partner produced (ANEP / AEP, $r = .78$, $p < .0006$; AEP / ANEP, $r = .65$, $p < .01$). These correlations make it clear that the students' performance was highly dependent upon the way the interaction unfolded. Taking into account the number of justifications added to the pieces of advice, the results allow us to conclude that being fictitiously assigned an expert position leads to better metacognitive performance than being assigned a nonexpert one.

In sum, this experiment revealed that telling students they are experts has a positive impact on metacognition. Holding such a position is apparently an effective way to improve performance. However, as pointed out in the introduction, to go further into the study of this role and its impact on behavior and performance, an individual's usual position of expertise should also be considered. The idea in this case would be to determine how students' usual and current positions of expertise jointly influence metacognition. This issue was examined in Study 2.

3.   STUDY 2

The purpose of this study was to explore the effects of students' usual and current positions of expertise, on their metacognitive performance. The participants' actual academic standing in English was used as their usual position of expertise. In English classes, low achievers frequently experience being in a nonexpert position (usual nonexpert), while high achievers frequently experience being in an expert position (usual expert). A current expert position was assigned to participants as in Study 1. Participants worked in pairs and had to converse in English about two English texts.

3.1 Method

3.1.1 Participants

The participants were 32 (20 males and 12 females) freshmen at a French university. Their average age was 19 years 3 months.

3.1.2   Material and procedure

The study had four main phases:

1. *Expertise evaluation and preliminary expertise assignment.* The participants were told to report their final marks in English (an integer between 0 and 20) for the tenth, eleventh, and twelfth grades. This was used later to categorize them as usual nonexperts (UNEP) or usual experts (UEP) in English. Then they individually took an English test designed to assess the reliability of the three grades reported, and later to arbitrarily assign each student a fictitious position of expertise. The maximum score was 31. The tests were graded by two English teachers.

2. *Main experiment.* The main phase of the experiment took place a week later. The students worked in pairs. Each pair contained two same-sex students with a very similar grade-point average. They were selected from two different curricula (geography, etc.) to minimize familiarity within pairs. Participants were assigned an arbitrary expert position (assigned nonexpert vs. assigned expert) using the same procedure as in Study 1.

Then each student in a pair was given a different English text and a short answer test. Syntactic and semantic mistakes had been inserted in the texts to test the students' metacognitive ability to detect errors (Baker, 1985; Englert et al., 1988; Paris & Oka, 1986; Yussen & Smith, 1990). The six questions on the short answer test were about the content of the partner's text. They were in French, and the participants had to produce a written answer in French to avoid a confounding effect of their English comprehension and their ability to write in English. The students were allowed 10 minutes to exchange information before answering the test questions. They were seated at the same table, separated from each other by a dividing wall made of cardboard so they could not see their partner's text or gestures. The 10-minute exchange period was audiotaped.

3. *Knowledge assessment.* The students' knowledge was assessed immediately after the experimental phase. To evaluate overall text comprehension, the participants were told to try to remember all the information they could about their own text and about their partner's text. They also had to take a recognition test of five items from each text, and to write down on a sheet of paper the mistakes they found in their text.

4. *Post-experimental evaluation.* The post-experimental evaluation was designed to determine how the students felt while interacting with their partner. They were told to state whether they thought the task was too difficult or too long, and whether it was interesting. They were requested to freely make comments about their feelings. Afterwards, before the participants left the experimental room, the reasons for the study were stated and they were told that the grade they had gotten on the English test was totally fictitious.

It was predicted that if the current and usual positions of expertise are independent, then whatever their true scholastic achievement level, AEP students –who were currently endowed with the social resource of expertise– should be more dominant (e.g., produce more words and use fewer compensatory strategies), feel more at ease (e.g., daring to answer more questions about the partner's text), and have higher cognitive (e.g., get better recall and recognition scores) and metacognitive (e.g., find more mistakes) performance than ANEP students. In contrast, if the current and usual positions of expertise are dependent, then based on Monteil's findings (Monteil, 1988, 1991, 1992; Monteil et al., 1996), these various types of performance should be better in usual experts when they are assigned an expert position than when they are assigned a nonexpert position; the opposite should be true for usual nonexperts. And there should be no main effect of current position of expertise.

3.1.3 Results

As in Study 1, the behaviors of the two students in a given pair were considered dependent upon each other. So on the different measures, two-factor ANOVAs with usual expertise as a between-subject factor and assigned expertise as a within-subject factor were computed. Frequencies were analyzed using the chi-square test.

Students' attitudes and feelings during interaction

The students' attitudes were examined through 10 attitude/feeling parameters. The number of speaking turns and the number of words produced, which are measures usually considered to reflect feelings of dominance (e.g., Takahashi, 1989; Zuengler, 1989), were analyzed. Any communication or compensatory strategies used during the interaction, taken to be indicative of the participants' difficulty, were noted (e.g., Poulisse, 1987; Faerch & Kasper, 1983). Four strategies were considered to reflect avoidance and message reduction: asking the experimenter for help, expressing an idea in French, resorting to language switching, and giving up on a message. It was also assumed that if the students were confident in their abilities, they would try to answer more questions about their partner's text than if they were not confident. Finally, the way the participants perceived the task was examined.

Table 1 summarizes the data about the students' attitudes and feelings while interacting. In support of relative independence between usual expertise and current expertise, there were fewer speaking turns for ANEP students than for AEP students ($F(1, 14) = 9.44, p < .01$). ANEP students produced fewer words than AEP students ($F(1, 14) = 75.85, p < .0001$). There was no significant correlation between these two variables. ANEP students asked the experimenter for help more frequently than did AEP students ($F(1, 14) = 72.61, p < .0001$). Compared to AEP students, they also used their native language more ($F(1, 14) = 24.44, p < .0001$), gave up on a message more frequently ($F(1, 14) = 12.70, p < .003$), and tried to answer fewer questions about their partner's text.

Table 1.
Mean score on the 9 attitude/feeling parameters, as a function of the students' usual and current positions of expertise in Study 2.

	Current Position of Expertise		
Number of Speaking Turns	Assigned Nonexpert	Assigned Expert	*Mean*
Usual Nonexpert	9.00	10.13	9.56
Usual Expert	6.88	8.38	7.63
Mean	*7.94*	*9.25*	
Number of Words Produced	Assigned Nonexpert	Assigned Expert	*Mean*
Usual Nonexpert	77.63	93.00	85.31
Usual Expert	88.00	107.13	97.56
Mean	*82.81*	*100.06*	
Asking Experimenter for Help	Assigned Nonexpert	Assigned Expert	*Mean*
Usual Nonexpert	4.50	1.25	2.87
Usual Expert	2.88	0.38	1.63
Mean	*3.69*	*0.81*	

(to be continued)

Table 1. (continued)
Mean score on the 9 attitude/feeling parameters, as a function of the students' usual and current positions of expertise in Study 2.

	Current Position of Expertise		
Speaking in Native Language	Assigned Nonexpert	Assigned Expert	*Mean*
Usual Nonexpert	7.75	5.88	6.81
Usual Expert	2.50	1.25	1.88
Mean	*5.13*	*3.56*	
Language Switching	Assigned Nonexpert	Assigned Expert	*Mean*
Usual Nonexpert	1.25	1.38	1.31
Usual Expert	1.50	0.50	1.00
Mean	*1.38*	*0.94*	
Giving Up on a Message	Assigned Nonexpert	Assigned Expert	*Mean*
Usual Nonexpert	1.75	1.25	1.50
Usual Expert	2.50	0.63	1.56
Mean	*2.13*	*0.94*	
Questions Answered	Assigned Nonexpert	Assigned Expert	*Mean*
Usual Nonexpert	3.75	5.38	4.56
Usual Expert	6.00	6.00	6.00
Mean	*4.87*	*5.69*	
Students who said "Task too difficult"	Assigned Nonexpert	Assigned Expert	*Mean*
Usual Nonexpert	100.00%	100.00%	100.00%
Usual Expert	75.00%	62.50%	68.75%
Mean	*87.50%*	*81.25%*	
Students who said "Task too long"	Assigned Nonexpert	Assigned Expert	*Mean*
Usual Nonexpert	75.00%	100.00%	87.50%
Usual Expert	87.50%	50.00%	68.75%
Mean	*81.25%*	*75.00%*	
Students who said "Task interesting"	Assigned Nonexpert	Assigned Expert	*Mean*
Usual Nonexpert	75.00%	50.00%	62.50%
Usual Expert	37.50%	25.00%	31.25%
Mean	*56.25%*	*37.50%*	

Other data support the hypothesized interdependence between the expertise assigned to the students and their usual position of expertise. This was true for the number of times a message was dropped ($F(1, 14) = 4.26$, $p < .05$). A planned contrast analysis revealed no significant difference among usual nonexperts (UNEP) between the ones assigned a nonexpert position and the ones assigned an expert position ($F(1, 14) = 1.13$, $p > .30$). Among usual experts (UEP), the number of times a message was dropped was higher when they were assigned a nonexpert than an expert position ($F(1, 14) = 15.83$, $p < .001$). UNEP students tried to answer more questions about the partner's text when assigned a fictitious expert position than when assigned a nonexpert position (z = -2.10, p < .02). There was no assigned-position effect for UEP students (z = 0.0, p = 1.0). Finally, more UNEP students than UEP students found the task too long, but only when they were assigned an expert fictitious position (χ^2 (1, N = 16) = 5.33, p < .02).

Very little language switching was observed. No significant assigned-position effect or interaction was observed on this parameter. There were no significant effects on the way students perceived the difficulty or interest level of the task.

Students' metacognition

The students' metacognitive activity was examined via four parameters: the number of students who found any mistakes, syntactic mistakes, semantic mistakes in their text, and the number of clarifying questions asked of the partner (Garner & Alexander, 1989).

Table 2.
Number of students reporting any mistakes, syntactic mistakes, and semantic mistakes, as a function of usual and current positions of expertise in Study 2.

	Current Position of Expertise		
Any Mistakes	Assigned Nonexpert	Assigned Expert	*Total*
Usual Nonexpert	2	7	9
Usual Expert	6	7	13
Total	8	14	
Syntactic Mistakes	Assigned Nonexpert	Assigned Expert	*Total*
Usual Nonexpert	0	1	1
Usual Expert	1	1	2
Total	1	2	
Semantic Mistakes	Assigned Nonexpert	Assigned Expert	*Total*
Usual Nonexpert	2	7	9
Usual Expert	5	7	12
Total	7	14	
Number of Clarifying Questions	Assigned Nonexpert	Assigned Expert	*Mean*
Usual Nonexpert	6.62	4.63	5.63
Usual Expert	8.00	7.75	7.88
Mean	*7.31*	*6.19*	

The results are shown in Table 2. The data revealed that fewer ANEP students than AEP students identified mistakes in their own text (χ^2 (1, N = 32) = 5.24, p < .02). The difference mainly occurred on semantic mistakes (χ^2 (1, N = 32) = 6.78, p < .01).

For the number of clarifying questions, there was an interaction effect between usual and current position of expertise (F(1, 14) = 5.44, p < .04). A planned contrast analysis revealed that UNEP students asked more questions when assigned a nonexpert position than when assigned an expert position (F(1, 14) = 14.22,

$p < .002$). For UEP students, the number of clarifying questions was not affected by the assigned position of expertise ($F(1, 14) = .22, p > .50$).

Students' cognitions: production and learning

The students' English speaking skills were assessed through three parameters: the number of grammatically correct sentences produced, the number of compound sentences produced, and the diversity of the vocabulary. Their learning was evaluated by means of five parameters: the score obtained on the short answer test about the partner's text, the recall score on the student's own text, the recall score on the partner's text, the recognition score on the student's own text, and the recognition score on the partner's text.

As for the attitude parameters, many of the findings support the relative independence of usual expertise and current expertise (Table 3). For English-speaking abilities, ANEP students produced fewer correct sentences ($F(1, 14) = 21.46, p < .0001$) and fewer compound sentences ($F(1, 14) = 13.40$, $p < .003$), and used a less diverse vocabulary ($F(1, 14) = 21.46, p < .0001$) than AEP students. For learning, ANEP students got a lower score on the test about the partner's text than did AEP students ($F(1, 14) = 44.80, p < .0001$). They also got a lower score on recall of their own text ($z = -1.60, p < .05$) and on recall of their partner's text ($F(1, 14) = 21.46, p < .0001$). In contrast, ANEP and AEP students had an equivalent score on recognition of their own text ($F(1, 14) = .03, p > .50$) and of their partner's text ($F(1, 14) = .03, p > .50$).

Only one interaction between current and usual position of expertise was observed: it was on diversity of vocabulary. The most interesting point in this interaction effect is that UNEP students assigned a fictitious expert position had the same score as UEP students assigned a fictitious nonexpert position ($F(1, 14) = 0$, $p = 1$).

4.   DISCUSSION

As in Study 1, the present data revealed a main effect of fictitious expertise on several aspects of performance, and specifically on its metacognitive aspects. Among the results, it is interesting to note, for instance, that an expert position led students to dare more to answer the test questions. Moreover, AEP students identified more mistakes in their text than did ANEP students, showing the positive effect of fictitious expert position on metacognitive activity. Mainly in support of the independence hypothesis between usual expertise and current expertise, what Study 2 showed was that, as a whole, a fictitious position of expertise promotes metacognition and student effectiveness. This supports the idea that a social position of expertise has the power to spontaneously trigger metacognitive activity without specific prompting.

Table 3
Mean score on the 8 cognition parameters, as a function of the students' usual and current positions of expertise in Study 2.

	Current Position of Expertise		
Correct Sentences	Assigned Nonexpert	Assigned Expert	*Mean*
Usual Nonexpert	2.88	5.50	4.19
Usual Expert	4.63	6.00	5.31
Mean	*3.75*	*5.75*	
Compound Sentences	Assigned Nonexpert	Assigned Expert	*Mean*
Usual Nonexpert	0.75	1.75	1.25
Usual Expert	2.63	3.75	3.19
Mean	*1.69*	*2.75*	
Diversity of Vocabulary	Assigned Nonexpert	Assigned Expert	*Mean*
Usual Nonexpert	2.25	5.88	4.06
Usual Expert	5.88	7.50	6.69
Mean	*4.06*	*6.69*	
Correct Answers about Text	Assigned Nonexpert	Assigned Expert	*Mean*
Usual Nonexpert	4.00	6.50	5.25
Usual Expert	6.63	8.13	7.38
Mean	*5.31*	*7.31*	
Recall of Own Text	Assigned Nonexpert	Assigned Expert	*Mean*
Usual Nonexpert	0.50	1.50	1.00
Usual Expert	4.75	6.00	5.38
Mean	*2.63*	*3.75*	
Recall of Partner's Text	Assigned Nonexpert	Assigned Expert	*Mean*
Usual Nonexpert	0.75	1.50	1.13
Usual Expert	2.00	3.75	2.88
Mean	*1.38*	*2.63*	
Recognition of Own Text	Assigned Nonexpert	Assigned Expert	*Mean*
Usual Nonexpert	3.13	3.75	3.44
Usual Expert	3.63	2.88	3.25
Mean	*3.38*	*3.31*	
Recognition of Partner's Text	Assigned Nonexpert	Assigned Expert	*Mean*
Usual Nonexpert	2.88	2.38	2.63
Usual Expert	2.13	2.75	2.44
Mean	*2.50*	*2.56*	

5.   GENERAL DISCUSSION AND CONCLUSION

The present experiments were prompted by the following question: Is modifying the characteristics of the context in which people are involved an efficient means of determining (promoting) metacognition and cognition even without providing specific instructions? The answer is clearly positive. Except for the ambiguous interaction effect between usual and current expertise for the number of clarifying questions (Study 2), most of the results reported here support the hypothesized influence of expertise position on the metacognitive and cognitive performance of students interacting in English as a foreign language (EFL). Consistently in both studies, students who were assigned a fictitious expert position (AEP) behaved more like experts than did students assigned a fictitious nonexpert position (ANEP), generally carried out more efficient metacognitive processing, and also produced better cognitive performance. As expected, it seems that an expert social position has the power to put one's metacognitive and cognitive potential to work and that a nonexpert social position, on the contrary, has the power to lead people to under-utilize their metacognitive and cognitive potential. What could lead students assigned an expert position to have spontaneously greater metacognitive and cognitive efficacy than students assigned a nonexpert position?

Schematically, one could say that a student's usual position of expertise reflects his/her cognitive resources, while a fictitious position of expertise is a social resource. One can assume in the present study that the social resource (the fictitious expert position) enhanced knowledge accessibility in memory. According to researchers who study the working self-concept (e.g., Markus & Kunda, 1986; Markus & Wurf, 1987; Markus & Nurius; 1986; Ruvolo & Markus, 1992), there are connections between certain characteristics of the situation and certain self-conceptions in memory. It is reasonable to go further and suggest that there are specific connections between certain characteristics of the situation and certain metacognitive activities, and between certain types of self-conceptions and certain metacognitive activities. These connections would be constructed through the subject's experiences. So a particular social position operating as an activation cue could lead to different effects, depending on the subject's personal history. In any case, social position appears to be a determinant of access to self-knowledge (Chambres & Martinot, 1999) and also to metacognitive processes, acting as a priming effect.

The present study provides some evidence that metacognitive activity can be induced by the social aspects of the situation, and more specifically, by the social position of expertise granted to the subject (characteristics of the social situation). Accordingly, persons who are good at a task (experts) can usually be differentiated from those who are less so (nonexperts) by the fact that their spontaneous metacognitive activity is greater in quantity and in quality. This may stem from a link between the expert social position and the expert processing mode, where planning, assessment, and regulation (i.e., metacognitive activity) play a crucial role. This mode, constructed gradually by the repetition of situations in which the subject is granted an expert status, is more likely to be implemented when the situation in which the subject is inserted places him/her in an expert role. The expert social position —among others no doubt— may reveal the subject's cognitive potential. It may promote the activities and performance characteristic of an expert. As such, if part of what differentiates experts from novices lies in their metacognitive activity, and if the social position partially determines the activity of experts, then a social insertion in which subjects perceive themselves as experts should lead to efficient metacognitive activity. Consequently, these subjects should excel to a greater extent than subjects led to see themselves as novices.

To conclude, two points brought out by the present study are worth stressing. Firstly, it seems important to consider performance as being more than just the consequence of the cognitive characteristics of the people who are performing. Secondly, the social aspects of expertise have to be regarded as a key component of metacognitive and cognitive expertise.

Notes

[1] The pragmatic index considered in the literature is the number of words produced.

[2] No instructions were given.

IV

WHAT CAN NONEXPERTS IN METACOGNITION OFFER TO METACOGNITIVE RESEARCH?

What can metacognition offer to them?

Chapter 1

The Metacognitive Implications of the Implicit-Explicit Distinction

Zoltan Dienes and Josef Perner
University of Sussex UK
University of Salzburg, Germany

Key themes: Defn / Proc / Theor

Key words: Implicit learning / Implicit knowledge / Higher order thought theory / Representation

Abstract: In this chapter we establish what it is for something to be implicit. The approach to implicit knowledge is taken from Dienes and Perner (1999) and Perner and Dienes (1999), which relates the implicit-explicit distinction to knowledge representations. To be clear about exactly what our claims are we first discuss what a representation is, what it is for a representation to represent something implicitly or explicitly and apply those concepts to knowledge. Next we show how maximally explicit knowledge is naturally associated with consciousness (according to the higher order thought theory). Then we discuss the relationships between explicit knowledge and metacognition, where metacognition is considered in terms of both its monitoring and control aspects, to shed light on conscious and unconscious perception, episodic memory, and volitional control. We will then show how implicit learning should be viewed in metacognitive terms, and conclude that people's relative lack of metaknowledge in implicit learning paradigms justifies the claim that people have acquired genuinely implicit knowledge.

1.   INTRODUCTION

In this chapter we will consider the relation between the implicit-explicit distinction and metacognition (Reder, 1996). To understand this relationship we will need to first consider what a representation is, because we subscribe to a representational theory of knowledge; i.e., we consider that when a person occurrently knows something, that is because they have formed a representation (be it connectionist or symbolic or something else) about what they know. We indicate how a representation can represent different contents implicitly or explicitly, and use this to derive a hierarchy of explicitness of knowledge (Dienes & Perner, 1999; Perner & Dienes, 1999). Explicitness will then be related to consciousness via the higher order thought theory. With this framework in place, we can finally consider metacognition in its monitoring and control aspects, and then look at the metacognitive approach to implicit learning.

2.   REPRESENTATIONS AND CONSCIOUSNESS

In order to clarify the relation between metacognition and the implicit-explicit distinction, we will first need to be clear about what representations are, and how they are related to consciousness. One can find considerable disagreement in the literature about the relation between representations and consciousness. For example, on the one hand, Whittlesea and Dorken (1997) asserted that people in general "do not have direct, conscious access to those representations" that underlie performance on tasks (p. 64); on the other hand, Dulany (1996) and Perruchet, Vinter, and Gallego (1997) believed that all mental representations are conscious. In order to make meaningful claims of either sort, we must first be clear what we mean by representation.

So what is a representation? Consider an unambiguous case of a representation: A map of a town. In this case, and in general, a representation consists of something physical (the representational medium, for example, paper and ink) that is about something else (the representational content, for example, the town). But how is it that an object –paper and ink– can acquire meaning, a content? Or consider a case closer to psychology. How could, say, a pattern of firing of a group of neurons in a person represent a cat? You might suggest –taking note of the way that neurophysiologists determine what a cell, or group of cells, code– that the pattern represents a cat if it is correlated with the presence of cats: Whenever you show a cat to the person, those neurons fire. Unfortunately, this does not quite do; it does not allow the person to misrepresent. If he saw a skunk on a dark night, the same neurons might fire. On the correlation story he has not misrepresented the skunk as a cat; he has just correctly detected a cat-OR-skunk-on-a-dark-night. But representations can misrepresent and any theory of representation must allow for that.

Correlations between patterns of neural activity and cats arise in people due to an evolutionary or learning history that has selected that pattern of activity because of the function it performs in dealing with cats. One might say the pattern has the function of indicating cats; or the function of producing further internal or behavioural reactions appropriate for dealing with real or imagined cats. According to one dominant (and we think persuasive) approach in philosophy, representations represent something precisely because of the functional role they play. Thus, on Dretske's (1988) approach, if A has the function of indicating B then A represents B. For example, if a pattern of neuronal activity has the function of indicating cats, then it represents "cat". If it fires because of a skunk on a dark night, then it has misrepresented the skunk as a cat. Function can be produced by evolution or learning, or, in the case of artifacts like a map, by our intentions.

Is there any reason why all representations, thus defined, should be conscious? Not at all, maps are not conscious. Imagine building a robot to interact with the world, and the robot will be conscious of some aspects of his world. It may be useful to have the activity in some circuit have the function of indicating a particular internal or external state of affairs. There seems to be no a priori reason why the content of all such representations should constitute the content of the robot's conscious experience. Perhaps the representation was useful simply temporarily to inform another process downstream of processing; or the problems it is used to solve are "local" problems that do not need to concern the processing system generally. In any case, the extent to which people have interesting unconscious representations is an open question, and an empirical question given a theory of consciousness.

The relationship between consciousness and representation may be partly open but the relationship is not one of complete independence. Our conscious states are typically characterized by being about things (Brentano, 1874); thoughts are always about what is thought, desires are always about what is desired. Some argue that all conscious states are about something (e.g., Tye, 1995), but it is enough to note that many conscious states are about something. Given a materialist theory of the mind, it follows that conscious states must be (in at least many cases) representational, because the states have a physical embodiment (the representational medium; that is, part of the brain) and are about something else (the representational content, the content of the conscious state). So the content of consciousness is just the content of some representation. In this sense we can say that at least some mental representations are conscious.

What makes some representations conscious (when others are not)? One might answer that all **mental** representations are conscious (e.g., Perruchet et al., 1997). One then needs an account of what makes a representation "mental". "Mental" has been defined as any state that could in principle become conscious (Searle, 1990). For example, states of detectors in the liver signaling the presence of glucose could not become conscious states, so they are not mental. Their unconscious status is no more mysterious than a map not being conscious (though the consciousness of mental states would remain mysterious). How does one view unconscious perception or unconscious learning if one assume that all mental states are conscious? A possible argument is that subliminal perception is not possible, because perception is a mental state, and all mental states are conscious. We believe this position has been falsified by the evidence (e.g., Debner & Jacoby, 1994; Merikle & Joordens, 1997). But a retreat position is available: the perceptual states controlling behaviour in a subliminal perception experiment are obviously ones that can not be made conscious, so they are not mental. Since this retreat position is always available (unless further stipulations about what counts as mental are made) whether the experimental evidence supports subliminal perception or not, it is not clear to us what work is being done by the claim "all mental representations are conscious". We will argue that some representations controlling behaviour are conscious, and that it is possible and testable that other representations controlling behaviour (occurrent representations resulting from perception, occurrent representations resulting from learning) are unconscious. In order to make this argument, we will need to distinguish implicit from explicit representations (according to the framework of Dienes and Perner, 1999) and employ a theory of consciousness (the higher order thought theory). Finally, we will be in a position to discuss how metacognition (the monitoring and control of such representations) is related to the implicit-explicit distinction.

3.   IMPLICIT VERSUS EXPLICIT REPRESENTATION AND KNOWLEDGE

According to Dretske (1988), if it is the function of state A in a representational medium to indicate B then A represents B. A has the function of indicating B partly because the state of A is used as information by the rest of the system to respond appropriately to B. Now for A to indicate anything, for it to be used as information, requires that at a minimum that the representational medium can go into two states. For example, if A represents "cat", then there should be one state for "cat" and another state for "not a cat" or "uncertain if cat or not-cat". We will define the explicit content of a representation in the following way: Distinctions (e.g., cat/not-cat) are explicitly represented only if there are corresponding distinctions in the representational medium. However, the explicit content of a representation rarely constitutes its entire content, as we will now begin to see.

A representation may express content that has a structure. But there is no reason why all the elements and relations in that structure must themselves be explicitly represented. Consider a device for distinguishing different animals. If you put a cat in front of its sensors, it goes into a "cat" state; if you put a dog there, it goes into a "dog" state, and so on. Thus, the distinction between cat and dog is explicitly represented, because differences in the device's representational medium correspond to the different animals placed before it. (Note that the representation explicitly represents "cat" because there are other representations that contrast with it.) But the full content expressed by the representation when the device goes into its "cat" state is more than just "cat"; rather the device is indicating (and has the function to indicate) at least that "this is a cat". We could not say anything less, for example, that it only expresses knowledge of cat-ness, or of the concept of cat. The device can convey information that "this is a cat", or "this is a dog" by going into different states. Yet, what are made explicit within the vocabulary of this device are only the properties of being-a-cat, being-a-dog, etc. That it is "this" rather than "that" object that is a cat is an element of the structure of the expressed content, an element that helps constitute the meaning of the representation, but there is no difference in the representational medium that corresponds to "this" rather than "that".

Based on the foregoing logic, we will distinguish explicit representation from something that is only implicitly represented in the following way: Any environmental feature or state of affairs that is not explicitly represented but forms part of the representational content is represented implicitly. Thus, in the example of the animal detector, the animal is represented explicitly, but the fact that it was **this** animal is represented only implicitly (the animal is explicit but the "this" is implicit). To give another example, the function of a bee dance is to indicate the location of nectar; this is its representational content. It represents the direction of the nectar explicitly, because the angle of the dance varies systematically with the direction of the nectar. However, the fact that it is about **nectar** (see Millikan, 1993, for the argument that the bee dance is indeed about nectar) is represented only implicitly. We will now apply the implicit-explicit distinction to what it is to have knowledge.

What is it to have knowledge? First there is the content of the knowledge: A proposition, i.e., something that can be true or false. This usually involves predicating a property (e.g., "is bald") to an individual (e.g., "the king of France").[1] Second, the content must be a fact at a given time. Third, there is a person ("I") having an appropriate relationship to this proposition, i.e., a relationship of knowing rather than, for example, wishing, guessing, considering or dreaming.

A representation functioning as knowledge need not make all this structure explicit. The following does constitute a fully explicit representation of the knowledge that the present king of France is bald "I know (that it is a fact) that the present king of France is bald". We will now consider ways in which a person may not represent this state of affairs fully explicitly, according to the taxonomy described by Dienes and Perner (1999).

At one extreme, the person may explicitly represent only a property of a presented object or event. For example, when a person is flashed the word "butter", during perception of the event they may not form an explicit representation of the full proposition "The word in front of me has the meaning butter". Instead the meaning butter is activated but it is not predicated of any particular individual (i.e., "the word in front of me"). The representational medium contains no distinction that indicates different individuals. So the full content of the proposition is not made explicit. But if the person reliably acts appropriately towards the stimulus (in a certain context) the representation is functioning as knowledge. Thus, its status as knowledge, the fact that the feature applies to a particular individual (presented word) is implicitly represented, by our definition. This is maximally implicit knowledge on our scheme. Consider for example a blindsight patient presented with a square or a circle in their blind field. They can reliably indicate whether the object is a square or a circle, but provide no evidence that anything more than "square" or "circle" has been explicitly represented about the fact that it is a square or circle presented to them (e.g., Weiskrantz, 1988).

We suggest that under subliminal conditions only the properties of a stimulus (the kind of stimulus) get explicitly represented (e.g., the word "butter"), not the fact that there is a particular stimulus event that is of that kind. This would be enough to influence indirect tests, in which no reference is made to the stimulus event (e.g., naming milk products), by raising the likelihood of responding with the subliminally presented stimulus ("butter" is listed as a milk product more often than without subliminal presentation). The stimulus word is not given as response to a direct test (e.g., Which word did I just flash?) because there is no representation of any word having been flashed. Performance on a direct test can be improved with instructions to guess, because this gives leave to treat the direct test like an indirect test, just saying what comes to mind first.[2]

At the next stage of explicitness, the person represents the full content of the proposition (i.e., including the individual that the property is predicated to) and then represents the temporal context of the fact and whether indeed it is a fact or not. This extra representation of time and factuality may seem gratuitous, but it is important for explicit memory rather than mere implicit memory (which can be just be based on maximally implicit knowledge, where just a property is represented explicitly): To recollect the past one must represent the past events as having taken place in the past.

At the final stage of explicitness, one represents that one knows a particular proposition. For example, in the case of perception, the knowledge is based on seeing and the perceptual process may yield the representation "I see that (it is a fact that) the word in front of me is butter". This representation would enable a person to confidently report on seeing the word butter; in other words it would enable conscious perception, as we will now see.

4.   HIGHER-ORDER THOUGHT THEORY OF CONSCIOUSNESS

What would make the perception of the word in front of you being butter a conscious perception? In general, under what conditions is a mental state (sensation, thought, desire, etc) a conscious mental state? We will answer this question by reference to the higher order thought theory of consciousness (e.g., Armstrong, 1980; Rosenthal, 1986, 2000a,b,c; Carruthers, 1992, in press), in particular Rosenthal's higher order thought theory, a philosophical theory of consciousness we find appealing for its simplicity and elegance. In order to have an account of a mental state, like a thought, being conscious, we need to consider the logical possibility of thoughts being unconscious, so we can consider what would make the mental state conscious independently of simply being a mental state. That is, to say that someone is thinking, we should not presume that they must be consciously thinking; they could be unconsciously thinking. With that proviso in mind, we can consider how we become conscious of events and things. In general, I can be conscious of things in two ways; by perception and by thinking. I can be conscious of a problem by thinking about a problem; I can be conscious of you by seeing you or just by thinking about you being there. If we flash a person either the word "butter" or the word "grass", and they can later make a forced choice discrimination above chance about the identity of the word, we can say he is conscious of the word because he saw the word. But by "conscious of the word" we do not necessarily mean consciously aware of the word or that he beheld the word with a conscious mental state. In a sense he is conscious of the word; but the seeing itself need not be a conscious mental state. For a mental state to be a conscious mental state, we should be conscious of the mental state. We could not claim that a person has a conscious mental state, and also claim that the person is not conscious of being in the mental state. According to Rosenthal, the relevant way of being conscious of the mental state is to have a thought about the mental state. For example, if the mental state is seeing that the word is butter, one becomes conscious of the mental state by thinking "I see that the word is butter"; because the state of affairs of the word being butter is now beheld with a conscious mental state, the person is consciously aware of the word being butter.

In general, according to these theories, it is a necessary and sufficient condition for conscious awareness of a fact that I entertain a second order thought that represents the first order mental state (in the example, the first order mental state is seeing that the word is butter; the second order thought is representing that I am seeing that the word is butter) But this is just the same as our requirement for knowledge to be fully explicit: The person must represent that they know (for example by seeing) that the word is butter. Our framework shows why explicitness is often intuitively felt to have something to do with consciousness.

The second order thought does not make itself, the second order thought, conscious, it just makes the first order thought that it is about conscious. The second-order thought "I see that the word is butter" only makes one consciously aware of the word being butter, not the fact that one sees that the word is butter. To be aware that one knows it by seeing, there needs to be a third-order thought that makes the second order thought conscious. Typically, when we consciously know a fact, we also know how we consciously know it. Normally, one could not sincerely claim "I am conscious of the word being butter" and at the same time deny having any knowledge of whether one sees the word, or hears about it, and so on. This fact provides strong evidence for higher order thought theories in humans. Presumably whatever mechanism produces second order thoughts is just the same that produces third order thoughts; and it would seem highly plausible that if a representation was available to the mechanism for second order thought, the output of the mechanism would be available for third order thoughts. At least, that would seem to be the simplest way for evolution to have set things up.[3] Thus, typically, according to the theory and as supported by the facts, one would expect people to be able to say how they are currently aware of something if they are able to say they are currently aware of it at all.[4]

5. METACOGNITION: MONITORING

According to Nelson and Narens, (1990) metacognition has both monitoring and control aspects to it. In this section we will consider metacognition as monitoring; in the next section we will consider the control aspect of metacognition. Metacognition literally means cognition about cognition. There is thus an obvious relation to higher order thought theory (a link discussed by Rosenthal, 2000a,b,c), since the latter claims that conscious mental states arise exactly from thinking about thinking. Fully explicit knowledge, in our sense, is thus a case of metacognition; what implicit representations lack is metacognitions about them (cf Kinoshita, this volume). Paris (this volume) discusses when metacognitions are harmful, benign, or useful; one use, of which we can be grateful, is in making us consciously aware.[5] Every moment of our waking life we are engaged in automatic and unconscious metacognitions providing us with all our conscious experiences. This is the pervasive sea of metacognitive monitoring in which we live.

Rosenthal argues that higher order thoughts make us consciously aware when they are (a) assertoric (they authoritatively assert that we are in a mental state); and (b) appear unmediated; that is, they are not the result of a conscious inference. If in a subliminal perception experiment, a subject thinks "I did not see anything. But, since I am forced to guess, 'butter' comes to mind easily. I must have seen the word butter", there is a higher order thought about seeing the word butter. But the thought arises as a conscious inference, and thus it does not make the subject conscious of seeing that the word was butter. The subject may just be conscious of inferring or guessing that the word was butter, but not conscious of seeing. An unmediated thought to the effect that they are guessing is formed, but not to the effect that they are seeing.

Further, according to our arguments, if a subject in a subliminal perception experiment when flashed the word "butter" just forms the maximally implicit representation "butter", the subject does not have any conscious experience caused by the representation. According to Dulany (1996) and Tzelgov, Ganor, and Yehene (1999), the formation of any semantic representation (e.g., the maximally implicit representation "butter") is sufficient for conscious experience. If, for example, one forced the subject to choose a word that may have been just flashed the subject may choose "butter" at above chance rates; therefore, the argument goes, the subject must have consciously seen the word butter. In this situation, according to us, the mechanisms brought into play by the attempt to guess use the unconscious representation "butter" to make a guess, and thus make it conscious as a guess. But the subject is not conscious of the seeing as seeing, so in this sense we can say the subject saw the word only unconsciously. (Further, conscious awareness of the word even just as a guess was only brought about by probing for the word; it was not automatically produced by the act of seeing.)

Searle (1983) argued that when we see an event, we experience the event as directly causing the visual experience. We don't have to follow a chain of reasoning to know the event caused the experience; the knowledge that the event caused the experience is part of the experience itself. That is, you know non-inferentially that the word "butter" directly caused your knowledge that the word butter was there. This is consistent with our claim that inferentially guessing cannot be regarded as a case of conscious seeing. But if the non-inferential understanding that the event directly caused the visual experience was necessary to all conscious seeing (as opposed to e.g., guessing what you must have seen), then it seems to follow that young children and animals do not consciously see (an implication pointed out by Armstrong, 1991), because they cannot make the conceptual distinction between experience and reality needed to understand that the experience was caused by the reality (Flavell, Flavell, & Green, 1983). The answer is that conscious seeing does not require this understanding; it just requires one to think "I see that the word is butter" with conviction and in a way that appears unmediated. Given an adult's understanding of seeing, "seeing that the word is butter" will mean to the adult that that the relevant state of affairs in the world –the word on the screen being butter– caused the visual experience, and this fact itself will appear (at least on reflection) to be part of the visual experience (giving vision what Searle calls a "self-referential" nature). That is, self-referentiality is part of how the adult understands vision; so when the adult thinks "I see that the word is butter", the self-referentiality is implicit in the use of the representation "see". However, the self-referentiality does not need to be explicitly represented in each episode of conscious seeing. It will be explicitly represented whenever the adult reflects on the seeing process; thus, it will seem to the adult that the experience of self-referentiality is always part of seeing. In fact, it only arises when the adult forms appropriate third-order thoughts. It is only there when the adult looks for it; thus, it appears to be always there. The child or the animal do not need to understand that seeing works this way; they just need some more primitive concept of seeing. Thus, children and animals, by using such concept of seeing as they do have, can have conscious visual experiences (but only when they use this concept in an assertoric way that does not appear mediated to them).

If one merely thought "I see that the word is butter", one would consciously see that the word is butter, but only in a conceptual way. Normally visual experiences have content that cannot be exhaustively described by concepts (e.g., Chrisley, 1996); for example, in looking at an apple, one may experience that the apple has a fine-grained shade of red for which one has no concept. This content not captured by the concepts the person actually possess has been called non-conceptual content (Cussins, 1992). Visual experiences normally have distinctively visual non-conceptual content. According to Rosenthal, we are conscious of our experiences only in the way they are represented to us by our higher order thoughts. Thus, when we are consciously aware of non-conceptual content, we must have predicated the non-conceptual content to the relevant object or event we are beholding and formed a higher order thought to the effect that we are seeing that non-conceptual content. The non-conceptual content becomes part of the higher order thought; only in this way could we be consciously aware of the non-conceptual content. Because such visual experiences have distinctively visual non-conceptual content, reflection on those experiences leads one to think that they are obviously visual experiences. But once again, one is consciously aware of the visual nature of those experiences only when one reflects on them with relevant third-order thoughts. It will seem to us that their visual nature is always apparent to us, because whenever we check, it is apparent to us for reasons (the presence of relevant non-conceptual content) that have been true all along.

Everything we have said above about perception applies to memory, with the necessary changes. For us to have an episodic memory of seeing butter on the list we must think the second-order thought[6] "I remember that I experienced that butter was on the list" with conviction and in a direct and unmediated way; i.e., the truth of the thought does not appear to the person to be known as a consequence of other thoughts and events. Such an authoritative unmediated thought is sufficient for us to know consciously something happened as part of our personal past. Genuine episodic memory also involves us being aware of the act of memory as an act of memory, and this involves forming a relevant third order thought to the effect that one knows one is remembering; just as in the visual case, where a third order thought is necessary to be aware one is seeing. Just as in vision where most acts of conscious seeing may only involve relevant second order thoughts, many acts of episodic memory (particularly when one is engrossed in memory) may involve only second order thoughts; but the third order thought will be generated whenever internally or externally probed for and help constitute the full experience of remembering.

Dokic (1997; see also Perner, 2000a) considered a case where a person believes they have experienced an event, but wonders if he believes this because he is really remembering or because he was told as a child. He asks his parents, and the parents assure him that he really experienced the event and no-one could have told him. So the person forms the representation "I remember I experienced the event", but this does not seem to be a genuine case of episodic memory. The reason why it does not seem to be genuine is for the same reasons guessing in subliminal perception experiments is not genuine conscious seeing. In the memory case, the person initially believes the thought "I experienced the event" may have been known by being told, and thus it is not a case of remembering one experienced the event at all. The parents' later comment leads the person to think "I remember I directly experienced the event" only as a conclusion derived from other people's comments, and one is conscious of its inferential nature (as in our vision example). If the person later forgot the conversation he had with the parents, but now experienced the thought "I remember I experienced the event" in what seems to him to be a direct and authoritative way then he would experience knowledge of the event as an episodic memory. If in fact the event never happened (he and his parents were wrong that it had happened) then he would still have an episodic memory, albeit a false one.

Adults understand memory in a self-referential way (Searle, 1983), they understand remembering must involve a real event directly causing the memory, and that the knowledge that the real event caused the memory must itself be caused by the event. This understanding of remembering can be implicit in the meaning of "remember" and need not be explicitly represented on every occasion something is remembered; the conscious awareness of having experienced a past event comes simply from an assertoric and non-inferential thought to the effect that one is remembering. A further relevant assertoric and non-inferential third order thought that one knows one is remembering provides the conscious awareness that one is remembering. As further argued by Perner (2000a), genuine recollections will involve representing the sensory content (and hence the non-conceptual content) involved in experiencing the event, representing it as part of the remembered event. This later step (combined with a relevant third order thought) creates what would be a conscious memory on Jacoby's (1991) account; and a "remember" rather than a "know" response according to the remember/know procedure (Gardiner, 1988; Tulving, 1985).

6.   METACOGNITION: CONTROL

In this section we discuss metacognition as a control process. As well as providing us with all our conscious experiences, another useful aspect of metacognition is that it also enables all acts of volitional control, as we shall now see. Almost continuously throughout our waking life we are engaged in automatic and unconscious metacognitions providing us with volitional control over our actions and mental processes. This is the pervasive sea of metacognitive control in which we live.

When we cognitively control our own cognitions, we are engaged in metacognition. Voluntary control is an example of metacognition. Voluntary or intentional control of knowledge means that one can use it intentionally. That is, one needs to represent that one intends to use that knowledge. One needs to reference the appropriate response as *something intended* and not, for example, as an existing fact. Thus, the factuality (or otherwise) of the content of the knowledge and the mental state by which one considers the content (i.e., desire) must be made explicit. In performing a voluntary action, the action is voluntary by virtue of forming a higher order thought to the effect that one is intending the action; implicit in the meaning of intending for adults will be the understanding that the action is performed by way of carrying out the intention of performing that very action (cf Searle, 1983). This analysis shows why the common notion that voluntary control is associated with explicitness is justified. Voluntary control is also shown to be essentially a metacognitive process, to involve second order thoughts, and hence consciousness.[7]

Perner (1998, in press b) presented a dual control model of action, in which there are two levels of control, vehicle and content control. Control of action can occur just at the level of representational vehicle: An action schema comes to control behaviour simply because of the existing associative links between the representation of current actual conditions –the schema's triggering conditions– and the production of the action. In this case, the action schema that controls behaviour is the one with most activation, and here activation is a property of the representational vehicle; the degree of activation does not represent the content of the schema, it just determines the probability with which it will control behaviour. In contrast to vehicle control, control of action can occur at the level of representational content. A representation is formed (e.g., from verbal instructions or mental planning) of the required mapping between conditions and actions ("if condition C then do action A") or simply of the desired action ("do A"). In content control, it is the content of this representation that determines which schema "comes to control behaviour; that is, the schema with the conditions and action described by this representation. This representation must represent conditions and actions at least fact explicitly because it states a hypothetical "If condition C..."; it should not in itself lead to registering that condition C has obtained, it simply states what to do if condition C were to obtain.[8] The representation also represents the action-to-be-performed as something needed and is therefore not actually a fact; the goal state of the completed action must therefore be represented fact explicitly. In content control, the representation of the appropriate condition-action mapping causes the relevant action schema to control behaviour, regardless of the existing strength of associative links between current actual conditions and particular actions. In vehicle control, there are the conditions and actions represented in the schema, which do not need to be represented fact explicitly; in content control, there is, in addition to the representations embodied in the schema themselves, the occurrent fact-explicit representation of the required actions that determines schema choice. For example, consider driving from work to the supermarket and the route taken is in part the same as the more normal route from work to back home. If one did not keep actively in mind the new action required at a crucial juncture (so content control fails) one would end up driving home (vehicle control determines behaviour; the action most strongly associated with current conditions is performed). The implicitly acquired control described by Reder (this volume) is an example of vehicle control.

Some tasks (the executive function tasks described by Norman and Shallice, 1986) necessarily involve content control, for example, inhibiting normal reactions in order to do something novel in a situation (Perner, 1998). This type of task requires one represent the novel action as something required, and therefore it must be represented fact explicitly. Conscious intentions use content control, because they represent desired condition-action mappings, i.e., they use fact-explicit representations to control schema choice. Conversely, vehicle control does not require conscious intentions. For example, Debner and Jacoby (1994) flashed a word to subjects and then asked them to complete a word stem with anything EXCEPT the word that had been flashed. The conscious intention to not use that word could inhibit the action schema responsible for completing with that word and allow other action schemata to control behaviour. Thus, for words flashed for a long enough duration, stems were completed with those words at below baseline levels. However, if words were flashed very quickly, they were not consciously perceived, no conscious intention could be formed that inhibited their normal use, and an action schema was chosen simply based on which became activated most strongly by the triggering stem. That is, only vehicle control was possible. In this situation, subjects completed stems with the flashed words at above baseline levels. (Of course, control occurs in the context of a hierarchy of goals; even vehicle control is relative to this context. Subjects would have had content control of the general action "complete the stem with **some** word".)

Content control only actually requires fact explicit representation; it does not require full explicitness, so it does not actually require **conscious** representations of required condition-action mappings. Perner (2000b) pointed out that our framework predicted the possibility of content control (i.e., the control required in executive function tasks) without conscious awareness. This seemed an unlikely prediction and led Perner to suggest the framework should be sent back to the drawing table. In fact, however, the predicted existence of content control without awareness is confirmed by hypnosis and related psychopathological states like hysteria, and everyday dissociative phenomena, which therefore provide supporting evidence for the validity of the framework. Sheehan and McConkey (1982) and Spanos (e.g., 1986) have emphasized the strategic goal-directed nature of hypnotic responding. A subject can be given a suggestion to count but always miss out the number "4". The inhibition of normal associations are required, so content control is required. Nonetheless, susceptible subjects will respond successfully to the suggestion (counting "1, 2, 3, 5, 6,..."), all the while affirming their ignorance that they are doing anything strange. Similarly, Spanos, Radtke, and Dubreuil (1982; Spanos, 1986) found that highly susceptible subjects suggested to forget certain words in any type of task given to them produced those words at a below baseline level in a word association test. This performance again calls for content control because the existing associations that would be produced by vehicle control must be suppressed. In general, virtually any arbitrary behaviour can be hypnotically suggested despite the fact that such behaviour might be novel to the person; it is highly plausible that many hypnotic responses are under content control. Yet highly susceptible subjects claim that their actions do not feel like normal consciously controlled actions; they seem strangely involuntary. And indeed they would seem involuntary if one had not represented the relevant goals as things to which the "I" had a mental-state relation (Kihlstrom, 1997), i.e., if ascent from explicit representation of activity to full explicitness had been inhibited.[9]

Content control of actions might be easier if one kept in mind not just declarative representations of the content of goals and condition-action mappings, but also representations of the appropriate mental states "I wish that...". That is, content control might be easier if performed with awareness rather than without. Perhaps the extra representations of mental states and the use of the "I" representation allows extra activation sources to feed to the controlling structures and support the controlling fact-explicit representation (cf Anderson, 1983; Kihlstrom & Cantor, 1984). A person particularly skilled at content control may be most able to engage in it even when the I and mental states are not being represented. That is, such a person may be particularly able to experience hypnotic effects. In sum, the prediction is highly hypnotizable subjects should be better than low hypnotizables at tasks requiring content control. Indeed, there is a large body of evidence for this claim; for example, highs can generate random numbers with a greater degree of randomness than lows (Graham & Evans, 1977; this is regarded as an executive task, Baddeley, 1986); and in selective attention tasks highs can select on the basis of representational content (semantic selection, or "pigeon holing", Broadbent, 1971) to a greater degree than lows, but they cannot filter according to purely sensory features any better than lows (Dienes, 1987).

7.   IMPLICIT LEARNING

The term implicit learning was coined by Reber (1967) to refer to the way people could learn structure in a domain without being able to say what they had learnt. Later, Broadbent and Aston (1978) independently applied the term "implicit" to such knowledge. Reber had looked at the way people learned artificial grammars; Broadbent looked at the way people learned to control dynamic systems. Both Reber and Broadbent found that people could make appropriate decisions (in deciding on grammaticality and setting the value of a control variable, respectively) without being able to explain why their decisions were correct; and both intuitively felt that the word "implicit" captured the nature of this learning. But what is implicit about implicit learning?

If people could describe the knowledge they had acquired the knowledge would have been represented at least fact explicitly. Anything we can state verbally we can consider whether it is true or not; hence all verbalizable knowledge is at least fact explicit. Further, by expressing the knowledge verbally, a person can consider their relation to the knowledge; if they correctly know that they know it, then the knowledge is fully explicit according to our framework. In order to test a hypothesis, a fact explicit representation must be considered ("If X is true, then..."), because conditional and counterfactual statements necessarily involve explicit consideration of factuality. Seeing why a hypothesis passes whatever test is set, is to see why the validated hypothesis is now part of one's knowledge. Hypothesis testing (when considered as such by the system that does it) is explicit learning. In contrast, the knowledge produced by implicit learning has not been represented as knowledge by the learning process. It's status as knowledge is left implicit in its functional role. The knowledge was acquired by the system in order to facilitate the very task the subject is engaged in; this is what makes it knowledge. For example, in the dynamic control tasks of Berry and Broadbent (1984), people appear to learn what actions lead to the goal in different specific situations to form a look-up table; and this look-up table determines future actions in the same situations (Dienes & Fahey, 1985). People do not explicitly remember these situations (Dienes & Fahey, 1998), they just respond appropriately to them.[10] People can respond appropriately without knowing they have knowledge; this lack of metacognition is what makes the knowledge implicit. Further, the knowledge need not be represented as factual or not; it's factuality is left implicit in the way it is simply taken as true. That is, according to our framework, implicit learning does indeed produce implicit knowledge. At least, this is what we believe the experimental evidence has shown, as we now describe. We will consider artificial grammar learning as a case in point (see Marescaux, Izaute & Chambres, this volume, for a complementary discussion of the dynamic control tasks).

In the artificial grammar learning task introduced by Reber (1967; see also his 1989; for other reviews see Berry & Dienes, 1993; Dienes & Berry, 1997; Shanks & St. John, 1994), a set of rules is used to determine the order that letters can appear in letter strings, which for example may be 5-8 letters long. The rules are sufficiently complex that the ordering of the letters at first seems quite arbitrary to a subject. Subjects are asked to observe, copy, or memorize the letter strings, but they are not told about the existence of the set of rules. After some minutes, the strings are taken away and the subjects are told of the existence of the set of rules, but not what they are. Subjects are asked to classify a new set of strings, half of which obey the rules and half of which do not. The basic finding is that people can classify at above chance rates (typically about 65%) without being able to say freely why they made the decisions they did.

Reber (1967) argued that people had induced rules specifying the structure of the letter strings. His claims about the implicit learning of rules went ignored for a decade or two, but then a flurry of interest started in the 1980's. Dulany, Carlson, and Dewey (1984), Perruchet and Pacteau (1990), and Dienes, Broadbent, and Berry (1991) argued that people had learned allowable small fragments of strings, for example, which bigrams (pairs of letters) occurred in the training strings, and to a lesser extent which trigrams, or higher order n-grams occurred. Such n-gram knowledge could either be learnt as rules which subjects consult explicitly; or as rules that govern subjects' performance but are represented only implicitly. In rule consulting, a rule like "T can follow M" is represented as a fact of the studied strings. Such declarative knowledge would typically be available for reflection on as knowledge. Alternatively, the knowledge may be represented in a fact implicit way, for example in a connectionist network (Dienes, 1992; Dienes, Altmann, & Gao, 1999; Dienes & Perner, 1996). Activation of an M node may lead to activation of the T node via a positive weight; the function of the weight is to code the fact that "T can follow M", but this is not explicitly represented as a fact or as knowledge by the weight.

When a subject comes to classify a string the rules the subject has implicitly or explicitly induced about the grammar are used to infer whether the string is grammatical. The subject forms a new piece of knowledge; e.g., "The test string TVXMMM is grammatical". We will call this knowledge a grammaticality judgement, in contrast to the knowledge used to make the judgement (the subject's personal grammatical rules). In order to determine experimentally whether any knowledge is implicit or explicit, we can assess the subject's ability to metacognitively reflect on the knowledge, for example, by asking the person to give a confidence rating on the grammaticality judgement. The situation is analogous to any situation in which a subject makes a metacognitive judgement about their knowledge. For example, consider a subject trying to retrieve the name of a famous person but they have not retrieved an answer yet. How might the person know that they know the answer? Koriat (in press; this volume) distinguished two ways of making such metacognitive judgements: "information-based" in which the person is aware of the inferences they make in forming a conclusion about their knowledge state; and "feeling-based", in which the true inferential basis of the judgements is not explicit, the person is only aware of the result of the inference as a directly-experienced feeling (e.g., the tip of the tongue state). This distinction is the same Rosenthal (2000a,b,c) makes between higher order thoughts that are based on conscious inferences and those that are not. It is only the latter that leads one to be conscious of a mental state and therefore cause a mental state to be a conscious mental state. Thus, if one judges that one knows the unretrieved famous name in a way that appears unmediated (i.e., the tip of the tongue state), one is conscious of the knowledge (but not in respect of all its content) by inferences that are themselves implicit and unconscious. On the other hand, if one judges that one knows the unretrieved famous name because of inferences of which one is conscious ("I suppose I must know the name, because I watched the news quite a bit at that time"), the knowledge of the name does not constitute a conscious mental state, but an implicit one, known about because of explicit, conscious inferences. This interplay between the implicit/explicit nature of the judgement and the inferences leading to the judgement may be part of the reason why different authors have different intuitions on the relation between metacognition and implicit cognition, as discussed by Koriat (see also the chapters in Reder, 1996).

When a subject judges a string to be grammatical, this may be based on inferences that the subject is conscious of as inferences leading to the conclusion that the string is grammatical. The inferential basis of the decision is then explicit. In contrast, implicit learning is a process by which rules are induced about the domain but they are not rules one consults, they are fact implicit, and the person is not conscious of the rules as rules about the domain. When they are applied, the subject is not directly aware of applying knowledge. How could we show experimentally that this was indeed the state of affairs in order to establish the existence of implicit learning?

One way of testing whether people are aware of their grammatical rules is to ask them to describe freely what rules they used. People are bad at describing the knowledge they have induced in an artificial grammar learning experiment (Reber, 1989; Mathews, Buss, Stanley, Blanchard-Fields, Cho, & Druhan, 1989; Dienes, Broadbent, & Berry, 1991). The sceptics however argue that is just because free report is an insensitive test, not because any piece of knowledge is in principle unavailable to free report (e.g., Shanks & St. John, 1994). If we knew exactly what type of knowledge structures and rules a subject had, we could ask people to judge whether each rule is one they possess and give a confidence rating to assess the subject's' assessment of their state of knowledge; unfortunately, we can never be quite sure exactly what rules a subject has induced (Marescaux & Chambres, 1999).

Fortunately, we can in principle determine the content and knowledge status of subjects' grammaticality judgements. As implicit learning researchers, the interesting issue is not really the implicit nature of the grammaticality judgements; it is the implicit nature of the grammatical rules. Nonetheless, the grammaticality judgements can, in certain circumstances, provide a window onto the implicit nature of the grammatical rules. If the grammatical rules are implicit and applied implicitly (i.e., the person does not explicitly represent that they are applying certain rules), the person will be unaware of the inferential basis of their grammaticality judgement. How might the subject decide what confidence rating to give to the grammaticality judgement? The subject may report that the judgement was a pure guess. Thus, if we took all the cases where the subject said the judgement was a pure guess, the implicit knowledge of the grammatical rules would lead the subject to still make correct responses at an above chance (or above control baseline) rate. This is the guessing criterion (Dienes, Altmann, Kwan, & Goode, 1995). The implicit grammaticality knowledge leads to implicit grammaticality judgements (implicit in the sense that the judgement is knowledge to the subject but not represented as knowledge by the subject). In addition, one can examine the relationship between confidence and performance over the whole range of confidence ratings given; this criterion, about to be explained, is called the "zero correlation criterion" (Dienes, Altmann, Kwan, & Goode, 1995).

Reber (reviewed in his 1989) and Dienes, Kurz, Bernhaupt, and Perner (1997) showed that (a) there are different strings to which subjects are differentially consistent in their responding; and (b) subjects are more consistent for strings to which they tend to make the correct response rather than the incorrect response. (a) is evidence that the learning/knowledge application system is treating itself as having different degrees of knowledge about different strings (in responding more consistently to strings it is treating itself as if it had more certain knowledge about those strings than strings it responds inconsistently to); (b) is evidence that it got this correct (as judged by the rules the experimenter had in mind). Are the different knowledge states the subjects treat themselves as being in explicitly represented as such? One can answer this question by determining whether increasing confidence is associated with an increasing tendency to give a correct response. A lack of relationship between confidence and performance (the zero correlation criterion) indicates that subjects do not know that they know; they do not have access to the different knowledge states they are in fact in as being different knowledge states.[11] As reviewed by Dienes and Berry (1997) and Dienes and Perner (in press), this has been found in a number of artificial grammar learning experiments for some types of stimuli (see also Marescaux, Izaute & Chambres, this volume, for application to the dynamic control tasks). The implicit and thus unconscious nature of the occurrent knowledge states underlying grammaticality judgements can be taken as a reflection of the implicit nature of the underlying grammar knowledge.

Unfortunately, the window provided by the grammaticality judgements on the implicit nature of the grammatical rules is not always a clear one (e.g., Whittlesea & Dorken, 1997). With practice on the task, subjects may come to base their confidence ratings on cues at least correlated with the knowledge status of the grammaticality judgements (these cues are not known, but could be: reaction times, string fluency, correct explicit knowledge). Indeed, Allwood, Granhag, and Johansson (in press) found that with a task involving a relatively small number of trials, the guessing criterion was satisfied and there was poor calibration of confidence and performance; on a task involving more trials calibration improved dramatically and when subjects claimed they were guessing they were indeed performing at chance.[12] Nonetheless, the result on the latter task leaves open the possibility that the grammar knowledge was quite implicit, given subjects' generally poor ability to freely report the bases of their decisions under conditions very similar to those of Allwood et al. How could one determine the implicit nature of the grammar rules in this situation?

In addition to looking at metacognitive monitoring, one can look at metacognitive control to determine the implicit status of grammar rules. Consistent with the logic of Jacoby (1991), if a subject were asked to complete a string with a letter in such a way that the rules were violated, implicit knowledge of the rules would be hard to inhibit. If the knowledge is applied by rule consulting, it is easy to not apply the rules; one just does not consult them. However, if the knowledge is not represented as knowledge, so it is not represented as the knowledge one has just learnt, there is no means to reference the knowledge by content control in order to inhibit its use. That is, if the knowledge is implicit but activated, the subject will have a tendency to use the knowledge to complete letter strings even when trying not to. This methodology has not been applied to Reber's artificial grammar learning task yet, but Goschke (1998) and Destrebecqz and Cleeremans (in press) applied the methodology to another implicit learning paradigm, the Sequential Reaction Time paradigm, in which a set of rules determine the order in which subjects should press a set of buttons. They found that after training, subjects still pressed the buttons according to the rules despite being told to press in a way that violated the rules. That is, the grammar knowledge could not be brought under content control, and thus its status as a particular body of knowledge must have been implicit. With Reber's artificial grammar learning paradigm, Dienes (1996; Dienes, Altmann, Tunney, & Goode, in preparation) showed that the grammatical status of to-be-ignored flanking strings affected the reaction time of subjects classifying target strings; subjects were faster when the flanking and target strings were consistent rather than inconsistent. That is, the flanking strings were automatically processed for grammatical status; the mere presence of the strings triggered the application of the relevant knowledge schema, indicating the use of vehicle control and thus implicit knowledge.

8. CONCLUSION

This chapter has taken the framework of Dienes and Perner (1999) to show the metacognitive implications of the implicit-explicit distinction in many domains. It has considered the metacognitive basis of the cognitive operations pervasive in all moments of waking life: seeing, perceiving, remembering, willing, and applying knowledge. The simple act of consciously seeing is deeply metacognitive. Understanding the nature of remembering, as much as perception, requires consideration of several layers of metacognition, even putting aside the more obvious metacognitions required to interactively search one's memory store to retrieve an obscure fact of one's past. When a cognitive operation is successful, but metacognition fails, the result is an unconscious mental state. We have argued, based on people's metacognitive failures, that people can perceive unconsciously, strategically act unconsciously, and acquire and apply knowledge of which they are not conscious. An interesting question is raised about the implicit basis of people's poor calibration of metacognitive judgements and their performance in other domains we have not discussed. We hope we can tempt metacognition researchers to look at implicit learning more closely, and implicit learning researchers to look at metacognition more closely.

Notes

[1] This is true, even of procedural knowledge. A procedure is of the general form "If condition X, then action Y". In a calculator, it may be: If "5 X 6" then show "30". The property of being 30 is predicated of the result of the operation 5 X 6. Note also that detailed perceptual properties can be predicated of individuals.

[2] It is the fact that the person can reliably identify the actually presented word (e.g., when given leave to guess) that entitles us to say the person has knowledge, and therefore allows us to talk about implicit **knowledge**. It is only in an appropriate supporting context that the representation functions as knowledge of a particular event. Nonetheless, we will loosely refer to the representation as providing implicit knowledge in all contexts. In many cases (e.g., Bridgeman, 1991; see Dienes & Perner, 1999), the visual system evolved the use of such (implicit) representations precisely because of their role in such supporting contexts, and so the proper function of the representation is indeed knowledge.

[3] According to Carruthers' (1992) potentialist higher-order thought theory, a representation is conscious if it is recursively available for successively highly order thoughts. It directly follows from this account that if you are conscious of X you are also potentially conscious of how you know X.

[4] This observation shows that the higher order thought theory is not just a conceptual analysis of how words are used; it has genuine explanatory power. Another illustration of the explanatory power of the higher order thought theory is that it corresponds to the measure of consciousness Cheesman and Merikle (1984; 1986) called the subjective rather than the objective threshold; it is the subjective threshold that appears to divide qualitatively different psychological processes.

[5] This begs the question of why second order thoughts may be useful from an evolutionary perspective; Miller (2000) argues eloquently that maybe natural selection had little to do with it; it may have been predominantly sexual selection.

[6] This may seem like a third order thought because one thinks that one remembers that one experienced; but the "experienced" is past tense and so not an occurrent mental state, but simply a fact of the past.

[7] There is an interesting symmetry with perception: The action must seem to be caused by the intention (higher order thought) in a way that appears unmediated; if the action appeared mediated, it would not be a voluntary action but the outcome of a voluntary action. Voluntary action *requires* unconscious processes of mediation, just as conscious perception requires the mechanisms mediating between first order mental states and higher order thoughts to be unconscious.

[8] Note that procedural knowledge - often represented in the form of procedures like "If condition C, then do action A" (e.g., Anderson, 1983) –does not require fact explicit representation. In fact, declarative knowledge differs from procedural knowledge precisely because declarative knowledge declares what is the case, i.e., represents factuality explicitly, whereas procedural knowledge need not. "If condition C, do action X" is a declarative representation of what a procedure may represent fact implicitly by virtue of implementing the right links between conditions and actions. Whenever, for example, the condition is occurrently represented in the procedure, the presence of the condition would be treated as a given because its factuality is taken for granted and the procedure would apply the action.

[9] The absence of second order thoughts would preclude the formation of a second order thought such as "I perform this action of raising my arm by way of carrying out this intention (of mine)". It is the absence of this "intention-in-action" (Searle, 1983) that makes the act feel involuntary. This analysis of hypnotic responding –appropriate first order control states in the absence of corresponding second-order thoughts– may account for many suggestions, like motor suggestions and some strategically-mediated cognitive ones. In addition, hypnotic hallucinations appear to rely on a complementary state of affairs: second order thoughts in the absence of the corresponding first order perceptual

states. One may experience being in a mental state (seeing, feeling pain) even though one is not really in it (as discussed by Rosenthal, 2000a,b,c for some non-hypnotic contexts). The prediction is that such illusory second-order thoughts should arise most often when: there is strong expectation that one will have the first order and higher order states; the person has vivid imagery and capacity for imaginative involvement; and the subject engages in appropriate fantasy simulations of the first order state (to produce sufficient first order information to trigger the primed second order thoughts). These are indeed important predictors of hypnotic responding (e.g., Kirsch, 1991; Spanos, 1986). A third route to hypnotic responding may be in the creation of different ""I"s (Kihlstrom, 1997), but the complexity of this route would presumably restrict its use to very few people.

[10] Contrast Whittlesea and Dorken's (1993) view that implicit learning is when we learn information for one purpose and do not realize it is relevant for another purpose; the usefulness for the latter purpose is left implicit in the knowledge as that knowledge was originally conceived by the learner. This is a meaning of implicit, but it is different to our meaning, and does not capture the nature of implicit learning as it seems to us: The knowledge can be best suited to the very purpose is was originally acquired for and still be implicit knowledge.

[11] Conversely, if (a) and (b) did not jointly hold, the zero correlation criterion would not indicate the existence of implicit knowledge (Dienes & Perner, 1996). If the subject consistently applies a partially correct rule, there is no reason why confidence in correct decisions should be different from confidence in incorrect decisions, regardless of whether the rule is implicit or explicit.

[12] The tasks differed in other respects as well; for example, a different grammar was used. It remains to be determined which factors were responsible for the difference in calibration.

Chapter 2

How Implicit is Implicitly Acquired Knowledge
From Dissociation to Subjective Threshold

Pierre-Jean Marescaux, Marie Izaute and Patrick Chambres
Université Blaise Pascal, Clermont-Ferrand, France

Key themes: Meth / Theor

Key words: Implicit learning / Implicit knowledge / Subjective tests of awareness

Abstract: In this chapter we first discuss why it has recently been suggested that there is an intersection between two research fields as distant as metacognition and implicit learning. One major issue for implicit learning research is to determine whether the resulting knowledge might be itself implicit, an issue which has usually been explored through the dissociation procedure. As a matter of fact, to examine whether people know they know - the so-called subjective threshold approach - is an approach that is thought to avoid some of the problems reported about the dissociation procedure. We then review empirical studies using this new approach in the three main experimental paradigms used to investigate implicit learning. In so doing, one experiment on the control of a complex system will be briefly reported. On the whole, the results suggest that participants often lack metaknowledge. However, the picture is still unclear because of a lack of real replications and the use of methods that cannot be really compared.

Repeated exposure to some complex stimulus environments can result in fine behavioral adjustments that apparently occur without any deliberate strategy to learn and that can be difficult to account for. Native language learning is a typical example of such an adaptability which is made possible thanks to implicit learning, a hypothetical process that has been studied in the laboratory over the last 30 years or so using three main experimental paradigms. In artificial grammar learning experiments, participants are typically asked to memorize - or even simply exposed to - letter strings generated by a formal grammar without being warned about the structured nature of the stimuli. Then, they are told that the strings they have seen were constructed with a complex set of rules and that they must classify new grammatical and ungrammatical strings according to what they know about the grammar. Their classification performance is above chance level, therefore testifying that they learned about the grammar, although they are quite unable to describe what the grammar is and how they performed their categorization (see, e.g., Reber, 1967; Reber & Lewis, 1977; Dienes, Broadbent, & Berry, 1991). Serial reaction time experiments are another ruse used to study implicit learning. Subjects must press a key as quickly as possible to locate the position of a target on a computer screen. Unbeknown to them, the target is moving according to some sophisticated sequential pattern. Reaction time decreases with practice and increases again if the regular display is disrupted. However, this sensitivity to the rule-governed environment is not accompanied by an ability to report the rules themselves (see, e.g., Lewicki, Czyzewska, & Hoffman,Czyzewska, & Hoffman, 1987; Lewicki, Hill, & Bizot, 1988; Cleeremans & McClelland, 1991). A third design consists of control tasks. In these experiments, participants manage a simulated system by means of one or two input variables so as to attain a target value for one or two output variables. Without receiving any explanation about the relationship between input and output variables, they nevertheless bring output ever closer to the target value with practice, although they cannot afterwards answer questions about how the system worked (Broadbent & Aston, 1977; Berry & Broadbent, 1984; Broadbent, Fitzgerald & Broadbent, 1986).

On the whole, the data base seems to be consistent with the idea that "*Implicit learning is the acquisition of knowledge that takes place largely independently of conscious attempts to learn and largely in the absence of explicit knowledge about what was acquired*". (Reber, 1993, p. 5). Although this definition is not accepted by all researchers (see, e.g., Frensch, 1998), it has the merit of highlighting two issues addressed in the field, as the term "implicit" has been used to label both the learning process and the resulting knowledge (see, e.g., Berry & Dienes, 1993). When learning is said to be implicit, this means that it is unintentional, passive, or even that it occurs in the absence of voluntary encoding strategies. The resulting knowledge has also been termed implicit, in the sense that it appears to be unconscious, unavailable to conscious awareness, or even difficult to express in free reports. Each of these facets is investigated using specific methods. The role of attention/volition is explored by examining the extend to which learning might be disturbed in the presence of attentional distraction (e.g., Frensch, Lin, & Buchner, 1998) or by instructions to search for the rules (Reber, 1976; Reber, Kassin, Lewis, & Cantor, 1980). The nature of the knowledge acquired - implicit versus explicit - is usually determined by means of the dissociation paradigm where two measures of knowledge are compared. The first one is a measure of information available "to the brain" - named α - which is typically a non-verbal performance such as the percentage of correct classifications in artificial grammar learning experiments -, and the other - the explicit measure - is intended to capture the information available to the "conscious part" of the brain - called β. Some knowledge might be characterized as implicit if "there is more in the brain than in consciousness", that is to say, if the information available to the brain is greater than the information available to conscious awareness or if $\alpha > \beta$ (see, e.g., Reber, 1993).

Beyond doubt, much has been (and still is) written about this approach, the difficulty lying entirely in finding a suitable measure of awareness. A first requirement of the procedure is that the test used to capture subjects' explicit knowledge must not leave any of the information available to awareness undetected. This condition refers to the exhaustiveness assumption (Reingold & Merikle, 1988) or to the sensitivity criterion (Shanks & St. John, 1994) and is likely to prove difficult to fulfill. Explicit knowledge has been frequently defined in terms of free reports, especially in a number of early studies (e.g., Reber, 1967; Lewicki, et al., 1988). The standard finding was that participants were unable to tell what the rules were and which aspects of the environment influenced their behavior, therefore suggesting that knowledge is implicit. However, given that debriefings were usually applied retrospectively with regard to the test intended to gather the information available to the brain, this outcome was considered by some skeptics to be only a very weak demonstration of implicit knowledge. One criticism has been that the absence of some of the retrieval cues makes it possible for forgetting to occur (e.g., Dulany, Carlson, & Dewey, 1984).

Another reason why free reports are suspected to underestimate β has been revealed by studies suggesting that the information responsible for performance change (i.e., α) may differ from the rules as they are conceived of by the experimenter (e.g., Dulany et al., 1984; Perruchet & Pacteau, 1990; Perruchet, Gallego, & Savy, 1990). Consequently, such information, if it is ever reported, may be underrated. This possibility refers to the concept of correlated hypotheses (Dulany, 1961; Dulany et al., 1984) or to the information criterion (Shanks & St. John, 1994). To illustrate this potential source of artifact, we may consider experiments with control tasks in which an increase in the ability to set output to target value is revealed with practice without a parallel improvement in the ability to answer questions about how the system worked or an ability to report the rule (Berry & Broadbent, 1984). If this pattern was originally interpreted as testifying that implicit knowledge of the rule was acquired, follow-on studies lent some support to the idea that learning to control the simulated system might be merely due to the acquisition of knowledge about "what to do in some situations of the system", just as if a look-up table in which successful actions are associated with related system states was progressively updated during learning (Marescaux, Luc, & Karnas, 1989; Dienes & Fahey, 1995). Consequently, to search for the rules in free reports may be a hopeless quest in such cases, because this information does not seem to be responsible for the behavioral changes. This could represent a real obstacle to the dissociation procedure, because environments as proposed in implicit learning experiments are typically complex, therefore allowing participants to respond in many ways that depart from the rules and that are difficult to guess by the experimenter (Berry & Dienes, 1993, chapter three).

The yoked subject technique employed by Mathews and associates might be a good way of circumventing this trap. The amount of explicit knowledge is then determined by the consequences that the free reports of participants exposed to a standard implicit learning procedure (e.g., exposure to grammatical strings) have on the behavior of untrained subjects (e.g., grammaticality judgment). If the performance of these yoked partners is enhanced in comparison to that of uninformed, entirely fresh novices, then there is evidence that the verbal accounts of the original participants contained information that was relevant for performing the task. In both artificial grammar learning (Mathews et al., 1989) and control tasks (Stanley, Mathews, Buss, & Kotler-Cope, 1989), this strategy clearly demonstrated that participants who received instructions from trained partners were helped (i.e., $\beta > 0$). However, these studies also showed that the performance of the yoked participants remained lower than the performance of the original learners. This pattern can be taken as evidence that the amount of implicit knowledge exceeds the amount of information available to awareness (i.e., $\alpha > \beta$). However, other accounts are also possible. Given that the free reports of the original learners were obtained after exposure to the material, forgetting might occur. Likewise, the yoked partners might have difficulty in understanding the instructions or might make mistakes in applying them. To sum up, the yoked subjects technique cannot guarantee exhaustiveness.

Given the risk that some explicit knowledge slips through the net with free reports, some authors have advocated the use of *objective tests of awareness* (e.g., Shanks & St. John, 1994). In fact, such tests share many characteristics with the implicit test (e.g., task demands, retrieval cues) but the participants are told that there is an underlying structure in the material they have seen and, in particular, they are urged to perform the objective test on the basis of their conscious knowledge about the complex arrangement. Once trained in a serial reaction time experiment for example, participants might be asked to generate parts of the sequences they were exposed to, either freely or with certain cues (Willingham, Nissen, & Bullemer, 1989; Shanks & Johnstone, 1998).

At first sight, objective tests may thus appear as a suitable way to capture explicit knowledge. Nevertheless, misgivings have also been reported about the relevance of this approach. A test of explicit knowledge is expected to be exclusive, that is to say, it must be able to select properly only conscious knowledge without any possibility for the intrusion of implicit knowledge. This condition refers to the exclusiveness assumption (Reingold & Merikle, 1988) and is difficult to meet with objective tests. Given that implicit knowledge is often thought to be inaccessible to voluntary control, it seems likely that cues offered by objective tests might trigger implicit knowledge, even though the participants are expressly asked to use only their explicit knowledge to respond to the test. The risk is therefore that β might be apparently equal to α, with the two tests measuring the same implicit information.

To avoid this type of confusion, Dienes and co-workers (Dienes & Berry, 1997; Dienes & Perner, 1999, this volume) have argued for the use of a subjective threshold, that is to say, that the boundary between implicit and explicit knowledge could be established by means of a metacognitive approach which involves examining the relationship between accuracy and confidence in forced-choice tests. In particular, two criteria were proposed. The first one, called the zero correlation criterion, requires us to consider how accuracy is correlated with confidence. If there is no positive relationship between these two measures, then one may infer that people do not know when they know and when they do not know. In this way, they lack metaknowledge. The second criterion, called the guessing criterion, makes it necessary to examine whether performance is above chance level when people say they are choosing at random. If accuracy is greater than chance, then there is some knowledge that is actually at work but which people does not know about. It therefore follows that people lack metaknowledge. Thus, the subjective threshold approach, like the dissociation procedure, is based on two measures, but one measure is a measure of knowledge and the other one is a measure of metaknowledge. Unlike the dissociation procedure, these two measures are not intended for a direct comparison[1]. Whether people are able to judge their own performance accurately is the point at issue. How implicit is implicitly acquired knowledge in terms of such an ability?

1. METAKNOWLEDGE IN ARTIFICIAL GRAMMAR LEARNING

Chan (1992, in Dienes & Berry, 1997) explored whether knowledge about an artificial grammar is implicit using the subjective threshold. He asked subjects to memorize a set of letter strings generated by a formal grammar. Then, he told them that the strings were constructed according to a complex set of rules and the subjects took a grammaticality test in which they rated their confidence in each decision they made. Chan found that accuracy was not correlated with confidence in the subsequent grammaticality test. However, when subjects were induced to search for the rules while memorizing the grammatical exemplars, there was a correlation between accuracy and confidence in the subsequent test. Chan therefore concluded that implicit learning, contrary to explicit learning, does not generate metaknowledge and that knowledge of an artificial grammar as it is usually learned (i.e., incidentally) might be implicit.

Likewise, Dienes, Altmann, Kwan, and Goode (1995) obtained some evidence that knowledge about an artificial grammar might be implicit rather than explicit. However, some of their results suggested the opposite. In their experiments, participants were first exposed to two sets of strings successively, each set being produced by a different formal grammar. Then, participants were given a list of strings that belonged to three categories. Some strings were grammatical according to the first grammar, some other strings obeyed the rules of the second grammar and the remainder of the strings infringed both grammars. In the grammaticality test, participants were asked to check only the strings that resembled those of either the first or the second set they had seen and gave a confidence rating for each decision. The results showed that participants had control over the application of their knowledge, that is to say, they could indeed identify the strings they had to check - the strings that belonged to the target grammar. Hence, their knowledge about the other grammar was not triggered despite the presence of cues in the forced-choice test (i.e., the strings generated by the grammar that was to be ignored). This was not really expected given the assumption that knowledge is implicit. Further, the authors found that when participants said they were guessing on the grammaticality test, they were nevertheless performing above chance level. Finally, Dienes et al. replicated Chan's finding that there was no relationship between accuracy and confidence in the grammaticality test after simple exposure to grammatical strings (i.e., under incidental learning conditions): the subjects were as confident in incorrect decisions as they were in correct decisions. However, this occurred only under specific circumstances. When participants were faced with a lot of stimuli and asked to state separately whether each of them belonged to the target grammar, then there was no relationship between accuracy and confidence. In contrast, when the stimuli were shown three by three, each stimulus of the target grammar being presented with two distractors, and the task was to choose which item obeyed the target grammar, then there was a relationship. To explain this discrepancy between testing conditions, Dienes et al. hypothesized that to show target strings with distractors, contrary to the standard yes-no procedure, might allow participants to realize that sometimes they hesitated between two or more items whereas sometimes they did not, and that they could therefore adjust their confidence rating according to the amount of uncertainty they felt. Nevertheless, this would not imply they knew about how they made the grammaticality judgments. To sum up, Dienes et al.'s experiments have provided evidence that implicit learning of an artificial grammar does not yield associated metaknowledge in terms of the guessing criterion, and partly in terms of the zero-correlation criterion. However, participants did not lack intentional control over their knowledge.

In a more recent study, Allwood, Granhag, and Johansson (2000) reported two experiments using calibration methods. In a first experiment, subjects were exposed to a standard implicit grammar learning procedure (i.e., with relatively few grammatical exemplars in the study phase). On average, realism was poor. Indeed, realism was good for grammatical strings only. With regard to the ungrammatical stimuli, an improvement in confidence was accompanied by an increase in the number of mistakes. After a careful scrutiny of the stimuli, the authors reasoned that grammaticality judgments might have been biased by the presence of one salient bigram (i.e., a combination of two letters). As a result, they controlled the material appropriately in a second experiment and then, realism was dramatically improved. Unfortunately, it is unclear whether realism was boosted by the really controlled material or by a change in the study phase. Actually, 500 grammatical strings were presented during learning, that is to say, far more than usually used in standard experiments (approximately 25 study exemplars). Thus, realism might have been enhanced simply because subjects were exposed to so many learning strings that they left the study phase with explicit knowledge (see also Wheaver & Kelemen, this volume, for a discussion about overlearning as a factor that inflates metacognitive accuracy).

2.   METAKNOWLEDGE IN SEQUENTIAL LEARNING

Shanks and Johnstone (1998) reported that there was no evidence of the existence of metaknowledge in a sequential learning task. Once practiced in a so-called "reaction time experiment", subjects were told that the stimulus followed some complex sequential pattern. They then participated in a free generation test in which they were required to type as many continuous parts of the sequences as they could. In a first experiment, subjects finally indicated if the sequences they had generated were familiar to them or if they thought they had produced the sequences by guessing. Three participants (out of 15) believed they were guessing. However, they still performed significantly above chance level in the free generation task. In a second experiment, the participants rated their confidence in the generated sequences. Both confidence and performance were higher in a group of subjects trained with a sequential pattern than in a group drilled with a nonrepeating sequence. However, a subset of the participants (7 out of 15) exposed to the regular material exhibited a level of confidence as low as that of the participants who had practiced with the nonrepeating stimuli. Nevertheless, these low-confident subjects performed significantly higher than those of the nonrepeating group. Hence, as argued by the authors, these results nicely confirmed those obtained by Dienes et al. (1995) suggesting knowledge acquired implicitly is not accompanied by metaknowledge. In this sense, it may be implicit.

3. METAKNOWLEDGE IN CONTROL TASKS

To date, there is no study on the control of complex systems that use the subjective threshold approach as recommended by Dienes and Berry (1997). In a rather different way, and given the look-up table account of learning in control tasks (Dienes & Fahey, 1995; Marescaux et al., 1989), Dienes and Fahey (1998, see also Dienes & Perner, this volume) examined whether the exploitation of the look-up table is accompanied by conscious recollection. In this study, subjects were first trained to control a dynamic simulated system and then respond to a questionnaire comprising different situations of the system. For each situation, they were asked which level of input would bring output to target value (the same target was required as was experienced during training) and whether they had seen the situation while interacting with the system. Some of the situations were system states subjects had come across during training and to which they had given a correct response (i.e., a response bringing output to the target value). Hence, the look-up table account predicts that there were responses available in memory for these situations. The crucial issue was then to know if subjects were aware of having the knowledge necessary to respond appropriately to these situations. The results showed that accuracy was not dependent on recognizing the situations, therefore suggesting that the look-up table is employed without any knowledge of its use, that is to say, without the corresponding metaknowledge.

However, this study did not provide any information about the guessing and the zero correlation criteria. To address these issues, we conducted an experiment in which fifty-seven unpaid Blaise Pascal University students were trained on the sugar factory task devised by Berry and Broadbent (1984). Participants were told to imagine they had to manage a factory so as to maintain its production at a constant amount of 9,000 tons of sugar per cycle. They performed four sets of thirteen trials. In this simulated system, controlling the production could be made by recruiting, on each trial, a number of workers who would participate in the production. Possible sugar production levels ranged between 1,000 and 12,000 tons (in multiples of 1,000). Similarly, recruitment values ranged between 100 and 1,200 (in multiples of 100). The relationship between work force and sugar production was computed by the equation $P = 20 * W - Po + R$, where P is the sugar production that will result from the work force used by the participant, W is this work force, Po is the sugar production on the previous trial, and R is a random term (either -1,000; 0 or +1,000 tons). This random term forced the participants to exert continuous control on the system. When the sugar production output as calculated by the equation was out of the permitted, it was set to the nearest permitted value (i.e., either 1,000 or 12,000 tons). The control task was run on a computer. The upper half of the screen held written information about the previous trial (i.e., the level of employment and the production reached). In the lower part of the screen, a graphical representation of the successive productions was progressively drawn. A horizontal line extending across the entire graph denoted the target production level.

After they had performed the control task, the participants responded to a questionnaire comprising 40 questions. Each question asked the participants to specify what level of work force might make it possible to attain a required target production output on the basis of a previous sugar factory episode (a previous episode was defined as three previous sugar production outputs). The questions were displayed on the computer screen in a format almost identical to that used during the control task itself. Twenty questions had a target production level of 9,000 tons whereas the other twenty questions required an output of 6,000 tons of sugar. The participants were asked to rate their confidence in each decision they took. When the question appeared on the screen, participants first gave the workforce they thought to be necessary to bring output to target and then rated their confidence in their decision on an ordinal scale comprising 5 points (i.e., from "not certain at all" to "not very certain", "reasonably certain", "nearly certain" and "absolutely certain").

Performance on each trial block was calculated by counting the hits which were defined as a resulting production on target or one level away from the target. Performance on a trial set therefore ranged between 0 and 30. Performance on the first and the last trial blocks was 6.82 and 10.30 respectively. A paired t test indicated that the improvement was significant; $t(56) = 4.46, p < .0005$. Performance on the questionnaire was calculated in such as way that it also ranged between 0 and 30 (for the details of the method which was used in previous studies, see, e.g., Marescaux et al., 1989). Accuracy on the questionnaire was 10.09, which was no different from the performance on the last trial block; $t(56) = .30, p > .05$. A confidence score was computed as the sum of the confidence levels given at each question (i.e., 1 for "not certain at all", 2 for "not very certain", and so on) divided by the number of questions. The confidence mean was 2.92. The guessing criterion requires us to compare the performance expected by chance with the performance attained when subjects say they are guessing. Due to both the difficulty of determining what might constitute random responding in control tasks (see, e.g., Dienes & Fahey, 1995) and the fact that the lowest level of confidence was not explicitly equated with guessing, this issue was addressed in the present experiment by examining whether participants performed better when they stated in the questionnaire that they had a very low level of confidence than when they were starting their training, that is to say, during the first trial block. The "not certain at all" confidence level was utilized by only 31 participants out of 57. For these 31 subjects, the low confidence score was 8.24 whereas their control task performance on the first trial set was 6.55. A paired t test did not indicate that the two scores were different; $t(30) = .96, p > .05$. The Goodman-Kruskal gamma statistic G was used to examine the relationship between accuracy and confidence across the whole questionnaire. For each participant, this statistic was computed on a contingency table that crossed the 5 levels of confidence (from "not certain at all" to "absolutely certain") with 5 levels of accuracy (i.e., response that brings output "exactly to target" vs. "to one production level away from target" vs. "to two levels away from target" vs. "to three levels away from target" vs. "to four or more levels away from target"). The G scores were then transformed into z scores. The G mean was .11 and the corresponding z mean was .40. These values were low and did not indicate any reliable relationship between confidence and accuracy. Thus, the guessing criterion and the zero-correlation criterion did not bring concordant results, the first one suggesting available metaknowledge and the second a lack of metaknowledge.

4. CONCLUDING REMARKS AND PROSPECTS FOR THE FUTURE

The subjective threshold approach that requires us to examine the relationship between confidence and accuracy in forced-choice tests is a radical shift in method to determine just how implicit implicitly acquired knowledge actually is. Given that it was only proposed recently (Dienes et al., 1995; Dienes & Berry, 1997; Dienes & Perner, 1999), it has been employed as yet in few empirical studies that have been reviewed in this chapter. Broadly speaking, the finding that seems to emerge most frequently from these studies is that knowledge acquired in the standard implicit learning experiments is not accompanied by corresponding metaknowledge and that it might therefore be implicit. Knowledge resulting from learning to control complex systems might not appear to escape the rule, as demonstrated by the experiment briefly reported here. Nevertheless, this general picture requires a number of comments.

First and because theoretical constructs are bolstered only by robust results, there is a need for replications. The accurate classification of new stimuli after exposure to letter strings generated by an artificial grammar is a well-established scientific fact that has been replicated many times. Unfortunately, not all the findings concerning implicit learning have been successfully reproduced in the same way. For example, inducing subjects to search for the rules while memorizing strings was reported as being detrimental to later classification performance (Reber, 1976; Reber et al., 1980) but this effect was not echoed by Dulany et al. (1984). Likewise, other failures have been recorded (e.g., Hayes & Broadbent, 1988 *vs.* Shanks, Green, & Kolodny, 1994). Therefore, one question that comes to mind is: can we observe the kind of regularity we are looking for? Yet, the question is not easy to answer, given the small number of studies using the subjective threshold approach. In addition, it should be noted that if a lack of metaknowledge is the most frequent outcome, this finding has been obtained through various routes that are not necessarily comparable.

By way of illustration, take the available studies on implicit grammar learning and suggestions resulting from the zero-correlation criterion. Chan (1992, in Dienes & Berry, 1997) found no relation between accuracy and confidence as measured by means of a correlation coefficient. Dienes et al. (1995) also examined this relationship and reached the same conclusion, but in a rather different manner. They averaged confidence ratings for correct and incorrect decisions and argued that a lack of metaknowledge could be inferred if the difference between the two scores was zero. Finally, Allwood et al. (2000) used various methods - calibration - correlation coefficient - difference in confidence for correct and incorrect decisions - and one of their two experiments provided evidence that metaknowledge was available in terms of the calibration and the difference score. However, the correlation coefficient was not significantly different from zero. Obviously, it is very hard to draw parallels between these studies that use different measures, all employed to gauge the relation between confidence and accuracy across the entire grammaticality test. In the latter case, there is evidence that the different measures did not present the same sensitivity[2]. It should be noted that the individual indicators are not designed to estimate the relationship between confidence and accuracy to the same extent. The calibration method is devised to appraise realism (i.e., whether confidence judgment is a fairly good predictor of performance). The correlation coefficient and the difference score are intended to examine whether accuracy increases as confidence does, but do not tackle the question of realism (e.g., a correlation can be positive in spite of an overall underconfidence). Thus, it would be of interest to conduct experiments that use the most relevant indexes relative to the subjective threshold approach and, hopefully, indexes that offer a good level of sensitivity. To this end, works discussing and comparing the advantages/disadvantages and sensitivity of techniques should help (see both Weaver & Kelemen; Olsson & Justin, this volume). Note that sensitivity is a problem of measurement (in the statistical sense) but also a problem in terms of the test itself. For example, the relationship between memory performance and the judgment of this performance generally increases with the number of alternatives proposed in the test (Schwartz & Metcalfe, 1994). It is worth noting that the literature on metacognition has a clear lead over the implicit learning literature with regard to these issues.

Still in line with the question outlined above, another comment concerns a possible confusion. Some studies may, at first sight, exhibit parallel results while really addressing different questions. Take the serial reaction time experiment conducted by Shanks and Johnstone (1998). Once trained, subjects were asked to freely generate as many parts of the sequences as they could and finally gave a confidence rating to indicate how successful they thought they had been in the whole free generation task. This way of capturing metaknowledge is open to a similar criticism that was leveled at free reports: confidence was measured retrospectively and might thus present a distorted image of the available metaknowledge. But this is not the whole story. It should be recognized that the relationship between confidence and accuracy can be analyzed only at a between-subjects level. Consequently, the lack of metaknowledge as observed in this study was not closely connected to the lack of metaknowledge found in the other grammar learning experiments that all used within-subjects designs (Chan, 1992, in Dienes & Berry, 1997; Dienes et al., 1995; Allwood et al., 2000). Probably between-subjects designs are less in line with the philosophy of the subjective threshold approach. To sum up these first comments, strong evidence of the lack of metaknowledge about implicitly acquired knowledge is lacking. Amongst the very few studies available, the issue has been explored using different methods and different indexes that do not allow for real comparisons to be made.

To address a different issue, the subjective threshold approach has been presented as a way of getting around the obstacles faced by the dissociation procedure. But is this approach problem-free?

The dissociation procedure is based on the comparison of two indexes, α which quantifies the information that is "available to the brain" and β which accounts for the explicitly available information. The avowed objective is clearly ambitious given the difficulty of using a test to capture all the explicit information but nothing more (i.e., the exhaustiveness and the exclusiveness requirements). Furthermore, even if we accept that a satisfactory test can be found, the comparison of the two measures is still not self-evident (see Footnote 1). In comparative terms, the subjective threshold approach does not attempt to perform these two measurements. It is based on the postulate that explicit knowledge will induce a certain realism when subjects judge their own performance unlike implicit knowledge that should be characterized by an absence of realism. If we subscribe to this postulate, the subjective threshold approach should not cause any problems if all the knowledge acquired during implicit learning is of the same type, i.e., either wholly implicit or wholly explicit.

However, supporters of the "wholly implicit" or "wholly explicit" theories are becoming increasingly rare (see, e.g., Berry, 1994). In this respect, certain experiments showing that trained subjects can pass on relevant information to novice participants, even though the latter do not achieve performances that are as good as their teachers', have suggested that at least a part of the knowledge acquired in implicit learning situations is explicit (Mathews et al., 1989; Stanley et al., 1989). What then would be the consequence for the metacognitive indexes if performance in a subjective test of awareness was based, as these studies suggest, on a refined mixture of implicit and explicit knowledge? It is highly probable that the partial realism induced by the explicit part of the knowledge would be masked by the lack of realism produced by the implicit part of the knowledge. This is a difficulty that may impair the relevance of the subjective threshold approach, alongside other potential problems reported elsewhere. For example, let us imagine that a participant responds to all items in the subjective test on the basis of a partially valid and explicit rule. The constant application of this rule would produce variations in the performance index (i.e., some responses would be correct and others false) but there is no reason to think that there would be any variation in the subject's confidence in the partial rule. In such a case, we should expect an absence of realism even though the participant is perfectly aware of the rule that he/she is applying (Dienes & Berry, 1997). A lack of realism would not necessarily indicate a lack of explicit knowledge. It might therefore be inadvisable to draw overhasty conclusions about the nature of the knowledge acquired during implicit learning on the basis of metacognitive indexes alone.

The comments above indicate a number of potential pitfalls concerning the subjective threshold approach. How real are these pitfalls? Only complementary research that should take the form of a comparison of different methods (i.e., different measures of explicit knowledge and different indexes of metaknowledge) can provide an answer. Clearly, work in this field still has a long way to go.

Notes

[1] In the dissociation procedure, α and β are destined for a direct comparison. However, these two measures often differ in a number of ways that could make the comparison hazardous. They may be not sampled on exactly the same stimuli under literally the same conditions. Likewise, they can be supported by different scales, etc.

[2] The amount of learning which might have result in explicit rather than in implicit knowledge in no way weakens the relevance of this comment.

Chapter 3

Calibration of Confidence among Eyewitnesses and Earwitnesses

Nils Olsson and Peter Juslin
Uppsala University, Sweden
Umeå University, Sweden

Key themes: Appl / Meth / Perf

Key words: Eyewitness / Earwitness / Witness / Confidence / Accuracy / Calibration

Abstract: One of the more alarming and intriguing results in forensic psychology is the weak relationship between confidence and accuracy in experimental studies of eyewitness identification. This relationship has traditionally been measured by the point-biserial correlation coefficient, r_{pb}. In the present chapter the confidence-accuracy relationship in witness identification is studied with two alternative and, as we argue, more suitable indices, namely **calibration** and **diagnosticity** analysis. When calibration analysis is applied to eyewitness identification, the participant (witness) is required to assess on a scale the subjective probability that the identified person is identical to the culprit. The subjective probabilities are compared to the corresponding relative frequencies of correct identifications. With the use of diagnosticity analysis of confidence, which is based on a modified form of Bayes' theorem, it is possible to determine the informational impact of positive identifications made with different levels of confidence.

We present three empirical studies. In Study I it was concluded from two experiments that eyewitness confidence can be both reasonably well calibrated and diagnostic, despite a low r_{pb}. Study II showed that in comparison to eyewitness identification in similar circumstances, **earwitness** accuracy is poorer, with overconfidence and low diagnosticity of confidence, even in easy tasks. In Study III, a meta-analysis showed that the measures r_{pb} and calibration were weakly correlated. A modest relation was observed between the r_{pb} and the diagnosticity index. The calibration and over/underconfidence scores co-varied with task difficulty. Overconfidence was again observed for voice identification tasks.

In the year of 1986 in central Stockholm the Swedish head of state, Olof Palme, was shot with two bullets in the back by a gunman. The victim and his wife were walking along the streets of downtown Stockholm after a cinema show when they were attacked. The perpetrator escaped after the firing. Later, a suspect was identified by the victim's wife in a lineup. The victim's wife claimed she had a good memory for faces and made her identification with high confidence. The suspect was found guilty by the first instance, but was freed by a court of appeal.

This example illustrates one frequent type of metacognitive judgment in real criminal trials, that is, a witness' confidence judgment in having made a correct identification of the culprit. That confidence judgments are taken seriously by police officers was shown in a nationwide survey of police officers in the United States, where 86% of the police officers said that they normally ask witnesses for a confidence judgment after the identification (Wogalter, Malpass, & Burger, 1993; cited in Malpass, Sporer, & Koehnken, 1996).

However, Seemungal and Stevenage (this volume) highlights that the question of whether a witness' confidence **really** is predictive of identification accuracy has been debated among forensic psychologists. This stems from the fact that in experimental studies the confidence-accuracy correlation is generally low, and also moderated by a number of cognitive, motivational, personality, and social factors.

1.   FACTORS THAT MODERATE THE CONFIDENCE-ACCURACY CORRELATION

In an early study, Deffenbacher (1980) found that on closer inspection the Confidence-Accuracy (CA) correlation varied significantly across studies. A further observation was that the CA correlation co-varied with the optimality of the information-processing conditions during encoding, storage, and retrieval of the witnessed event. This lead Deffenbacher to conclude that the CA relation was correspondingly high when conditions were conductive to forming and holding a clear, accurate memory, or:

> "when confidence ceases to track memory accuracy, an eyewitness might then tend to express a particular level of confidence whether correct or incorrect, a level determined for a particular witness perhaps by personality variables. That is, though different witnesses would possess different confidence levels, variation of confidence scores within witnesses would be rather low. If the accuracy rate were low enough, very near chance or the guessing level, for example, a zero correlation could also result from confidence scores showing very little variability across witnesses as well, tending to cluster at the low end of the rating scale. Here there would be little variability between or within witnesses."
> (Deffenbacher, 1980, p. 246)

That is, when the information processing conditions are less optimal as, for example, when the perpetrator is disguised and the exposure duration is brief, the witness is less accurate on the identification test and confidence is less reliable. In these circumstances, confidence is probably based on other factors than the strength of the memory trace (e.g., the witness' personality). This in turn results in no variation in confidence judgments within the participants. Second, very low or high optimality can also constrain variability affecting both within- and between-participant correlations (i.e., ceiling and floor effects).

Consistently, with the optimality hypothesis, Cutler and Penrod (1989) and Brigham (1990) reported that the CA relation was stronger in conditions where the targets were distinctive in appearance compared to conditions with less distinctive targets. Also consistent with the claims by Deffenbacher is the work by Seemungal and Stevenage (this volume) which shows that the CA relation is stronger when the witness can form a clear, distinctive memory of an event and can mentally re-experience that event.

Contemporaneous with Deffenbacher, Leippe (1980) suggested that variation between studies could also be due to the presence or absence of reconstructive memory processes and/or suggestive social influence. For example, reconstructive processes in memory might influence identification accuracy while having less effect on confidence. Social influence processes, on the other hand, might influence confidence judgments while having less of an effect on the accuracy of the identification.

"[It] can now be seen that two features of human memory and cognition—their unconscious operation and their dynamic, integrative nature—define a system that seems indeed capable of altering memory and confidence in orthogonal directions, especially in the context of powerful and rich social situations. (Leippe, 1980, p. 271)"

Leippe's framework later inspired a number of additional studies (e.g., Luus & Wells, 1994a; Shaw, 1996; Wells & Bradfield, 1998), which all have confirmed the initial tentative findings by Leippe.

2.   METHODOLOGICAL DEVELOPMENT

While the research cited above has been concerned with **moderator** variables for the CA relation (e.g., degree of optimality, social influence), other research has been concerned with **methodological** issues involved in measuring the CA relation (e.g., Cutler & Penrod, 1988; Juslin, Olsson, & Winman, 1996; Lindsay, Read, & Sharma, 1998; Luus & Wells, 1994b; Olsson, 2000; Weingardt, Leonesio, & Loftus, 1994; Wells, 1993). In a traditional study, confidence is assessed on a category scale and these assessments are correlated with the binary outcome, correct or incorrect identification, by means of a point-biserial correlation coefficient, r_{pb}. While the r_{pb} has been the standard measure, weaknesses of the correlation as a CA measure have been highlighted in the recent literature (Juslin et al., 1996; Lindsay et al., 1998; Weingardt et al., 1994).

One criticism against the correlation measure is that a low point-biserial correlation, r_{pb}, is, in principle, compatible with good or even perfect **calibration** (realism) of the confidence assessments (Juslin et al., 1996). Further, the r_{pb} provides no information about whether witnesses **over- or underestimate** the probability of a correct identification. A low r_{pb} is compatible with witnesses that make realistic confidence judgments, systematically over-estimate the probability of a correct identification, or systematically under-estimate the probability of a correct identification. This would appear to be information of crucial interest to the forensic system.

In calibration studies, realism of confidence is investigated by comparing subjective probabilities with corresponding objective probabilities. The witnesses are well calibrated, or realistic, in their confidence assessments, if the subjective probabilities are realized in terms of the corresponding relative frequencies (e.g., across all identifications made with 90% confidence, 90% should be correct). In principle, the calibration analyses provides the objective frequentistic probability of a correct identification as a function of confidence level. This analysis highlights the issue of whether the witnesses over- or underestimate the probability of a correct limitation. The main methodological limitation of calibration analysis is that the outcome of the analysis depends on the base-rate of culprit-absent line-ups. To the extent that the base-rate in the experiment departs markedly from the base-rate in real lineups, the results may fail to generalize to real forensic settings (the same appears to be true of the r_{pb}, though). This problem is mitigated by the fact that the outcome of a calibration analysis can be corrected for other assumptions about the base-rate (see Juslin et al., 1996).

A second problem with the correlation is that it provides almost no information about whether confidence is diagnostic or not, in the sense that it should be of use when evaluating eyewitness identifications made with different levels of confidence. **Diagnosticity** indices are derived by computing the likelihood ratios for a correct identification as a function of confidence level (Wells & Lindsay, 1985). To the extent that confidence is useful for assessing the accuracy of identification, the likelihood ratios should increase with confidence (see Wells & Lindsay, 1985, or Juslin et al, 1996, on the computations involved). As with calibration analysis, however, a low r_{pb} is compatible both with virtually no diagnosticity as well as with extremely high diagnosticity. Diagnosticity has the additional virtue of being independent of the base-rate of culprit-absent lineups in the experiment. Diagnosticity, of course, goes to the very heart of the question that is of relevance to the forensic system: should we assign more weight to a witness with high than low confidence?

The reasons why both calibration and diagnosticity analysis may imply different conclusions from correlation analysis are essentially the same. First, a correlation measure only provides information about co-variation, not about the probability of a correct identification. Second, correlation measures are heavily affected by the confidence distributions elicited by specific and arbitrary experimental arrangements. If, for example, all participants are presented with the same encoding and identification conditions, there is little cause for stimulus-related variation in confidence. In contrast, both calibration analysis and likelihood ratios are computed **conditional** on specific confidence levels and therefore are independent of the distribution across confidence levels.

For these reasons, it has been proposed that the weaknesses of the correlation index can be overcome by using measures of calibration analysis and diagnosticity (Juslin et al., 1996). Note also that the differences between the measures may provide a partial explanation for the discrepant conclusions about the CA relation we find among forensic psychologists, on the one hand, and lay-people, on the other. One possibility may simply be that lay-people and the judicial system in general are mistaken. Another possibility, however, may be that the correlation analysis largely fail to provide the information relevant to assessing the usefulness of the CA relation. The intuition of lay people may fall closer to the aspects addressed by calibration and diagnosticity analysis –and perhaps appropriately so.

In a series of studies, we applied calibration and diagnosticity analysis to experiments on witness identification. Of primary interest was to investigate whether the conceptual differences between the measures outlined above also have important empirical implications. In Study I, calibration and diagnosticity was applied to eyewitness identification. In Study II, the same measures were applied to earwitness identification in three experiments. In Study III, a meta-analysis of the relation between the traditional point-biserial correlation and the alternative measures of calibration and diagnosticity was performed using fifty-two data sets from seven studies on witness identification.

3.   EMPIRICAL STUDIES

Investigations of the CA relation in witness identification have, with few exceptions, relied on simulated stimulus events (Wells, 1993). Typically, the participants are exposed to film scenarios, live stagings, or slide sequences. After a retention interval, they are asked to identify a persons from the event in a lineup or photo-spread, if possible, and to make a confidence judgment. In the experiments presented below, we apply this traditional method to both eyewitness and earwitness identification (further described below).

In the literature on witness identification, two types of confidence judgments have been investigated: Pre-decision confidence is expressed prior to the identification, that is, before the witness has seen the lineup or photo-spreads (analogous to the delayed judgments of learning, dJOLs, in the verbal learning domain). Post-decision confidence is obtained after an identification, that is, the witness states how confident he/she is that the identification was correct. These latter confidence ratings differ from feeling of knowing ratings, FOKs, in that they are given after every recognition judgment, not just after recall failures. In general post-identification confidence is more strongly related to accuracy (Narby, Cutler, & Penrod, 1996). In the experiments reported here only post-identification confidence is analyzed and discussed.

3.1   Study I (Juslin, Olsson, & Winman, 1996): Eyewitness Identification

The purpose of the experiment was to collect calibration data for eyewitness identifications with photo-spreads under a sample of realistic circumstances. Based on an extensive body of empirical data collected on calibration in other domains (e.g., Lichtenstein, Fischhoff, & Phillips, 1982, for a review), we hypothesized that: (a) there is a positive relation between subjective probability (confidence) and objective probability (relative frequency) also in eyewitness identification, even when the correlation is moderate or low. (b) This relationship should be robust and obtain at both high and low attention and for both shorter and longer retention intervals. The latter prediction was motivated by the fact that, whereas over- or underconfidence varies across different domains in previous research, the positive relation between objective and subjective probability is almost always observed.

The procedure of the experiment followed the standard eyewitness identification paradigm. The participants viewed a video-filmed theft under conditions created to promote incidental learning and were later required to identify the two persons ("culprits") that performed the theft in two separate photo-spreads, one for each culprit. To attain forensic relevance, the "culprits" were photographed at the Police Department in Uppsala and the photos of the foils were selected by experienced police officers from the photo material (mug-shots) used by the Police Department in Uppsala in regular police investigations. The foils in the photo-spreads were selected in two different ways: either to satisfy a **culprit description** or for maximal **suspect-similarity** (where the suspect is either innocent or identical to the culprit). (See Wells, 1993, for a discussion of the forensic relevance of this distinction.). The participants returned after one hour or one week to identify both a central and a peripheral culprit (i.e., the culprits differed in salience and exposure time in the video film).

The calibration analysis revealed a clear positive relationship between subjective probability (confidence) and objective probability of a correct identification in all conditions. Both overall identification performance and calibration was better in the culprit-description than the suspect-similarity condition. Consistently with the second hypothesis, the calibration curves were little affected by the salience of the culprit (central *vs.* peripheral) or the retention interval (1 hour *vs.* one week). The left-hand side of Figure 1 exemplifies calibration curves. The diagnosticity analysis showed that the likelihood ratio increased from about 1 at confidence .1 and .2 to 16 at confidence .9 and 1.0 (right-hand side of Figure 1).

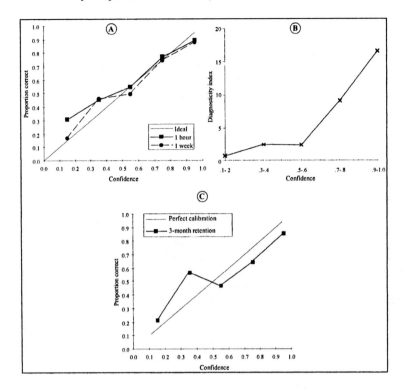

Figure 1. (A) Calibration curve and (B) diagnosticity index as a function of confidence in experiment 1. (C) Calibration curve from experiment 2.

The point-biserial correlations were relatively high, the r_{pb} was .55 in the culprit-description condition and .48 in the suspect-similarity condition, as compared to the average of .25 reported in the meta-analysis by Bothwell, Deffenbacher and Brigham (1987). That is, we succeeded in showing that confidence can be well calibrated and diagnostic, but the correlations were high as well. The question remained as to whether we can identify empirical circumstances where the witnesses are well calibrated despite a moderate or low r_{pb}.

The aim of Experiment 2 was to design an experiment where the correlation is lower. Half of the subjects saw the same stimulus films as in the above experiment, the other half saw shorter versions of the same films, created by selecting a 15 second sequence from the original version (short exposure). For half of the subjects the retention interval was one week (as in one condition of the Experiment 1), for the other half, the retention interval was three months (long retention interval). These manipulations should make identification harder and lead to a lower correlation. In Experiment 2 there again was a clear positive relation between subjective and objective probability with reasonable calibration, even under the more extreme conditions (e.g., 3-month retention). The point-biserial correlation was .34.

To summarize, the empirical data reported in these two experiments, based on the authentic photo material and procedures used by the Swedish Police in real crime investigations, indicate that, at least under some circumstances, witnesses can be reasonably well calibrated, despite a low r_{pb}. Notably, although these experiments do not involve misleading post-event information or other similar manipulations known to adversely affect the CA relation (see Wells, Malpass, Lindsay, Fisher, Turtle, & Fulero, 2000 for a recent review of these factors) they do implement a number of variables of clear forensic relevance, like incidental learning, short exposures and fairly long retention intervals.

3.2   Study II (Olsson, Juslin, & Winman, 1998): Earwitness Identification

The purpose of the first experiment of Study 2 was to investigate calibration of **earwitness** identification and to compare these results with those on **eyewitness** identifications obtained in Study 1. Do the results of reasonably good calibration and high diagnosticity for face identification –at least, in the circumstances administered in Study 1– generalize to earwitness identification of voices in similar circumstances? The two later experiments aimed to validate and confirm the observed difference in performance and calibration for eyewitnesses versus earwitnesses. The procedure and the participant population were similar to those in Study I for eyewitness identification.

The participants listened to a tape with four persons discussing what could be interpreted as criminal activities. The conversation on the tape concerned the arrival of a new shipment of a substance not specified in the conversation. Later the participants were required to identify the four voices in four separate voice lineups with eight voices in each "lineup". In order to ascertain the robustness of the CA relation we used two different exposure time at encoding, two different retention intervals and two different encoding instructions. The overall picture from the calibration curves for earwitnesses, was that accuracy and calibration was much worse compared to the eyewitnesses. Indeed, the calibration curve for the earwitnesses was virtually flat, with extreme overconfidence bias.

In Experiment 2, the purpose was to equate the estimator variables even more carefully. Specifically, we tried to equate the discriminative difficulty of the face and voice stimuli by presenting the participants with a representative distribution of face and voice features encountered within the same random sample of persons. We selected 32 persons, 16 females and 16 males, from a population of undergraduate students at Uppsala University. Photos and voice samples from these same 32 persons were used as stimuli. The idea was that this procedure would approximate the ecological distributions of voice and face characteristics, in a way that allows us to compare the recognizability of voices and faces from the same random sample of stimulus persons. The experimental procedure was simplified to an old/new recognition task, with strictly identical experimental procedures for faces and voices. The interesting question was: Will the same difference be observed in these circumstances, with reasonable calibration for faces and extreme overconfidence bias for voices?

The calibration curve for faces indicated very good calibration while there was strong overconfidence for almost all confidence categories in the voice condition. There was a sharp increase in diagnosticity for the faces, whereas the voices were subject to a much more modest increase which did not appear until the highest confidence category. One explanation for the difference in recognizability of voices and faces which has been proposed is the interference hypothesis, which states that the interference in memory is more profound for voices (Hammersley & Read, 1996). To test the interference hypothesis, we designed a third experiment where we reduced the number of training stimuli in each modality dramatically to only one, minimizing the interference. In both the voice- and face-conditions, there was a positive relation between confidence and the objective probability of a correct identification. In the voice-condition there was clear overconfidence even when the proportion correct was high (.73). In the face condition there was slight underconfidence. Calibration curves and diagnosticity functions from Experiment 3 of Study II are presented in Figure 2.

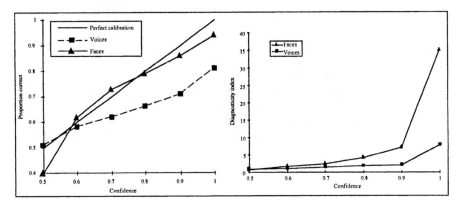

Figure 2. Calibration curves and diagnosticity indices for both voice and face identifications of experiment 3, Study II.

In sum, despite our efforts to rule out artifactual accounts of the observed difference between face and voice identification the difference persisted: There was good calibration and high diagnosticity for eyewitness identification of faces, but poor calibration with overconfidence and low diagnosticity for earwitness identification of voices.

3.3   Study III (Olsson, 2000): A Meta-Analysis

Because more studies had been conducted after Study I and Study II, the time was appropriate to do a meta-analysis of the relation between the measures using several relatively large empirical data sets. More specifically, in Study III the aim was to (a) Quantitatively compare the traditional correlation measure of the CA relation (i.e., r_{pb}) with the calibration and diagnosticity indices. When applied to the same empirical data sets, do they in general suggest the same or divergent conclusions? (b) Compare the calibration and diagnosticity of confidence for eyewitness and earwitness identification.

An aggregated analysis of the data from seven studies on eyewitness and earwitness identification was performed, where both the traditional and the alternative measures were computed. The criteria for inclusion were the following: (1) The study was an experimental study of eyewitness or earwitness identifications.

(2) The dependent measures of the study contained both r_{pb} and indices of calibration and diagnosticity. These studies provided 52 independent data points, with 28 independent data points with auditory voice identification tasks, and 24 independent data points with visual face identification tasks. The participant sample size of the 52 conditions was 780 participants. The average r_{pb} in these data was .30, a value that is close to the average correlation of .29 reported by Bothwell et al., (1987) in a meta-analysis of studies of the CA relation in eyewitness identification.

The standard measure of calibration is the mean squared deviation between the subjective and objective probability, where a score of zero indicates perfect calibration (see, e.g., Yates, 1990, for details). Overall, the measures of calibration and r_{pb} were uncorrelated, $r = -.11$, *ns*. The scatterplot is presented in the left-side panel of Figure 3. For approximately one third of the data points, the calibration score is zero or almost zero (close to perfect calibration) despite a highly variable r_{pb} (range = .00 - .63). There was likewise a low and non-significant relation between r_{pb} and diagnosticity of confidence ($r_{pb} = .31$, *ns.*).

In addition to the comparison of the measures of the CA relation, a comparison between the CA relation in the visual and auditory modality was made. Recall that earlier individual studies in Study II had shown a tendency for earwitnesses to be more overconfident than eyewitnesses. In the aggregated analysis, earwitnesses were overestimating their accuracy by 43% across conditions where the probability was assessed on a **full-range scale** between 0 and 1 and by 8% across the conditions where confidence was assessed on a half-range scale between .5 and 1 (i.e., in two-alternative tasks). In contrast, participants in eyewitness tasks were only slightly overconfident across the full-range conditions and even somewhat underconfident across the half-range conditions (see right-side panel of Figure 3).

However, it is important to note that in studies of calibration, task-difficulty tends to covary with over/underconfidence (**O/U**), a phenomenon referred to as the **hard-easy effect** (Lichtenstein, Fischhoff, & Phillips, 1982). Specifically, overconfidence is more common for tasks with a low proportion correct. Taking this into account, the difference in overconfidence bias between the two modalities might be caused by the fact that the eyewitness tasks were easier overall. The relation between confidence and accuracy indeed co-varied with the level of difficulty in the expected manner (see the right-side panel of Figure 3). Thus, for difficult tasks, participants tended to be overconfident, for easy tasks they tended to be underconfident. As demonstrated in Juslin, Winman and H. Olsson (2000), however, the psychological interpretation of the hard-easy effect is seriously complicated by the presence of a number of statistical and measurement artifacts. More important is that Figure 3 illustrates that there is also a main effect of auditive voice identification versus visual face identification that holds regardless of the task difficulty. That is, regardless of the difficulty (proportion correct), earwitness identification appears more prone to elicit overconfidence.

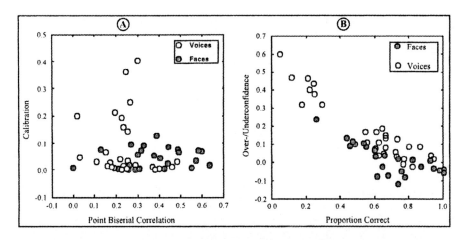

Figure 3. The relation between point-biserial correlation and calibration (A) and (B) Over-/underconfidence for different proportions of correct identifications for face identifications and voice identifications.

4. DISCUSSION

Regarding the measures, the analysis of the empirical data showed, first, that the alternative measures of calibration and diagnosticity of confidence were largely uncorrelated with the traditionally used correlation measure (i.e., r_{pb}). Second, the low correlation between the r_{pb} and the other indices holds both for auditory and visual identifications. Third, in several conditions involving eyewitnesses, the calibration score was close to zero, that is, indicating an almost a perfect correspondence between subjective probabilities and objective probabilities. Fourth, in some conditions where the calibration was almost zero (perfect) a highly variable r_{pb} was observed. This latter result is in line with the conceptual difference between the measures discussed in earlier sections. Thus, the arguments initially made by logical considerations of the r_{pb} index as a measure of the CA relation proved to have important empirical implications as well.

4.1 How to Measure the Confidence-Accuracy Relationship

What are the implications for further research? Table 1 summarizes some of the properties of the measures of the CA relation discussed in this chapter. As Table 1 indicates, r_{pb} gives an overall estimate of the **co-variation** between confidence and accuracy. One can note that the r_{pb} can be computed either between participants or within participants. When a r_{pb} is computed between participants, it assesses whether those participants who are most confident about their memories are also the most accurate. Within-participants r_{pb} is informative about whether identifications made with high confidence by a particular witness are more accurate than identification made with low confidence by the same witness.

Eyewitness research has almost exclusively focused on between-subject correlations (Bornstein & Zickafoose, 1999; Smith, Kassin, & Ellsworth, 1989). One reason is that the correlation across large numbers of participants will come near a good estimate of the CA relation for any particular participant (Bothwell et al., 1987). Between-subject correlations can be useful in court trials where two witnesses differ in their confidence levels. Thus, the benefit to this design is enhanced external validity relative to the within-participant designs.

As pointed out above, r_{pb} also has serious limitations. One major limitation concerns the information conveyed by a correlation. The common situation of applied interest is that the court is faced with a witness identification made with a stated level of confidence. Now assume that the court is told that the point-biserial correlation between confidence and accuracy is .3 (or that this is the information available to a forensic expert that appears at the trial). What is the appropriate logical inference in regard to the reliability of the identification?

It appears from the previous literature, that a r_{pb} of .3 in general (and implicitly) has been taken to imply that confidence is an information of little use to the court. This inference is simply not valid. The low correlation is compatible with both poor and perfect calibration. If the witness expresses high confidence and is well calibrated, the objective probability that the identification is correct is correspondingly high, despite the low r_{pb}. Likewise, the low r_{pb} is perfectly consistent with high diagnosticity of confidence. In this case, an identification made with high confidence should have a profound effect on the decision.

At a first glance the measures of calibration (together with the measure over/underconfidence) and diagnosticity seems to have many advantages over the r_{pb} (see Table 1). However, there are limitations with these methods too. The calibration scale demands very careful instructions to the participant. The instructions might be difficult to comprehend for special populations. Future research should investigate whether it is possible for, say, children at 12 years of age (and other non-student populations) to understand and use the subjective probability scale. Moreover, as already pointed out, calibration analysis is sensitive to the base-rate of culprit-absent lineups in the experiment (although the consequences of other base-rates can be ascertained post hoc, see Juslin et al., 1996). Finally, to get reliable estimates of the relative frequency of correct identification at each confidence levels, one needs a large number of experimental eyewitness identifications.

Table 1.
An Overview of the Information Gain and Advantages/Disadvantages with Each Measure.

	Point-biserial correlation	Calibration index and over/underconfidence	Diagnosticity index
Information gain	• overall covariation between confidence and accuracy • no information about the cause of low relation, e.g., over-or under-confidence? (-)	• overall relation between subjective probabilities and objective frequencies • accuracy at each level of confidence • informative about over-or under-estimation	• is used for determining posterior probability after identification for each confidence level
Disadvantages (-)/ advantages (+)	• is dependent on the confidence distribution in particular studies (-) • can give misleading results due to constrained variation in experiments, both continuous/ dichotomous variable affected (-) • possible to extrapolate despite restricted variance with regression line (+) • call for perfect discrimination only (-) • ambiguous scale (-) • covariation difficult to apply in court • normally gives a lower population estimate than other correlation indices (-)	• independent of confidence distribution (+) • is effected by base rates (which can be corrected with formula) (-) • less informative for confidence categories not used (-) • works with less than perfect discrimination (+) • less ambiguous scale (+) • provide information relevant in court (+) • instructions can be difficult to comprehend (-)	• independent of confidence distribution (+) • not effected by base rates (+) • can be difficult to obtain enough data points in experiments (-) • provide information relevant in court (+) • difficult to obtain prior probabilities (-)

In regard to diagnosticity, the studies we have performed indicate that it can be difficult to obtain the minimum amount of data points required for the analysis. This measure requires both identifications of the culprit and of the innocent suspect, but unfortunately identifications of innocent suspects were seldom made. This was true for several experiments discussed here. The crucial point is of course that only small portions of false identifications are used in the diagnosticity analysis (i.e., those of an innocent suspect). One solution is to have participants confront more than one lineup, but this strategy inevitably leads, if more than say three lineups per person are used, to questions of ecological validity, since it is unusual that the witness in real life identifications are confronted with more than one lineup.

The sensible conclusion seems to be, first, that interpretations of the forensic usefulness of the CA relation on the basis of a CA correlation should be exercised with extreme care. Second, whenever possible, the analysis of the CA relation should be supplemented by calibration and diagnosticity analysis, and, when possible, by both.

4.2   The Confidence-Accuracy Relationship for Faces Versus Voices

Another theme of our investigations was a comparison of the CA relation in the two modalities (i.e., auditory and visual) of concern to the forensic system. Earwitness identification, in contrast to eyewitness identification has not received much attention from psychological researchers (e.g., Yarmey, 1994). Earwitness testimony is less frequently used in court, even if there are criminal cases where voice identification can be used, for example when the victim is blind, or the perpetrator is masked, when the area is in darkness, or when the only contact with the perpetrator is via telephone. In general, the recognition of unfamiliar voices has been found to be variable, and often quite poor (Hammersley & Read, 1996). In regard to the CA of voice identification, there are as yet no systematic reviews, although the findings from individual studies show non-significant CA correlations (Yarmey, 1986).

How can the difference in calibration for earwitnesses and eyewitnesses be explained? One can speculate that the task in normal life is mostly to identify already familiar voices where there are contextual cues present. In contrast, in experiments neutral brief passages are used as a rule and the contextual cues are eliminated. Investigating these speculations further in a later study it was shown that calibration for familiar voices were much better than for unfamiliar voices under identical experimental conditions (Olsson, 1999). Further, one might speculate that the difference between earwitnesses and eyewitnesses regarding the CA relation is simply due to differing expertise. That is, we are all "experts" at recognizing faces because we use this method all the time to identify people, whereas voices are used to make such decisions much less often. One can speculate that such repeated practice leads to the use of more valid cues for metamemory judgments (see Koriat and Shitzer-Reichert, this issue, for a classification and discussion of metamemory cues). Further evidence that there is something "special" about face recognition comes from neuropsychological studies (prosopagnosia), single unit recordings in monkeys (selective responding to faces), developmental studies (faster eye tracking for faces), and standard memory research (the face inversion effect); (Farah, Wilson, Drain, & Tanaka, 1998).

Regarding calibration and expertise in general, research has shown that for example professional bridge players, meteorologists, and auditors can be well calibrated in their restricted domain (Allwood & Granhag, 1999). Applying the "expert hypothesis" to voice recognition, suggests possible work on blind participants' voice identification abilities, that is, to compare blind participants' earwitness abilities (especially calibration) with sighted participants' eyewitness abilities.

Authors note.
The research reviewed in this chapter was supported by a grant to the second author from the Swedish Council for Research in the Humanities and Social Sciences.

Chapter 4

Using state of Awareness Judgements to Improve Eyewitness Confidence-Accuracy Judgements

Florence V. Seemungal and Sarah V. Stevenage
Centre for Criminological Research and Probation Studies, University of Oxford, UK
Department of Psychology, University of Southampton, UK

Key themes: Appl / Meth / Perf

Key words: Eyewitness / Confidence / Accuracy / Remember/know / Children / Detail type

Abstract: Two experiments with adults (Experiment 1) and 8-9 year olds (Experiment 2) are reported which examined the effect of the state of awareness at retrieval to eyewitness accuracy, confidence and the reliability of the confidence-accuracy (CA) association. The novelty of the research is the application of the remember/know model to facilitate CA resolution. The recall of central and peripheral details was assessed 24 hours after a video event was shown. Adults were more accurate and confident for all details they remembered than knew. Remembering improved CA resolution, but only for central details. Children's accuracy, but not confidence in memory, was better for remember-based retrieval. Neither retrieval state nor detail assisted children to make reliable CA judgements. The research revealed first, the selective effect of remembering in CA resolution. Second, the components of remembering, such as context reinstatement and introspection, can overcome better central detail memory. Third, police interviewing techniques can potentially benefit from encouraging witnesses to reflect upon how they retrieve information and to report only what was personally experienced and remembered, than known.

Eyewitness testimony is of paramount importance. An accurate witness can provide vital information that clarifies an incident, initiates the search for a suspect, and sways a jury to convict or acquit a defendant. Witnesses attempt to convince others of the reliability of their memories through their expressions of confidence, for example, 'I am sure that the defendant was armed with a gun!' One would expect confident witnesses to be more accurate than those persons who are less certain of what they experienced. However, the psychological literature reveals that witnesses are not always accurate in their recollections of an event (see Wright &Davies, 1999 for recent reviews). Moreover, confident witnesses are not necessarily more accurate than those persons who express doubts about their knowledge (e.g., Robinson & Johnson, 1998) although Olsson and Juslin's chapter in Section Four report good CA calibration. When expressions of confidence lead to the mis-identification of suspects this can have life-threatening consequences. Olsson and Juslin provide a realistic example based on the shooting of the Swedish head of state in 1986.

The ability to match confidence with accuracy is represented in the confidence-accuracy (CA) relationship. Being confident when accurate and less certain when inaccurate demonstrates efficient memory monitoring. Koriat and Shitzer-Reichert's chapter in Section One highlighted first, the importance of assessing the reliability of metacognitive judgements; and second, the mechanisms by which individuals adapt their behaviour in line with efficient memory monitoring. These two issues will be examined with adults (Experiment 1) and children (Experiment 2). The main assumption underlying the present research is that a witness's state of awareness at the time information is retrieved is related to the accuracy of that report, the confidence with which the information is given, and the strength of the CA association.

Requesting witnesses to reflect upon, to identify how their knowledge was obtained, and the mental origins of their experiences, encourages efficient memory-monitoring. This should increase the reliability of CA judgements and benefit both the witness and the listener. The novelty of the current research is the application of the remember/know procedure to identify the specific mental retrieval state that accompanies a strong confidence-accuracy association.

The reliability of the CA association reflects the contents of the material being reported. Modest CA correlations are obtained for eyewitness memory compared to stronger correlations for general knowledge events (e.g., Bornstein & Zickafoose, 1999; Perfect &Hollins, 1996). Such evidence raises serious concerns given the weight jurors place on a witness's expressions of confidence to establish accuracy and credibility in the courtroom (e.g., Brewer, Potter, Fisher, Bond, &Luszez, 1999; Shaw, Garcia & McClure, 1999). Witnesses easily conform to the accounts of more confident witnesses (Wright, Self & Justice, 2000). Similarly, police officers rely on the level of confidence and the retrieval state of witnesses as measures of accuracy (Kebbell & Milne, 1998). These measures are incorporated in the criterion-based content analysis (CBCA) for detecting deception in witness testimony. The CBCA explicitly identifies the richness, contextual details, subjective mental states and the thoughts and feelings underlying memories as a measure of the authenticity of the reports (see Vrij & Akehurst, 1998 for a review). Given the heavy reliance on confidence as a predictor of accuracy, research into the metacognitive conditions that facilitate better CA judgements is relevant.

The weak to modest CA association reported in the eyewitness literature may be due to the following reasons. First, the element of surprise in becoming a witness may reduce accuracy for specific types of details, without altering confidence. In contrast, memory monitoring is efficient for judgements of learning (see Moulin, Perfect & Fitch's in this volume; Son & Metcalfe, 2000). Second, memories of a witnessed incident are a combination of the observer's reflections and reconstruction of that incident. Reconstructive memory processes weaken the CA association (Leippe, 1980). Third, the 'truth' of an eye-witnessed event is difficult to verify, compared to general knowledge events, and weak CA resolution is attributed to the lack of feedback inherent in witness observations (Wells, Lindsay & Ferguson,

1979). Fourth, the controlled, artificial nature of psychological experiments reduces the forensic realism and the variation in the data needed to produce strong CA correlations (Gruneberg & Sykes, 1993). Olsson and Juslin's chapter in this volume suggest that ceiling or floor effects in the data affect the CA correlation. Heterogeneous test items are associated with higher CA correlations because witnesses find some questions easier to answer than others and they are better able to match confidence and accuracy. Kebbell, Wagstaff and Covey (1996) report more reliable CA correlations for easy than hard test items.

The recall of critical details, central to an event as well as the peripheral details of an event are evaluated because it is forensically relevant and they also constitute heterogeneous test items. Accuracy and confidence are greater for central than peripheral details (e.g., Burke, Heuer &Reisberg, 1992; Migueles & Garcia-Bajos, 1999). Thus the CA association is expected to be stronger for central detail memory. However, there may be scope for significant improvement in the recall accuracy of peripheral details. Accurate peripheral details guide police investigations and they increase the perceived credibility of a witness in the eyes of the jury (e.g., Bell & Loftus, 1989; Heath, Grannemann, Sawa & Hodge, 1997). Consequently, the identification of a state of awareness that facilitates peripheral detail memory is a high priority.

1. THE ROLE OF STATE OF AWARENESS IN IMPROVING MEMORY AND METAMEMORY

The connection between retrieval conditions and accuracy has theoretical support. Deffenbacher's (1980) 'optimality hypothesis' links the strength of the CA association to the information processing conditions present during the encoding, storage and retrieval of material. Given the unexpected nature of some crime events, optimal encoding and storage conditions are not present. Nevertheless, an interviewer can encourage an optimal *retrieval* condition by directing witnesses to be aware of how their information was recollected. Tulving (1985) identified two states of awareness at retrieval, 'remembering' and 'knowing'. 'Remembering' is defined as autonoetic or self-knowing consciousness, characterised by the conscious awareness of past general events or a specific target item and its related contextual details. Visual or auditory memory prompt the feeling that the information was 'remembered'. In contrast, 'knowing' is described as noetic consciousness, characterised by a sense of familiarity of past events without the contextual details that would give rise to the knowledge of specific information.

The distinction between 'remembering' and 'knowing' draws theoretical support from the Source Monitoring Framework (SMF) presented by Johnson and Raye (1981). The SMF claims that the perceptual experiences of an event are encoded and stored alongside the contextual and source details. Accurate recollection of the accompanying context can facilitate memory of details specific, including the source of the information, because a richer network of associations can be activated. The ability to recall the source of an event is a powerful factor in determining accuracy of event recall itself (Henkel, Franklin &Johnson, 2000; Multhaup, De Leonardis & Johnson, 1999). Tulving's (1985) 'remember' state of awareness is associated with context reinstatement and it provides the conditions necessary for both memory and source monitoring. Source monitoring studies demonstrate the benefit of a 'remember' retrieval state to source accuracy and confidence of the narrator (e.g., Henkel, Johnson & DeLeonardis Leonardis,, 1998; Johnson, Nolde & DeLeonardis Leonardis,, 1996).

Research modelled after the remember/know procedure provide participants with descriptions of the two states of awareness and subsequently ask them to identify which mental state accompanied their retrieval of some previously presented material. Another way of improving memory monitoring is to ask individuals to provide a confidence judgement in the accuracy of their memory. People can regulate the information they choose to report or withhold (Koriat & Goldsmith, 1996). Consequently, information provided with a high degree of confidence is likely to be accurate than inaccurate. Remembering is associated with greater accuracy and confidence than knowing for word recall (Toplis, 1997, Experiment 1), word recognition (Gardiner & Java, 1991; Tulving, 1985, Experiment 1), and autobiographical reports (Conway, Collins, Gathercole &Anderson, 1996; Hyman, Gilstrap, Decker & Wilkinson, 1998).

The remember/know paradigm is not without criticism. A debate exists between those who consider remembering and knowing to be independent processes (Duzel, Yonelinas,Mangun, Heinze & Tulving, 1997; Tulving, 1983; 1985) and those who believe that a knowing state is implicitly achieved when someone remembers an experience (Gardiner, Gawlick & Richardson-Klavehn, 1994; Jacoby, Yonelinas &Jennings, 1997; Knowlton, 1998). Robinson and Johnson (1998) caution that introspective memory techniques, such as monitoring one's state of awareness in order to make a 'remember/know' distinction, can inflate confidence without regard for the accuracy of the recollected information. Despite these limitations, the positive effect of a 'remember' state on accuracy and confidence for general knowledge and autobiographical memory is expected to extend to eyewitness recall.

Experiment One examines the relationship between the state of awareness at retrieval to accuracy, confidence and the confidence-accuracy association. The CA association was measured using Goodman-Kruskal's gamma which is suitable for evaluating ordinal data containing tied scores (Wright, 1996). Perfect and colleagues assess the CA reliability for eyewitness memory using gamma (e.g., Perfect & Hollins, 1996; Hollins & Perfect, 1997). The evidence from source monitoring and remember/know studies suggest that eyewitness performance on all three measures would improve for remember-based responses.

2.   EXPERIMENT ONE

2.1   Method

Design. A 2 x 2 mixed factorial design was used in which State of Awareness (remember, know) and Detail Type (central, peripheral) were within-subjects variables. Participants were presented with information from a video-taped and an audio-taped event to evaluate source accuracy.

Participants. One hundred and sixty-seven A' Level students and Southampton University undergraduates (113 women, 54 men) ranging in age from 16-35 years (M = 19 years) participated in the study.

2.1.1 Materials.

To-be-remembered event. The video information, a novel event, was a film clip of a movie lasting 1 minute, 15 seconds. The film depicted a chase in which four men, one armed with a gun, pursued an man and a woman. Eight 'central' detail questions were devised based on events critical to the plot and actions performed by the main characters. Eight 'peripheral' detail questions were created relating to the background scenery and plot irrelevant material shown in the clip. The definition of central and peripheral details was modelled after Burke et al. (1992). Three independent raters viewed the clip and generated the questions. Inter-rater reliability was 95 percent across all the test items. The audio information was an extension of the film clip presented as an audio taped report, lasting 1 minute 24 seconds. Seven central and 7 peripheral detail questions were asked. Despite attempts to separate central and peripheral details, there is the possibility that these distinctions are blurred. This would reduce the effect of detail type on performance.

Questionnaire. Thirty-one questions were devised, the first of which was a practise question and formed no part of the data analysis. The order of the questions was listed in the chronological order in which the material was presented so that answers to earlier questions could not inform answers to later questions on the test. Participants either filled in the answer, gave a 'do not know' response, or indicated if they feel they would know the answer if they saw it, a 'feeling of knowing' judgement.

Instructions. The instructions were verbally administered and written on the test questionnaire. Definitions of remembering and knowing were modelled after (Tulving, 1983, 1985; Gardiner, Java and Richardson-Klavehn, 1996).

"When you answered the question, if you remembered SEEING or HEARING in your mind the information you needed to answer the question, then you REMEMBER the answer. If instead you simply had a feeling that 'I just know' the answer because it was familiar to me, then you KNOW the answer. Remembering is accompanied by a mental image or other auditory details, but knowing is not. Please do not guess and try to be as accurate as possible. If you cannot answer the question, I want you to tell me if this was because (a) you did not know the answer or (b) you feel you would know the answer if you saw it"

Participants were given an example of the difference between remembering and knowing and a manipulation check was conducted to ascertain that they understood the task and the instructions.

2.1.2 Procedure.

Participants watched the film clip in groups of 12-18 students. The audio material was presented 20 minutes later. For half the sample the procedure was reversed and the audio material presented first. Twenty-hours later a surprise memory test was administered. For each answered item on the recall test participants made three subsequent judgements: (1) a rating of confidence by means of a 5-point

Likert Scale (where 1 = not very confident, and 5 = very confident); (2) a source judgement, video or audiotape; and (3) a remember or know judgement.

2.2   Results

Responses were classified as accurate, inaccurate, do not know, or feeling of knowing. Only the video data was analysed because the focus is on the state of awareness accompanying the CA association, rather than source accuracy. Feeling of knowing judgements to unanswered questions were evaluated on a subsequent recognition test, but the data are not discussed. Unless specified, the effects of retrieval state and detail were analysed using a two way, repeated measures Analysis of Variance (ANOVA). The mean number of correct and incorrect responses, proportion of accurate responses and confidence are summarised by retrieval state and detail in Table 1.

Table 1.
Mean number of correct responses for the video information (out of 16) and proportion accuracy across detail type and state of awareness judgement for adult witnesses, together with confidence ratings when accurate (standard deviations shown in brackets).

	Central Details		Peripheral Details	
	Know	Remember	Know	Remember
No. correct responses	.64 (.96)	1.90 (1.90)	1.00 (1.25)	2.20 (1.79)
No. incorrect responses	.58 (.86)	.84 (1.20)	.69 (1.00)	.83 (1.09)
Proportion Accurate	.47 (.37)	.73 (.33)	.57 (.38)	.71 (.36)
Confidence when accurate	2.66 (1.10)	3.90 (.91)	3.90 (.13)	2.96 (1.09)

Mean number of accurate responses. Remembering was associated with more accurate responses than knowing (F (1, 166) = 84.47, MSE = 254.11, p < .001). Accurate peripheral details outnumbered central details (F (1, 166) = 22.54, MSE = 3.01, p < .001).

Proportion Accurate. The proportion of accurate responses was calculated for each individual in relation to the total number of retrieval attempts. There were 70 cases containing responses in all the experimental conditions. The ANOVA analysis confirmed the benefits of 'remembering' to recall accuracy (F (1, 69) = 27.13, MSE = 2.74, p < .025). Detail type was unrelated to accuracy (F (1, 69) = 1.57, MSE = .08, p > .05) and the interaction between retrieval state and detail was non-significant (F (1, 69) = 2.91, MSE = .24, p > .05).

Confidence in accurate responses. Confidence increased for remember-based responses (F (1, 39) = 30.40, MSE = 47.57, p < .001) but it did not vary by detail type (F (1, 39) = 2.46, MSE = .87, p > .05). The interaction between retrieval state and detail was non-significant (F (1, 39) = 1.46, MSE = .84, p > .05).

An analysis of accurate and inaccurate responses revealed that central details accurately remembered attracted higher confidence ratings than central details inaccurately remembered (F (1, 56) = 29.78, MSE = 13.13, p < .001). The mean and (standard deviation) scores were 3.65 (1.00) and 2.97 (.90) respectively. Similarly, peripheral details accurately remembered were more confidently expressed than peripheral details inaccurately remembered (F (1, 65) = 27.76, MSE = 9.67, p <

.001). The mean and (standard deviation) scores were 3.64 (1.04) and 3.10 (1.04) respectively. There was no difference in confidence for central details accurately and inaccurately known (F (1, 39) < 1, MSE = .05, p > .05). The mean and (standard deviation) scores were 2.64 (.93) and 2.65 (.98) respectively. There was no difference in confidence between peripheral details accurately and inaccurately known (F (1, 46) = 2.98, MSE = 1.31, p > .05). The mean and (standard deviation) scores were 2.95 (1.11) and 2.72 (1.11) respectively. In summary, remembering was associated with recall accuracy, confidence and it lowered confidence for inaccurate responses.

   Confidence-Accuracy Association. Gamma correlations were calculated for each participant across the experimental conditions. The mean, and significance of the CA correlation calculated from a one-sample t-test, are displayed in Table 2.

Table 2.
Mean confidence-accuracy gamma correlation (and standard deviation) across detail type and state of awareness for adult witnesses.

	Central Details	Peripheral Details
Know	-.08 (.16)	.28 (.15)
Remember	.55 (.09) *	.35 (.11)*

*p < .05 (2-tailed)

   A Wilcoxon signed ranks, 2-tailed test assessed the effect of retrieval state to the CA correlation. Remembering facilitated the mean central detail CA correlation more than knowing (z = 2.37, p < .025). The mean (and sum) of the ranks in which remembering facilitated the central detail CA correlation was 4.93 (34.50), while the mean (and sum) of the ranks in which a know state improved the central detail CA correlation was 1.50 (1.50). Retrieval state was unrelated to the peripheral detail CA correlation (z = 1.63, p > .05). The mean (and sum) of the ranks in which remembering facilitated the peripheral detail CA correlation was 0.00 (0.0), but the mean (and sum) of the ranks in which a know mental state improved the central detail CA correlation was 1.50 (1.50).

   Detail type was unrelated to the CA correlation reported during 'remembering' (z = 1.24, p > .05). The mean (and sum) of the ranks in which the mean central detail CA correlation was higher than the mean peripheral detail CA correlation was 13.80 (138.00). The mean (and sum) of the ranks in which the mean peripheral detail CA correlation was higher than the mean central detail CA correlation was 7.20 (72.00). Likewise, detail type was unrelated to the CA correlation during a 'know' retrieval state (z = .28, p > .05). The mean (and sum) of the ranks in which the mean central detail CA correlation was higher than the mean peripheral detail CA correlation was 5.92 (35.50), but the mean (and sum) of the ranks in which the mean peripheral detail CA correlation was higher than the mean central detail CA correlation was 7.08 (42.50). The data must be treated with caution because of the low number of participants in some conditions. However, the results are relevant because of the current paucity of data in this area.

2.3   Discussion

Experiment One evaluated the effect a witness's retrieval state has on accuracy, confidence and CA judgements. The SMF and remember/know models suggest that performance is better during a 'remember' retrieval state. The data supported these expectations. Memory for critical, central details are assumed to be better encoded and reported than peripheral information (e.g., Migueles & Garcia-Bajos, 1999). However, the central detail accuracy bias reported in the literature was eliminated in the present study. Weaker peripheral memory traces appeared to be more accessible during a 'remember' than a 'know' retrieval state. The data conformed to Tulving's (1985) expectations that a weaker memory trace can be accessed with a richer, retrieval cue. The results are forensically relevant given the importance of accurately reporting peripheral details to police inquiries and the credibility of a witness.

The value of the present data lie not only in establishing that accuracy and confidence improve with the ability to 'remember' events, but in identifying the conditions under which a CA association is reliable. This occurred when witnesses reported central details. Koriat (1998) felt that people are generally accurate in their memory-monitoring. Experiment One revealed that witnesses who are given the opportunity to think about, report how their knowledge was derived and who evaluate perceived accuracy, are more efficient at matching confidence and accuracy than is suggested in the eyewitness literature.

Koriat and Shitzer-Reichert's chapter identified age-related differences in memory monitoring in relation to judgements of learning (JOL). Developmentalists express concern about the reliability of children's eyewitness memory. Given the benefits of a 'remember' retrieval state to adult performance, the exploration of the role of retrieval-state to children's accuracy and confidence-accuracy judgements is a clear next step.

3.   EXPERIMENT TWO

There is a practical reason for investigating the reliability of children's evidence. Between October 1994 and April 1995 1,561 child witnesses testified in court, the majority were between 10 and 15 years. Of these witnesses 88 percent were alleged victims and 59 percent involved a single child witness (Davies, Wilson, Mitchell & Milsom, 1995). Home Office Statistics for England and Wales in 2000 revealed that 7,500 10-11 year olds and 21,700 12-14 year olds were found guilty or cautioned by the courts for various offences (Johnson, 2001).

Judges evaluate the quality of a witness's memory on an individual basis, but psychological evidence reveals a developmental difference in ability. Recall and source monitoring accuracy improve with age, with older children performing better than younger ones, though less well than adults (Foley & Ratner, 1998; McBrien & Dagenbach, 1998; Quas, Goodman, Bidrose, Pipe, Craw & Ablin, 1999; Shrimpton, Oates & Hayes, 1998). Reliable meta-memory judgements require children to be able to engage in source monitoring and to report only from personal experience (Poole & Lindsay (1998). The emphasis on 'personal experience' fits Tulving's (1985) description of autonoetic or self-knowing consciousness. If children are unable to remember an incident they are likely to report what they know from previous experiences. Fabricating or embellishing a fact jeopardises their credibility in the courtroom and the value of the testimony. The influence of retrieval strategies and detail type on CA judgements are considered. Mention is made of the effect of stress on CA processing because young children may become more stressed than older ones during an interview. The effect of stress or on memory is moderated by factors including conditions at retrieval and the type of detail reported.

Inaccuracies in memory are attributed to the inability to initiate retrieval strategies and to conduct exhaustive memory searches. Some theorists believe that children lack this skill (Ochsner, Zaragoza & Mitchell, 1999), but others disagree and propose instead that children simply do not use retrieval strategies spontaneously (Flavell & Wellman, 1977). Therefore, children would benefit from retrieval guidance and contextual cues (Gee & Pipe, 1995). Flavell (1999) advocated for research to identify how children relate their mental state to behaviour. It is hoped that in the present experiment directing children to think about how their information was obtained, would improve accuracy and CA judgements in the same way as it assisted adults in Experiment One. The ability to engage in introspection commences at an early age and 6 year olds can differentiate between remembering, knowing and guessing (Perner & Ruffman, 1995). Eight year olds are more accurate when they remembered than knew words and objects previously shown to them (Toplis, 1997). It is expected that a 'remember' retrieval state would assist children to match confidence and accuracy judgements.

Meta-memory efficiency relates to the type of detail recalled. Prosecutors are interested in the central details of an offence while defence barristers focus on the peripheral details surrounding the incident (Davies et al., 1995). The court assumes that young witnesses possess an equivalent ability to report the central, critical details along with the minutiae or peripheral details. In contrast, empirical research reveals that children are more accurate and less suggestible to misleading or post event information when reporting central details (Cassel & Bjorklund, 1995; Gobbo, 2000). Less is known about the effect of detail type on the CA association, so the present study fills this gap.

Stress at the time of exposure to an event affects the encoding of information. Anxiety during recollection influences the willingness and ability to report information, as well as beliefs in the certainty of knowledge. Children's reliability in reporting details of a medical examination revealed that embarrassment reduces disclosure and accuracy (Goodman, Quas, Batterman-Faunce, Riddlesberger, & Kuhn, 1994). This could potentially weaken the ability to calibrate confidence and accuracy. Seven, eight and eleven year olds are more accurate in reporting emotional than non-emotional behaviours described in narratives (Davidson, Luo & Burden, 2001). However, emotional arousal may impair children's memory for peripheral details as it does with adults (Burke et al., 1992; Christianson, 1992). Consequently, there may be a difference in the accuracy with which child-witnesses to abuse and child-victims of abuse report events.

There is a paucity of research on the effect of stress on children's CA processing although predictions can be made from adults' performance. Highly anxious individuals suffer from test anxiety during questioning and although they may be as accurate in recall as less anxious people, they lack confidence in their knowledge (Noland & Markham, 1998). Interestingly, pressuring adult witnesses to report details leads to an increase in both accurate *and* inaccurate information, but does not impair meta-cognitive accuracy (Winningham & Weaver III, 2000). Some aspects of the legal procedure create anxiety such as the mode of interrogation used, the social demand to conform to the authority figure of the interviewer, repeated interviewing, hostile or lengthy cross examination, requests to remember the minutiae of an event after a delay or failure to understand a question.

Psychological findings have influenced UK legislation. Provisions are made for children in the 'Memorandum of Good Practice on Video-Recorded Interviews with Child Witnesses for Criminal Proceedings' (1992), the Criminal Justice Act, 1988, and the Youth Justice and Criminal Evidence Act (1999). They have the opportunity of giving video-taped evidence, instead of, or in addition to a written statement. This is useful for young children who have limited verbal skills as video evidence provides a fuller picture of the way they respond to questioning. Young witnesses need not be actually present in the courtroom when they testify. They can be questioned and cross examined via a live video-link from an interviewing suite to the court. Children reported being more relaxed giving evidence on tape than testifying in court (Davies et al., 1995) and this is likely to improve accuracy and confidence in memory. Judges and barristers remove their wigs and gowns when defendants under 17 are in the Crown Court. These measures make court proceedings less formal and intimidating to children and ultimately to assist them in improving the quality of their evidence.

Experiment Two responds to the call for research to examine the strengths and weaknesses of children's memory monitoring efficiency (Bruck, Ceci & Hembrooke, 1998). Primary consideration is given to the role of the retrieval state to CA processing. A secondary issue is the effect of detail type on performance.

3.1   Method

Design. The experimental design was identical to that used in Experiment 1.

Participants. One hundred and eighty-one children (93 girls, 88 boys) ranging in age from 9-10 years (M = 9 years, 5 months), participated in the study. The children were recruited from 4 primary schools in Southampton.

Materials. All materials were identical to those used in Experiment 1. However, the instructions were simplified for use with children (e.g., 'how confident are you that your answer is correct' was changed to 'how sure are you that your answer is correct'). Instructions were administered to children verbally and written on the questionnaire. Feedback from participants revealed that the descriptions of the 'remember' and 'know' mental states, the task and the instructions were understood.

Procedure. This was identical to that used in Experiment 1.

3.2   Results

The results were analysed in the same way as Experiment 1. The mean number of correct and incorrect responses, proportion of accurate responses and confidence are displayed across retrieval state and detail in Table 3.

Table 3.
Mean number of correct responses for the video information (out of 16) and proportion accuracy across detail type and state of awareness judgement for child witnesses, together with confidence ratings when accurate (standard deviations shown in brackets).

	Central Details		Peripheral Details	
	Know	Remember	Know	Remember
No. correct responses	.59 (.99)	2.64 (2.10)	.60 (1.00)	2.59 (2.16)
No. incorrect responses	.56 (.08)	1.65 (.11)	.76 (.10)	1.91 (.16)
Proportion Accurate	.54 (.40)	.67 (.31)	.49 (.42)	.67 (.32)
Confidence when accurate	3.55 (1.36)	3.50 (1.08)	3.47 (1.00)	3.58 (.93)

Mean number of accurate responses. Remembering facilitated accuracy (F (1, 180) = 142.29, MSE = 738.07, $p < .001$) but there was no difference in the number of accurate central and peripheral details reported (F (1, 180) < 1, MSE = .11, $p > .05$).

Accuracy. There were 53 cases containing data across the experimental conditions.

The ANOVA analysis confirmed the advantage of remembering to accuracy (F (1, 52) = 9.95, MSE = 1.195, $p < .001$). Detail type was unrelated to accuracy (F (1, 52) < 1, MSE = .03, $p > .05$) and the interaction between retrieval state and detail was non-significant (F (1, 52) < 1, MSE = .07, $p > .05$).

Confidence in accurate responses. Unlike adults, children's confidence was unaffected by their retrieval state (F (1, 26) < 1, MSE = .02, $p > .05$) and detail type (F (1, 26) < 1, MSE = .0001, $p > .05$). The interaction between retrieval state and detail was non-significant (F (1, 26) < 1, MSE = .46, $p > .05$).

Confidence in accurate and inaccurate responses. The data patterned those obtained with adults. Confidence was higher for central details accurately than inaccurately remembered (F (1, 108) = 30.14, MSE = 15.69, $p < .001$). The mean and (standard deviation) scores were 3.79 (1.00) and 3.26 (1.05) respectively. Similarly, confidence was higher when peripheral details were accurately than inaccurately remembered (F (1, 103) = 12.83, MSE = 4.92, $p < .001$). The mean and (standard deviation) scores were 3.75 (1.00) and 3.44 (.95) respectively. There was no difference in confidence for central details accurately and inaccurately known (F (1, 27) < 1, MSE = .32, $p > .05$). The mean and (standard deviation) scores were 3.75 (1.11) and 3.60 (1.27) respectively. Confidence was also equivalent for peripheral details accurately and inaccurately known (F (1, 30) = 3.57, MSE = 1.27, $p > .05$). The mean and (standard deviation) scores were 4.11 (1.11) and 3.83 (1.12) respectively.

Confidence-Accuracy Association. The mean CA gamma correlations and significance are summarised across retrieval state and detail in Table 4.

Table 4.
Mean confidence-accuracy gamma correlation (and standard deviation) across detail type and state of awareness for child witnesses.

	Central Details	Peripheral Details
Know	.14 (.91)	.40 (.77)*
Remember	.28 (.76)**	.16 (.79)

* $p < .05$ (2-tailed) ** $p < .001$ (2-tailed)

The results of a Wilcoxon signed ranks test revealed no significant difference between remembering and knowing to the mean central detail CA correlation (z = .11, p > .05). The mean (and sum) of the ranks in which remembering facilitated the central detail CA correlation was 5.50 (11.00), while the mean of the ranks in which a know mental state improved the central detail CA correlation was 2.50 (10.00). Retrieval state was also unrelated to the mean peripheral detail CA correlation (z = 1.47, p > .05). The mean (and sum) of the ranks in which remembering facilitated the peripheral detail CA correlation was 1.00 (1.00), while the mean of the ranks in which a know mental state improved the peripheral detail CA correlation was 3.00 (9.00).

There was no effect of detail type on CA judgements derived during a remember retrieval state (z = .98, p > .05); the mean (and sum) of the ranks in which the central detail CA correlation was higher than the peripheral detail CA correlation was 25.58 (767.50), while the mean (and sum) of the ranks in which the peripheral detail CA correlation was higher than the central detail CA correlation was 26.60 (558.50). Detail type was also unrelated to the CA correlation during a 'know' retrieval state (z = .11, p > .05); the mean (and sum) of the ranks in which the central detail CA correlation was higher than the peripheral detail CA correlation was 3.67 (11.00). While the mean (and sum) of the ranks in which the peripheral detail CA correlation was higher than the central detail CA correlation was 3.33 (10.00).

3.3   Discussion

When children can 'remember' an incident they are more accurate, but not more confident, than when they 'know' the information. As a result the reliability of their CA judgements did not improve when they reported information they 'remembered seeing'. This suggests that accuracy and confidence are independent, rather than inter-related constructs (Leippe, 1980). The factors that enhance accuracy may not have the same effect on confidence, hence CA resolution is impaired. Alternatively, confidence judgements may be relatively stable whilst accuracy tends to vary more (Thompson &Mason, 1996). Although there was no overall effect of retrieval state or detail to the reliability of CA judgements, resolution was better for central details 'remembered' and peripheral details 'known'.

Three important findings are highlighted. First, 8 and 9 year olds can engage in memory monitoring sufficiently to be aware of, and to identify, how their memories were accessed. Second, the ability to reinstate, contextualise and retrieve associated details that accompany the process of 'remembering' transcends the age of the narrator and the content of the material reported. Children's eyewitness memories proved to be more reliable than is reported in some studies (e.g., Gobbo, 2000). Third, the data offered evidence that the central detail accuracy bias reported in the literature disappears for remember-based retrieval.

4.   GENERAL DISCUSSION

The two experiments reported in this chapter represent the first empirical investigation of the importance of the state of awareness accompanying eyewitness reports in assisting witnesses to match confidence and accuracy. The theoretical implications and practical applications of the research are outlined.

Recall accuracy. The improvements to word and autobiographical recall for remember-based recollection extended to eyewitness descriptions of persons and events. The memory literature reports a central detail accuracy bias but participants were equally accurate in answering all questions. Taken together the data suggest that a witness who remembers the information that he or she reports, is likely to be a more valuable witness than another witness who simply knows that an incident occurred. The knowledge that a 'remember' state of awareness accompanies accurate responses can be used to guide witnesses during questioning. Two interview techniques, the CBCA which was previously described and the Cognitive Interview (see Memon & Highman, 1999 for a review), currently used by the police in the United Kingdom incorporate context reinstatement and the phenomenological experiences of the interviewee.

Confidence. The remember/know model and the SMF stipulate that efficient memory and source monitoring increase the criterion necessary for accuracy and subsequently boosts confidence in recollections. The data derived from adult witnesses confirmed that confidence is higher during a 'remember' than a 'know' retrieval state. However, children's perceptions of their accuracy remained unchanged when they remembered the event, although their accuracy improved. It is possible that children feel less confident in their recall ability when there is a delay in reporting events. With delay children can remember content details sufficiently to accurately answer a question, but they may fail to remember the time and place where those events occurred (Newcombe & Siegal, 1997). It appears that the inability to engage in source monitoring affects another type of memory monitoring, confidence in memory.

Confidence-Accuracy Association. When adults remembered answers it facilitated reliable CA judgements, but only for central details. This result is not surprising when one considers that it is easier to remember salient, critical events that were attended to and well encoded. Children's CA judgements were statistically significant for central details they remembered and peripheral details they knew, but there was no overall effect of retrieval state, or detail type, to the strength of the CA correlation.

5. CONCLUSION

The data confirmed that the ability to remember events manifests itself in accuracy, confidence and reliable CA judgements. Meta-memory is enhanced by the ability to mentally re-experience and contextualise an event. Future studies need to consider the extent to which an eyewitness's retrieval state influences juror perceptions of that person's accuracy, confidence, and overall credibility. Jurors may attach different weights to statements in which a witness claims to 'know' a crime occurred as opposed to another witness who can 'remember' the crime. This is based on evidence that jurors are swayed by powerful words (Schooler, Clark & Loftus, 1988). Although both witnesses may have useful information about the incident, the present research reveals that the quality of remember-based recollections constitutes the more reliable testimony.

Varied situations and accuracy: concluding remarks

Marie Izaute, Patrick Chambres, Pierre-Jean Marescaux and Laurence Paire-Ficout
Université Blaise Pascal, Clermont-Ferrand, France

Three terms are central to this volume: Process, Function and Use. As we have already mentioned in the Preface, this volume was designed to show how the concept of metacognition is used and studied from several different but complementary angles. It demonstrates that many interesting connections can be made between research that deals with the processes of metacognition and that concerned with metacognitive functions and roles. Typically, the former has focused on the processes underlying metacognitive monitoring and control and with the dynamic of these processes as they mediate learning and remembering. The latter examines how and when people use their knowledge about their own thinking to guide their actions. This might occur when an airplane pilot changes course because he senses a more efficient route, or when a teacher changes her instructional style to challenge a student more.

Our aim was therefore to compare these "process" and "function" perspectives as well as to present the aspect of the "use" of metacognition. To what extent do the methods, tools, and the questions resulting from metacognition relate to fields such as eyewitness testimony or implicit learning? Finally, we address the question of how non-experts in the field of metacognition can provide us with models for consideration or, more specifically, how considerations resulting from the organization of representations can clarify the relation between consciousness and metacognition (Dienes & Perner, this volume, IV-1).

In fact, this volume contributes to the initial, fundamental stages in the synergism which is emerging from the meeting of these crucial complementarities and we shall see how they can be brought together for the benefit of both scientific knowledge and real-world application. The work on education by Hacker, Dunlosky and Graesser (1998) has already made a contribution to this attempt as do the examples given by Koriat and Shitzer-Reichert (this volume, I-1) at the end of their chapter. In each section, we emphasize the attempt to bring together and compare these different perspectives. Our conclusion will not consist of categorizing these three aspects of metamemory. Our objective will instead be to stress the complementarity of these perspectives in terms of certain key questions relating to metacognition. To shed specific light on these different angles of research, we have chosen in this conclusion to concentrate on two questions which we consider to be central to this volume: first, how can the various aspects combine, to illuminate and complement one another depending on the experimental or natural situations that are being studied and, second, how does accuracy –a point which is central metacognition– act in a complementary way depending on the different perspectives?

Historically, as several authors writing here have pointed out (Paris, this volume, III-1; Koriat & Shitzer-Reichert, this volume, I-1; Efklides, this volume, I-2), it was Flavell (1971) who gave birth to this discipline. According to Flavell (1979), a number of different characteristics are central to situations of metacognition: "My present guess is that metacognitive experiences are especially likely to occur in situations that stimulate a lot of careful, highly conscious thinking: in a job or school task that expressly demands that kind of thinking; in novel roles or situations, where every major step you take requires planning beforehand and evaluation afterwards; where decisions and actions are at once weighty and risky. Such situations provide many opportunities for thoughts and feelings about your own thinking to arise and, in many cases, call for the kind of quality control that metacognitive experiences can help supply" (Flavell, 1979, p. 909). In this volume, we present an illustration of the diversity of contexts in metacognitive studies. As we shall see in this initial section, learning, problem solving, strategy selection, airplane piloting and eyewitness reports all testify to the metacognitive basis of the cognitive operations pervasive in all moments of waking life.

1.   FROM READING AND LEARNING TO WEIGHTY AND RISKY SITUATIONS

What are the conditions and contexts under which metacognition is initiated or plays a supporting role? "Metacognition cannot be extricated from the context and appraised or studied independent of the task and purpose" (Paris, this volume, III-1). This is because any context is composed of many different elements, as a result of which a "function" and a "process" approach make it possible to identify the shared characteristics and how they focus on complementary aspects. This work provides a number of illustrations relating to various fields: the reading of texts, learning, problem-solving, strategy selection in higher-risk situations such as flying a fighter aircraft or acting as an eye-witness. Initially, we shall identify the aspects of metacognition involved in each of these contexts.

When studying new material, people normally monitor the extent to which they have mastered different parts of that material and control the allocation of learning resources accordingly (Koriat & Shitzer-Reichert, this volume, I-1; Moulin, Perfect & Fitch, this volume, I-3). In the situations presented in this volume, we can identify the metacognitive knowledge of expert subjects as well as that of others or the effect of greater familiarity with a specific field of activity. An example of the study of new material can be found in the field of in reading and text comprehension. A major issue in the metacognition of text comprehension literature is to understand why people's monitoring of text comprehension appears so poor. Rouet and Eme's proposition (this volume, III-2) is that text-based learning difficulties have to do with what students know (or don't know) about texts and comprehension tasks, the metatextual knowledge. For these authors, metacognitive knowledge involves a variety of dimensions of knowledge about the structural and functional properties of text. For example, they propose the identification of the functions of texts' basic features such as headings and paragraphs. Two studies were reported. The first shows that children (10-11 years old) still have a lot to learn about texts, comprehension and study strategies. The second study examines college students. The results reveal a massive increase in metatextual knowledge, although it is also clear that some student cannot define advanced features of texts (e.g., what is an index, what is it for?). It is not just the nature of metatextual knowledge that varies but also the knowledge of ways to improve the comprehension of text. Depending on the level of expertise, there is a greater level of diversity accompanied by a more appropriate utilization.

Moreover, Chambres, Bonin, Izaute and Marescaux (this volume, III-4) present an original aspect of expertise. For them, experts' metacognitive superiority is probably due to their competence level, but also to their "social position of expertise". The authors define this social position of expertise as an individual's perception of his or her relative degree of expertise. In an experimental study, they examined a conversation between two students who are using English as a foreign language. Students assigned an expert position produced more justifications associated with each orally-produced piece of advice, and identified more mistakes in their own texts than students in a non-expert position. These initial studies, which center on a somewhat functional approach, identify the variety of metacognitive knowledge as well as the use of this knowledge in the school context.

Remaining within a school context and using mathematical tasks, Efklides (this volume, I-2) contribution focuses on the study of the diversity of metacognitive evaluations. Efklides examines interrelations between the various metacognitive experiences such as feeling of confidence, feeling of familiarity, feeling of difficulty, the estimated correctness of the solution, and feeling of satisfaction. She consider how these evaluations change as a function of the stages of problem-solving: in advance of problem solving, planning phase and output of response phase and depending on task difficulty. In an illustrative study, described in this chapter, the author presented two mathematical tasks of differing complexity to students of 7th to 9th grade. The results suggested that task difficulty mainly influenced the intensity of the interrelations between the metacognitive feelings rather than the pattern of the relations. Unlike the initial examples, we have to consider here how a central factor can intervene in the various stages of the solving of a mathematical task.

Similarly, Cary and Reder (this volume, II-1) focus on the study of a process selection strategy, and evaluate the ways in which it is possible, across different experimental contexts, to identify functioning or decisions based on criteria that are common to all these contexts. They established that strategy selection varies across and within-individuals in response to dynamic features of the environment. Strategy selection was affected by two types of factors: intrinsic and extrinsic factors. One extrinsic factors is prior history of success with a strategy. The influence of this factor has been shown to affect strategy choice in several domains, including, for example, runway selection in an Air Traffic Control Task (Reder & Schunn, 1999).

This factor, history of success, contributes to what Valot (this volume, III-3) defines as the level of pleasure during the professional activity of piloting an airplane. In effect, the evaluation of pleasure depends on whether the person eventually decides that their personal objectives were met or not. This is an aspect of metacognitive knowledge reported by Valot in an unusual contribution. This author examines the role and content of metacognitive knowledge of operators involved in tasks that are highly dynamic, risky, and of a high level of cognitive complexity. Two studies of the activity of single-seater and two-seater combat aircraft pilots are reported. For Valot, three aspects are specific to this professional situation: evaluation of the level of pleasure, uncertainty and risk management. In particular in the "risk management" field the author emphasizes that it is crucial to assess the integrity of a person and the safety of a technical system. An heuristic was identified in which a pilot can only distribute his attention between roles and actions up to a certain point; beyond this point, excessive sharing can lead the pilot to run the risk of losing control of the situation.

Risk management is also involved at a fundamental level in eye-witness situations (Olsson & Juslin, this volume, IV-3; Seemungal & Stevenage, this volume, IV-4). In this situation, the point is that two different aspects are important, both the possible answer (a candidate response for the subject) and the requirements of the situation (the consequences of providing the response)?. This decision involves an evaluation of the risks, which may be too high and prevent the subject from responding, or acceptable and lead to the decision to provide a response. In effect, eye-witnesses to accidents evaluate the accuracy of what they have seen, and assess the implications of their testimony in order to decide whether to reveal what they know or think they know. An accurate witness can provide vital information that clarifies an incident, initiates the search for a suspect, and sways a jury to convict or acquit a defendant. Seemungal and Stevenage, in their chapter shows that confidence in the veracity of one's memories is boosted when the person can recall not only the event but also details of its context.

To what extent does the importance of accuracy differ depending on the activity in question? To what extent are the metacognitive knowledge or evaluations produced by an individual determined or modified by the situation? Using the example of a laboratory situation or a situation from everyday life, Koriat and Goldsmith (1996) show how subjects can include regulatory components in their responses if the objective of the task requires this. The authors have shown that a high level of external requirements (high motivation level) results in a reduction in the global number of provided responses coupled to an equivalent number of correct responses compared with the forced response condition, while also provoking a reduced number of incorrect responses.

In the same manner, the psychological literature reveals that witnesses are not always accurate in their recollections of an event, and that confident witnesses are not necessarily more accurate than those persons who are less certain about their knowledge (Seemungal & Stevenage, this volume, IV-4). The evaluation of this accuracy is problematic. Olsson and Juslin (this volume, IV-3) make the important methodological point that an observed correlation between performance and confidence only provides information about co-variation, not about the probability of a correct identification. In contrast, the computation of both calibration analyses and likelihood ratios is conditional on specific confidence levels and therefore independent of the distribution across confidence levels.

2. ACCURACY IN A FUNCTIONAL AND PROCESS PERSPECTIVE

Metacognitive knowledge and the outcome of metacognitive processes should be accurate. How should the question of accuracy be phrased? Within a functional perspective the question is how and when people use their knowledge about their own thinking and how it is that they are more accurate when they use their metacognitive knowledge? In a process perspective, the question is how accurate are metacognitive judgements and what are the factors that affect their accuracy?

A number of studies have examined accuracy and changes in accuracy as a function of the studied population. The question raised by Moulin et al. (this volume, I-3) is what the Alzheimer's Disease study can tell us about metacognition? In particular, they present novel empirical data that examines the nature of metamemory monitoring at encoding for repeated items using a Judgement of Learning (JOL) procedure. For the JOL data, they found that, whereas the older adult control group made predictions of performance that were in line with item repetitions, predicting higher performance for items seen on the third occasion than on the first, the Alzheimer Disease patients were insensitive to repetition in their JOLs. These patients were not aware of repetitions. However, the memory performance (recall and recognition) indicated that participants suffering from Alzheimer's Disease and older adult control groups benefited from repeated presentation of to-be-remembered items. Unlike Kinoshita (this volume, II-2) who defends the position that implicit memory and metacognition are unrelated, these authors suggest that some aspects of metamemory are implicit and others explicit.

Using an approach close to that adopted by Kinoshita (this volume, II-2), Marescaux, Izaute and Chambres (this volume, IV-2) suggest clarifying the distinction between implicit and explicit learning by using concepts and methods from research in metacognition. In the implicit learning situations, the examination of the knowledge reported by participants may make it possible to distinguish between explicit and implicit knowledge. One criterion, called the guessing criterion, requires us to examine whether performance is above chance level when people are told to choose at random. If accuracy is above chance, then there is actually some knowledge at work, and people are not aware of. It therefore follows that people are lacking metaknowledge. Dienes and Perner (this volume, IV-1) suggest that people's relative lack of metaknowledge in implicit learning paradigms justifies the claim that they have acquired genuinely implicit knowledge. Are differences in the evaluation of accuracy, therefore, a consequence of a lack of knowledge, the consequence of the use of implicit knowledge, or the consequence of an imprecision in the evaluation processes? As far as this last question is concerned, Weaver and Kelemen (this volume, I-4) investigated the reliability of individual differences in metacognitive accuracy in two experiments, examining within-subjects performance on four different tasks, ease of learning, feeling of knowing, judgement of learning and text comprehension monitoring. What is unique about these studies is the inclusion of measures of individual differences in metacognitive accuracy that are based on within-person evaluations. The question is how does subjects' accuracy change as a function of the tasks? As the authors point out, "the summary of these results is simple but powerful: while memory performance and confidence were stable across both time and task, metacognitive accuracy was not". Metamemory accuracy appears to reflect differences attributable to factors such as the conditions at time of judgement, the type of items being used, delay between prediction and test, type of processing used, retrieval fluency, and familiarity.

One example that is well represented in the present volume is cue familiarity (Cary & Reder, this volume, II-1; Lories, this volume, II-3). In answering general information questions, a rapid feeling of knowing (FOK), which may involve cue familiarity, develops during the early stage of memory retrieval (e.g., Reder & Ritter, 1992). In his chapter, Lories (this volume, II-3) reports experimental data about the accuracy of the FOK as a predictor of response correctness under various conditions of time pressure. The participants were asked to press a button whenever a question was presented that they thought they could answer, but they were given only a short time window in which to make this decision. The results support the idea that accuracy, when properly defined, remains under time pressure.

Another example of the variation in accuracy is reported in the volume. The variation relates as a function of the characteristics of the population (young, old; expert, non-expert, etc.) Here, Koriat and Shitzer-Reichert (this volume, I-1) report a study concerned with two factors that have been found to have marked effects on the accuracy of item-by-item JOLs among adults as well as among children. The two factors included repeated practice studying the same materials, and the elicitation of JOLs immediately after study or after an interval. Within a more functional perspective, accuracy seems to be the result of an adaptive capability. Acting dynamically when learning something new, children seem able to adapt their strategies as a function of the problems they address. What guides children's choices seems to be the effectiveness of one strategy compared to others (Cary & Reder, this volume, II-1).

When metacognitive experiences (process perspective) are based on the explicit use of a belief or theory, their accuracy should depend greatly on the validity of the underlying theories or beliefs. It is these theories or beliefs that have received a great deal of attention in the context of studies of metacognitive knowledge (functional perspective). The previous elements focus mainly on theoretical questions about metacognition that appear in various domains of research. In each domain, researchers have also attempted to link theory to specific applications. An interplay between process and function is widespread throughout many areas of psychology and is a promising approach for developing a theory that will be highly relevant to improving people's lives. This volume promotes a greater dialogue between the two approaches to metacognition. A combination of the two approaches is likely to offer interesting and important new avenues for investigation.

References

Afflerbach, P.P. (1990). The influence of prior knowledge and text genre on readers' prediction strategies. *Journal of Reading Behavior, 22,* 131-148.

Alexander, P.A., Schallert, D., & Hare, V. (1991). Coming to terms: How researchers in learning and literacy talk about knowledge. *Review of Educational Research, 61,* 315-343.

Allwood, C.M., & Granhag, P.A. (1996). Considering the knowledge you have: Effects on realism in confidence judgments. *European Journal of Cognitive Psychology, 8,* 235-256.

Allwood, C.M., & Granhag, P.A. (1999) Feelings of confidence and the realism of confidence judgments in everyday life. In P. Juslin, & H. Montgomery (Eds.) *Judgment and decision making: Neo-Brunswikian and process-tracing approaches* (pp. 123-146). Mahwah, NJ: Erlbaum.

Allwood, C.M., Granhag, P.A., & Johansson, H. (2000). Realism in confidence judgments of performance based on implicit learning. *European Journal of Cognitive Psychology, 12,* 165-188.

Amalberti, R. (1995). Diagnostic et prise de décision dans le contrôle de processus. In R. Ghiglione & J-F. Richard (Eds.), *Cours de psychologie, Vol. 6, Processus et applications* (pp. 397-413). Paris: Dunod.

Amalberti, R. (1996). *La conduite des systèmes à risque.* Paris: Presses Universitaires de France.

Amalberti, R., & Hoc, J.M. (1998). Analyse des activités cognitives en situation dynamique : pour quels buts ? comment ? *Le Travail Humain, 61,* 209-234.

American Psychiatric Association (1987). *Diagnostic and statistical manual of mental disorders, 3rd ed. (revised),* Washington DC: Author.

Anderson, J.R. (1983). *The architecture of cognition.* Cambridge, MA: Harvard University Press.

Anderson, J.R. (1990). *The adaptive character of thought.* Hillsdale, NJ: Lawrence Erlbaum Associates

Anderson, J.R. (1996). ACT: A simple theory of complex cognition. *American Psychologist, 51,* 355-365.

Anderson, J.R., Reder, L.M., & Lebière, C. (1996). Working memory: Activation limitations on retrieval. *Cognitive Psychology, 30,* 221-256.

Ardelt, M. (1997). Wisdom and life satisfaction in old age. *Journals of Gerontology, 52B,* 15-27.

Arkes, H.R., Christensen, C., Lai, C., & Blumer, C. (1987). Two methods of reducing overconfidence. *Organizational Behavior and Human Decision Processes, 39,* 133-144.

Armstrong, D.M. (1980). *The nature of mind and other essays.* Cornell University Press.

Armstrong, D.M. (1991). Intentionality, perception, and causality: reflections on John Searle's intentionality. In E. Lepore & R. Van Gulick (Eds.), *John Searle and his critics* (pp. 149-158). Basil Blackwell.

Atkinson, R.C., & Juola, J.F. (1973). Factors influencing speed and accuracy of word recognition. In S. Kornblum (Ed.), *Attention and Performance IV*, New York: Academic Press.

Bäckman, L., & Lipinska, B. (1993). Monitoring of general knowledge: Evidence for preservation in early Alzheimer's disease, *Neuropsychologia, 31*, 335-345.

Bacon, E., Danion, J., Kauffmann-Muller, F., Schelstraete, M-A., Bruant, A., Sellal, F., & Grange, D. (1998) Confidence level and feeling of knowing for episodic and semantic memory: An investigation of lorazepam effects on metamemory. *Psychopharmacology, 138*, 318-325.

Baddeley, A.D. (1986). *Working memory.* Oxford: Oxford University Press.

Bainbridge, L. (1980-81). Le contrôleur de processus, *Bulletin de psychologie, 34*, 813-832.

Baker, L. (1985). How do we know when we don't understand? Standards for evaluating text comprehension. In D.L. Forrest-Pressley, G.E. MacKinnon, & T.G. Waller (Eds.), *Metacognition, cognition, and human performance (Vol. 1)*, (pp. 155-205). London: Academic Press.

Bandura, A. (1977). Self-efficacy: Towards a unifying theory of behavioral change. *Psycholigical review, 84*, 191-215.

Barnes, A.E., Nelson, T.O., Dunlosky, J., Mazzoni, G., & Narens, L. (1999). An integrative system of metamemory components involved in retrieval. In D. Gopher & A. Koriat (Eds.), *Attention and Performance XVII - Cognitive Regulation of Performance: Interaction of Theory and Application* (pp. 287-313). Cambridge, MA: MIT Press.

Bastien, C., & Richard, J-F. (1995). La résolution de problèmes. In R. Ghiglione & J-F. Richard (Eds.), *Cours de psychologie, Vol. vol 6 : Processus et applications* (pp. 379-396). Paris: Dunod.

Bateson, G. (1995). *Vers une écologie de l'esprit* (Vol. 1). Paris: Editions du Seuil.

Begg, I., Duft, S., Lalonde, P., Melnick, R., & Sanvito, J. (1989). Memory predictions are based on ease of processing. *Journal of Memory and Language, 28*, 610-632.

Bell, B.E., & Loftus, E.F. (1989). Trivial persuasion in the courtroom: The power of (a few) minor details. *Journal of Personality and Social Psychology, 56*, 669-679.

Benjamin, A.S., & Bjork, R.A. (1996). Retrieval fluency as a metacognitive index. In L.M. Reder (Ed.), *Implicit memory and metacognition* (pp. 309-338). Hillsdale, NJ: Erlbaum.

Benjamin, A.S., Bjork, R.A., & Schwartz, B.L. (1998). The mismeasure of memory: When retrieval fluency is misleading as a metamnemonic index. *Journal of Experimental Psychology: General, 127*, 55-68.

Bentler, P.M. (1995). *EQS. Structural Equations Program Manual.* Encino, CA: Multivariate Software, Inc.

Berry, D.C. (1994). Implicit learning: Twenty-five years on. A tutorial. In C. Umiltà, & M. Moscovitch (Eds.). *Attention and Performance XV.* Cambridge, Mass.: MIT Press.

Berry, D.C., & Broadbent, D.E. (1984). On the relationship between task performance and associated verbalizable knowledge. *Quarterly Journal of Experimental Psychology, 36A*, 209-231.

Berry, D.C., & Dienes, Z. (1993). *Implicit learning: Theoretical and empirical issues.* Hove, England: Lawrence Erlbaum.

Beyer, S., & Bowden, E.M. (1997). Gender differences in self-perceptions: Convergent evidence from three measures of accuracy and bias. *Personality and Social Psychology Bulletin, 23*, 167-172.

Bjork, E.L. (1999).Assessing our own competence: Heuristics and illusions. In D. Gopher & A. Koriat (Eds.), *Attention and Performance XVII - Cognitive regulation and performance: Interaction of theory and application* (pp. 435-459). Cambridge, NJ: MIT Press.

Bjorklund, D.F., & Douglas, R.N. (1997).The development of memory strategies. In N. Cowan (Ed.), *The development of memory in childhood.* (pp. 201-246). Hove, UK: Psychology Press Publishers.

Borkowski, J.G., Carr, M., Rellinger, E., Pressley, M. (1990). Self-Regulated cognition: interdependence of metacognition, attributions, and self-esteem. In B.F. Jones, & L. Idol (Eds.), *Dimensions of thinking and cognitive instruction* (pp. 53-92). Hillsdale, NJ: Lawrence Erlbaum.

Bornstein, B.H., & Zickafoose, D.J. (1999). "I know I know it, I know I saw it": The stability of the confidence-accuracy relationship across domains. *Journal of Experimental Psychology: Applied, 5,* 76-88.

Bothwell, R.K., Deffenbacher, K.A., & Brigham, J.C. (1987) Correlation of eyewitness accuracy and confidence: Optimality hypothesis revisited, *Journal of Applied Psychology, 72,* 691-695.

Brand-Gruwel, S., Aarnoutse, C.A.J., & van den Bos, K.P. (1998). Improving text comprehension strategies in reading and listening settings. *Learning and Instruction, 8,* 63-81.

Brandt, J. (1991). The Hopkins Verbal Learning Test: Development of a new memory test with six equivalent forms. *The Clinical Neuropsychologist, 5,* 125-142.

Brentano, F. von (1874/1970). *Psychology from an empirical standpoint.* (Edited by O.Kraus, translated by L.L. McAllister.) London: Routledge

Brewer, N., Potter, R., Fisher, R.P., Bond, N., & Luszez, M.A. (1999). Beliefs and data on the relationship between consistency and accuracy of eyewitness testimony. *Applied Cognitive Psychology, 13,* 297-313.

Brickman, P., & Bulman, R.J. (. (1977). Pleasure and pain in social comparison. In J.M. Suls & R.L. Miller (Eds.), *Social comparison processes: Theoretical and empirical perspectives* (pp. 149-186). Washington, DC: Hemisphere.

Bridgeman, B. (1991). Complementary cognitive and motor image processing. In G. Obrecht & L.W. Stark (Eds), *Presbyopia research: From molecular biology to visual adaptation.* Plenum Press.

Brigham, J.C. (1990). Target person distinctiveness and attractiveness as moderator variables in the confidence-accuracy relationship in facial identification. *Basic and Applied Social Psychology, 11,* 101-115.

Britt, M.A., & Gabrys, G.L. (in prep.). *Teaching advanced literacy skills for the World Wide Web.* Manuscript in preparation.

Broadbent, D.E. (1971). *Decision and stress.* New York: Academic Press.

Broadbent, D.E., & Aston, B. (1978). Human control of a simulated economic system. *Ergonomics, 21,* 1035-1043.

Broadbent, D.E., Fitzgerald, P., & Broadbent, M.H.P. (1986). Implicit and explicit knowledge in the control of complex systems. *British Journal of Psychology, 77,* 33-50.

Brooks, L. (1978). Non-analytic concept formation and memory for instances. In E. Rosch & B.B. Lloyd (Eds.). *Cognition and categorization.* Hillsdale, NJ: Erlbaum.

Brown, A.L. (1978). Knowing when, where, and how to remember: A problem of metacognition. In R. Glaser (Ed.), *Advances in instructional psychology* (pp. 77-165). Hillsdale, NJ: Lawrence Erlbaum Associates.

Brown, A.L. (1980). Metacognitive development and reading. In R. Spiro, B. Bruce, & W, Brewer (Eds.), *Theoretical issues in reading comprehension* (pp. 453-481). Hillsdale, NJ: Lawrence Erlbaum Associates.

Brown, A.L., Armbruster, B.B., & Baker, L. (1986). The role of metacognition in reading and studying. In J. Orasanu (Ed.) *Reading Comprehension: From Research to Practice (pp. 49-75).* Hillsdale, N.J: Lawrence Erlbaum Associates.

Brown, A.L., Bransford, J.D., Ferrara, R.A., & Campione, J.C. (1983). Learning, remembering, and understanding. In J.H. Flavell & E.M. Markman (Eds.), *Carmichael's manual of child psychology* (Vol. 1, pp. 77-166). New York: Wiley.

Bruck, M., Ceci, S.J., & Hembrooke, H. (1998). Reliability and credibility of young children's reports. *American Psychologist, 53(2)*, 136-151.

Burke, A., Heuer, F., & Reisberg, D. (1992). Remembering emotional events. *Memory and Cognition, 20(3)*, 277-290.

Butterfield, E.C., Nelson, T.O., & Peck, V. (1988). Developmental aspects of the feeling of knowing. *Developmental Psychology, 24*, 654-663.

Carlson, R.A. (1997). *Experienced cognition.* Mahwah, NJ: Erlbaum.

Carruthers, P. (1992). Consciousness and concepts. *Proceedings of the Aristotelian Society, Supplementary Vol. LXVI*, 42-59.

Carruthers, P. (in press). *Phenomenal consciousness naturally.* Cambridge: Cambridge University Press.

Cary, M., & Carlson, R.A. (1995). Control of a fluent cognitive routine: Running arithmetic. *Unpublished manuscript.*

Cary, M., & Carlson, R.A. (1999) External support and the development of problem solving routines. *Journal of Experimental Psychology: Learning, Memory, and Cognition, 25*, 1053-1070.

Cassel, W.S. & Bjorklund, D.F. (1995). Developmental patterns of eyewitness memory and suggestibility. *Law and Human Behaviour, 19(5)*, 507-332.

Cataldo, M.G., & Cornoldi, C. (1998). Self-monitoring in poor and good reading comprehenders and their use of strategy. *British Journal of Developmental Psychology, 16*, 155-165.

Caverni, J.-P. (1988). Psychologie de l'expertise. *Psychologie Française, 33*, 114-125.

Chambres, P. (1993). Social comparison and knowledge construction. *Learning and Instruction, 3*, 23-38.

Chambres, P. (1995). Influence of an expert social position on incidental learning: The role of metacognitive activity. *International Review of Social Psychology, 1*, 79-99.

Chambres, P., & Marescaux, P.-J. (1998). Fictitious Social Position of Competence and Performance in a Second Language Interaction Situation: an experimental approach. *European Journal of Psychology of Education, XIII*, 411-430.

Chambres, P., & Martinot, D. (1999). Relationship between academic standing and academic self-beliefs. *European Psychologist, 4*, 19-32.

Cheesman, J., & Merikle, P.M. (1984). Priming with and without awareness. *Perception and Psychophysics, 36*, 387-395.

Cheesman, J., & Merikle, P.M. (1986). Distinguishing conscious from unconscious perceptual processes. *Canadian Journal of Psychology, 40*, 343-367.

Chrisley, R.L. (1996). *Non-conceptual psychological explanation: Content and computation.* D.Phil. thesis, University of Oxford.

Christensen, H., Kopelman, M.D., Stanhope, N., Lorentz, L., & Owen, P. (1998). Rates of forgetting in Alzheimer dementia. *Neuropsychologia, 36*, 547-557.

Christianson, S.A. (1992). Emotional stress and eyewitness memory: A critical review. *Psychological Bulletin, 112(2)*, 284-147.

Chun, M.M., & Jiang, Y. (1998). Contextual cueing: Implicit learning and memory of visual context guides spatial attention. *Cognitive Psychology, 36*, 28-71.

Clark, S.E., & Gronlund, S.D. (1996). Global matching models of recognition memory: How the models match the data. *Psychonomic Bulletin and Review, 3*, 37-60.

Cleeremans, A., & McClelland, J.L. (1991). Learning the structure of event sequences. *Journal of Experimental Psychology: General, 120*, 235-253.

Conway, M.A., Collins, A.F., Gathercole, S.E., & Anderson, S.J. (1996). Recollections of true and false autobiographical memories. *Journal of Experimental Psychology: General, 25,* 69-95.

Correa, D.D., Graves, R.E., & Costa, L. (1996). Awareness of memory deficit in Alzheimer's disease patients and memory impaired older adults. *Aging, Neuropsychology and Cognition, 3,* 215-228.

Costermans, J., Lories, G., & Ansay, C. (1992). Confidence level and feeling of knowing in question answering: The weight of inferential processes. *Journal of Experimental Psychology: Learning, Memory, and Cognition, 18,* 142-150.

Covington, M.V. (1992). *Making the grade: A self-worth perspective on motivation and school reform.* Cambridge: Cambridge University Press.

Crawford, J.D., & Stankov, L. (1996). Age differences in the realism of confidence judgments: A calibration study using tests of fluid and crystallized intelligence. *Learning Disabilities Research and Practice, 8,* 83-103.

Crick, F.C. (1994). *The astonishing hypothesis.* New York: Simon & Schuster.

Critchfield, T.S. (1996). Self-report about performance under time pressure: bias and discriminability. *The Psychological record, 46,* 333-350.

Cross, D.R., & Paris, S.G. (1988). Developmental and instructional analyses of children's metacognition and reading comprehension. *Journal of Educational Psychology, 80,* 131-142.

Cussins, A. (1992). Content, embodiment and objectivity: the theory of cognitive trails. *Mind, 101,* 651-688.

Cutler, B.L., & Penrod, S.D. (1988). Improving the reliability of eyewitness identification: Line-up construction and presentation. *Journal of Applied Psychology, 73,* 281-290.

Cutler, B.L., & Penrod, S.D. (1989). Moderators of the confidence-accuracy correlation in face-recognition: the role of information processing and base-rates. *Applied Cognitive Psychology, 3,* 95-107.

Damasio, A.R. (1994). *Descartes' error.* New York: Picador.

Darling, S., Sala, S.D., Gray, C., & Trivelli, C. (1998). Putative functions of the prefrontal cortex: Historical perspectives and new horizons. In G. Mazzoni & T.O. Nelson (Eds.), *Metacognition and cognitive neuropsychology: Monitoring and control processes.* (pp. 53-95). Mahwah, NJ: Lawrence Erlbaum Associates.

Davidson, D., Luo, Z. & Burden, M.J. (2001). Children's recall of emotional behaviours, emotional labels, and non-emotional behaviours: Does emotion enhance memory? *Cognition and Emotion, 15(1),* 1-26.

Davidson, J.E., Deuser, R., & Sternberg, R.J. (1994). The role of metacognition. In J. Metcalf & A.P. Shimamura (Eds.), *Metacognition: Knowing about Knowing* (pp. 207-226). Cambridge, MS: MIT Press.

Davies, G.M., Wilson, C., Mitchell, R. & Milsom, J. (1995). Videotaping children's evidence: An evaluation. *Home Office Report.*

Debner, J.A., & Jacoby, L.L. (1994). Unconscious perception: Attention, awareness, and control. *Journal of Experimental Psychology: Learning, Memory, and Cognition, 20,* 304-317.

Deffenbacher, K.A. (1980). Eyewitness accuracy and confidence: Can we infer anything about their relationship? *Law and Human Behaviour, 4,* 242-260.

Dennett, D.C. (1991). *Consciousness explained.* London: Penguin Press.

Dennett, D.C. (1996). *Kinds of minds: Toward an understanding of consciousness.* New York: Basic Books.

Dermitzaki, I. (1997). *The relations between dimensions of the self concept, level of cognitive development, and school performance* [in Greek]. Unpublished doctoral dissertation, Aristotle University of Thessaloniki, Greece.

Dermitzaki, I., & Efklides, A. (2000, May). *Goal orientations and their effect on self-concept and metacognition.* Paper presented at the 7th Workshop on Achievement and Task Motivation: An International Conference, Leuven, Belgium.

Dermitzaki, I., & Efklides, A. (2001). Age and gender effects on students' evaluations regarding the self and task-related experiences in mathematics. In S. Volet & S. Jarvela (Eds.), *Motivation in learning contexts: Conceptual advances and methodological implications* (pp. 271-293). Amsterdam: Elsevier.

Destrebecqz, A., & Cleeremans, A. (in press). Can sequence learning be implicit? New evidence with the Process Dissociation Procedure. *Psychological Science.*

Dienes, Z. (1987). *Selective attention: Relevance to hypnosis and hypnotizability.* Thesis submitted in partial fulfillment of the requirements for Master of Arts (Hons), School of Behavioural Sciences, Macquarie University.

Dienes, Z. (1992). Connectionist and memory array models of artificial grammar learning. *Cognitive Science, 16,* 41-79.

Dienes, Z. (1996). *How unconscious is the transfer of knowledge of artificial grammars across domains?* Invited paper presented at the 1996 Annual Conference of the British Psychological Society, Brighton, 11-14 April, 1996.

Dienes, Z., & Berry, D.C. (1997). Implicit learning: below the subjective threshold. *Psychonomic Bulletin and Review, 4,* 3-23.

Dienes, Z., & Fahey, R. (1995). The role of specific instances in controlling a dynamic system. *Journal of Experimental Psychology: Learning, Memory, and Cognition, 21,* 848-862.

Dienes, Z., & Fahey, R. (1998) The role of implicit memory in controlling a dynamic system. *Quarterly Journal of Experimental Psychology, 51A,* 593-614.

Dienes, Z., & Perner, J. (1996) Implicit knowledge in people and connectionist networks. In G. Underwood (Ed), *Implicit cognition* (pp. 227-256), Oxford University Press.

Dienes, Z., & Perner, J. (1999). A theory of implicit and explicit knowledge. *Behavioral and Brain Sciences, 22,* 735-755.

Dienes, Z., & Perner, J. (in press). A theory of the implicit nature of implicit learning. In Cleeremans, A., & French, R. (Eds), *Implicit learning and knowledge of the real world.* Psychology Press.

Dienes, Z., Altmann, G.T.M., & Gao, S-J. (1999). Mapping across domains without feedback: A neural network model of implicit learning. *Cognitive Science, 23,* 53-82.

Dienes, Z., Altmann, G.T.M., Kwan, L., & Goode, A. (1995). Unconscious knowledge of artificial grammars is applied strategically. *Journal of Experimental Psychology: Learning, Memory, and Cognition, 21,* 1322-1338.

Dienes, Z., Broadbent, D.E., & Berry, D.C. (1991). Implicit and explicit knowledge bases in artificial grammar learning. *Journal of Experimental Psychology: Learning, Memory, and Cognition, 17,* 875-882.

Dienes, Z., Kurz, A., Bernhaupt, R., & Perner, J. (1997). Application of implicit knowledge: deterministic or probabilistic? *Psychologica Belgica, 37,* 89-112.

Dillon, A. (1994) *Designing Usable Electronic Text: Ergonomics Aspects of Human Information Usage.* London: Taylor and Francis

Dillon, A., & Gabbard, R. (1998). Hypermedia as an educational technology: A review of the quantitative research literature on learner comprehension, control and style. *Review of Educational Research, 68,* 322-349.

Dokic, J. (1997). *Two metarepresentational theories of episodic memory.* Paper presented at the Annual Meeting of the ESPP in Padua, Italy August 1997.

Donaldson, W. (1996). The role of decision processes in remembering and knowing. *Memory and Cognition, 24,* 523-533.

Downes, J.J. (1988). Memory for repetitions and word fragment completion in normal, depressed and demented elderly. In M.M. Gruneburg, P.E. Morris, & R.N. Sykes (Eds.) *Practical Aspects of Memory - Volume 2: Clinical and Educational Implications.* Wiley: Chichester.

Dreher, M.J., & Guthrie, J.T. (1990). Cognitive processes in textbook chapter search tasks. *Reading Research Quarterly, 25,* 323-339.

Dretske, F. (1988). *Explaining behaviour: Reasons in a world of causes.* Cambridge (Massachusetts), London: The MIT Press.

Duffy, G.G., & Roehler, L.R. (1989). The tension between information-giving and mediation. In J. Brophy (Eds.), *Advances in Research on Teaching,* (pp. 1-33). London: JAI Press Inc.

Dufresne, A., & Kobasigawa, A. (1989). Children's spontaneous allocation of study time: Differential and sufficient aspects. *Journal of Experimental Child Psychology, 47,* 274-296.

Dulany, D.E. (1961). Hypotheses and habits in verbal 'operant conditioning'. *Journal of Abnormal and Social Psychology, 63,* 251-263.

Dulany, D.E. (1996). Consciousness in the explicit (deliberative) and implicit (evocative). In J.D. Cohen & J.W. Schooler (Eds), *Scientific approaches to the study of consciousness* (pp. 179-212). Erlbaum: Hillsdale, NJ.

Dulany, D.E., Carlson, R.A., & Dewey, G.I. (1984). A case of syntactical learning and judgement: How concrete and how abstract? *Journal of Experimental Psychology: General, 113,* 541-555.

Dunlosky, J., & Hertzog, C. (1998). Training programs to improve learning in later adulthood: Helping older adults educate themselves. In D.J. Hacker, J. Dunlosky, & A.C. Graesser (Eds.), *Metacognition in educational theory and practice.* (pp. 249-276). Mahwah, NJ: Lawrence Erlbaum Associates.

Dunlosky, J., & Nelson, T.O. (1992). Importance of the kind of cue for judgements of learning (JOL) and the delayed-JOL effect. *Memory and Cognition, 20,* 374-380.

Dunlosky, J., & Nelson, T.O. (1994). Does the sensitivity of judgments of learning (JOLs) to the effects of various study activities depend on when the JOLs occur? *Journal of Memory and Language, 33,* 545-565.

Dunlosky, J., & Nelson, T.O. (1997). Similarity between the cue for judgments of learning (JOL) and the cue for test is not the primary determinant of JOL accuracy. *Journal of Memory and Language, 36,* 34-49.

Dunlosky, J., & Schwartz, B.L. (1995, November). *Does relational information affect people's predictions of eventual free recall?* Poster session presented at the 36th annual meeting of the Psychonomic Society, Los Angeles.

Dunlosky, J., Nelson, T.O., Ishikawa, T., Domoto, P.K., Wang, M., Roberson, I., & Ramsay, D.S. (1998). Inhalation of 30% Nitrous Oxide impairs people's learning without impairing people's judgements of what will be remembered. *Experimental and Clinical Psychopharmacology, 6,* 77-86.

Duzel, E., Yonelinas, A.P., Mangun, G.R., Heinze, H., & Tulving, E. (1997). Event-related brain potential correlates of two states of conscious awareness in memory. *Proceedings of the National Academy of Science USA, 94,* 5973-5978.

Edwards, D., & Hardman, L. (1989). "Lost in hyperspace": cognitive mapping and navigation in a hypertext environment. In R. McAleese (Ed.) *Hypertext: Theory into Practice* (pp. 105-125). Oxford (U.K.): Intellect.

Efklides, A. (2001). Metacognitive experiences in problem solving: Metacognition, motivation, and self-regulation. In A. Efklides, J. Kuhl, & R.M. Sorrentino (Eds.), *Trends and prospects in motivation research* (pp. 297-323). Dordrecht, The Netherlands: Kluwer.

Efklides, A., & Demetriou, A. (1989). *Image of cognitive self, task knowledge, and cognitive performance.* Unpublished manuscript, Aristotle University of Thessaloniki, Greece.

Efklides, A., & Tsiora, A. (in press). Metacognitive experiences, self-concept, and self-regulation. *Psychologia: An International Journal of Psychology in the Orient.*

Efklides, A., & Vauras, M. (Guest Eds.). (1999). Metacognitive experiences and their role in cognition [Special issue]. *European Journal of Psychology of Education, 14*(4).

Efklides, A., Demetriou, A., & Metallidou, Y. (1994). Structure and development of propositional reasoning ability: Cognitive and metacognitive aspects. In A. Demetriou & A. Efklides (Eds.), *Intelligence, mind, and reasoning* (pp. 151-171). Amsterdam: Elsevier.

Efklides, A., Papadaki, M., Papantoniou, G., & Kiosseoglou, G. (1997). The effects of cognitive ability and affect on school mathematics performance and feelings of difficulty. *The American Journal of Psychology, 110*(2), 225-258.

Efklides, A., Papadaki, M., Papantoniou, G., & Kiosseoglou, G. (1998). Individual differences in feelings of difficulty: The case of school mathematics. *European Journal of Psychology of Education, XIII*(2), 207-226.

Efklides, A., Samara, A., & Petropoulou, M. (1996). Micro- and macro- development of metacognitive experiences: The effect of problem solving phases and individual differences [in Greek]. *PSYCHOLOGY, The Journal of the Hellenic Psychological Society, 3*, 1-20.

Efklides, A., Samara, A., & Petropoulou, M. (1999). Feeling of difficulty: An aspect of monitoring that influences control. *European Journal of Psychology of Education, 14*(4), 461-476.

Ehrlich, M.F., Kurtz-Costes, B., Rémond, M., & Loridant, C. (1995). Les différences individuelles dans la compréhension de l'écrit: Facteurs cognitivo-linguistiques et motivationnels. *Cahiers d'acquisition et de la pathologie du langage, 13*, 37-58.

Elio, R., & Scharf, P.B. (1990). Modeling novice-to-expert shifts in problem-solving strategy and knowledge organization. *Cognitive Science, 14*, 579-639.

Eme, E., & Rouet, J-F. (2001). Les connaissances métacognitives en lecture-compréhension chez l'enfant et chez l'adulte. *Enfance, sous presse.*

Englert, C.S., & Raphael, T.E. (1989). Developing successful writers through cognitive strategy instruction. In J. Brophy (Eds.), *Advances in Research on Teaching (Vol. 1)*, (pp. 105-151). London: JAI Press Inc.

Englert, C.S., Raphael, T.E., Fear, K.L., & Anderson, L.M. (1988). Student's metacognitive knowledge about how to write informational texts. *Learning Disability Quarterly, 11*, 18-46.

Erickson, M.A., & Kruschke, J.K. (1998). Rules and exemplars in category learning. *Journal of Experimental Psychology: General, 127*, 107-140.

Faerch, C., & Kasper, G. (1983). *Strategies in interlanguage communication.* London, England: Longman.

Farah, M.J., Wilson, K.D., Drain, M., & Tanaka, J.N. (1998). What is "special" about face perception? *Psychological Review, 3*, 482-498.

Fischer, P.M., & Mandl, H. (1984). Learner, text variables and the control of text comprehension and recall. In, H. Mandl, N. Stein &, T. Trabasso (Eds.), *Learning and Comprehension of Text* (pp. 213-254). Hillsdale, NJ: Lawrence Erlbaum Associates.

Flavell, J.H. (1971). First Discussant's Comments: What is Memory Development the Development of? *Human Development, 14*, 272-278.

Flavell, J.H. (1979). Metacognition and cognitive monitoring: A new area of cognitive-developmental inquiry. *American Psychologist, 34,* 906-911.

Flavell, J.H. (1981). Cognitive Monitoring. In P. Dickson (Ed.) *Children's Oral Communication Skills* (pp. 35-60). New York: Academic Press.

Flavell, J.H. (1999). Cognitive Development: Children's knowledge about the mind. *Annual Review of Psychology, 50,* 21-45.

Flavell, J.H. (1999). Remembering specific episodes of a scripted event. *Journal of Experimental Child Psychology, 73,* 266-288.

Flavell, J.H., & Wellman, H.M. (1977). Metamemory. In R.V. Kail, & J.W. Hagen (Eds.), *Perspectives on the Development of Memory and Cognition* (pp. 3-33). Hillsdale, NJ: Erlbaum.

Flavell, J.H., Flavell, E.R., & Green, F.L. (1983). Development of the appearance-reality distinction. *Cognitive Psychology, 15,* 95-120.

Fodor, J. (1983). *The modularity of mind.* Cambridge, MA: MIT/Bradford Press.

Foley, M.A. & Ratner, H.A. (1998). Distinguishing between memories for thoughts and deeds: The role of prospective processing in children's source monitoring. *British Journal of Developmental Psychology, 16,* 465-484.

Folstein, M.F., Folstein, S.E., & McHugh, P.R. (1975). Mini-Mental State: A practical method for grading the cognitive state of the patient for the clinician. *Journal of Psychiatric Research, 12,* 189-198.

Forbus, K.D., Gentner, D., & Law, K. (1994). MAC/FAC A model of similarity based retrieval. *Cognitive Science, 19,* 141-205.

Forster, K.I., & Davis, C. (1984). Repetition priming and frequency attenuation in lexical access. *Journal of Experimental Psychology: Learning, Memory and Cognition, 10,* 680-698.

Frensch, P.A. (1998). One concept, multiple meanings: On how to define the concept of implicit learning. In M.A. Stadler & P.A. Frensch (Eds.). *Handbook of implicit learning.* Sage Publications, Thousand Oaks.

Frensch, P.A., & Sternberg, R.J. (1989). Expertise and intelligent thinking: When is it worse to know better? In R.J. Sternberg (Eds.), *Advances in the Psychology of Human Intelligence (Vol. 5),* Broadway: Lawrence Erlbaum Associate Publisher.

Frensch, P.A., Lin, J., & Buchner, A. (1998). Learning versus behavioral expression of the learned: The effects of a secondary tone-counting task on implicit learning in the serial reaction task. *Psychological Research, 61,* 83-99.

Frijda, N. (1986). *The emotions.* Cambridge, UK: Cambridge University Press.

Frost, P.J., & Weaver, III, C.A. (1997). Overcoming misinformation effects in eyewitness memory: Effects of encoding time and event cues. *Memory, 4,* 1-12.

Gardiner, J.M. (1988). Functional aspects of recollective experience. *Memory and Cognition, 16,* 309-313.

Gardiner, J.M., & Java, R.I. (1991). Forgetting in recognition memory with and without recollective experience. *Memory and Cognition, 19(6),* 617-623.

Gardiner, J.M., & Parkin, A.J. (1990). Attention and recollective experience in recognition memory. *Memory and Cognition, 18,* 579-583.

Gardiner, J.M., Gawlick, B., & Richardson-Klavehn, A. (1994). Maintenance rehearsal affects knowing, not remembering – elaborative rehearsal affects remembering, not knowing. *Psychonomic Bulletin and Review, 1(1),* 107-110.

Gardiner, J.M., Java, R.I., & Richardson-Klavehn, A. (1996). How level of processing really influences awareness in recognition memory. *Canadian Journal of Experimental Psychology-Revue Canadienne de Psychologie Experimentale, 50(1),* 114-122.

Garner, R., & Alexander, P.A. (1989). Metacognition: Answered and unanswered questions. *Educational Psychologist, 24*, 143-158.

Garner, R., Macready, G.B., & Wagoner, S. (1984). Reader's acquisition of the components of the text-lookback strategy. *Journal of Educational Psychology, 76*, 300-309.

Gass, S., & Varonis, E. (1985). Variation in native speaker speech modification to nonnative speakers. *Studies in Second Language Acquisition, 7*, 37-57.

Gee, S., & Pipe, M.E. (1995). Helping children to remember: The influence of object cues on children's accounts of a real event. *Developmental Psychology, 31(5)*, 746-758.

Gentner, D., Rattermann, M.J., & Forbus, K.D. (1993). The roles of similarity in transfer: Separating retrievability from inferential soundness. *Cognitive Psychology, 25*, 524-575.

Gilbert, D.T., Giesler, R.B., & Morris, K.A. (1995). When comparisons arise. *Journal of Personality and Social Psychology, 69*, 227-236.

Gillingham, M.G. (1996). Comprehending electronic text. In H. van Oostendorp & S. de Mul (Eds.) *Cognitive aspects of electronic text processing* (pp. 77-98). Norwood, NJ: Ablex.

Glenberg, A.M., & Epstein, W. (1985). Calibration of comprehension. *Journal of Experimental Psychology: Learning, Memory, and Cognition, 11*, 702-718.

Glenberg, A.M., & Epstein, W. (1987). Inexpert calibration of comprehension. *Memory and Cognition, 15*, 84-93.

Glenberg, A.M., Sanocki, T., Epstein, W., & Morris, C. (1987). Enhancing calibration of comprehension. *Journal of Experimental Psychology: General, 116*, 119-136.

Glover, J.A. (1989). Improving readers' estimates of learning from text: The role of inserted questions. *Reading Research Quarterly, 28*, 68-75.

Glucksberg, S., & McCloskey, M. (1981). Decisions about ignorance: Knowing that you don't know. *Journal of Experimental Psychology: Human Learning and Memory, 7*, 311-325.

Gobbo, C. (2000). Assessing the effects of misinformation on children's recall: How and when makes a difference. *Applied Cognitive Psychology, 14*, 163-182.

Goethals, G.R. (1986). Social comparison theory: Psychology from the lost and found. *Personality and Social Psychology Bulletin, 12*, 261-278.

Gombert, J.E. (1990). *Le développement métalinguistique*. Paris: Presses Universitaires de France.

Goodman, G.S., Quas, J.A., Batterman-Faunce, J.M., Riddlesberger, M. and Kuhn, J. (1994). Predictors of accurate and inaccurate memories of traumatic events experienced in childhood. *Consciousness and Cognition, 3*, 269-294.

Goschke, T. (1998). Implicit learning of perceptual and motor sequences: Evidence for independent learning systems. In M.A. Stadler & P.A. French (Eds), *Handbook of implicit learning* (pp. 401-444). London: Sage Publications.

Graham, C., & Evans, F.J. (1977). Hypnotizability and the deployment of waking attention. *Journal of Abnormal Psychology, 86*, 631-638.

Green, A.J.K., & Gilhooly, K.J. (1992). Empirical advances in expertise research. In M.T. Keane, & K.J. Gilhooly (Eds.), *Advances in the psychology of thinking (Vol. 1)*, (pp. 45-70). Exeter: BPCC Wheatons.

Greene, J.D.W., Baddeley, A.D., & Hodges, J.R. (1996). Analysis of the episodic deficit in early Alzheimer's disease: Evidence from the doors and people test. *Neuropsychologia, 34*, 527-551.

Grober, E., & Kawas, C. (1997). Learning and retention in preclinical and early Alzheimer's disease. *Psychology and Aging, 12*, 183-188.

Gronlund, S.D., & Ratcliff, R. (1989). Time course of item and associative information: implications for global memory models. *Journal of Experimental Psychology: Learning, Memory, and Cognition, 15*, 846-858.

Gruneberg, M.M., & Sykes, R.N. (1993). The generalisability of confidence-accuracy studies in eyewitnessing. *Memory, 1(3)*, 185-189.

Guthrie, J.T. (1988). Locating information in documents: examination of a cognitive model. *Reading Research Quarterly, 23*, 178-199.

Hachinski, V.C., Linnette, D.I., Zilhka, E., DuBoulay, G.H., McAllister, V.L., Marshall, J., Russel, R.W.R., & Symon, L. (1975). Cerebral bloodflow in dementia. *Archives of Neurology, 32*, 632-637.

Hacker, D.J. (1998). Definitions and empirical foundations. In D.J. Hacker, J. Dunlosky, & A.C. Graesser (Eds.), *Metacognition in educational theory and practice* (pp. 1-23). Mahwah, NJ: Lawrence Erlbaum Associates.

Hacker, D.J. (1998). Self-regulated comprehension during normal reading. In D.J. Hacker, J. Dunlosky, & A. C. Graesser (Eds.), *Metacognition in educational theory and practive* (pp. 165-191). Mahwah, NJ: Lawrence Erlbaum Associates.

Hacker, D.J., Dunlosky, J., & Graesser, A.C. (Eds.) (1998). *Metacognition in educational theory and practice*. Mahwah, NJ: Lawrence Erlbaum Associates.

Hammersley, R., & Read, J.D. (1996). Voice identification by humans and computers. In S.L. Sporer, R.S. Malpass, & G. Koehnken (Eds.), *Psychological issues in eyewitness identification* (pp. 117-153). Mahwah, NJ: Erlbaum.

Hart, J.T. (1965). Memory and the feeling-of-knowing experience. *Journal of Educational Psychology, 56*, 208-216.

Harter, S. (1999). *The construction of self*. New York: Guilford Press.

Hayes, N.A., & Broadbent, D.E. (1988). Two modes of learning for interactive tasks. *Cognition, 28*, 249-276.

Heath, W.P., Grannemann, B.D., Sawa, S.E., & Hodge, K.M. (1997). Effects of detail in eyewitness testimony on decisions by mock jurors. *Journal of Offender Rehabilitation, 25*, 51-71.

Henkel, L.A., Franklin, N., & Johnson, M.K. (2000). Cross-modal source monitoring confusion between perceived and imagined events. *Journal of Experimental Psychology: Learning, Memory and Cognition, 26(2)*, 321-335.

Henkel, L.A., Johnson, M.K., & De Leonardis, D.M. (1998). Aging and source monitoring: Cognitive processes and neuropsychological correlates. *Journal of Experimental Psychology: General, 127(3)*, 251-268.

Heun, R., Burkhart, M., Wolf, C., & Benkert, O. (1998). Effect of presentation rate on word list learning in patients with dementia of the Alzheimer type. *Dementia and Geriatric Cognitive Disorders, 9*, 214-218.

Hinsley, D.A., Hayes, J.R., & Simon, H.A. (1977). From words to equations: Meaning and representation in algebra word problems. In P.A. Carpenter & M.A. Just (Eds.), *Cognitive processes in comprehension*. (pp. 89-106). Hillsdale, NJ: Lawrence Erlbaum Associaties.

Hintzman, D.L. (1986). "Schema abstraction" in a multiple-trace memory model. *Psychological Review, 93*, 411-428.

Hirshman, E., & Master, S. (1997). Modeling the conscious correlates of recognition memory: Reflections on the Remember-Know paradigm. *Memory and Cognition, 25*, 345-351.

Hockley, W.-E., & Murdock, B.B. Jr. (1987). A decision model for accuracy and response latency in recognition memory. *Psychological Review, 94*, 341-358.

Hollins, T.S., & Perfect, T.J. (1997). The confidence-accuracy relation in eyewitness event memory: The mixed question type effect. *Legal and Criminological Psychology, 2*, 205-218.

Holyoak, K.J., & Koh, K. (1987). Surface and structural similarity in analogical transfer *Memory and Cognition, 15*, 332-340.

Hyman Jr., I.E., Gilstrap, L.L., Decker, K., & Wilkinson, C. (1998). Manipulating remember and know judgements of autobiographical memories: An investigation of false memory creation. *Applied Cognitive Psychology, 12*, 371-386

Izaute, M., Larochelle, S., Morency, J., & Tiberghien, G. (1996). La validité du sentiment de savoir au rappel et à la reconnaissance [Validity of FOK in recall and recognition]. *Canadian Journal of Experimental Psychology, 50*, 163-181.

Jacobs, J.E., & Paris, S.G. (1987). Children's metacognition about reading: Issues in definition, measurement, and instruction. *Educational Psychologist, 22*, 255-278.

Jacoby, L.L. (1991). A process dissociation framework: Separating automatic from intentional uses of memory. *Journal of Memory and Language, 30*, 513-541.

Jacoby, L.L., & Kelley, C.M. (1987). Unconscious influences of memory for a prior event. *Personality and Social Psychology Bulletin, 13*, 314-336.

Jacoby, L.L., & Whitehouse, K. (1989). An illusion of memory: flase recognition influenced by unconscious perception. *Journal of Experimental Psychology: General, 118*, 126-135.

Jacoby, L.L., Kelley, C.M., & Dywan, J. (1989). Memory attributions. In H.L.I. Roediger & F.I.M. Craik (Eds.), *Varieties of memory and consciousness: Essays in honour of Endel Tulving* (pp. 391-422). Hillsdale, N.J.: Erlbaum.

Jacoby, L.L., Yonelinas, A.P., & Jennings, J.M. (1997). The relation between conscious and unconscious (automatic) influences: A declaration of independance. In J.D. Cohen and J.W. Schooler (eds), *Scientific Approaches to Consciousness*. (pp. 13-48). Lawrence Erlbaum Associates, Inc.

Jameson, K.A., Narens, L., Goldfarb, K., & Nelson, T.O. (1990). The influence of near-threshold priming on metamemory and recall. *Acta Psychologica, 73*, 55-68.

Jausovec, N. (1994). Metacognition in creative problem solving. In M.A. Runco (Ed.), *Problem finding, problem solving and creativity* (pp. 77-95). Norwood, NJ: Ablex publishing corp.

Jensen, R., & Benel, R. (1977). *Judgement evaluation and instuction in civil pilot training.* Springfield VA: FAA National Technic Information service.

Johnson, K. (2001). Cautions, Court Proceedings and Sentencing: England and Wales, 2000. *Home Office Report*, 20/01.

Johnson, M.K., & Raye, C.L. (1981). Reality monitoring. *Psychological Review, 88(1)*, 67-85.

Johnson, M.K., Hashtroudi, S., & Lindsay, D.S. (1993). Source monitoring. *Psychological Bulletin, 114*, 3-28.

Johnson, M.K., Nolde, S.F., & De Leonardis, D.M. (1996). Emotional focus and source monitoring *Journal of Memory and Language, 35*, 135-156.

Johnston, W.A., Dark, V.J., & Jacoby, L.L. (1985). Perceptual fluency and recognition judgments. *Journal of Experimental Psychology: Learning, Memory and Cognition, 11*, 3-11.

Johnston, W.A., Hawley, K.J., & Elliott, J.M.G. (1991). Contribution of perceptual fluency to recognition memory judgments. *Journal of Experimental Psychology: Learning, Memory and Cognition, 17*, 210-233.

Juslin, P., Olsson, N., & Winman, A. (1996). Calibration and diagnosticity of confidence in eyewitness identification: Comments on what can be inferred from the low confidence-accuracy correlation. *Journal of Experimental Psychology: Learning, Memory, and Cognition, 22*, 1304-1316.

Juslin, P., Winman, A., & Olsson, H. (2000). Naive empiricism and dogmatism in confidence research: A critical examination of the hard-easy effect. *Psychological Review, 107*, 384-396.

Kamas, E.N., & Reder, L.M. (1995). The role of familiarity in cognitive processing. In R.F. Lorch Jr., & E.J. O'Brien, (Eds), *Sources of coherence in reading* (pp. 177-202). Hillsdale, NJ: Lawrence Erlbaum Associates.

Kamas, E.N., Reder, L.M., & Ayers, M.S. (1996). Partial Matching in the Moses illusion: Response bias not sensitivity. *Memory and Cognition*, 24, 687-699.

Kebbell, M.P., & Milne, R. (1998). Police officers' perceptions of eyewitness performance in forensic investigations. *The Journal of Social Psychology*, *138(3)*, 323-330.

Kebbell, M.P., Wagstaff, G.F., & Covey, J.A. (1996). The influence of item difficulty on the relationship between eyewitness confidence and accuracy. *British Journal of Psychology*, 87, 653-662.

Kelemen, W.L. (2000). Metamemory cues and monitoring accuracy: Judging what you know and what you will know. *Journal of Educational Psychology*, 92, 800-810.

Kelemen, W.L., & Creeley, C.E. (2001). Caffeine (4 mg/kg) influences sustained attention and delayed free recall but not memory predictions. *Human Psychopharmacology: Clinical and Experimental*, 16, 309-319.

Kelemen, W.L., & Weaver, III, C.A. (1997). Enhanced metamemory at delays: Why do judgments of learning improve over time? *Journal of Experimental Psychology: Learning, Memory, and Cognition*, 23, 1394-1409.

Kelemen, W.L., & Winningham, R.G. (unpublished manuscript). *Practice improves mean metacognitive accuracy but not the stability of individual differences.*

Kelemen, W.L., Frost, P.J., & Weaver, III, C.A. (2000). Individual differences in metacognition: Evidence against a general metacognitive ability. *Memory and Cognition*, 28, 92-107.

Kelemen, W.L., Winningham, R.G., Renken, A.E., Frost, P.J., & Weaver, III, C.A. (1998, November). *Transfer appropriate monitoring: Matching prediction and retrieval conditions improves metacognitive performance.* Paper presented at the 39th annual meeting of the Psychonomic Society. Dallas.

Kelley, C.M., & Jacoby, L.L. (1996). Memory attributions: Remembering, knowing, and feeling of knowing. In L.M. Reder (Ed.), *Implicit memory and metacognition*. Mahwah, N.J.: Erlbaum.

Kelley, C.M., & Lindsay, D.S. (1993). Remembering mistaken for knowing: Ease of retrieval as a basis for confidence in answers to general knowledge questions. *Journal of Memory and Language*, 32, 1-24.

Kihlstrom, J.F. (1997). Consciousness and me-ness. In J.D. Cohen & J.W. Schooler (Eds), *Scientific approaches to consciousness*. New Jersey: Erlbaum.

Kihlstrom, J.F., & Cantor, N. (1984). Mental representations of the self. In L. Berkowitz (Ed.), *Advances in experimental social psychology (Vol 17)*, (pp. 2-47). New York: Academic Press.

King, J.F., Zechmeister, E.B., & Shaughnessy, J.J. (1980). Judgments of knowing: The influence of retrieval practice. *American Journal of Psychology*, 93, 329-343.

Kinoshita, S. (1995). The word frequency effect in recognition memory versus repetition priming. *Memory and Cognition*, 23, 569-580.

Kinoshita, S., Karayanidis, F., Woollams, A., & Tam, P.S. (1997). An ERP study of masked priming effect on recognition memory. *Paper presented at the 38th Annual Meeting of the Psychonomic Society*, Philadelphia, PA.

Kintsch, W. (1988). The role of knowledge in discourse comprehension: A construction Integration model. *Psychological Review*, 95, 163-182.

Kintsch, W. (1998). *Comprehension: a paradigm for cognition*. Cambridge, MA: Cambridge University Press.

Kirsch, I. (1991). The social learning theory of hypnosis. In Lynn, S.J., & Rhue, J.W. (Eds) *Theories of hypnosis: Current models and perspectives* (pp. 439-465). The Guilford Press: New York

Knowlton, B.J. (1998). The relationship between remembering and knowing: A cognitive science perspective. *Acta Psychologia, 98(2-3),* 253-265.

Koivisto, M., Portin, R., Seinela, A., & Rinne, J. (1998). Automatic influences of memory in Alzheimer's disease. *Cortex, 34,* 209-219.

Koriat, A. (1993). How do we know that we know? The accessibility model of the feeling of knowing. *Psychological Review, 100,* 609-639.

Koriat, A. (1994). Memory's knowledge of its own knowledge: The accessibility account of the feeling of knowing. In J. Metcalfe & A.P. Shimamura (Eds.), *Metacognition: Knowing about knowing* (pp. 115-136). Cambridge, MA.: MIT Press.

Koriat, A. (1995). Dissociating knowing and the feeling of knowing: Further evidence for the accessibility model. *Journal of Experimental Psychology: General, 124,* 311-333.

Koriat, A. (1996). Metamemory: the feeling of knowing and its vagaries. M. Sabourin, F. Craik, & M. Robert (Eds.), *XXVI International congress of psychology,* Vol. 2 (pp. 461-479), Montreal: Psychology Press Ltd.

Koriat, A. (1997). Monitoring one's own knowledge during study: A cue-utilization approach to judgments of learning. *Journal of Experimental Psychology: General, 126,* 349-370.

Koriat, A. (1998). Illusions of knowing: The link between knowledge and metaknowledge. In V.Y. Yzerbyt, G. Lories, & B. Dardenne. (Eds.), *Metacognition: Cognitive and Social Dimensions.* (pp.16-34). Thousand Oaks, CA: Sage.

Koriat, A. (1998). Metamemory: The feeling of knowing and its vagaries. In M. Sabourin, F. Craik, & M. Robert (Eds). *Advances in psychological science, Vol. 2: Biological and cognitive aspects* (pp. 461-469). Hove, England: Psychology Press.

Koriat, A. (2000). The feeling of knowing: Some metatheoretical implications for consciousness and control. *Consciousness and Cognition, 9,* 149-171.

Koriat, A., & Goldsmith, M. (1996). Monitoring and control processes in the strategic regulation of memory accuracy. *Psychological Review, 103,* 490-517.

Koriat, A., & Levy-Sardot, R. (1999). Processes underlying metacognitive judgments: Information-based and experience-based monitoring of one's own knowledge. In S. Chaiken & Y. Trope (Eds.). *Dual Process Theories in Social Psychology* (pp. 483-502). New York: Guilford Publications.

Koriat, A., & Levy-Sardot, R. (2000a). Conscious and unconscious metacognition: A rejoinder. *Consciousness and Cognition, 9,* 193-202.

Koriat, A., & Levy-Sardot, R. (2000b). *The combined contributions of the cue-familiarity and accessibility heuristics to feelings of knowing* (IIPDM Rep. No. 160). Haifa, Israel: University of Haifa, Institute of Information Processing and Decision Making.

Koriat, A., & Levy-Sardot, R. (2001). The combined contributions of the cue-familiarity and the accessibility heuristics to feelings of knowing. *Journal of Experimental Psychology: Learning, Memory and Cognition, 27,* 34-53.

Koriat, A., Goldsmith, M., Schneider, W. (1999). *Metamemory processes mediate the credibility of children's memory reports.* Paper presented at the 3rd meeting of the Society of Applied Research in Memory and Cognition, University of Colorado, Boulder, Colorado, July, 1999.

Koriat, A., Goldsmith, M., Schneider, W., & Nakash-Dura, M. (in press). The credibility of children's testimony: Can children control the accuracy of their memory? *Journal of Experimental Child Psychology.*

Koriat, A., Lichtenstein, S., & Fischhoff, B. (1980). Reasons for confidence. *Journal of Experimental Psychology: Human Learning and Memory, 6,* 107-118.

Kreutzer, M.A., Leonard, C., & Flavell, J.H. (1975). An interview study of children's knowledge about memory. *Monographs of the Society for Research in Child Development, 40* (1, Serial no. 159).

Laird, J.E., Newell, A., & Rosenbloom, P.S. (1987) Soar: An architecture for general intelligence. *Artificial Intelligence, 33,* 1-64.

Lave, J., & Wenger, E. (1991). *Situated learning: Legitimate peripheral participation.* New York: Cambridge University Press.

Lee, C.M., & Jackson, R.F. (1992). *Faking it.* Portsmouth,NH: Heinemann.

Leippe, M.R. (1980). Effects of integrative memorial cognitive processes in the correspondence of eyewitness accuracy and confidence. *Law and Human Behavior, 4,* 2611-274.

Lemaire, P., & Reder, L.M. (1999) What affects strategy selection in arithmetic? The example of parity and five effects on product verification. *Memory and Cognition, 27,* 364-382.

Leonesio, R.J., & Nelson, T.O. (1990). Do different metamemory judgments tap the same underlying aspects of memory? *Journal of Experimental Psychology: Learning, Memory, and Cognition, 16,* 464-470.

Lewicki, P., Czyzewska, M., & Hoffman, H. (1987). Unconscious acquisition of complex procedural knowledge. *Journal of Experimental Psychology: Learning, Memory, and Cognition, 13,* 523-530.

Lewicki, P., Hill, T., & Bizot, E. (1988). Acquisition of procedural knowledge about a pattern of stimuli that cannot be articulated. *Cognitive Psychology, 20,* 24-37.

Lewis, W.D., Canby, H.S., & Brown, T.K., Jr.(Eds.). (1946). *The Winston Dictionary* (College ed.). New York: Collier.

Lichtenstein, S., Fischhoff, B., & Phillips, L.D. (1982). Calibration of subjective probabilities: the state of the art up to 1980. In D. Kahneman, P. Slovic, & A. Tversky (Eds.), *Judgment under uncertainty: Heuristics and biases* (pp. 306-334). New York: Cambridge University Press.

Light, L.L. (1991). Memory and aging: Four hypotheses in search of data. *Annual Review of Psychology, 42,* 333-376.

Lin, L., & Zabrucky, K.M. (1998). Calibration of comprehension: Research and implications for education and instruction. *Contemporary Educational Psychology, 23,* 345-391.

Lindsay, D.S., Read, J.D., & Sharma, K. (1998). Accuracy and confidence in person identification: The relationship is strong when witnessing conditions vary widely. *Psychological Science, 9, 215-218.*

Lipinska, B., & Bäckman, L. (1996). Feeling of knowing in fact retrieval: Further evidence for preservation in early Alzheimer's disease. *Journal of the International Neuropsychological Society, 2,* 350-358.

Lockl, K., & Schneider, W. (submitted). Developmental trends in children's feeling-of-knowing judgments. *Developmental Science.*

Long, M.H. (1983). Native speaker/non-native speaker conversation and the negotiation of comprehensible input. *Applied Linguistics, 4,* 126-141.

Lonka, K., Lindblom, Y., & Maury, S. (1994). The effect of study strategies on learning from text. *Learning and Instruction, 4,* 253-271.

Lorch, R.F., Jr., Lorch, E.P., & Klusewitz, M.A. (1993). College students' conditional knowledge about reading. *Journal of Educational Psychology, 85,* 239-252.

Lories, G., & Petre, A. (unpublished). On the accuracy of a rapid Feeling of Knowing. *unpublished manuscript.*

Lories, G., & Schelstraete, M-A. (1998). The feeling of knowing as a judgment. In V.Y. Yzerbyt, G. Lories, & B. Dardenne (1998). *Metacognition: Cognitive and social dimensions* (pp. 53-68). London: Sage.

Lories, G., Dardenne, B., & Yzerbyt, V.Y. (1998). From social cognition to metacognition. In V.Y. Yzerbyt, G. Lories, & B. Dardenne (Eds.), *Metacognition: Cognitive and social dimensions* (pp. 1-15). London: Sage.

Lories, G., Engels, S., & Petre, A. (unpublished). Reminding and retrieval in speeded conditions. *unpublished manuscript.*

Lovelace, E.A. (1984). Monitoring future recallability during study. *Journal of Experimental Psychology: Learning, Memory and Cognition, 10,* 756-766.

Lovelace, E.A., & Marsh, G.R. (1985). Prediction and evaluation of memory performance by young and old adults. *Journal of Gerontology, 40,* 192-197.

Lovett, M.C., & Anderson, J.R. (1996). History of success and current context in problem solving. *Cognitive Psychology, 31,* 168-217.

Lovett, S.B., & Flavell, J.H. (1990). Understanding and remembering: Children's knowledge about the differential effects of strategy and task variables on comprehension and memorization. *Child Development, 61,* 1842-1858.

Lovett, S.B., & Pillow, B.H. (1995). Development of the ability to distinguish between comprehension and memory: Evidence from strategy-selection tasks. *Journal of Educational Psychology, 87,* 523-536.

Luus, C.A.E., & Wells, G.L. (1994a). The malleability of eyewitness confidence: co-witness and perseverance effects. *Journal of Applied Psychology, 79,* 714-723.

Luus, C.A.E., & Wells, G.L. (1994b). Eyewitness identification confidence. In D.F. Ross, J.D. Read, & M.P. Toglia (Eds.), *Adult eyewitness testimony: Current trends and developments* (pp. 348-362). New York: Cambridge University Press.

Maggi, B. (1996). La régulation du processus d'action de travail. In P. Cazamian, F. Hubault, & M. Noulin (Eds.), *Traité d'ergonomie.* Toulouse: Octarès.

Maki, R.H., & Berry, S.L. (1984). Metacomprehension of text material. *Journal of Experimental Psychology: Learning, Memory, and Cognition, 10,* 663-679.

Maki, R.H., & Swett, S. (1987). Metamemory for narrative text. *Memory and Cognition, 15,* 72-87.

Maki, R.H., Jonas, D., & Kallod, M. (1994). The relationship between comprehension and metacomprehension ability. *Psychonomic Bulletin and Review, 1,* 126-129.

Malpass, R.S., Sporer, S.L., & Koehnken, G. (1996). Conclusion. In S.L. Sporer, R.S. Malpass, & G. Koehnken (Eds.), *Psychological issues in eyewitness identification* (pp. 117-153). Mahwah, NJ: Erlbaum.

Mandler, G. (1980). Recognizing: The judgment of previous occurrence. *Psychological Review, 87,* 252-271.

Mandler, G., Nakamura, Y., & van Zandt, B.J.S. (1987). Nonspecific effects of exposure on stimuli that cannot be recognized. *Journal of Experimental Psychology: Learning, Memory and Cognition, 13,* 646-648.

Marescaux, P.-J., & Chambres, P. (1999). What is the cat in complex settings? *Behavioral and Brain Sciences, 22,* 773-774.

Marescaux, P.-J., Luc, F., & Karnas, G. (1989). Modes d'apprentissage sélectif et non-sélectif et connaissances acquises au contrôle d'un processus: évaluation d'un modèle simulé. *Cahiers de Psychologie Cognitive, 9,* 239-264.

Markus, H.R., & Kunda, Z. (1986). Stability and malleability of the self-concept. *Journal of Personality and Social Psychology, 51,* 858-866.

Markus, H.R., & Nurius, P.S. (1986). Possible selves. *American Psychologist, 41,* 954-969.

Markus, H.R., & Wurf, E. (1987). The dynamic self-concept: a social psychological perspective. *Annual Review of Psychology, 38,* 299-337.

Mathews, R.C., Buss, R.R., Stanley, W.B., Blanchard-Fields, F., Cho, J.R., & Druhan, B. (1989). The role of implicit and explicit processes in learning from examples: A synergistic effect. *Journal of Experimental Psychology: Learning, Memory, and Cognition, 15,* 1083-1100.

Mazzoni, G., & Cornoldi, C. (1993). Strategies in study time allocation: Why is study time sometimes not effective? *Journal of Experimental Psychology: General, 122,* 47-60.

Mazzoni, G., & Nelson, T.O. (Eds.). (1998). *Metacognition and cognitive neuropsychology: Monitoring and control processes.* Mahwah, NJ: Lawrence Erlbaum Associates.

Mazzoni, G., Cornoldi, C., & Marchitelli, G. (1990). Do memorability ratings affect study-time allocation? *Memory and Cognition, 18,* 196-204.

McBrien, C.M. & Dagenbach, D. (1998). The contributions of source misattributions, acquiescence, and response bias to children's false memories. *American Journal of Psychology, 111(4),* 509-528.

McGlynn, S.M., & Kaszniak, A.W. (1991). When metacognition fails: Impaired awareness of deficit in Alzheimer's disease. *Journal of Cognitive Neuroscience, 3,* 183-189.

McKenzie, C.R.M. (1998). Taking into account the strength of an alternative hypothesis. *Journal of Experimental Psychology: Learning, Memory, and Cognition, 24,* 771-792.

McKhann, G., Drachman, D., Folstein, M.F., Katzman, R., Price, D., & Stadlan, E.M. (1984). Clinical diagnosis of Alzheimer's disease: Report of the NINCDS-ADRDA Work Group under the auspices of Department of Health and Human Services Task Force on Alzheimer's disease. *Neurology, 34,* 939-944.

Memon, A., & Highman, P.A. (1999). A review of the cognitive interview. *Psychology, Crime and Law, 5,* 177-196.

Merikle, P.M., & Joordens, S. (1997). Parallels between perception without attention and perception without awareness. *Consciousness and Cognition, 6,* 219-236.

Merikle, P.M., & Reingold, E.M. (1991). Comparing direct (explicit) and indirect (implicit) measures to study unconscious memory. *Journal of Experimental Psychology: Learning, Memory and Cognition, 17,* 224-233.

Metallidou, P., & Efklides, A. (2001). The effects of general success-related beliefs and specific metacognitive experiences on causal attributions. In A. Efklides, J. Kuhl, & R.M. Sorrentino (Eds.), *Trends and prospects in motivation research* (pp. 325-347). Dordrecht, The Netherlands: Kluwer.

Metcalfe, J. (1996). Metacognitive processes. In E.L. Bjork & R.A. Bjork (Eds.), *Memory.* (pp. 381-407). New York: Academic Press.

Metcalfe, J., & Shimamura, A. (1994). *Metacognition: Knowing about knowing.* Cambridge, MA: Bradford Books.

Metcalfe, J., Schwartz, B.L., & Joaquim, S.G. (1993). The cue-familiarity heuristic in metacognition. *Journal of Experimental Psychology: Learning, Memory, and Cognition, 19,* 851-864.

Migueles, M., & Garcia-Bajos, E. (1999). Recall, recognition, and confidence patterns in eyewitness testimony. *Applied Cognitive Psychology, 13,* 257-268.

Miller, G. (2000). *The mating mind: How sexual choice shaped the evolution of human nature.* London: Heinemann.

Millikan, R.G. (1993). *White queen psychology and other essays for Alice.* Cambridge, MA: Bradford Books/MIT-Press.

Miner, A.C., & Reder, L.M. (1994). A new look at feeling of knowing: Its metacognitive role in regulating question answering. In J. Metcalfe, & A.P. Shimamura (Eds.), *Metacognition: Knowing about knowing.* (pp. 47- 70). Cambridge, MA: Bradford.

Mitchell, K.J., Johnson, M.K., Raye, C.L., & d'Esposito, M. (2000). fMRI evidence of age-related hippocampal dysfunction in feature binding in working memory. *Cognitive Brain Research, 10,* 197-206.

References

Monteil, J.-M. (1988). Comparaison sociale, stratégies individuelles et médiation socio-cognitives. Un effet de différenciations comportementales dans le champ scolaire. *European Journal of Psychology of Education, 3,* 3-18.

Monteil, J.-M. (1991). Social regulations and individual cognitive function: effects of individuation on cognitive performance. *European Journal of Social Psychology, 21,* 225-237.

Monteil, J.-M. (1992). Toward a social psychology of cognitive functioning: Theoretical outline and empirical illustrations. In M. Von Cranach, W. Doise, & G. Mugny (Eds.), *Social representations and the social bases of knowledge* (pp. 42-55). Berne: Hubert.

Monteil, J.-M., Brunot, S., & Huguet, P. (1996). Cognitive performance and attention in the classroom: An interaction between past and present academic experiences. *Journal of Education Psychology, 88,* 242-248.

Moscovitch, M. (1989). Confabulation and the frontal systems: Strategic versus associated retrieval in neuropsychological theories of memory. In H.L.I. Roediger & F.I.M. Craik (Eds.), *Varieties of memory and consciousness: Essays in honour of Endel Tulving.* Hillsdale, N.J.: Erlbaum.

Moscovitch, M. (1992). Memory and working-with-memory: A component process model based on modules and central systems. *Journal of Cognitive Neuroscience, 4,* 257-267.

Moulin, C.J.A. (submitted). Sense and sensitivity: Metacognition in Alzheimer's disease. Chapter to appear in Perfect, T.J. & Schwartz, B.L. (Eds.) *Applied Metacognition.* Cambridge University Press.

Moulin, C.J.A., Perfect, T.J., & Jones, R.W. (2000a). Evidence for intact memory monitoring in Alzheimer's disease: Metamemory sensitivity at encoding. *Neuropsychologia, 38,* 1242-1250

Moulin, C.J.A., Perfect, T.J., & Jones, R.W. (2000b). The Effects of Repetition on Allocation of Study Time and Judgements of Learning in Alzheimer's Disease, *Neuropsychologia, 38,* 748-756

Moulin, C.J.A., Perfect, T.J., & Jones, R.W. (2001). Global predictions of memory in Alzheimer's disease: Evidence for preserved metamemory monitoring, *Aging, Neuropsychology and Cognition, 7,* 230-244.

Multhaup, K.S., De Leonardis, D.M., & Johnson, M.K. (1999). Source memory and eyewitness suggestibility in older adults. *Journal of General Psychology, 126(1),* 74-84.

Murdock, B.B. Jr. (1982). A theory for the storage and retrieval of item and associative information. *Psychological Review, 89,* 609-626.

Murdock, B.B. Jr. (1987). Serial-order effects in a distributed-memory model. In D.S. Gorfein, & R.R. Hoffman (Eds). *Memory and learning: The Ebbinghaus Centennial Conference,* (pp. 277-310). Hillsdale, NJ: Lawrence Erlbaum Associates, Inc.

Myers, M., & Paris, S.G. (1978). Children's metacognitive knowledge about reading. *Journal of Educational Psychology, 70,* 680-690.

Narby, D.J., Cutler, B.L., & Penrod, S.D. (1996). The effects of witness, target, and situational factors on eyewitness identifications. In S.L. Sporer, R.S. Malpass, & G. Koehnken (Eds.), *Psychological Issues in Eyewitness Identification* (pp. 117-153). Mahwah, NJ: Erlbaum.

Narens, L., Jameson, K.A., & Lee, V.A. (1994). Subthreshold priming and memory monitoring. In J. Metcalfe & A.P. Shimamura (Eds.), *Metacognition: Knowing about knowing* (pp. 71-92). Cambridge, MA: MIT Press.

Nelson, T.O. (1984). A comparison of current measures of the accuracy of feeling-of-knowing predictions. *Psychological Bulletin, 95,* 109-133.

Nelson, T.O. (1988). Predictive accuracy of the feeling of knowing across different criterion tasks and across different subject populations and individuals. In M.M. Gruenberg, P.E.

Morris, & R.N. Sykes (Eds.), *Practical aspects of memory: Current research and issues (Vol. 1)*, (pp. 190-196). New York: Wiley.

Nelson, T.O. (1993). Judgments of learning and the allocation of study time. *Journal of Experimental Psychology: General, 122*, 269-273.

Nelson, T.O. (1996a). Consciousness and metacognition. *American Psychologist, 51*, 102-116.

Nelson, T.O. (1996b). Gamma is a measure of the accuracy of predicting performance on one item relative to another item, not of the absolute performance of an individual item. *Applied Cognitive Psychology, 10*, 257-260.

Nelson, T.O., & Dunlosky, J. (1991). When people's judgments of learning (JOLs) are extremely accurate at predicting subsequent recall: The "delayed-JOL effect." *Psychological Science, 2*, 267-270.

Nelson, T.O., & Dunlosky, J. (1994). Norms of paired-associate recall during multitrial learning of Swahili-English translation equivalents. *Memory, 2*, 325-335.

Nelson, T.O., & Leonesio, R.J. (1988). Allocation of self-paced study time and the "labor-vain effect". *Journal of Experimental Psychology: Learning, Memory, and Cognition, 14*, 676-686.

Nelson, T.O., & Narens, L. (1980). Norms of 300 general-information questions: Accuracy of recall, latency of recall, and feeling-of-knowing ratings. *Journal of Verbal Learning and Verbal Behavior, 19*, 338-368.

Nelson, T.O., & Narens, L. (1990). Metamemory: A theoretical framework and some new findings. In G.H. Bower (Ed.), *The psychology of learning and motivation (Vol. 26, pp 125-173)*. San Diego, USA: Academic Press.

Nelson, T.O., Dunlosky, J., White, D.M., Steinberg, J., Townes, B.D., & Anderson, D. (1990). Cognition and metacognition at extreme altitudes on Mount Everest. *Journal of Experimental Psychology: General, 119*, 367-374.

Nelson, T.O., Gerler, D., & Narens, L. (1984). Accuracy of feeling of knowing judgments for predicting perceptual identification and relearning. *Journal of Experimental Psychology: General, 113*, 282-300.

Nelson, T.O., Graf, A., Dunlosky, J., Marlatt, A., Walker, D., & Luce, K. (1998). Effects of acute alcohol intoxication on recall and on judgments of learning during the acquisition of new information. In G. Mazzoni & T.O. Nelson (Eds.), *Metacognition and cognitive neuropsychology: Monitoring and control processes* (pp. 161-180). Mahwah, NJ: Erlbaum.

Nelson, T.O., Leonesio, R.J., Landwehr, R.S., & Narens, L. (1986). A comparison of three predictors of an individual's memory performance: The individual's feeling of knowing versus normative feeling of knowing versus base-rate item difficulty. *Journal of Experimental Psychology: Learning, Memory, and Cognition, 12*, 279-287.

Nelson, T.O., McSpadden, M., Fromme, K., & Marlatt, G.A. (1986). Effects of alcohol intoxication on metamemory and on retrieval from long-term memory. *Journal of Experimental Psychology: General, 115*, 247-254.

Newcombe, P.A., & Siegal, M. (1997). Explicitly questioning the nature of suggestibility in pre-schoolers memory and retention. *Journal of Experimental Child Psychology, 67*, 185-203.

Nhouyvanisvong, A., & Reder, L.M. (1998). Rapid feeling-of-knowing: A strategy selection mechanism. In V.Y. Yzerbyt, G. Lories, & B. Dardenne (Eds.), *Metacognition: Cognitive and social dimensions*. (pp. 35-52). London: Sage.

Nhouyvanisvong, A., & Reder, L.M. (1998). Rapid FOK: A strategy selection mechanism. In V.Y. Yzerbyt, G. Lories, & B. Dardenne. *Metacognition: Cognitive and social dimensions*, (pp. 35-52). Thousand Oaks, CA: Sage Publications.

Noland, J. & Markham, R. (1998). The accuracy-confidence relationship in an eyewitness task: anxiety as a modifier. *Applied Cognitive Psychology*, 12, 43-54.

Norman, D.A., & Shallice, T. (1986). Attention to Action. Willed and automatic control of behavior.. In R.J. Davidson, G.E. Schwartz, & D. Shapiro (Eds.), *Consciousness and self-regulation (Vol. 4)*, (pp. 1-18). New York: Plenum.

Nosofsky, R.M. (1986). Attention, similarity, and the identification-categorization relationship. *Journal of Experimental Psychology: General, 115*, 39-57.

Oakhill, J. (1994). Individual differences in children's text comprehension. In M.A. Gernsbacher (Ed.) *Handbook of Psycholinguistics* (pp. 821-848). New York, NY: Academic Press.

Ochsner, J.E., Zaragoza, M.S., & Mitchell, K.J. (1999). The accuracy and suggestibility of children's memories for neutral and criminal eyewitness events. *Legal and Criminological Psychology*, 4, 135-147.

Olsson, N. (1999). Recognizing familiar versus unfamiliar voices. *Manuscript submitted for publication*. Department of Psychology, Uppsala University.

Olsson, N. (2000). A comparison of correlation, calibration, and diagnosticity as measures of the confidence-accuracy relationship in witness identification. *Journal of Applied Psychology, 4*, 504-511.

Olsson, N., Juslin, P., & Winman, A. (1998). Realism of confidence in earwitness versus eyewitness identification. *Journal of Experimental Psychlogy: Applied, 4*, 101-118.

Palincsar, A.S., & Brown, A.L. (1984). Reciprocal teaching of comprehension-fostering and comprehension-monitoring activities. *Cognition and Instruction, 1*, 117-175.

Palincsar, A.S., & Brown, A.L. (1987). Enhancing instructional time through attention to metacognition. *Journal of Learning Disabilities, 20*, 60-75.

Palincsar, A.S., & Ransom, K. (1988). From the mystery spot to the thoughtful spot: The instruction of metacognitive strategies. *Reading Teacher, 41*, 784-789.

Pappas, B.A., Sunderland, T., Weingartner, H.M., Vitiello, B., Martinson, H., & Putnam, K. (1992). Alzheimer's disease and feeling of knowing for knowledge and episodic memory. *Journal of Gerontology: Psychological Sciences, 47*, 159-164.

Paris, S.G., & Byrnes, J.P. (1989). The constructivist approach to self-regulation and learning in the classroom. In B. Zimmerman & D. Schunk (Eds.), *Self-regulated learning and academic achievement: Theory, research, and practice,* (pp. 169-200). New York: Springer-Verlag.

Paris, S.G., & Jacobs, J.E. (1984). The benefits of informed instruction for children's reading awareness and comprehension skills. *Child Development, 55*, 2083-2093.

Paris, S.G., & Lindauer, B.K. (1982). The development of cognitive skills during childhood. In B. Wolman (Ed.), *Handbook of developmental psychology.* (pp. 35-60). Englewood Cliffs, NJ: Prentice-Hall.

Paris, S.G., & Oka, E.R. (1986). Children's reading strategies, metacognition, and motivation. *Developmental Review, 6*, 25-56.

Paris, S.G., & Paris, A.H. (2001). Classroom applications of research on self-regulated learning. *Educational Psychologist, 36*(2), 89-101.

Paris, S.G., & Winograd, P.W. (1990). How metacognition can promote academic learning and instruction. In B.J. Jones & L. Idol (Eds.), *Dimensions of thinking and cognitive instruction (*pp. 15-51). Hillsdale, NJ: Lawrence Erlbaum Associates.

Paris, S.G., Byrnes, J.P., & Paris, A.H. (2001). Constructing theories, identities, and actions of self-regulated learners. In B. Zimmerman & D. Schunk (Eds.), *Self-regulated learning and academic achievement Theoretical perspectives, 2nd Ed.* (pp. 253-287). Mahwah, NJ: Erlbaum

Paris, S.G., Cross, D.R., & Lipson, M.Y.L. (1984). Informed strategies for learning: A program to improve children's reading awareness and comprehension. *Journal of Educational Psychology, 76,* 1239-1252.

Paris, S.G., Lipson, M.Y.L., & Wixson, K.K. (1983). Becoming a strategic reader. *Contemporary Educational Psychology, 8,* 293-316.

Paris, S.G., Wasik, B.A., & Turner, J.C. (1991). The development of strategic readers. In R. Barr, M. Kamil, P. Mosenthal, & P.D. Pearson (Eds.), *Handbook of reading research,* 2nd ed., (pp. 609-640). New York: Longman.

Patton, J.H., Weaver, III, C.A., Burns, K.D., Brady, M.D., & Bryant, D.S. (1991, April). *Cognitive impulsivity and cognitive skills.* Paper presented at the 37th annual meeting of the Southwestern Psychological Association, New Orleans.

Pavot, W., Fujita, F., & Diener, E. (1997). The relation between self-aspect congruence, personality and subjective well-being. *Personality and Individual Differences, 22,* 183-191.

Perfect, T.J., & Hollins, T.S. (1996). Predictive feeling of knowing judgements and postdictive confidence judgements in eyewitness memory and general knowledge. *Applied Cognitive Psychology, 10,* 371-382.

Perfect, T.J., Watson, E.L., & Wagstaff, G.F. (1993). The accuracy of confidence ratings associated with general knowledge and eyewitness memory. *Journal of Applied Cognitive Psychology, 78,* 144-147.

Perfetti, C.A. (1985). *Reading Ability.* New York: Oxford University Press.

Perner, J. (1998). The meta-intentional nature of executive functions and theory of mind. In P. Carruthers and J. Boucher (Eds), *Language and thought* (pp. 270-283). Cambridge: Cambridge University Press.

Perner, J. (in press, a). Episodic Memory: Essential distinctions and developmental implications. In C. Moore & K. Skene (Eds.). *The self in time: Developmental issues.* Erlbaum.

Perner, J. (in press, b). Dual control and the causal theory of action: The case of non-intentional action and causal self-reference. In N. Eilan & J. Roessler (Eds), *Agency and self-awareness.* Oxford: Oxford University Press.

Perner, J., & Dienes, Z. (1999). Deconstructing RTK: How to Explicate a Theory of Implicit Knowledge. *Behavioural and Brain Sciences, 22,* 790-808.

Perner, J., & Ruffman, T. (1995). Episodic memory and autonoetic consciousness: Developmental evidence and a theory of childhood amnesia. *Journal of Experimental Child Psychology, 59,* 516-548.

Perruchet, P., & Pacteau, C. (1990). Synthetic grammar learning: Implicit rule abstraction or explicit fragmentary knowledge? *Journal of Experimental Psychology: General, 119,* 264-275.

Perruchet, P., Gallego, J., & Savy, I. (1990). A critical reappraisal of the evidence for unconscious abstraction of deterministic rules in complex experimental situations. *Cognitive Psychology, 22,* 493-516.

Perruchet, P., Vinter, A., & Gallego, J. (1997). Implicit learning shapes new conscious percepts and representations. *Psychonomic Bulletin and Review, 4,* 43-48.

Pica, T. (1987). Second-language acquisition, social interaction, and the classroom. *Applied Linguistics, 8,* 3-21.

Pinard, A. (1992). Métaconscience et métacognition. *Canadian Psychology, 33,* 27-40.

Pintrich, P.R. (2000). The role of goal orientation in self-regulated learning. In M. Boekaerts, P. Pintrich, & M. Zeidner (Eds.), *Handbook of self-regulation* (pp. 452-502). NY: Academic Press.

Pintrich, P.R., & Schrauben, B. (1992). Students' motivational beliefs and their cognitive engagement in classroom academic tasks. In D.H. Schunk & J.L. Meece (Eds.), *Student perception in the classroom* (pp. 247-266). Hillsdale, NJ: Lawrence Erlbaum Associates.

Poole, D.A., & Lindsay, D.S. (1998). Assessing the accuracy of young children's reports: Lessons from the investigation of child sexual abuse. *Applied and Preventive Psychology, 7,* 1-26.

Poulisse, N. (1987). Problems and solutions in the classification of compensatory strategies. *Second Language Research, 3/2,* 141-153.

Pressley, M., Borkowski, J.G., & O'Sullivan, J. (1985). Children's metamemory and the teaching of memory strategies. In D.L. Forrest-Pressley, G.E. MacKinnon, & T. Gary Waller (Eds.), *Metacognition, cognition, and human performance (Vol. 1)*, (pp. 111-153). London: Academic Press.

Pressley, M., Borkowski, J.G., & Schneider, W. (1987). Cognitive strategies: Good strategy users coordinate metacognition and knowledge. In R. Vasta & G. Whitehurst (Eds.), *Annals of child development* (Vol. V, 575-582). Greenwich, CT: JAI.

Pressley, M., Snyder, B.L., Levin, J.R., Murray, H.G., & Ghatala, E.S. (1987). Perceived readiness for examination performance (PREP) produced by initial reading of text and text containing adjunct questions. *Reading Research Quarterly, 22,* 219-236.

Pressley, M., Woloshyn, V., & Associates. (1995). *Cognitive strategy instruction that really improves children's academic performance* (2nd Ed.). Cambridge, MA: Brookline.

Pulford, B.D., & Colman, A.M. (1997). Overconfidence: Feedback and item difficulty effects. *Personality and Individual Differences, 23,* 125-133.

Quas, J.A., Goodman, G.S., Bidrose, S., Pipe, M.E., Craw, S. & Ablin, D.S. (1999) Emotion and memory: Children's long term remembering, forgetting, and suggestibility. *Journal of Experimental Child Psychology, 72,* 235-270.

Rabinowitz, J.C., Ackerman, B.P., Craik, F.I.M., & Hinchley, J.L. (1982). Aging and metamemory: The roles of relatedness and imagery. *Journal of Gerontology, 37,* 688-695.

Rajaram, S. (1993). Remembering and knowing: Two means of access to the personal past. *Memory and Cognition, 21,* 89-102.

Raphael, T.E., & Pearson, P.D. (1985). Increasing students' awareness of sources of information for answering questions. *American Educational Research Journal, 22,* 217-235.

Rawson, K.A., Dunlosky, J., & Thiede, K.W. (2000). The rereading effect: Metacomprehension accuracy improves across reading trials. *Memory and Cognition, 28,* 1004-1010.

Reber, A.S. (1967). Implicit learning of artificial grammar. *Journal of Verbal Learning and Verbal Behavior, 6,* 855-863.

Reber, A.S. (1976). Implicit learning of synthetic languages: the role of instructional set. *Journal of Experimental Psychology: Human Learning and Memory, 2,* 88-94.

Reber, A.S. (1989). Implicit learning and tacit knowledge. *Journal of Experimental Psychology: General, 118,* 219-235.

Reber, A.S. (1993). *Implicit learning and tacit knowledge: An essay on the cognitive unconscious.* New York: Oxford University Press.

Reber, A.S., & Lewis, S. (1977). Implicit learning: an analysis of the form and the structure of a body of tacit knowledge. *Cognition, 5,* 333-361.

Reber, A.S., Kassin, S.M., Lewis, S., & Cantor, G. (1980). On the relationship between implicit and explicit modes in the learning of a complex rule structure. *Journal of Experimental Psychology: Human Learning and Memory, 6,* 492-502.

Reder, L.M. (1982). Plausibility judgments versus fact retrieval: Alternative strategies for sentence verification. *Psychological Review, 89,* 250-280.

Reder, L.M. (1987). Strategy selection in question answering. *Cognitive Psychology, 19*, 90-138.

Reder, L.M. (1988). Strategic control of retrieval strategies. In G. Bower (Ed.). *The psychology of learning and motivation. (Vol. 22)*, (pp. 227-259). San Diego, CA: Academic Press.

Reder, L.M. (1996). Different research programs on metacognition: Are the boundaries imaginary? *Learning and Individual Differences, 8*, 383-390.

Reder, L.M. (Ed.) (1996). *Implicit memory and metacognition.* Hillsdale, NJ: Erlbaum.

Reder, L.M., & Kusbit, G.W. (1991). Locus of the Moses Illusion: Imperfect encoding, retrieval, or match? *Journal of Memory and Language, 30*, 385-406.

Reder, L.M., & Ritter, F.E. (1992). What determines initial feeling of knowing? Familiarity with question terms, not with the answer. *Journal of Experimental Psychology: Learning, Memory, and Cognition, 18*, 435-451.

Reder, L.M., & Schunn, C.D. (1996). Metacognition does not imply awareness: Strategy choice is governed by implicit learning and memory. In L.M. Reder (Ed.). *Implicit Memory and Metacognition.* (pp. 45-77). Mahwah, NJ: Erlbaum.

Reder, L.M., & Schunn, C.D. (1999). Bringing together the psychometric and strategy worlds: Predicting adaptivity in a dynamic task. In D. Gopher & A. Koriat (Eds.). *Cognitive regulation of performance: Interaction of theory and application. Attention and Performance XVII.* (pp. 315-342). Cambridge, MA: MIT Press.

Reder, L.M., & Weber, K.H. (1997, November). *Spatial habituation and expectancy effects in a negative priming paradigm.* Paper presented at the annual meeting of the Psychonomics Society, Philadelphia, PA.

Reingold, E.M., & Merikle, P.M. (1988). Using direct and indirect measures to study perception without awareness. *Perception and Psychophysics, 44*, 563-575.

Renken, A.E., & Weaver, III, C.A. (2000). *Transfer-Appropriate Monitoring of text comprehension monitoring: Matching prediction and retrieval conditions improves predictions of performance.* Paper presented at the 41st annual meeting of the Psychonomic Society: New Orleans.

Richardson-Klavehn, A., Gardiner, J.M., & Java, R.I. (1996). Memory: Task dissociations, process dissociations and dissociations of consciousness. In G. Underwood (Ed.), *Implicit cognition* (pp. 85-158). Oxford: Oxford University Press.

Rijsman, J.B. (1974). Factors in social comparison of performance influencing actual performance. *European Journal of Social Psychology, 4*, 279-311.

Rijsman, J.B. (1983). The dynamics of social competition in personal and categorical comparison-situations. In W. Doise, & S. Moscovici (Eds.), *Current Issues in European Social Psychology* (pp. 279-312). Cambridge: Cambridge University Press.

Riley, V. (1996). Operator reliance on automation. In R. Parasurama & M. Mouloua (Eds.), *Automation and human performance: Theory and application* (pp. 19-35). Mahwah, N.J.: Laurence Erlbaum.

Ripoll, T. (1998). Why this makes me think of that. *Thinking and Reasoning, 4*, 15-43.

Ripoll, T. (1999). A comparison between Keane (1987) and Ripoll (1998): Studies on the retrieval phase of reasoning by analogy. *Thinking and Reasoning, 5*, 189-191.

Roberts, M.J., & Erdos, G. (1993). Strategy selection and metacognition. *Educational Psychology, 13*, 259-266.

Robinson, M.D. , & Johnson, J.T. (1998) How not to enhance the confidence-accuracy relation: The detrimental effects of attention to the identification process. *Law and Human Behavior, 22(4)*, 409-428.

Robinson, M.D., Johnson, J.T., & Herndon, F. (1997). Reaction time and assessments of cognitive effort as predictors of eyewitness memory accuracy and confidence. *Journal of Applied Psychology, 82*(3), 416-425.

Roebers, C.M., Moga, N., & Schneider, W. (in press). The role of accuracy motivation on children's and adults' event recall. *Journal of Experimental Child Psychology.*

Rosenthal, D.M. (1986). Two concepts of consciousness. *Philosophical Studies, 49,* 329-359.

Rosenthal, D.M. (2000a). Consciousness, Content, and Metacognitive Judgments, *Consciousness and Cognition, 9,* 203-214.

Rosenthal, D.M. (2000b). Metacognition and Higher-Order Thoughts (extended response to commentaries), *Consciousness and Cognition, 9,* 231-242.

Rosenthal, D.M. (2000c).."Consciousness and Metacognition", in Daniel Sperber (Ed.), *Metarepresentation: Proceedings of the Tenth Vancouver Cognitive Science Conference.* New York: Oxford University Press.

Ross, B.H. (1984). Remindings and their effects in learning a cognitive skill. *Cognitive Psychology, 16,* 371-416.

Ross, B.H. (1989). Distinguishing types of superficial similarities: Different effects on the access and use of earlier problems. *Journal of Experimental Psychology: Learning, Memory, and Cognition, 15,* 456-468.

Rouet, J-F., & Chollet, C. (2000). The acquisition of information search skills in 9 to 13 year-old students. Paper presented at the *Tenth Annual Meeting of the Society for Text and Discourse.* Lyon, France: July.

Rouet, J-F., Britt, M.A., Mason, R.A., & Perfetti, C.A. (1996). Using multiple sources of evidence to reason about history. *Journal of Educational Psychology, 88,* 478-493.

Rouet, J-F., Favart, M., Britt, M.A., & Perfetti, C.A. (1997). Studying and using multiple documents in history: Effects of discipline expertise. *Cognition and Instruction, 15,* 85-106.

Rubin, D.C., & Friendly, M. (1986). Predicting which words get recalled: Measures of free recall, availability, goodness, emotionality, and pronouncability for 925 nouns. *Memory and Cognition, 14,* 79-94.

Ruvolo, A., & Markus, H.R. (1992). Possible selves and performance: The power of self-relevant imagery. *Social Cognition, 10,* 95-124.

Samurcay, R., & Hoc, J.M. (1988). De l'analyse du travail à la spécification des aides dans les environnements dynamiques. *Psychologie française, 33,* 187-196.

Scardamalia, M., & Bereiter, C. (1987). Knowledge telling and knowledge transforming in written composition. In S. Rosenberg (Ed.) *Advances in applied psycholinguistics: Vol. 2, reading, writing and language learning.* Cambridge, England: Cambridge University Press.

Schacter, D.L., Harbluk, J.L., & Mclachlan, D.R. (1984). Retrieval without recollection: an experimental analysis of source amnesia. *Journal of Verbal Learning and Verbal Behavior, 23,* 593-611.

Schneider, W. (1985). Developmental trends in the metamemory-memory behavior relationship: An integrative review. In D.L. Forest-Pressley, G.E. MacKinnon, & T.G. Waller (Eds.), *Metacognition, cognition, and human performance* (Vol. 1, pp. 57-109). Orlando, FL: Academic Press.

Schneider, W., & Pressley, M. (1997). *Memory development between 2 and 20.* New York, NY: Springer-Verlag.

Schneider, W., Visé, M., Lockl, K., & Nelson, T.O. (in press). Developmental trends in children's memory monitoring: Evidence from a judgment-of-learning (JOL) task. *Cognitive Development.*

Schoenfeld, A. (1992). Learning to think mathematically: Problem solving, metacognition, and sense making in mathematics. In D. Grouws (Ed.), *Handbook of research on mathematics teaching and learning* (pp. 334-370). New York: Macmillan.

Schooler, L.J., Clark, C.A., & Loftus, E.F. (1988). Knowing when memory is real. In M.M. Gruneberg, P.E.Morris & D. Sykes. (eds), *Practical Aspect of Memory: Current and Research Issues. (Vol. 1,* pp.83-88). John Wiley and Sons Ltd.

Schraw, G., & Impara, J.C. (2001). *Issues in the measurement of metacognition.* Lincoln, NE: Buros Institute of Mental Measurements.

Schraw, G., & Roedel, T.D. (1994). Test difficulty and judgment bias. *Memory and Cognition, 22,* 63-69.

Schraw, G., Dunkle, M.E., Bendixen, L.D., & Roedel, T.D. (1995). Does a general monitoring skill exist? *Journal of Educational Psychology, 87,* 433-444.

Schunk, D.H. (1996). *Theories of learning* (2nd edition). Englewood Cliffs, NJ: Prentice-Hall.

Schunk, D.H., & Rice, J.M. (1987). Enhancing comprehension skill and self efficacy with strategy value information. *Journal of Reading Behavior, 19,* 285-302.

Schunn, C.D., & Reder, L.M. (1998). Strategy adaptivity and individual differences. In D.L. Medin (Ed.). *The psychology of learning and motivation.* (pp. 115-154). New York: Academic Press.

Schunn, C.D., Reder, L.M., Nhouyvanisvong, A., Richards, D.R., & Stroffolino, P.J. (1997). To calculate or not to calculate: A source of activation confusion model of problem familiarity's role in strategy selection. *Journal of Experimental Psychology: Learning, Memory, and Cognition, 23,* 3-29.

Schwartz, B.L. (1994). Sources of information in metamemory: Judgments of learning and feeling of knowing. *Psychonomic Bulletin and Review, 1,* 357-375.

Schwartz, B.L., & Metcalfe, J. (1992). Cue familiarity but not target retrievability enhances feeling-of-knowing. *Journal of Experimental Psychology: Learning, Memory, and Cognition, 18,* 1074-1083.

Schwartz, B.L., & Metcalfe, J. (1994). Methodological problems and pitfalls in the study of human metacognition. In J. Metcalfe & A. P. Shimamura (Eds.), *Metacognition: Knowing about Knowing.* (pp. 93-113). Cambridge, MA: MIT Press.

Schwartz, B.L., Benjamin, A.S., & Bjork, R.A. (1997). The inferential and experiential bases of metamemory. *Current Directions in Psychological Science, 6,* 132-137.

Searle, J.R. (1983). *Intentionality.* Cambridge: Cambridge University Press.

Searle, J.R. (1990). Consciousness, explanatory inversion, and cognitive science. *Behavioural and Brain Sciences, 13,* 585-642.

Selinker, L., & Douglas, D. (1985). Wrestling with 'context' in interlanguage theory. *Applied Linguistics, 6,* 190-204.

Shafto, M., & McKay, D.G. (2000). The Moses, Mega-Moses and Armstrong illusions: integrating language comprehension and semantic memory. *Psychological Science, 11,* 372-378.

Shanks, D.R., & Johnstone, T. (1998). Implicit knowledge in sequential learning tasks. In M.A. Stadler & P.A. Frensch (Eds.). *Handbook of implicit learning.* Sage Publications, Thousand Oaks.

Shanks, D.R., & St. John, M.F. (1994). Characteristics of dissociable human learning systems. *Behavioural and Brain Sciences, 17,* 367-448.

Shanks, D.R., Green, R.E., & Kolodny, J.A. (1994). A critical examination of the evidence for unconscious (implicit) learning. In C. Umiltà, & M. Moscovitch (Eds.). *Attention and Performance XV.* Cambridge, Mass.: MIT Press.

Shaw, J.S., Garcia, L.A., & McClure, K.A. (1999). A lay perspective on the accuracy of eyewitness testimony. *Journal of Applied Social Psychology, 29(1),* 52-71.

Shaw, J.S., III. (1996). Increases in eyewitness confidence resulting from postevent questioning. *Journal of Experimental Psychology: Applied, 2,* 126-146.

Shaw, R.E., Mace, W.M., & Turvey, M. (1995). Resources for ecological psychology. In P. Hancok, J. Flach, J. Caird, & K. Vincente (Eds.), *Local application of the ecological approach to human-machine systems* (pp. 1-4). Hillsdale New Jersey: Lawrence Erlbaum.

Sheehan, P.W., & McConkey, K.M. (1982). *Hypnosis and experience: The exploration of phenomena and process.* Hillsdale, NJ: Erlbaum.

Shiffrin, R.M., & Schneider, W. (1977). Controlled and automatic human information processing: II. Perceptual learning, automatic attending, and a general theory. *Psychological Review, 84,* 127-190.

Shimamura, A.P., & Squire, L.R. (1986). Memory and metamemory: A study of feeling-of-knowing phenomenon in amnesic patients. *Journal of Experimental Psychology: Learning, Memory and Cognition, 12,* 452-460.

Shimamura, A.P., Janowsky, J.S., Squire, L.R. (1991). What is the role of frontal lobe damage in memory disorders? In H.S. Levin, H.M. Eisenberg, & A.L. Benton (Eds.), *Frontal lobe function and dysfunction* (pp.173-197). New York: Oxford University Press.

Shrimpton, S., Oates, K., & Hayes, S. (1998). Children's memory of events: Effects of stress, age, time delay and location of interview. *Applied Cognitive Psychology, 12,* 133-143.

Siegler, R.S. (1987). The perils of averaging data over strategies: An example from children's addition. *Journal of Experimental Psychology: General, 116,* 250-264.

Siegler, R.S. (1988). Strategy choice procedures and the development of multiplication skill. *Journal of Experimental Psychology: General, 117,* 258-275.

Siegler, R.S., & Shrager, J. (1984). Strategy choices in addition and subtraction: How do children know what to do? In C. Sophian (Ed.), *Origins of cognitive skills* (pp. 229-293). Hillsdale, NJ: Lawrence Erlbaum Associates.

Slife, B.D., & Weaver, III, C.A. (1992). Depression, cognitive skill, and metacognitive skill. *Cognition and Emotion, 6,* 1-22.

Smith, V.L., Kassin, S.M., & Ellsworth, P.C. (1989). Eyewitness accuracy and confidence: Within versus between-subjects correlations. *Journal of Applied Psychology, 74,* 356-359.

Son, L.K., & Metcalfe, J. (2000). Metacognitive and control strategies in study-time allocation. *Journal of Experimental Psychology: Learning, Memory and Cognition, 26,* 204-221.

Spanos, N.P. (1986). Hypnotic behaviour: A social-psychological interpretation of amnesia, analgesia, and "trance logic". *The Behavioural and Brain Sciences, 9,* 449-502.

Spanos, N.P., Radtke, H.L., & Dubreuil, D.L. (1982). Episodic and semantic memory in post-hypnotic amnesia: A re-evaluation. *Journal of Personality and Social Psychology, 43,* 565-573.

Spellman, B.A., & Bjork, R.A. (1992). When predictions create reality: Judgments of learning may alter what they are intended to assess. *Psychological Science, 3,* 315-316.

Stankov, L., & Crawford, J.D. (1996). Confidence judgments in studies of individual differences. *Personality and Individual Differences, 21,* 971-986.

Stanley, W.B., Mathews, R.C., Buss, R.R., & Kotler-Cope, S. (1989). Insight without awareness: on the interaction of verbalization, instruction and practice in a simulated process control task. *Quarterly Journal of Experimental Psychology, 41A,* 553-577.

Subbotin, V. (1996). Outcome feedback effects on under- and overconfident judgments (general knowledge tasks). *Organizational Behavior and Human Decision Processes, 66,* 268-276.

Sun, R. (2000). *Explicit and implicit processes of metacognition* (Tech. Rep. No. TR-00-001). Columbia, MO: University of Missouri, CECS Department.

Swanson, H.L. (1990). Influence of metacognitive knowledge and aptitude on problem-solving. *Journal of Educational Psychology, 82*, 306-314.

Takahashi, T. (1989). The influence of the listener in L2 speech. In S. Gass, C. Madden, D. Preston, & L. Selinker (Eds.), *Variation in second language acquisition: psycholinguistic issues* (pp. 245-279) Multilingual Matters Ltd: Clevedon, UK.

Thagard, P., Holyoak, K.J., Nelson G., & Goschfeld, D. (1990). Analog retrieval by constraint satisfaction. *Artificial Intelligence, 46*, 259-310.

Thiede, K.W. (1999). The importance of monitoring and self-regulation during multi-trial learning. *Psychonomic Bulletin and Review, 6*, 662-667.

Thiede, K.W., & Dunlosky, J. (1994). Delaying students' metacognitive monitoring improves their accuracy in predicting their recognition performance. *Journal of Educational Psychology, 86*, 290-302.

Thiede, K.W., & Dunlosky, J. (1999). Toward a general model of self-regulated study: An analysis of selection of items for study and self-paced study time. *Journal of Experimental Psychology: Learning, Memory, and Cognition, 25*, 1024-1037.

Thompson, W.B., & Mason, S.E. (1996). Instability of individual differences in the association between confidence judgments and memory performance. *Memory and Cognition, 24*, 226-234.

Toplis, R. (1997). Recollective experiences in children and adults: A comparative study. Doctoral dissertation, University of East London, London.

Tulving, E. (1983). *Elements of Episodic Memory*. Oxford Psychology Series No. 2. Oxford: Oxford University Press.

Tulving, E. (1983). *Elements of episodic memory*. Oxford: Clarendon Press.

Tulving, E. (1985). Memory and consciousness. *Canadian Psychology, 26*, 1-12.

Tulving, E. (1994). Foreword. In J. Metcalfe, & A.P. Shimamura (Eds.), *Metacognition: Knowing about knowing* (pp. vii-x). Cambridge, MA: MIT Press.

Tversky, A., & Kahneman, D. (1973). Availability: A heuristic for judging frequency and probability. *Cognitive Psychology, 5*, 207-232.

Tye, M. (1995). *Ten Problems of Consciousness: A Representational Theory of the Phenomenal Mind*. MIT Press: Cambridge.

Tzelgov, J., Ganor, D., & Yehene, V. (1999). Automatic processing results in conscious representations. *Behavioral and Brain Sciences, 22*, 786-787.

van den Broek, P., Young, M., Tzeng, Y., & Linderholm, T. (1999). The landscape model of reading: Inferences and the online construction of a memory representation. in H. van Oostendorp & S.R. Goldman (Eds.), *The construction of mental representations during reading* (pp. 71-98). Mahwah, NJ: Lawrence Erlbaum Associates.

van Dijk, T.A., & Kintsch, W. (1983). *Strategies of Discourse Comprehension*. Hillsdale, NJ: Lawrence Erlbaum Associates.

Verfaellie, M., & Cermak, L.S. (1999). Perceptual fluency as a cue for recognition judgments in amnesia. *Neuropsychology, 13*, 198-205.

Vrij, A., & Akehurst, L. (1998). *Verbal communication and credibility: Statement validity assessment. In A. Memon, A. Vrij, & R. Bull (Eds.). Psychology and Law: Truthfulness, Accuracy and Credibility of Victims, Witnesses and Suspects.* (pp. 3-31), Maidenhead: McGraw Hill.

Vygotsky, L. (1962). *Thought and language*. Cambridge, MA; MIT Press.

Wagner, R.K., & Sternberg, R.J. (1987). Executive control in reading comprehension. In B.K. Britton & S.M. Glynn (Eds.) *Executive Control Processes in Reading* (pp. 1-22). Hillsdale, N.J.: Lawrence Erlbaum Associates.

Walczyk, J.J., & Hall, V.C. (1989). Is the failure to monitor comprehension an instance of cognitive impulsivity? *Journal of Educational Psychology, 81*, 294-298.

Watkins, M.J., & Gibson, J.M. (1988). On the relation between perceptual priming and recognition memory. *Journal of Experimental Psychology: Learning, Memory and Cognition, 14,* 477-483.

Weaver, III, C.A. (1990). Constraining factors in calibration of comprehension. Journal of Experimental Psychology: *Learning, Memory and Cognition, 16,* 214-222.

Weaver, III, C.A., & Bryant, D.S. (1995). Monitoring of comprehension: The role of text difficulty in metamemory for narrative and expository text. *Memory and Cognition, 23,* 12-22.

Weaver, III, C.A., & Kelemen, W.L. (1997). Judgments of learning at delays: Shifts in response patterns or increased metamemory accuracy? *Psychological Science, 8,* 318-321.

Weaver, III, C.A., Bryant, D.S., & Burns, K.D. (1995). Comprehension monitoring: Extensions of the Kintsch and van Dijk model (pp. 177-193). In C.A. Weaver, III, S. Mannes, & C.R. Fletcher (Eds). *Discourse comprehension: Essays in honor of Walter Kintsch.* Hillsdale, NJ: Lawrence Erlbaum Associates.

Weaver, III, C.A., Winningham, R.G., & Renken A.E. (unpublished manuscript). *Transfer appropriate processing: Matching prediction and retrieval conditions improves metacognitive performance of text.*

Weingardt, K.R., Leonesio, R.J., & Loftus, E.F. (1994). Viewing eyewitness research from a metacognitive perspective. In J. Metcalfe, & A.P. Shimamura (Eds.), *Metacognition: Knowing about knowing* (pp. 157-184). Cambridge, MA: MIT Press.

Weiskrantz, L. (1988). Some contributions of neuropsychology of vision and memory to the problem of consciousness. In A.J. Marcel & E. Bisiach (Eds.), *Consciousness in contemporary science* (pp. 183-199). Oxford: Clarendon Press.

Weiskrantz, L. (1997). *Consciousness lost and found: A neuropsychological exploration.* Oxford, UK: Oxford.

Wellman, H.M. & Gelman, S.A. (1992). Cognitive development: Foundational theories of core domains. *Annual Review of Psychology, 43,* 337-375.

Wells, G.L. (1993). What do we know about eyewitness identification? *American Psychologist, 48,* 553-571.

Wells, G.L., & Bradfield, A.L. (1998). "Good, you identified the suspect": Feedback to eyewitnesses distorts their reports of the witnessing experience. *Journal of Applied Psychology, 83,* 360-376.

Wells, G.L., & Lindsay, R.C.L. (1985). Methodological notes on the accuracy -confidence relation in eyewitness identification. *Journal of Applied Psychology, 70,* 413-419.

Wells, G.L., Lindsay, R.C.L., & Ferguson, T.J. (1979). Accuracy, confidence, and juror perceptions in eyewitness identifications. *Journal of Applied Psychology, 64(4),* 440-448.

Wells, G.L., Malpass, R.S., Lindsay, R.C.L., Fisher, R.P., Turtle, J.W., & Fulero, S.M. (2000). *From the lab to the police station: a successful application of eyewitness research. American Psychologist, 6,* 581-598.

Wharton, C.M., Holyoak, K.J., Downing, P.E., Lange, T.E., Wickens, T.D., & Melz, E.R. (1994). Below the surface: Analogical similarity and retrieval competition in reminding. *Cognitive Psychology, 26,* 64-101.

Wheeler, M.A., Stuss, D.T., & Tulving, E. (1997). Toward a theory of episodic memory: The frontal lobes and autonoetic consciousness. *Psychological Bulletin, 121,* 331-354.

Whitten, W.B., & Bjork, R.A. (1977). Learning from tests: Effect of spacing. *Journal of Verbal Learning and Verbal Behavior, 16,* 465-478.

Whittlesea, B.W.A. (1993). Illusions of familiarity. *Journal of Experimental Psychology: Learning, Memory, and Cognition, 19,* 1235-1253.

Whittlesea, B.W.A., & Dorken, M.D. (1993). Incidentally, things in general are particularly determined: An episodic processing account of implicit learning. *Journal of Experimental Psychology: General, 122,* 227-248.

Whittlesea, B.W.A., & Dorken, M.D. (1997). Implicit learning: Indirect, not unconscious. *Psychonomic Bulletin and Review, 4,* 63-67.

Whittlesea, B.W.A., & Williams, L.D. (1998). Why do strangers feel familiar, but friends don't? The unexpected basis of feelings of familiarity. *Acta Psychologica, 98,* 141-166.

Whittlesea, B.W.A., & Williams, L.D. (2000). The source of feelings of familiarity: The discrepancy-attribution hypothesis. *Journal of Experimental Psychology: Learning, Memory and Cognition, 26,* 547-565.

Whittlesea, B.W.A., Jacoby, L.L., & Girard, K. (1990). Illusions of immediate memory: Evidence of an attributional basis for feelings of familiarity and perceptual quality. *Journal of Memory and Language, 29,* 716-732.

Wiley, J., & Voss, J.F. (1999). Constructing arguments from multiple sources: Tasks that promote understanding not just memory for text. *Journal of Educational Psychology, 91,* 301-311.

Willingham, D.B., Nissen, M.J., & Bullemer, P. (1989). On the development of procedural knowledge. *Journal of Experimental Psychology: Learning, Memory, and Cognition, 15,* 1047-1060.

Winningham, R.G., & Weaver, III, C.A. (2000). The effects of pressure to report more details on memories of an eyewitness event. *European Journal of Cognitive Psychology, 12,* 271-282.

Woken, M.D., & Swales, J. (1989). Expertise and authority in native/non-native conversations: the need for a variable account. In S. Gass, C. Madden, D. Preston, & L. Selinker (Eds.), *Variation in second language acquisition: psycholinguistic issues* (pp. 211-227). Clevedon, UK: Multilingual Matters Ltd.

Wood, J.V. (1989). Theory and research concerning social comparisons of personal attributes. *Psychological Bulletin, 106,* 231-248.

Wood, J.V. (1996). What is social comparison and how should we study it? *Personality and Social Psychology Bulletin, 22,* 520-537.

Wright, D.B. (1996). Measuring feeling of knowing: Comment on Schraw (1995). *Applied Cognitive Psychology, 10,* 261-268.

Wright, D.B., & Davies, G.M. (1999). Eyewitness Testimony. In F Durso, R.S. Nickerson, R.W. Schvaneveldt, S.T. Dumais, D.S. Lindsay & M.T.H. Chi (Eds.), *Handbook of Applied Cognition,* Chichester: Wiley.

Wright, D.B., Self, G., & Justice, C. (2000). Memory conformity: Exploring misinformation effects when presented by another person. *British Journal of Psychology, 91,* 189-202.

Yarab, P.E., Sensibaugh, C.C., & Allgeier, E.R. (1997). Over-confidence and under-performance: Men's perceived accuracy and actual performance in a course. *Psychological Reports, 81,* 76-78.

Yarmey, D. (1986). Verbal, visual, and voice identification of a rape suspect under different levels of illumination. *Journal of Applied Psychology, 3,* 363-370.

Yarmey, D. (1994). Earwitness evidence: Memory for a perpetrator's voice. In D.F. Ross, J.D. Read, & M.P. Toglia (Eds.), *Adult eyewitness testimony: Current trends and developments* (pp. 362-385). New York: Cambridge University Press.

Yates, J.F. (1990). *Judgment and decision making.* Englewood Cliffs, NJ: Prentice Hall.

Yuill, N., & Oakhill, J. (1991). *Children's problems in text comprehension: An experimental investigation.* New York, NY: Cambridge University Press.

Yussen, S.R., & Smith, M.C. (1990). Detecting general and specific errors in expository texts. *Contemporary Educational Psychology, 15,* 224-240.

Zimmerman, B.J., & Schunk, D.H. (2001). *Self-regulated learning and academic achievement.* New York: Springer-Verlag.

Zuengler, J. (1989). Performance variation in NS-NNS interactions: Ethnolinguistic difference, or discourse domain? In S. Gass, C. Madden, D. Preston, & L. Selinker (Eds.), *Variation in second language acquisition: psycholinguistic issues* (pp. 228-244). Clevedon, UK: Multilingual Matters Ltd.

Author Index

Lories, G., VII, IX, XII, 18, 19, 21, 29, 89, 92, 95, 98, 231, 237, 247
Lovelace, E.A., 151, 247
Lovett, M.C., 63, 64, 68, 69, 71, 72, 73, 247
Lovett, S.B., 119, 247
Luc, F., 187, 190, 192, 248
Luce, K., 52, 251
Luo, Z., 221, 237
Luszez, M.A., 214, 235
Luus, C.A.E., 199, 247
M
Mace, W.M., 133, 257
Macready, G.B., 154, 241
Maggi, B., 147, 248
Maki, R.H., 50, 51, 53, 248
Malpass, R.S., 198, 203, 248, 259
Mandl, H., 118, 119, 240
Mandler, G., 78, 81, 248
Mangun, G.R., 216, 239
Marchitelli, G., 6, 248
Marescaux, P.-J., XII, 3, 72, 149, 151, 179, 180, 181, 185, 187, 190, 192, 236, 248
Marescaux, P-J., VII, X, XII, 227, 229, 231
Markham, R., 221, 251
Markus, H.R., 107, 162, 248, 255
Marlatt, G.A., 52, 251
Marsh, G.R., 151, 247
Marshall, J., 39, 242
Martinot, D., 151, 162, 236
Martinson, H., 34, 252
Mason, R.A., 117, 255
Mason, S.E., 52, 53, 224, 258
Master, S., 84, 88, 243
Mathews, R.C., 180, 187, 194, 248, 258
Maury, S., 128, 247
Mazzoni, G., 3, 6, 15, 43, 62, 234, 248
McAllister, V.L., 39, 242
McBrien, C.M., 220, 248
McClelland, J.L., 186, 236
McCloskey, M., 90, 91, 242
McClure, K.A., 214, 257
McConkey, K.M., 177, 257
McGlynn, S.M., 35, 248
McHugh, P.R., 39, 241
McKay, D.G., 94, 96, 257
McKenzie, C.R.M., 30, 248
McKhann, G., 38, 39, 248
McLachlan, D.R., 83, 256
McSpadden, M., 52, 251

Melnick, R., 49, 50, 234
Melz, E.R., 95, 97, 259
Memon, A., 224, 248
Merikle, P.M., 81, 169, 183, 186, 188, 236, 248, 249, 254
Metallidou, P., 20, 249
Metallidou, Y., 20, 240
Metcalfe, J., 2, 3, 5, 36, 43, 50, 51, 62, 67, 103, 193, 214, 249, 256, 257
Migueles, M., 215, 219, 249
Miller, G., 183, 249
Millikan, R.G., 170, 249
Milne, R., 214, 244
Milsom, J., 220, 221, 237
Miner, A.C., 21, 22, 66, 91, 249
Mitchell, K.J., 220, 249, 251
Mitchell, R., 220, 221, 237
Moga, N., 15, 255
Monteil, J.-M., 151, 156, 249
Morency, J., 91, 243
Morris, C., 49, 51, 242
Morris, K.A., 150, 242
Moscovitch, M., IX, 78, 82, 83, 86, 249
Moulin, C.J.A., VIII, XII, 4, 8, 33, 34, 35, 36, 39, 42, 45, 52, 214, 228, 231, 249, 250
Multhaup, K.S., 215, 250
Murdock, B.B., 97, 243, 250
Murray, H.G., 49, 253
Myers, M., 119, 121, 128, 250
N
Nakamura, Y., 81, 248
Nakash-Dura, M., 15, 246
Narby, D.J., 201, 250
Narens, L., 1, 2, 3, 15, 21, 22, 34, 37, 44, 49, 50, 52, 54, 62, 66, 85, 103, 173, 234, 244, 250, 251
Nelson G., 258
Nelson, T.O., V, 1, 2, 3, 4, 5, 6, 8, 12, 13, 15, 20, 21, 22, 30, 34, 36, 37, 42, 44, 47, 48, 49, 50, 51, 52, 53, 54, 55, 62, 66, 85, 96, 97, 102, 103, 105, 173, 234, 236, 239, 244, 246, 248, 250, 251, 256
Newcombe, P.A., 224, 251
Newell, A., 64, 246
Nhouyvanisvong, A., 66, 67, 68, 89, 91, 92, 93, 94, 251, 256
Nissen, M.J., 188, 260
Noland, J., 221, 251
Nolde, S.F., 215, 244

Subject Index

Printed in the United States
42003LVS00002B/183

9 781402 071348